BELFAST AND DERRY IN REVOLT

A New History of the Start of the Troubles

SIMON PRINCE

GEOFFREY WARNER

IRISH ACADEMIC PRESS
DUBLIN • PORTLAND, OR

First published in 2012 by Irish Academic Press

2 Brookside,	920 NE 58th Avenue, Suite 300
Dundrum Road,	Portland, Oregon,
Dublin 14, Ireland	97213-3786 USA

www.iap.ie

British Library Cataloguing in Publication Data
An entry can be found on request

ISBN 978 0 7165 2997 2 (cloth)
ISBN 978 0 7165 2998 9 (paper)

Library of Congress Cataloging-in-Publication Data
An entry can be found on request

Printed by Good News Digital Books, Ongar, Essex

Contents

Acknowledgements

Both of us would like to begin by acknowledging the incalculable debt that we owe to Paul Bew and Lisa Hyde. Among many, many other things, we would like to thank Paul and Lisa for introducing us to each other and encouraging us to work together. We would also like to thank the staffs of the National Archives in London, the National Archives of Ireland in Dublin and the Public Record Office of Northern Ireland in Belfast – and particularly David Huddleston whose advice and help on the location and declassification of documents was indispensable; the McClay Library at Queen's University Belfast and especially Diarmuid Kennedy, in charge of Special Collections; the Linen Hall Library in Belfast; the newspaper libraries in Belfast and Colindale; the Bodleian Library at Oxford University; the Imperial War Museum; Derry City Council's Archive Service; and the Institute of Advanced Legal Studies in London. Thanks to Will Liddle for the maps and to the team at Irish Academic Press for their sterling work in getting the book ready for publication. We owe a debt to fellow scholars of Northern Ireland's troubled past, too: Paul Arthur, Guy Beiner, Aaron Edwards, Richard English, James Greer, Brian Hanley, Tom Hennessey, Liam Kelly, Brendan Lynn, Marc Mulholland, Niall Ó Dochartaigh, Henry Patterson, Bob Purdie and Graham Walker.

GEOFFREY WARNER: I would like to express my thanks to the following people, without whose help my contribution to this book would never have been written: Jane Liddle, whose efforts halved the time required in the archives and libraries of London and Belfast and who provided constant encouragement during the research process and the writing-up; to Fathers Keenan, McMunro and Mac Manuis for access to the valuable chronicles of St Matthew's Church and the Clonard Monastery in Belfast; to Briege Rice, for much appreciated help in the latter stages of research; to Bob Purdie for reading through early drafts and providing invaluable comments; to Martin Parker, whose computing skills ensured that an ageing desktop survived long enough to see the completion of the text; and to two men, one a former member of the IRA and the other of the UVF, who were participants in some of the events described in the book and who gave generously of their time in answering my questions and explaining their own positions. Given the circumstances, it is even more important than usual to emphasize the customary caveat that the conclusions reached and the views expressed in the book are those of the author alone.

SIMON PRINCE: I have accumulated many scholarly debts in working on this book. My greatest debt is to Roy Foster who signalled that I was heading down a dead end, guided me in a different direction and encouraged me to wander all over the road and indeed off it, too. I have also benefitted enormously from the support that I have received from Richard English, Ian McBride and Richard Bourke; my contribution to this book would not have been written without them. Bob Purdie, Patrick Maume, Briege Rice, Erika Hanna, Robert Lynch, Margaret O'Callaghan, Graham Walker, Dominic Bryan, Kieran McEvoy, Catherine Merridale, Michael Drolet, Elizabeth Elbourne, Frances Flanagan, Sarah Stoller, Lorenzo Bosi, Jeremy Varon, Ruud van Dijk and Chris Reynolds all took the trouble to read early forms of some of the chapters, and I am deeply grateful for their incisive comments. During the course of researching and writing my contribution to this book, many other people have helped me in different ways and I am glad to have this chance to thank them: Giogros Antoniou, Lauren Arrington, Pamela Ballinger, John Bew, Eugenio Biagini, Jessie Blackbourn, Dani Blaylock, the late Kevin Boyle, Mike Broers, Tony Coughlan, Tony Craig, Gianluca De Fazio, Anne Devlin, Michael Fanning, Diarmaid Ferriter, Martyn Frampton, Ultán Gillen, Clive Holmes, Eamonn Hughes, Roy Johnston, the late Tony Judt, Tara Keenan Thomson, Michael Kerr, Frances Lannon, Jane Liddle, Maria Luddy, Brendan 'Bik' McFarlane, Leo McGann, Marisa McGlinchey, Cillian McGrattan, Peter McLoughlin, Caroline Magennis, Jonathan Moore, Ellie Nairne, Caoimhe Ni Dháibhéid, Eunan O'Halpin, Senia Paseta, Tamson Pietsch, Paul Readman, Colin Reid, the Rice family, Daniel Sherman, Robert Tombs, Jon Tonge, Brian Walker and Rakefet Zalashik. (As ever, not all of those I thank agree with all the arguments I have made nor do they bear any responsibility for any errors.) I owe debts to institutions as well as individuals because Lady Margaret Hall, Oxford, the Institute of Irish Studies, Queen's University Belfast, and the History Department, King's College London, have each provided me with an academic home over the last four years. 'Writing a book,' George Orwell argued, 'is a horrible, exhausting struggle, like a long bout of some painful illness.' So, I want to end by thanking my best friends and my family for nursing me through this second bout: Tom Parkin, Nick Dale and Corin Spencer-Allen; my sister Sarah, my father Keith and my mother Margaret. I have dedicated this book to my mother, who deserves much better.

List of Abbreviations

BBC	British Broadcasting Corporation
BHAC	Belfast Housing Action Committee
CCDC	Central Citizens Defence Committee
CIA	Central Intelligence Agency
CND	Campaign for Nuclear Disarmament
CS	O-Chlorobenzylidene Malonontrite
DCAC	Derry Citizens Action Committee
DCDA	Derry Citizens Defence Association
DHAC	Derry Housing Action Committee
DUAC	Derry Unemployed Action Committee
ECHR	European Convention on Human Rights
EOKA	National Organization of Cypriot Fighters
GOC	General Officer Commanding
GPO	General Post Office
IRA	Irish Republican Army
ITN	Independent Television News
MP	Member of Parliament
NICRA	Northern Ireland Civil Rights Association
NIHT	Northern Ireland Housing Trust
NILP	Northern Ireland Labour Party
PD	People's Democracy
RIC	Royal Irish Constabulary
RTÉ	Raidió Teilifís Éireann
RUC	Royal Ulster Constabulary
SDA	Shankill Defence Association
SNCC	Student Non-violent Co-ordinating Committee
UCDC	Ulster Constitution Defence Committee
UDI	Unilateral Declaration of Independence
UDR	Ulster Defence Regiment
UPV	Ulster Protestant Volunteers

USC	Ulster Special Constabulary
UTV	Ulster Television
UVF	Ulster Volunteer Force
VSC	Vietnam Solidarity Campaign
YUHAC	Young Unionist Housing Action Committee

Maps

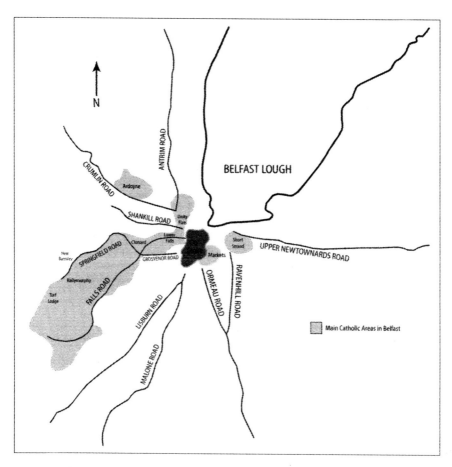

1. Main Catholic Areas in Belfast

Belfast and Derry in Revolt

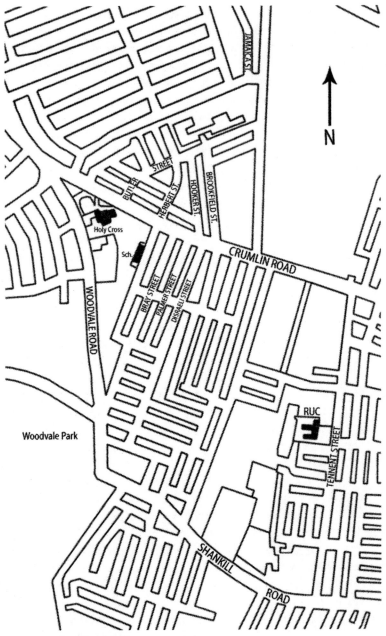

2. The Crumlin Road Interface

3. East Belfast

4. The Falls-Shankill Interface

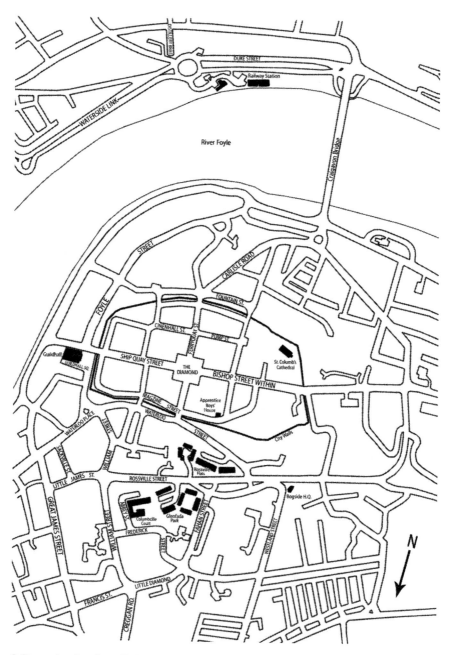

5. Derry, showing the walled city, the Waterside and the Bogside

Introduction

'The beginning, in which was conceived the end, could not but continue to shape the middle part of the story'

– Elizabeth Bowen

We could have chosen any number of beginnings. In Derry, at the close of the 1950s, five children almost died in the fire that burned down the hut which was their family's home.[1] In Belfast, on the night of 14/15 August 1969, a 9-year-old boy was killed by machine-gun fire as nearby streets burned.[2] In Derry, during the last week of June 1970, two young girls died in the fire that burned through their house after their father's attempts to make a bomb in the kitchen caused an explosion.[3] But, the choice of beginnings that has been offered here would lock in different narrative meanings. Brian Friel's play *Freedom of the City*, which is set in Derry at the start of 1970, brilliantly illustrates how narrative brings together identity, causality, agency and trajectory across time. An American sociologist's expert testimony, a children's rhyme, a priest's sermon and an army officer's press statement give different explanations of what has caused the violence: poverty, the unfinished Irish revolution, the injustice inflicted upon the local Catholic community and terrorism.[4] All narratives, including historical ones, are constructions and all narratives, even ones which insist they are simply stories, offer ways of viewing the world. So, we have chosen to begin by explaining how we constructed our historical narrative and why we are asking, not what caused the Troubles to start, but rather, how the violence of the start of the Troubles was produced.

There are books that are perfect and then there are books that actually get published. This, obviously, is one of the latter. We will make no attempt to pass off our work as the definitive history or the full story of the start of the Troubles, especially as our focus is just on Belfast and Derry. This book is not the final word on the subject, and we expect our arguments to be assessed and tested by others. To lubricate this communication – which we hope will be with historians of different countries, with academics from related disciplines and with wider publics – some methodological niceties need to be observed. Our aim is to present the most convincing interpretation of the past which we can construct from available sources. As Peter Mandler has reasoned, 'while our evidence is partial, some of it is better than the rest, and some better suited than the rest to addressing certain problems'.[5] We are not asking, once again, what the origins of the Troubles were, but instead how the form of the conflict in Northern Ireland changed.[6] The violence produced in Belfast and Derry at the end of the period examined in our book was such that the conflict had taken on the form of a civil war. (We are using here the political scientist Stathis Kalyvas's broad definition of civil war as 'armed conflict within the boundaries of a recognized sovereign entity between parties subject to a common authority at the outset of the hostilities'.)[7] As we are addressing a new question, we have drawn on primary sources that have not been used before and we have also examined for ourselves ones that have because other scholars were pursuing other problems when they were in the archives. That said, this book could not have been written without the pathbreaking work done on Northern Ireland by historians, political scientists, sociologists, anthropologists, lawyers and literary critics; the choice we have made to try, wherever possible, to base our arguments upon primary sources is a methodological one. Most of our extensive debts are paid, as much as they can be, up front in the acknowledgements rather than in instalments spread throughout the text.

'Historians,' Joseph Ruane and Jennifer Todd claim, 'in contrast [to social scientists], tend to work more empirically and intuitively'– and, 'without explicit theoretical reflection', 'crucial issues can be elided'.[8] (The use of 'explicit' matters here: all historians employ theories, it is just that some are more explicit and thoughtful about this than others.) This criticism is echoed by Mandler. 'Why,' he asks, 'are we so conservative in our use of theory?' Mandler suggests not only that 'we refresh ourselves with ... draughts of theory', but also that 'we need to explore [the] theoretical work being done ... not thirty or a hundred years ago, but recently'.[9] This is advice worth following. So, when our archival research carried us to a point where our intuition told us we needed help from our neighbours in the academy, we chose to look for it. Contemporary theory, to use Mandler's term, is indeed refreshing, but we have tried to drink responsibly by testing these theories with our own evidence and keeping hold of the historian's sober recognition of how alien and complex the past is. Still, objections could be raised that we have merely been taking small sips of contemporary theory; we would counter, however, that we have again been simply staying within our limits, as we have been given a fixed number of words in which to answer our question. Similar complaints could be made about our use of comparison, and we would give a similar explanation for our approach. While, ideally, a comparative framework should be set out and primary research should be conducted, this is actually just one end of a continuum: every historical narrative is comparative, even when the comparisons are implicit.[10] We have chosen to draw explicit, albeit brief, comparisons in our book because, first and foremost, contemporaries often located themselves within international contexts. Answering our question has required us to take account of how people's mental worlds stretched beyond the streets of Belfast and Derry.

As will soon become clear, one of us has made more use of theory and comparison than the other. We are advancing broadly the same arguments in this book, yet we nonetheless have chosen to allow each other plenty of room for personal styles, emphases and interpretations by writing separate narratives on Belfast (Geoffrey Warner) and on Derry (Simon Prince). Our different voices reinforce and open up reflection on the fact that our new history is a narrative and therefore is contingent upon the choices we have made as historians. Such a structure has other advantages, too, as it keeps calling the reader's attention to the differences between the start of the Troubles in the two cities that were, usually, at the heart of developments. We, it is perhaps worth stressing again, are not claiming to be presenting an Olympian view of the whole of Northern Ireland. Despite these narrative demands, we are confident that readers will take in their stride the book's shifts of perspective, place and period; after all, to quote Roy Foster, modern Irish writers have had 'neither the time nor the inclination for novels that were formal in conception and linear in structure'.[11] This book is meant to be read from cover to cover because from conception to completion, this has been our intention. Indeed, we would have chosen to construct our respective narratives quite differently if they were going to be separated out into two books instead of being put inside the same covers. That said, while the whole is greater than its parts, we have accepted that, in these hard-pressed times, this is a lot to ask of readers and so we have tried, in various ways, to make it easier to consume the book in bits. For those reviewers who are in a hurry, we will treat you to sweeping statements about our underlying assumptions in the introduction's remaining paragraphs.

'It is quite possible,' muses John Whyte, 'that, in proportion to size, Northern Ireland is the most heavily-researched area on earth'.[12] For our particular period, this famous quotation should be reworked: It is quite possible that, in relation to its importance, Northern Ireland is one of the least researched areas of the 'global Sixties'. The 'Surrealist Map of the World' depicts an island of Ireland which, due to its contribution to art, dwarfs Britain and many other European countries; a map of the 'global Sixties' that reflected political impact would almost certainly feature a huge Ireland as well.[13] But, even on this expanded area, are we not still covering well-trodden ground? Well, modern Irish historians are right to be proud of how our discipline punches above its weight – however, we would be wrong to let our skill at the sweet science blind us as to what division we belong in. For example, two recent, impressive publications on the Troubles from our academic neighbours cite as the standard works for this period political science books from the last century.[14] Bob Purdie's *Politics in the Streets* and Niall Ó Dochartaigh's *From Civil Rights to Armalites* owe their continuing relevance to the quality of the writing and the research; they also owe it to having had the field largely to themselves. History students starting post-graduate research today that touches on the start of the Troubles will start off reading political science books based on doctoral dissertations which were started before they were born. Of course, as we have made clear above and will below, too, the existing literature consists of much more than these two books. Nonetheless, the frequency with which both *Politics in the Streets* and *From Civil Rights to Armalites* appear in footnotes and reading lists deals a body blow to the received wisdom that the start of the Troubles has been overburdened with research.

What, then, is 'new' about our 'New History'? Firstly, this book has drawn upon new sources. 'Much of what has been written about this period,' as Henry Patterson pointed out in 2008, 'has as yet made little use of the wealth of governmental archive material now available.'[15] There are, of course, exceptions, notably the pioneering work of Thomas Hennessey on the origins and evolution of the Troubles.[16] Following in the footsteps of Hennessey and others, following different research questions and following different methodologies, we have used primary sources that were overlooked by and/or unavailable to previous scholars. We therefore have also been able to relate the streets to the authorities much more closely than even Hennessey could do – which matters because the actions and identities of the people on the streets cannot be understood without examining the actions and identities of the people in authority, and vice versa.[17] Secondly, this book has drawn upon new scholarship. In the last decade or so, historians of the American civil rights movement have pushed back its chronological and geographical boundaries; this has transformed the comparisons that can be made between developments on either side of the Atlantic. Research on the complicated linkages between non-violence, self-defence and armed struggle has been especially useful here. As has recent work on gender, material culture, riots, social movements, individual memory, collective memory, narrative and the dynamics of violence in civil wars.

So, we have tested ideas, hypotheses and arguments against a wealth of systematically gathered and interrogated primary sources – and we have changed our views as the evidence has compelled (indeed, we have broken away from our earliest work on Northern Ireland). After all of this, what basic conclusion have we reached about the Troubles? That it was, essentially, a political conflict.[18] The concept of ethnic conflict, in contrast, depends upon people, either as perpetrators, participants or victims, being completely interchangeable; cultures, in this interpretation, are given agency, while individual actors are reduced to following a script handed down to them.[19] Arguments that 'natural' ties can inspire communal action are falling out of favour in the academy, but the view nonetheless lingers that there is something special about ethnic identities compared to other identities in the turn to violence. Despite this seeming to be simple common sense, however, making direct causal links between ethnicity and conflict is much more problematic than it first appears. Inter-communal relations across the world and across history are usually peaceful and co-operative, even where and when inequality and discrimination exists.[20] Ethnic identity, moreover, is a subset of a broader identity category in which membership is determined by attributes associated with, or thought to be associated with, descent and in which the intrinsic characteristics are constrained change and visibility; most arguments about how ethnic divisions lead to violence, though, require ethnic identities to be fixed and assume that they can be distinguished from other group identities, including descent-based ones.[21] The example of India since independence is helpful here. The political scientist Paul Brass has found 'an overarching discourse of Hindu-Muslim relations' that explains 'all incidents involving members of these ... communities in terms of the eternal differences between them'. This discourse, among other things, displaces blame from democratic politics, which is the context that gives meaning to the idea of a Hindu 'majority' and a Muslim 'minority' and which fixes these identities. Hindu-Muslim riots are not a spontaneous upsurge in ethnic animosities, but rather a particularly brutal form of electioneering that only happen in certain Indian states.[22] Similarly, the start of the Troubles was not the beginning of the latest round in a centuries-old quarrel between Protestants and Catholics; it was part of the unfinished Irish revolution, the struggle over what democracy meant in theory and how it should then be applied in practice. Peter Hart, following Charles Tilly's classic definition of revolution, calculates that the Irish one ended with the Civil War.[23] That said, when it comes to answering our question, it is more appropriate to borrow and adapt François Furet's definition of the French Revolution, according to which the Revolution ended, in a narrower political sense, with the second founding of the Third Republic and, in a wider ideological sense, with the decline of communism.[24] In Northern Ireland, during our period of study, the modern democratic ideologies of constitutional nationalism, republicanism, socialism and unionism were still struggling for mastery. The question of who ruled and by what right had not been settled: the Irish revolution, in this sense, had not ended.

Prioritizing politics does not mean overlooking Northern Ireland's many fiscal, economic, social and cultural problems or, indeed, people's personal problems. (It should be noted here that while we have questioned the role of ethnic cleavages in the production of violence, there is no question that the communal divide was important.) We are political historians; nonetheless, as James Vernon recommends, 'the questions we ask, not the territories we claim dominion over, should be our guide'.[25] This book is a 'fox', not a 'hedgehog', and we have chosen to let it race through different fields, including social, cultural, intellectual, military, international and urban histories.[26] That said, Northern Ireland's other problems entered into the production of the violence of the start of the Troubles by becoming objects of political contention within a political 'game' which was gaining new players and new rules. It is the production of the violence, not the causes of the conflict, that concern us. Violence, it is usually assumed, is something that naturally emerges when a conflict boils over, yet there is, as the sociologist Rogers Brubaker and the political scientist David Laitin point out, a 'lack of strong evidence showing that higher levels of conflict ... lead to higher levels of violence'. They conclude that 'Violence is not a quantitative degree of conflict but a qualitative form of conflict'.[27] Although the violence of the start of the Troubles was linked to the unresolved Irish revolution, the underlying conflict cannot explain where, when and how violence was produced – nor who produced it.

Politics, it should be conceded here, was marginal to most people's lives at the start of the Troubles. Consequently, there are many Belfasts and Derrys, each with their own history and their own memory, which have not made it into this book. Certain readers may not recognize their memories of 'their' city in how we, two outsiders, have chosen to present our research. This is not something we can choose simply to ignore, especially as everybody who takes part in a public debate should show equal respect to all people. But, what does this, in practice, mean for us? As far as matters of reason and evidence are concerned, we have not thought of our readers as primarily members of particular communities, but instead have thought of them as individuals capable of evaluating and criticizing our arguments and sources. History is universal: its writers and its readers cannot claim special privileges for themselves just because they belong to a specific group, even if they are victims.[28] Indeed, the novelist and critic Zadie Smith, writing about America's 'civil rights generation', warns that 'bitter struggles deform their participants in subtle, complicated ways', such as instilling the 'idea that one should speak one's ... allegiance first and the truth second'. That said, as Smith goes on to acknowledge, 'the black movement had to yell with a clear and unified voice, or risk not being heard at all', and so criticisms should not be made without 'context', 'empathy' and 'understanding'.[29] The Derry Citizens Defence Association, through its lawyers, asked for the same thing – pleading with the Scarman Tribunal, which was inquiring into the events of the Battle of the Bogside, to 'place' 'individual acts' in a 'more sympathetic light' by considering 'background and circumstances'.[30] We have chosen to be critical, yet we have also chosen to try to be civil.

Some readers, however, may be concerned that we have not turned our book into a site of resistance. If we have not sided with the 'victims', does that not mean, then, that we have sided with the 'perpetrators'? (We will not pursue here the argument that it would be anachronistic to work as historians within these terms.) Well, 'victim' and 'perpetrator' made their way into historical writing via research on the Third Reich (although most historians now reject these labels because they fail to capture the complexity of what happened); so, like the leading authority on the Holocaust, we will answer that 'Explaining is not excusing; understanding is not forgiving'.[31] Richard J. Evans has gone further still, complaining that the 'growing tendency' 'in favour of the exercise of moral judgment' has led to 'analysis, argument and interpretation' getting pushed aside.[32] This holds for Northern Ireland, too, as assigning blame – stating that the origin of the conflict lies in, say, imperialism or a clash of cultures – fails to explain how, where and when violence was produced at the start of the Troubles in Belfast and Derry. Moreover, making moral judgments is not as simple as handing out white and black hats.[33] For example, John Hume, the 'apostle of non-violence in this part of the world', faced forceful accusations during the autumn of 1969 from both Unionists and socialists that he partly bore responsibility for the violence on the streets.[34] According to the Derry Labour Party, Hume had taken the 'tiger for a walk on a leash made of thread' and was now, with 'sick-making ... saintliness', 'whining that "it's not my fault"'.[35] Anyway, is it actually in the interests of those for whom the struggle continues to present the past as a morality play? 'By idolizing those whom we honor,' a close friend of Martin Luther King once cautioned, 'we fail to realize that we could go and do likewise'.[36]

'[I]t must be understood that it is none of our function to make moral judgments,' announces the character of the judge who chairs the tribunal in *Freedom of the City* into the deaths of three civilians at the hands of the British army. Later, in the theatre of the play, the sociologist's oral evidence is interrupted as the victims stagger on to the stage to tell their own stories.[37] Their truth has broken through the totalizing narrative mouthed by the academic outsider. But, has it? Objectivity lies at the sum total of all possible subjectivities; although it can never be reached, it can be approached by shifting perspectives. While Friel's account provides us with a recognizable portrayal, which transcends factual detail, of what pain and loss feel like, a historical account offers a different route back to the past, one which can answer different questions.[38] We have chosen to look closely at what was happening on the streets in Belfast and Derry and at how this was situated in local, regional and international contexts. Of course, there is still much that we have overlooked. So, while we believe we have something new to say, we do not pretend to have said everything that there is to say.

NOTES

1. *Derry Journal*, 6 November 2009.
2. Marshall autopsy report, 15 August 1969, Belfast, Public Record Office of Northern Ireland (PRONI), BELF/6/1/1/2
3. INTSUM, 24 to 30 June 1970, London, National Archives, WO/305/3355; *Derry Journal*, 30 June 1970.
4. B. Friel, *Freedom of the City* (London: Faber and Faber, 1974).
5. P. Mandler, 'The Problem with Cultural History', *Cultural and Social History*, 1, 1 (January 2004), pp. 94–117, pp. 94–5.
6. On the origins of the Troubles, see, for example, H. Patterson, *Ireland since 1939: The Persistence of Conflict* (Dublin: Penguin Ireland, 2006); T. Hennessey, *Northern Ireland: The Origins of the Troubles* (Dublin: Gill & Macmillan, 2005); P. Dixon, *Northern Ireland: The Politics of War and Peace* (Basingstoke: Palgrave Macmillan, 2001); N. Ó Dochartaigh, *From Civil Rights to Armalites: Derry and the Birth of the Irish Troubles* (Cork: Cork University Press, 1997); J. Ruane and J. Todd, *The Dynamics of Conflict in Northern Ireland: Power, Conflict and Emancipation* (Cambridge: Cambridge University Press, 1996); B. Purdie, *Politics in the Streets: The Origins of the Civil Rights Movement in Northern Ireland* (Belfast: Blackstaff Press, 1990).
7. S. Kalyvas, *The Logic of Violence in Civil War* (Cambridge: Cambridge University Press, 2006), p. 17.
8. Ruane and Todd, *The Dynamics of Conflict in Northern Ireland*, p. 3.
9. Mandler, 'The Problem with Cultural History', p. 116.
10. S. Berger, 'Comparative History', in S. Berger, H. Feldner and K. Passmore (eds), *Writing History: Theory & Practice* (London: Arnold, 2003), pp. 161–79, p. 161.
11. R. Foster, 'The Story of Ireland', in R. Foster (ed.), *The Irish Story* (London: Penguin, 2001), pp. 1–22, p. 3. For Foster's latest thinking on Irish narratives, see R. Foster, *Words Alone: Yeats and his Inheritances* (Oxford: Oxford University Press, 2011).
12. J. Whyte, *Interpreting Northern Ireland* (Oxford: Oxford University Press, 1990), p. xviii.
13. *Variétés*, June 1929.
14. P. McLoughlin, *John Hume and the Revision of Irish Nationalism* (Manchester: Manchester University Press, 2010), p. 18; K. McEvoy, 'What Did the Lawyers Do During the "War"? Neutrality, Conflict and the Culture of Quietism', *Modern Law Review*, 74, 3 (May 2011), pp. 350–84, p. 357.
15. H. Patterson, 'The British State and the Rise of the IRA, 1969–71: The View from the

Conway Hotel', *Irish Political Studies*, 23, 4 (December 2008), pp. 491–511, p. 491.

16. Hennessey, *Northern Ireland*; T. Hennessey, *The Evolution of the Troubles 1970–72* (Dublin: Irish Academic Press, 2007).

17. See D. McAdam, S. Tarrow and C. Tilly, *Dynamics of Contention* (Cambridge: Cambridge University Press, 2001).

18. This scholarly argument was pioneered in R. Bourke, *Peace in Ireland: The War of Ideas* (London: Pimlico, 2003).

19. S. Kalyvas, 'The Ontology of "Political Violence": Action and Identity in Civil Wars', *Perspective on Politics*, 1, 3 (September 2003), pp. 475–494, p. 481.

20. A. Lawrence and E. Chenoweth, 'Introduction', in E. Chenoweth and A. Lawrence (eds), *Rethinking Violence: States and Non-State Actors in Conflict* (Harvard, MA: MIT Press, 2010), pp. 1–19, pp. 8–10.

21. K. Chandra, 'What Is Ethnic Identity and Does It Matter?' *Annual Review of Political Science*, 9 (June 2006), pp. 397–424.

22. P. Brass, 'Foucault Steals Political Science', *Annual Review of Political Science*, 3 (June 2000), pp. 305–30, pp. 325–6.

23. P. Hart, *The IRA at War 1916–1923* (Oxford: Oxford University Press, 2003), pp. 10 and 27.

24. F. Furet, *Interpreting the French Revolution* trans. E. Forster (Cambridge: Cambridge University Press, 1981), pp. 81–9.

25. J. Vernon, *Hunger: A Modern History* (Cambridge, MA: Harvard University Press, 2007), p. ix.

26. I. Berlin, *The Hedgehog and the Fox: Essays on Tolstoy's View of History* (London: Weidenfeld and Nicolson, 1953). Hedgehogs see the world through the lens of one big idea; foxes draw on many little ideas to understand the world.

27. R. Brubaker and D. Laitin, 'Ethnic and Nationalist Violence', *Annual Review of Sociology*, 24 (August 1998), pp. 423–52, p. 426.

28. S. Collini, *That's Offensive! Criticism, Identity, Respect* (London: Seagull Books, 2010).

29. Z. Smith, 'Speaking in Tongues', *New York Review of Books*, February 26, 2009.

30. DCDA's submission to the Scarman tribunal, [Summer 1971], London, Institute of Advanced Legal Study, Scarman submissions.

31. C. Browning, *The Path to Genocide: Essays on Launching the Final Solution* (Cambridge: Cambridge University Press, 1992), p. xx.

32. R. Evans, 'Introduction', *Journal of Contemporary History*, 39, 2 (April 2004), pp. 163–7.

33. See, for example, T. Shanahan, *The Provisional Irish Republican Army and the Morality of Terrorism* (Edinburgh: Edinburgh University Press, 2009).

34. J. Hume's evidence to the Scarman Tribunal, 14 November 1969, London, Institute of Advanced Legal Study, Scarman minutes of evidence, pp. 16 and 48.

35. 'Labour and Civil Rights', 4 October 1969, Belfast, Linen Hall Library, P1618.

36. D. Garrow, *Bearing the Cross: Martin Luther King, Jr., and the Southern Christian Leadership Conference* (New York, NY: William Morrow, 1999 edn.), p. 625.

37. Friel, *Freedom of the City*.

38. The British army intelligence summary records, despite 'rumours, alarms and excursions', 'there was very little trouble' – and there were no killings. INTSUM, 4 to 10 February 1970, NA, WO/305/3350.

1

Before October

INTRODUCTION

'Every Irishman,' wrote John Steinbeck in 1953, 'sooner or later makes a pilgrimage to the home of his ancestors.' But, the American novelist continued, 'He wouldn't stay there if you gave him the place.' Steinbeck and his wife found Derry to be a 'city which is somber even ... in sunlight' – 'and a desolation came over us'. He asked the 'not-the-real-porter' in their hotel: '"Has all illegality gone out of this rebellious island in three generations?"' The 'sad-looking man' did not 'make out my meaning'.[1] When the fortieth anniversary of the start of the civil rights movement was marked in Derry, a veteran activist also did not make out his meaning. The Derryman somehow managed to claim that Steinbeck, 'antenna alert', 'realised that this community around him would soon uprise'. 'It [i.e. the civil rights movement] was a natural, organic, reflex uprising.'[2]

The metaphor that injustice produced a build up of pressure which was not released by reforms and so eventually exploded in violence is a common one across history; it is also one that is powerful enough to result in evidence to the contrary being ignored. Metaphor clearly matters. It is a property of concepts and of words; it offers help with understanding ideas as well as with enjoying language; it often links together things that are not similar at all; it is an essential part of how humans think about their worlds.[3] This chapter argues that for Derry before October 1968 and the emergence of the civil rights movement, another metaphor from the natural sciences is more appropriate. Evolution, put simply, involves adaptation, whereby an organism over time becomes better able to live in its habitat, and mutation, in which a dramatic change to a species – often induced by an external shock – leads to the pace of development being accelerated. Once Northern

Ireland had been created during the early 1920s, the arrangements did not stay static: politics, society, economics and culture were always in flux, with each change opening up possibilities of further changes. Derry Catholics, workers and women as well as middle-class men, were able to find new ways to push at the boundaries of Unionist control and secure tangible reforms. What was important was not frustration with the lack of rights, but instead fresh power to fight for those rights. Most groups and individuals, though, shied away from direct confrontation, and the few which did not tended to launch futile attacks on the system's strongest points. In the second half of the 1960s, however, radicals from the Labour Party and the Republican movement borrowed and adapted a new transnational form of political action – and this was to change the situation dramatically.

Although the chapter draws upon urban history, among other specialisms, its focus is not on the city itself but on local politics before October 1968. The first section introduces Derry through the stories of working-class Catholic women, which are developed into a contextualized case study of social and political activism prior to the civil rights era. The next section examines two of the main strategies employed by Derry Catholics in their efforts to reshape the city: direct action and self help. While they are separated out here to make them more convenient to study, the strategies were generally used in combination with each other. The third section explores the different approaches taken by the Unionists, in Derry and at Stormont, as they sought to retain control. Reform was seen by some Unionists to be a way of crushing and co-opting a range of internal and external challenges to the party's dominant position. A reform could throw up temporary and uneasy coalitions between surprising allies, on both sides of the debate. The Londonderry Area Plan, for example, was backed not just by Unionists but by Nationalists as well. The moderate leadership of the self-help movement, in contrast, lined up with the radicals to oppose aspects of the plan to develop Derry. The final section describes how the leftists formulated a new strategy which broke out of the limits set by bounded reform and started a revolution. The chapter thus ends with the political actors who brought the 'before-October' period to an end.

WINTER IN SPRINGTOWN

'Winter was for back lanes, cinema, Christmas presents, school competitions, dances and a sight that made my father smile: my mother standing with her back to the range, legs spread, skirt hitched up, warming her bum.'[4] Nell McCafferty seems here to be selling her Irish childhood spent in the Bogside. With Ireland changing utterly in the years around the millennium, the reading public often clutched at books that carried them back to a lost time which was more innocent and more certain.[5] In fact, *Nell* relates the young McCafferty's uncertainties about herself to the larger uncertainties of living in Derry during the 1950s. 'On winter nights,' McCafferty recalls, she sat like a 'cat', 'watching': she saw husbands strike their wives, she saw two boys standing apart because they had been raped together, she saw a nervous girl who was pimped out by her father, she saw illicit affairs, she saw pregnancies outside of marriage and she saw teenagers of both sexes who desired her. This is community viewed in the harsh winter light or through the gloom, not bathed in the warm glow from hearths and oil lamps.[6] Admittedly, while McCafferty may be recalling the memories that are remembered best and writing with scorching honesty, *Nell* should still be read as a reconstruction of her youth made in late middle age.[7] Nonetheless, the book remains a warning against the will-o'-the-wisps of idealized communities. As another Derry civil-rights activist told an interviewer in 1979, 'I never looked upon a sense of community born out of desperation as anything healthy'.[8]

It is a different winter and it is a different story from McCafferty, this time she is telling someone else's – Peggy Deery's. The 'one thing for a Catholic mother to do in Derry on a fine, wintry, Sunday afternoon', McCafferty explains, was to 'stroll...in the city cemetery'. Deery was barely a decade older than McCafferty, but her biological clock had a mechanism that dated back to the Victorian era: she gave birth to her fourteenth child in her late thirties and may have had pregnancies into her forties if her husband had lived.[9] At the start of the 1960s, one third of Derry's population was under 14 years of age, as compared with one quarter in Britain.[10] Nineteenth-century patterns survived in the shirt factories, too, where 90 per cent of employees were women – one fifth of the total workforce – and their hours varied as their lives and the economy changed.[11] For many mothers, with two, demanding roles to fulfil, a Sunday in the cemetery was 'a comparative treat', offering 'a rich source of gossip, speculation and tribal perspective'. The children, who came from homes that lacked gardens, played among the graves, and may have noticed that the Protestant high crosses tended to be grander than the Catholic low tombstones.[12]

Looking out from a hill of the dead upon a city that was slowly dying, the families could see this and other divisions among the 50,000 people living there. St Columb's Church, Long Tower, sat at the heart of Derry and was dedicated to the monk who had founded a settlement there in the sixth century.[13] Rising above this Catholic church was the Church of Ireland Bishop's Palace and a short distance away was the Anglican cathedral of St Columb's, which had been built by the City of London in the early seventeenth century. The new city of Londonderry, as it was named in the royal charter, was one of the last of Europe's bastides, providing defences for the Protestants from England and Scotland who had been settled there during the plantation of Ulster. Derry's walls were never breached, not even when James II's soldiers laid siege to Derry in the second year of the War of the League of Augsburg. The loyal order of the Apprentice Boys, which had its hall inside the old city, continued to mark this epic with annual commemorations, remembering both triumph and treachery.[14] At the end of the eighteenth century, the Catholic population outside the walls in what became the Bogside area, which had been reclaimed from the River Foyle, began to grow rapidly – and from 1920 to 1923 Derry was run by a nationalist and Sinn Féin council. When the Irish Republican Army (IRA) began its offensive, the resulting loyalist backlash initiated a cycle of reprisals which left the city ravaged by fire and eighteen people dead in just a single week during the summer of 1920. Afterwards, however, Derry's Irish Revolution was comparatively peaceful, as local Republicans thought violence was counter-productive and headquarters wanted recruits to be sent south to fight.[15] Still, the new Northern Irish Government decided to abolish proportional representation and Derry duly returned a Unionist council again. As late as the mid-1930s, Stormont believed that 'the fate of [the] constitution was on a knife edge' and that it was therefore 'defensible' to gerrymander Derry 'on the basis that the safety of the state is the supreme law'. In a 'Nationalist city', a 'Unionist majority [was] secured by a manipulation of ward boundaries, for the sole purpose of retaining...control'.[16] The gerrymander was copper-fastened by the property franchise, which put rateable values above population sizes and which deprived more Catholics than Protestants of the vote.[17] In 1958, the Unionist Chief Whip cautioned party grandees that 'if we were to allow universal suffrage', 'we may lose Derry'.[18] Partition deformed the city in another way: Donegal, which had once been inside its hinterland, was now part of a different state and the local economy was hit by the loss. War and welfare eventually pulled the city out of the slump. On the slopes of the Creggan, which lay above the cemetery, a vast public housing estate was built in the post-war years – and on these foundations were being built dreams of indoor toilets and bathrooms.[19] Some of the mothers had not waited for the state to solve Derry's chronic housing problems and were living with their families in huts that had been put up for the American naval personnel stationed in the north east of Ireland during the Second World War. (The North Atlantic Treaty Organization forces posted to Derry were fighting the Cold War from new bases.) The Deerys were among the first squatters in Springtown Camp.[20]

Although desperation had pushed them to go outside the law, most of the Springtown squatters, Protestant and Catholic, had wanted to remain respectable. So, they worked hard to transform temporary barracks into permanent family homes and they were also happy for Londonderry Corporation to take over the management of the site and charge them rent.[21] However, despite all that was achieved through self-help and pressurizing the authorities into action, Springtown was still a dangerous, depressing and disease-ridden place for the hundreds of people who lived there. Many residents, including Deery, chose to emigrate rather than suffer through another winter waiting for the council to give them a decent house – in a ward where their vote would not wreck the gerrymander.[22] During the winter, families had, as one father put it, to risk 'fire or freeze', and in November 1959 an oil heater set fire to one of the huts and five children almost died. This was the spark that began an eight-year campaign to get homes for the remaining residents.[23]

On a march through the city in January 1963, one of the placards carried the slogan 'Springtown – Derry's Little Rock'.[24] Comparing their plight to that of African Americans in Arkansas framed the Springtown struggle as a moral one conducted within the system. But, the two movements were linked by more than a metaphor. The protests of poor African American and Irish Catholic women were politicizing their identities as mothers and wives who were working for their homes, families and communities.[25] The Student Non-violent Co-ordinating Committee (SNCC) in the United States referred to these local leaders as 'mamas'. 'There is always a "mama",' explained a SNCC activist in 1962, 'usually a militant woman in the community, outspoken, understanding and willing to catch hell.'[26] When Springtown's 'mammies', led by Sadie Campbell, opened the campaign in November 1959 by occupying the council chamber, they stressed that they were there to demand their citizenship rights on behalf of their husbands, some of whom had served in the army, and of their young children.[27] The respectability that they had battled so hard to hold onto in the camp was now another weapon in their hands. Respectability was a tactic that had long been used by American 'mamas', too. Racists defended segregation by portraying blacks as naturally lazy, ignorant and irresponsible. So, civil rights activists behaved in accordance with prevailing middle-class standards of respectability and thus turned this stereotype back on the segregationists; they made themselves seem deserving of full citizenship and their opponents appear as little more than animals.[28] In Northern Ireland, as a prominent Tyrone Unionist told the party leadership in 1950, the authorities often assumed that 'Respectable families' were 'PROTESTANT FAMILIES!'[29] The Springtown 'mammies' employed respectability to overcome these sectarian and class prejudices. It helped them prove that they were not to blame for their problems and that the authorities were failing in their moral duties under the welfare state.[30] (The welfare state was neither an historical inevitability nor a monolith, but rather a contingent and hybrid achievement – one that gave the 'mammies' new opportunities and new objectives.)[31] The press photographs taken at the October 1960 occupation show that the protesters were smartly dressed, their faces were made up and their hair was in a permanent wave.[32] The last was the ultimate symbol of post-war respectability, marking women out from those at the very bottom of society who had unkempt greasy hair.[33] The 'mammies' fighting the Springtown campaign were to prove a greater threat to Unionist power than the 'boys' fighting the IRA's Border Campaign.

That threat, though, should not be exaggerated nor should it be simplified. The Springtown campaign did prefigure some of the tactics that would be used at the end of the 1960s, yet it followed established political practices as well. The Springtown protesters occupied the council chamber, disrupted the corporation's meetings, squatted in houses, staged marches that ignored the city's sectarian geography and courted the media; they also asked their local MP to help, wrote to the Prime Minister, organized petitions, sent delegations to the authorities and appealed to the courts.[34] The campaign did open with young, working-class women entering the political sphere, yet it closed with middle-aged, middle-class men cutting a deal. The Springtown Camp Housing Committee was all male, and they were negotiating with men in the corporation, Londonderry Rural District Council, the local business community and the Northern Irish Government.[35] The campaign did show up the failings of Unionists and Nationalists, yet it demonstrated how flexible and effective they could be, too.[36] Nationalist politicians gave constructive support to the campaign from the first protest and Unionist councillors and ministers re-housed hundreds of families and turned the empty site into an industrial estate.[37] A range of strategies – direct action, self help and parliamentary politics – had together solved the immediate problem of Springtown Camp. That said, this approach was not capable of transforming Derry's political injustices: Stormont and its subordinate councils were providing houses and jobs to retain Unionist control.

IRISH ACTION

With the Second World War giving way to struggles to build a 'New Jerusalem' and to break the old colonial system, Eddie McAteer was elected to Stormont hopeful that Irish self-determination could finally be respected. He pushed out time-serving hacks within the Nationalist Party and led into office a younger political generation who wanted to pursue the interests of their constituents with greater energy.[38] However, with the return of cold wars, international and Irish, McAteer wondered whether there were roads, other than those marked constitutional and physical force, for the nationalist people to advance down. In the pamphlet *Irish Action*, published in 1948, McAteer invoked 'the mighty spirit of the late Mahatma [i.e. Mohandas Gandhi]', who had 'pointed a third road', that of 'non-co-operation, no violence [sic]'.[39]

A decade later, as another political generation stepped into the public sphere, self-help was mapped out by some as the road to take. When the first Credit Union branch was formed in Derry, the treasurer wrote an article about how 'the spirit which brings men together to co-operate' should be 'brought to bear on...problems at the local level', so as to 'lead to...gradual growth and prosperity'.[40] 'If any community needs self-help,' he later observed, 'it is this one'.[41] In Derry before October 1968, direct action and self-help played key roles in reshaping the city – within, of course, the limits set by Unionist control.

Questions about the origins of the direct-action and self-help traditions are unanswerable and distracting (as such questions so often are).[42] This section will instead consider early attempts in the post-war years to adapt these indigenous traditions to transnational trends and for changed local circumstances. With *Irish Action*, for instance, McAteer was recognizing that Gandhi had forged a new weapon (one that had helped end British rule) and that the welfare state had created new vulnerabilities. 'If the British Government's only answer to our pleadings is that the problem is not urgent,' he argued, 'then let us make it urgent!' Non-violence is not about petitioning the powerful, it is itself a distinct form of power.[43] McAteer laid out the methods he thought would make the problem urgent, would make the 'local misgovernment' practised by Unionists 'impossible'. These ranged from 'acting stupid' when dealing with officials to holding back taxes and occupying public buildings.[44] McAteer himself refused to pay his rates, which led to a court case in 1951. The following year, he tried to force his way onto the Mayor of Derry's chair, a gesture which symbolized that power in the city rightly lay with nationalists.[45] But, McAteer seemed to be the only one taking part in his campaign. Among the millions of other Irish nationalists, it was treated with indifference and, in some cases, outright hostility; as early as January 1949 the *Irish Times* commented: 'McAteer's formula can only lead to disaster'.[46] There were flaws in the formula, not least of which were McAteer's beliefs that 'organisation has distinct disadvantages' and that '[e]ach individual must constitute a complete action cell'; when, in fact, the success of a non-violent campaign depends heavily upon numbers and discipline.[47] The 'science of non-violence', to use Gandhi's phrase, would be experimented with again and again in Derry before October 1968.[48]

McAteer's experiences were not unique. Unearthing an idea that was rooted in the history and culture of India and transplanting it to foreign soil was far from easy, and many times the seed of the idea failed to bloom around the world.[49] Pacifists and civil rights activists in the United States were among those who admired Gandhi's 'soul force' and were ploughing on with efforts to grow non-violent movements. Indeed, by the second half of the 1950s, as the Springtown campaign showed, the variety of non-violent direct action that people were trying to introduce to Derry was American rather than Asian. As early as the inter-war years, the radical theologian Reinhold Niebuhr, who sympathized with the black struggle and would later influence Martin Luther King's thinking, had seen that it would be 'hopeless' to expect racial equality to come by 'trusting in the moral sense of the white race' or through 'violent revolution'. He, too, believed that the way ahead was instead along Gandhi's third road; 'non-violence', claimed Niebuhr, 'is a particularly strategic instrument for an oppressed group which is hopelessly in the minority'.[50] Although Gandhi maintained that the object of non-violent struggle was to convert rather than coerce the opponent, his civilized form of warfare had not just relied upon suffering love.[51] Niebuhr noted that 'political realism [had] qualified religious idealism' and that Gandhi's campaigns did 'coerce and destroy'. Economic boycotts, the refusal to use courts and schools, the illegal production of salt and tax strikes compelled the British Viceroy to act – to crack down with violence or to start up negotiations. Non-violence was therefore best understood as a 'type of coercion'. But, where violence would push the sides to a conflict increasingly apart, non-violence would keep open the lines of communication and the chance of a settlement. Niebuhr also drew attention to how using non-violence would further weaken an opponent by 'rob[bing] [him] of the moral conceit by which he identifies his interests with the peace and order of society'. The authorities and their apologists might still try to brand the protesters as terrorists, traitors and criminals, yet neutral elements both inside and outside the dominant group would most likely see through these underhand tactics. Non-violence would help win widespread support at home and abroad, neutralize the security forces and bring about defections. Niebuhr predicted that the 'emancipation of the Negro race in America probably waits upon the adequate development of this kind of social and political strategy'; he was right.[52] However, it took years to perfect the formula. Non-violence did not come naturally to African Americans anymore than it had to Indians or would to Derry's Catholics; non-violence had to be taught and enforced, and that required institutions and organization. So, over three decades were to pass between the theologian making his prophesy and King using 'a Niebuhrian stratagem of power' to win the great non-violent victories for civil rights at Birmingham and Selma, Alabama, in 1963 and 1965.[53]

With the IRA coming to terms with defeat in the early 1960s, these victories did not go unnoticed; some leading Republicans began to argue that military action alone would not succeed and that direct action, among other strategies, should also be tried.[54] Once again, Irish traditions and foreign fashions were woven together and fitted to the local situation. In January 1964, a new IRA volunteer, Eamon Melaugh, took out an advertisement in the *Derry Journal* which asked, 'are you concerned about unemployment, emigration?'[55] Melaugh wished to 'contact men of action prepared to do something concrete about these social evils'. Just ten people answered his call – and eight of them had jobs. 'It seems incredible that out of a total of 2,740 unemployed men only two should inquire about my advertisement', he complained to the *Derry Journal* six months later. Melaugh, though, still wanted to take Derry's unemployed out of 'apathy' and into jobs, and he still believed that 'Direct action must be taken'.[56] At the start of 1965, Melaugh finally succeeded in forming the Derry Unemployed Action Committee (DUAC); but he continued to have problems finding men of action.[57] The first protests were therefore more of a guerrilla marketing campaign than a campaign to disrupt local government so much that their opponents would be forced to negotiate a settlement. When Londonderry Corporation met in January 1965, Melaugh led in the DUAC and told the 'bigots' 'We do not intend to allow the business of this meeting to go on'. He made the front page of the *Derry Journal*.[58] From the thirty who had attended the inaugural meeting, the DUAC's membership was grown over a number of weeks through meetings and marches until there were enough people to bring traffic to a halt around the Guildhall during a visit by the Minister of Commerce.[59] This early momentum was not sustained, however, and the DUAC's activities were limited to greeting politicians with pickets or being greeted by them at Stormont and Westminster.[60] Ahead of the fiftieth anniversary of the Easter Rising, the IRA volunteers parked this protest vehicle – but they remained on what one of them had described as the 'road' of 'action, passive resistance and self-help'.[61]

The self-help tradition in Derry was closely connected with the Catholic Church. Rejected by Belfast, London and Dublin at the close of the Irish Revolution, Northern Catholics were given a home by Rome: a Catholic counter-society within the new Protestant state. There were Catholic schools, hospitals and voter registration associations – all of which depended upon the laity giving both their money and their time.[62] When Derrymen tried to reinvigorate their city's self-help tradition, the foreign model that inspired them was also Catholic. The Credit Union movement, as the Derry branch's treasurer, John Hume, explained in the press, was 'Catholic in origin' and had been 'endorsed down the years by many eminent Church leaders'.[63] Hume himself was a product of the Catholic counter-society and, in turn, felt a responsibility to this society; yet, he was a beneficiary of the welfare state, too, and an example of what could and could not be achieved under Stormont. The 1947 Education Act as well as the Catholic Church had provided the Bogside boy with a route – via St Columb's College and Maynooth – out of poverty and into the professions. The Credit Union's 'practical Christianity' now offered the chance of a route out for the community as a whole. Within eight years, the Derry branch had attracted around 6,200 members, loaned out over £1,000,000 and moved into a 'splendid new £26,000 headquarters'.[64] Such was the extent of this achievement that Hume advanced from a branch treasurer through the Northern chapter and the all-Ireland league to become a director on the world governing body.[65] The local was tied to the global.

'The movement creates self-help,' Hume told the Chamber of Commerce in October 1966, 'out of which will rise other things.'[66] That summer, the Derry Housing Association, which had been founded by Father Anthony Mulvey and was chaired by Hume, had bought a two-and-a-half acre site at the edge of the city on which it was putting up thirty-two semi-detached houses. By the start of 1967, Hume was telling the first annual general meeting that the 'only final answer' was the 'provision of homes on a large scale and at speed'.[67] The help in reaching this ambitious goal, though, was not only going to come from within the community itself. When the association drew up plans to build 211 houses, the authorities agreed a loan of £800,000 to pay for the entire cost of the project.[68] The housing associations created in Northern Ireland during the 1960s essentially owed their existence to the post-war expansion of the state. As Hume admitted, they had received 'endorsement and excellent assistance from the Ministry of Development'.[69] The Catholic counter-society in Derry was working with the Protestant state; social teaching which had been developed in opposition to socialism was being used by Hume and Mulvey in conjunction with collectivist legislation. Indeed, as early as 1947, the Catholic Church had set up a social services centre, funded by collections, to help their flock receive the benefits owed to them by the welfare state.[70] The people of Derry were travelling down roads that merged and parted in ways that may have seemed surprising, but the debates over tactics and strategies were about what practical steps to take next rather than about academic points of interest. Hume's attempts to guide both communities along twisting paths in 1965 led them to lose what they had set out to find and instead put them, by chance, on the road to what a Nationalist councillor described as the 'prospect of a revitalised city'.[71]

THE WEST'S ASLEEP

In the autumn of 1958, the Unionist MP for the City of Londonderry wrote to the Northern Irish Prime Minister about the likelihood of more factories coming to his constituency. To Viscount Brookeborough's dismay, Teddy Jones was lobbying against this happening. 'No government', Brookeborough confided to his diary, 'can stand idly by and allow possible industries not to develop'.[72] This nonetheless was the approach that he and his successor, Terence O'Neill, generally ended up taking. From the late 1950s onwards, Londonderry Unionists, who saw 'industrial expansion in Ulster [as] a most dangerous thing', were allowed to let their city gradually die rather than risk losing control of it.[73] With the staple industries of shipbuilding and linen in long-term decline and the major employer, Birmingham Sound Reproducers, laying off workers, the number of people signing on was to pass over 5,000 in the first months of 1967.[74] But, this meant that Catholic emigration was far outstripping immigration and that the gerrymander was protected. Catholics were also being pushed out of

Derry by the chronic housing shortage. In 1963, for example, thirty-three families moved into new homes provided by the corporation and ten times that figure put in fresh applications.[75] The Northern Ireland Housing Trust (NIHT) – the public body charged with supplementing private and local authority house building – had made up for some of the corporation's failings; the Unionist council, though, restricted most of the NIHT's activities to the overwhelmingly Catholic South Ward, as the trust did not allocate tenancies on a directly sectarian basis.[76] So, by 1966, the NIHT was giving notice that there was 'virtually no land left for housing within the city boundary'.[77] The corporation had helped make Derry one of the most overcrowded cities in the whole of Britain and Ireland and had stranded hundreds of families on the waiting list for public housing.[78] But, this meant that the North and Waterside wards kept their Protestant majorities and that the gerrymander was protected. Stormont only abandoned its malign neglect when the local Unionists came close to losing control of Derry in 1965, during a crisis which was sparked by British officials deciding that the second city should not get the second university and which saw Jones fighting for the best interests of all his constituents.

The Lockwood Committee, which was charged by the new O'Neill Government with making recommendations about higher education, was led by its British members.[79] They followed long-standing British practices for selecting a location for a new university, which was to leave the process mired in the bog of Northern Irish politics. The authorities in Coleraine, a solidly Unionist town in County Londonderry, had noticed that the new universities of Sussex and Essex had been built near to the south coast because of the availability of seaside lodgings.[80] Putting up students in boarding houses cost much less than providing them with halls of residence. Coleraine's bid as a result focused on how close it was to the resort towns of Portrush and Portstewart. The Derry bodies, in contrast, had not done such thorough research; so, the city's Magee University College was presented as an asset rather than a liability. The committee recognized Magee for what it was: a college that had a Byzantine system of administration, incompetent staff and bad relations with Queen's University Belfast. Magee could not be used as a nucleus for the second university. The committee therefore dealt Derry a double blow by advising the government at the end of 1964 to choose Coleraine and to close Magee.[81] O'Neill, who had been part of the 1949 enquiry into the college's affairs and still recalled his bruising encounters with the Magee lobby, had no intention of agreeing to this second recommendation. Jones concurred with his Prime Minister that a future had to be found for Magee. Working closely with the Minister of Education, he started to broker a settlement that was acceptable to Magee's trustees and faculty.[82] Admittedly, when other figures in the local party came to Stormont on 19 February 1965, they again brought up concerns to do with how industrial development would make it difficult to 'retain our position' – yet, they also begged O'Neill to give Magee one of the new university's departments.[83] The government, however, was more impressed by the previous day's visitors from Derry: a motorcade made up of about 2,000 vehicles that had carried 'all creeds and classes and all shades of political opinion' to the seat of power as a protest against Lockwood preferring Coleraine to their city.[84] 'What happens there is my problem,' Jones had told the Cabinet Secretary two weeks before the demonstration, 'but only to some extent because...such an infection could well spread'.[85] Derry was 'in revolt' and was now Stormont's problem.[86]

The University for Derry Committee had been formed by a group of 'business and professional men', Protestants and Catholics, in January 1965 after news about the Lockwood report leaked out to Magee's trustees.[87] Hume was chosen to front the campaign; he did not belong to any political party, his Credit Union work had made him a community leader and he was young enough not to have any serious enemies. Derry's four main Churches were brought on board and issued a joint statement welcoming the 'beginning [of] a period of greater co-operation among all the citizens for the ... development of their city'.[88] To show that there was also 'no suggestion of any division of opinion in our ranks by reason of differing political views', Hume chaired a meeting in the Guildhall at which Nationalist, Liberal and Labour MPs as well as the Unionist Mayor, Albert Anderson, spoke.[89] The drive to unite Derry behind the campaign accelerated with the motorcade and with the plan to bring the city to a 'standstill'.[90] 'Clergy of all denominations', purred the *Derry Journal*, 'joined with business and professional men, factory workers, dockers, school teachers and students in a motorcade which varied from the stately limousine to furniture vans, coal lorries and bread vans'. They left behind a city where 'shops, schools and public houses [were] closed' and 'most traffic [was] stopped'. When the motorcade arrived, Hume stood on the steps of Stormont with the leaders of Nationalism and Unionism in Derry by his side and with thousands of citizens at his back.[91]

What worried Jones was not so much the civic unity as the unionist divisions.[92] The president of the Rotary Club, a prominent member of the chamber of commerce and the city solicitor were on the committee; so, not everyone in the local elite was prepared to keep placing control above development.[93] Inside the parliamentary party, there were backbenchers who were also unhappy that the west of the province was losing out on investment. For other MPs, those who resented how O'Neill was taking power to the centre and taking the hand of Irish nationalism, the second university was just another issue on which they could attack their leader.[94] Although the government made the vote on the *Lockwood Report* into a vote of confidence, four Unionist backbenchers sided with the opposition or abstained.[95] One of the rebels, Robert Nixon, would later whisper to the press that 'nameless, faceless men' in the local party had conspired to stop the new university being built in a 'Papist city'.[96] But, as the *Derry Journal* pointed out, 'apart from the colourful touch which Dr Nixon gave to them, the…same allegations have been going the rounds in the city for a considerable time'.[97] In February 1964, for instance, the newspaper had claimed that there was a 'deep political motive' behind 'the grandiose project of a brand new city in North Armagh – planted…where there is the most solid support for the Unionist Government'.[98] These suspicions were seemingly confirmed when the Englishman heading up the project resigned on the grounds that Craigavon was 'basically unwise' and that Derry should have been developed into 'the city in the playground' instead.[99] For the *Derry Journal*, this was 'both an indictment of and a challenge to [the] glaring indifference to the future of Derry' shown by 'the kept Corporation'.[100] The controversy over the new university caused this infection to spread. By the end of March 1965, the *Londonderry Sentinel* was reporting that the 'cries that the West is being isolated are just as strong from the Government's supporters as from its enemies'.[101] Jones sent a copy of the newspaper to the cabinet office so Stormont could 'see how the wind blows': 'The Editor, as the Prime Minister knows, is a member of the Council of the Londonderry and Foyle Unionist

Association, no less' and he 'is...urg[ing] that the Unionist Party should select "new blood" – candidates who will oppose Government policy'.[102] While Jones was not thrown aside by the local association, he nonetheless faced a serious challenge from the Liberal Claude Wilton in the November 1965 elections. Hume, who was serving as Wilton's election agent, told a rally that the origin of the 'plan' to 'destroy Derry' could be traced to 'fourteen years ago when the Unionist Party met to select...Jones'.[103] The Unionists came away from the election with a victory that felt more like a defeat, as Jones's majority was cut to only 1,014 and he left the count to be greeted by shouts of 'Lundy', the name of the man who was remembered as the traitor of the 1689 siege.[104] Three centuries later, a sizeable number of Protestants saw Derry beset by socio-economic forces and Jones as someone who was selling out its future.

As Protestants were fighting each other behind the old walls on that November night, resources were already starting to flow towards Derry to relieve this new siege.[105] A month before, the Minister of Development, Bill Craig, had informed the corporation that he was 'anxious for the creation of a "masterplan" for the development of the north west' and that he intended to 'get rid of the idea that the Government...is neglecting Derry'.[106] Professor Tom Wilson's 1965 economic programme for Northern Ireland, which was published at a time when over 400 urban renewal schemes were underway across the United Kingdom, had also concluded that 'a development plan [for Derry] is needed, and should be put in hand'; but, the civil service had cautioned that 'the attitude of the City [i.e. the corporation] to modern planning [is] so completely obstructive that one cannot conscientiously advise this course at present'.[107] The crisis, however, had made the problem urgent and had forced Stormont to change its position. O'Neillism was now going to be extended to the western borders: jobs and houses would be provided, with the short-term aim of buying off discontent and with the ultimate goal of helping Irish nationalism and the coarser aspects of unionism to wither away.[108] Out of office, O'Neill put this latter idea in a particularly patronizing way when he explained to a journalist that 'cars and television sets' would lead 'Roman Catholics' to 'live like Protestants'.[109] Nonetheless, northern Europe's ruling classes had long believed in 'the civilizing effect of things' – that things would guide the poor away from 'superstition and sloth' towards a (Protestant) regime of 'domestic economy and self-improvement'.[110] Border Unionists, in contrast, remained 'sure that the Nationalists here with us who would prefer the butter on their bread in this world are very few compared to those who would prefer it in the next'.[111] The clash over the different approaches to retaining control was at its most raw when the leading Londonderry Unionist, Gerald Glover, met Junior Development Minister Brian McConnell at the end of 1966 to discuss housing. Glover was fixated upon holding on to a rural district council ward, paranoid about what the NIHT was doing, doubtful that any houses were needed at all and unwilling to address the wider questions. 'What really mattered,' McConnell countered, 'was the preservation of Londonderry itself.' The Minister insisted that at least 7,000 new homes were on the way over the next fifteen years and that the 'sensible thing appeared to be that we should build up our majority in electoral divisions that we were likely to win rather than create large minorities in ones that we were going to lose'. The former Mayor was reminded that Craig had 'asked for an all-over plan from the Londonderry Unionists but this had never been received' – and now it was too late. Despite threatening to walk out, Glover eventually accepted that Stormont was in control.[112]

The Belfast-based James Munce Partnership, which had been awarded the contract to produce the area plan, also had to put up with the tantrums of Londonderry's grandees. When the planners were introduced to the steering committee in February 1966, Anderson reproached them for trying to involve the wider public in the process and claimed that 'WE are the people'. While the Unionists on the steering committee were working to hold the planners back, the Nationalist councillors were working with them to push things forward. James Doherty, McAteer's closest political ally, believed that here was his city's last, best hope and he therefore devoted himself to the project.[113] His faith was rewarded. At the launch of the approved plan in March 1968, Doherty praised 'this vital programme', especially the 'scientific analysis of our besetting problems of employment and housing'.[114] He had embraced the language of post-war British planning, which spoke of 'seemingly logical and unambiguous solutions to previously intractable urban problems'; Derry had become a problem to be solved rather than a place of history, memory and identity.[115] The plan promised an 'expanded Londonderry Urban Area...at the heart of a Crescent of population growth and industrial expansion' that was to be linked up to the 'Belfast Region' by 'improved road communications'. Vacant factories were to be used again, existing businesses were to recruit more workers, new industrial estates were to be occupied – and, as result, 'the minimum manufacturing employment needs of the Area will be met'.[116] Just over a year before the launch, Glover had told McConnell that the 'figure of 7,000 houses by 1981 was quite fanciful and unrealistic', but the plan now set a 'conservative' target of 9,600 new homes.[117] Within the expanded urban area, a population of close to 100,000 were going to live, work and play (the plan provided for new restaurants and cafes, more parkland, a regional sports complex and a marina on the Foyle) in a city that was 'landscaped' and 'open'. The old walls were to be 'cleared of adjacent buildings' and 'floodlit'; the socio-economic forces that had been kept at bay were to be welcomed by them into a city that nonetheless was to remain Unionist.[118]

The Londonderry Area Plan was a major victory in the city's struggle against poverty. However, while the plan was being given a triumphant reception in London's Guildhall, the man who had led the campaign that had manoeuvred Stormont into changing its strategy was fighting against this very settlement. Hume's Housing Association had appealed against the corporation refusing planning permission for a residential development on a site that the James Munce Partnership had instead zoned for industry. In his evidence at the hearing, Hume maintained that the housing situation was not 'a problem' but rather 'an emergency that requires immediate attention'; how much longer would the '29 families where husband and wife lived apart, usually with their parents, their children divided between them or, in a few cases, in children's homes' be asked to wait?[119]

This was a question that divided those people in Derry who were opposed to Unionism. After Doherty had voted to turn down Hume's application, the Nationalist councillor had used a speech in Manchester to argue that the 'present position in [the] city was that development meant loss of Unionist power – and power means everything'.[120] The *Derry Journal*, which usually backed the party line, had found this reasoning 'unconvincing': 'The provision of no less than 700 homes is too substantial a measure of relief in such an acute housing situation to be turned down in favour of a proposed, but still...distant future'.[121]

This split over whether to be patient with the plan or to act immediately drained away yet more of the momentum that had built up behind Hume during the early protests over the second university. The urgency that had existed in February 1965 had faded. Starting with Magee's trustees and faculty, the government had succeeded in buying off large parts of the uneasy coalition put together by the University for Derry Committee.[122] Hume, too, had unwittingly played a role in containing the crisis, as he had drawn back from the direct-action tactics that had brought Derry to a standstill and had pushed Stormont into getting involved. Although the campaign had continued even after MPs had voted for Coleraine, O'Neill had been left unmoved by Hume's speeches and by a petition calling for an inquiry into Nixon's accusations.[123] The tight City election and the disturbances following the count had been more of a concern to Stormont, yet they were still just weak echoes of what had happened at the beginning of 1965.[124] In his *Letter from Birmingham Jail*, King explained that: 'The purpose of our direct action program is to create a situation so crisis packed that it will inevitably open the door to negotiation'.[125] The University for Derry Committee had almost accidentally achieved this goal, if only for a brief moment; the Republican and Labour lefts now consciously set out to find the formula for non-violence that would send the city into sustained disorder.[126]

WHAT'S LEFT

Another McCafferty story: it is one that has been misremembered, yet in such a way as to lend a suitably cinematic quality to her introduction to the men and women who transformed her life and her city. 'One gloomy autumn afternoon [in 1967]', she begins, 'Eamonn McCann came down the street, bursting with energy...I complained of boredom. Why didn't I come up to the Londonderry Labour Party headquarters that night and help in the forthcoming general election campaign? he asked.'[127] In fact, McCann was in London during 1967, the next election in Derry was a May 1968 by-election and McCafferty was away for almost the whole of that spring.[128] While these details had faded, certain memories of McCafferty's old comrades continued to blaze bright: Cathy Harkin was 'separated from her violent husband', 'rearing a son' and believed that 'one day we would run Derry'; Dermie McClenaghan 'loved Frank Sinatra', 'worried about his family' and lived near a 'corner bookies' on which someone had graffitied 'We want better odds'; Ivan Cooper, 'the only Protestant', 'managed [a] factory' and 'thought life was a breeze'. But, they were all outshone by McCann, with his 'Elvis sideboards', 'brilliant orator[y]' and 'breathtaking' good looks.[129]

Other Derry radicals, such as McClenaghan and Melaugh, also remember how McCann 'brought a lot of energy' and 'a lot of positive ideas' back with him from London in the spring of 1968.[130] McCann himself recalled coming home convinced that he 'could sweep up the local, parochial politics…by introducing an international dimension'.[131] 'Youthful dissidence' was 'a world-wide phenomenon', the Central Intelligence Agency told President Lyndon Johnson in September 1968: 'Because of the revolution in communications, the ease of travel and the evolution of society everywhere'.[132] The State Department agreed that the upheavals were 'truly international', that young people facing similar political problems were looking to their contemporaries in foreign countries for help solving them.[133] McCann, thinking back forty years on, linked 'direct action' with this 'wider perspective': 'direct action was…the hallmark of the radical movement …in London and across the world', the 'tactic of the civil rights movement [and] of the anti-Vietnam war movement'.[134] (Although there is, of course, an element of recasted memories here, McCann has consistently taken this line over the decades.) The 'global Sixties' was an external shock to the local political system.

During the second half of the 1960s, the civil rights and anti-war movements radicalized non-violence and helped build up links between activists around the world. In 1966, Stokely Carmichael, the then chair of SNCC, began calling for 'black power' – which came to stand for armed self-defence, for political and cultural self-determination and for international solidarity. This did not, though, mark the end of the civil rights movement after a decade of successes. Black power grew out of the long-standing black self-help tradition and of the general black opposition to imperialism.[135] These were roots that black power shared with the civil rights movement, too, and both sets of activists worked together to transform citizenship and democracy in America.[136] Carmichael's ambitions also went beyond the United States, leading him to embark upon a tour of foreign countries throughout 1967 that was to bring him to London in July for the Dialectics of Liberation Congress.[137] The head of its planning committee wanted this event to bring together 'groups [from] all over the world [that] are doing much the same' and to 'get this transnational network established'.[138] One of the connections made was between Carmichael and McCann.[139] When Carmichael addressed the congress, he declared that black militants were 'going to extend our fight internationally and hook up with the Third World [because] the fight must come from the Third World'.[140] A few months later, McCann's *Irish Militant* newspaper, which 'carried' the 'banner' of the 'Fourth International', urged its readers to 'do what the Afro-Americans are doing'.[141]

An African-American radical was also among the star performers at another European congress which had been organized to 'commence the co-ordinated battle against imperialism': the International Vietnam Congress held in West Berlin during February 1968.[142] Although she did not mention his name in her article, Ulrike Meinhof, who was on a winding road from pacifism to armed struggle herself, quoted him urging the packed hall to move from 'protest to resistance'.[143] The West German New Left had been taking inspiration from African Americans since the start of the decade; exchange students had returned home after participating in civil rights campaigns as evangelists for non-violent direct action.[144] With the escalation of both police brutality and the Vietnam War, however, radicals were now borrowing and adapting the black power narrative and its fantastic promise of global revolution. As one of them summarized it, 'the intelligentsia...must unite with the suffering masses of the Third World and themselves employ illegal, direct action against the state apparatus to weaken the imperialist powers'.[145] Black power – especially the strand that posed as urban guerrillas fighting a national liberation struggle in America's ghettos – served as a stepping stone between very different worlds and helped make the leap of imagination taken by the New Left appear more plausible.

Foreign delegations came away from the International Vietnam Congress eager to put into practice what they had seen and heard in West Berlin.[146] French militants, for example, took illegal, direct action against the Paris offices of American Express by smashing its windows in March 1968. A number of student radicals from the Nanterre campus were arrested and this, in turn, led to rival leftist groups coming together to invade the administration building.[147] Like their comrades at West Berlin's Free University, the Nanterre activists disrupted classes, occupied buildings, staged pickets, showed films on Cuba and China, went on marches, insulted staff and their fellow students, covered walls in political and obscene graffiti and held seemingly endless meetings.[148] They also turned non-violence into a euphemism. The March occupation caused 15,000 francs' worth of property damage; the Enragés in particular were referencing, not King or even SNCC, but the Watts rioters, who had set their black Los Angeles ghetto ablaze in August 1965.[149] The French philosopher Raymond Aron described these tactics as 'non-violent violence'.[150]

Britain's Vietnam Solidarity Campaign (VSC), with which McCann was heavily involved, had also sent a delegation to West Berlin, and they had asked their German hosts to act as movement consultants.[151] While London's demonstrations may not have matched the militancy of those taking place on the continent, British-based Trotskyites were nonetheless part of the global trend.[152] In the autumn of 1967, ahead of the March on the Pentagon and the solidarity marches around the world, the *Irish Militant* argued that one of the 'duties to Vietnam' owed by 'socialists in Western Europe' was to provide a 'diversion of attention'. 'It [i.e. the day of marches] will be the first occasion that the imperialists have been confronted in all countries of the world at the same time'.[153] Activists in London confronted the police outside the American embassy in Grosvenor Square, which left thirty-nine officers injured and fifty-three people in the cells; the VSC was pleased with these results and planned to return in greater numbers the following spring. Among the groups brought on board by the VSC to help organize the first Grosvenor Square march was the Stop-it Committee, whose chair had collected Carmichael at Heathrow airport back in July 1967.[154] On 4 December 1967, the committee held a meeting at Conway Hall to announce that the anti-war movement had reached 'a new stage – resistance': 'Because the American Government has so callously ignored marches, protests and reasoned dissent on an international...level, more extreme forms of action are necessary'. Three weeks before the march, in late February 1968, the Metropolitan Police Special Branch was expecting it to be 'violent, paralleling recent demonstrations on the continent'.[155] It was and it did. The *Guardian* concluded that 'the demonstrators seemed determined to stay until they had provoked a violent response of some sort from the police, and this intention became paramount once they entered Grosvenor Square'.[156] Whitehall was convinced that a 'disciplined gang' from West Germany – 'acknowledged experts in methods of riot against police' – had played a leading role in this confrontation.[157] Some qualifications need to be made here: newspapers were framing marches as law-and-order issues and so were panicking about violence and praising the police; officials were predisposed to find evidence of subversion; leftists were making exaggerated claims to pull in the media and push the authorities into overreacting.[158] Still, as a Special Branch report from September 1968 noted, there had been a 'radical change over the last few years…from orderly, peaceful, co-operative meetings and processions to passive resistance and "sit downs" and now to active confrontation'.[159]

McCann returned to Derry after the first Grosvenor Square march.[160] Whenever McCann was asked to remember the civil rights era during the lead up to the fortieth-anniversary commemorations, he was keen to stress this hostility to his new strategy and to its global frame of reference.[161] His 'memory of it' was that 'the moderates' 'resented the Socialist element…importing other experiences and other ideas'.[162] McCann could have drawn a dividing line between the Old and New Lefts, too. C. Desmond Greaves, the chief of the London-based Connolly Association and a veteran British Communist, had identified civil rights as Unionism's weak spot back in 1955; he had also taken the orthodox position that a movement should be patiently built up from within Ireland's Labour parties and trade unions.[163] Although the Northern Ireland Civil Rights Association (NICRA), which was founded in Belfast at the start of 1967, fell short of Greaves's original vision (the Labour movement was underrepresented, other opposition groups were overrepresented), a close comrade, Betty Sinclair, came to head up the committee. She resisted attempts to take politics on to the streets and then, having lost the internal debate, restricted the protests that did take place.[164] As a young Communist in the inter-war years, Sinclair had witnessed what had happened when the Marxist Revolutionary Workers' Group had gone on to the streets: the 1935 Orange marching season in Belfast had brought communal violence and the decline of Sinclair's party.[165] This fear of sectarian confrontation was shared by many within the

Northern Ireland Labour Party (NILP) as well.[166] So, recalled McClenaghan, 'when Eamonn came to Derry and joined the Labour Party he immediately, immediately caused division...just because of what he was politically'.[167] By May 1968, the *Derry Journal* was reporting rumours that the branch was split and Anderson, the Unionist candidate in the by-election, was claiming a 'red fringe' had taken 'control'.[168] A new formula of non-violence was going to be trialled in Derry.

The Labour candidate, the English-born Janet Wilcock, was calling for the same far-reaching reforms as the Derry Housing Action Committee (DHAC), which had recently brought together left-wingers in her party and in the local Republican Club.[169] Barely a month after the area plan had been launched, the DHAC burst into the Guildhall to tell Nationalists as well as Unionists that change needed to come immediately. The group's spokesman demanded that the corporation should extend the city boundary to make more space available for new homes and should embark upon a crash house-building programme.[170] The novelty of direct action attracted the attention of the local media, with this disruption of the March meeting of the council making the front page of the *Derry Journal*.[171] The radicals returned the following month, yet this time the report was tucked away in the inside pages.[172] During June 1968, the DHAC succeeded in getting back into the headlines by blocking the main road through the Bogside for three hours with a caravan that had been home to a young family of four for three years. While the disorder did force the corporation to promise to take up this family's case, the radicals nonetheless warned that there would be 'a much bigger demonstration', 'if nothing materialised by Saturday next'.[173] This was an unrealistic deadline, and so, a week later, the DHAC and the caravan returned.[174] When a policeman asked Melaugh why he was stopping traffic, the officer was told to 'bring this matter to Court' – 'then I will get the publicity I am looking for'. Wilcock was bound over to keep the peace for two years and afterwards issued a statement reaffirming the DHAC's commitment to 'non-violent, militant action although it be illegal'.[175]

Like their foreign comrades, the Derry radicals were now seeking confrontation. As McCann wrote in his 1974 memoir, 'our conscious, if unspoken, strategy was to provoke the police into overreaction and thus spark off mass reaction against the authorities'.[176] The term 'provocation', with its implications for the question of who was responsible for the violence of the start of the Troubles, is controversial; yet, it was also one which was often used by activists around the world in the late 1960s. For example, the leader of the Resistance, an American anti-war group, said in September 1967 that its aim was to 'provoke confrontation'. West German leftists claimed the 'protest violence' of the Easter 1968 marches was a way of 'provoking the state' and an article in the July–August 1968 issue of the *New Left Review* advised student radicals to behave 'provocatively...to the extent that they [i.e. the university authorities] *need* to use force'.[177] What, though, did contemporaries mean when they referred to 'provocation' and indeed to 'violence'? During the Birmingham campaign, King explained to 'the white moderate who is more devoted to "order" than to justice' that 'we who engage in non-violent direct action are not the creators of tension. We merely bring to the surface the hidden tension that is already alive.'[178] A month after her husband was murdered, Coretta Scott King 'remind[ed]' Americans about this hidden violence: 'starving a child is violence. Suppressing a culture is violence... Contempt for poverty is violence.'[179] McCann wanted to reveal the violence, broadly defined, that he believed lay behind the Prime Minister's liberal mask: 'O'Neill talked about progress but he would go back to the old Unionist background of open suppression'.[180] The radicals intended to test this hypothesis. On 5 September 1968, the DHAC informed the media that they were going to 'fight to force the powers-that-be to act' – to build 'houses for the homeless or a new wing to Crumlin Road Prison'.[181]

Everyone in Derry, McCann acknowledged, knew that the 'one certain way to ensure a head-on clash with the authorities was to organize a non-Unionist march through the city centre'.[182] As the *Derry Journal* pointed out in the summer of 1968, during 'the past twenty years several attempts have been made by the Nationalist Party...to demonstrate in...the main thoroughfares of the city. They were met by the imposition of the Special Powers Act and on two occasions police batons were out'.[183] The theory was simple, but putting it into practice was not. In line with other western countries (including Britain and the Republic of Ireland), Northern Ireland had become less repressive throughout the 'long 1960s'.[184] Rome in March, West Berlin in April, Paris in May and Chicago in August – these vicious clashes were the exceptions rather than the rule in 1968. Brutal repression of demonstrations by the forces of law and order was relatively rare.[185] This development had, in fact, helped to create the space for direct action to operate; the West German sociologist Jürgen Habermas argued that the leftists were 'exploiting the unexpected latitude granted by liberal institutions'.[186] So, the failure of the Derry radicals to engineer a confrontation at their first attempt was to be expected. In July 1968, the Labour and Republican left proposed to mark the centenary of the Marxist martyr James Connolly's birth by holding a march that would pass through the city walls. The Royal Ulster Constabulary (RUC) responded by entering into a series of discussions with the organizers about finding a different, less provocative route and, after finally choosing to ban the march, by stationing only a few officers at the edge of the rally which was held instead. The leftists had cautioned that 'If peaceful demonstrations are to be banned, can anyone be surprised if there are demonstrations in future of a non-peaceful nature?'[187] However, under pressure from some of the politicians who had agreed to take part, the radicals had made a tactical retreat and had put on an event that the *Derry Journal* described as 'very orderly'.[188] Fionnbarra Ó Dochartaigh, an IRA volunteer who had been involved with both McCann and the Connolly Association during a brief stay in London, hinted that this would not happen again.[189] 'On future occasions,' he told the crowd of around 600 people, 'the question of a police ban...would be a matter for meeting in a different manner.'[190]

The Derry radicals were given their second chance by NICRA's choice in August 1968 to 'challenge...by more vigorous action than Parliamentary questions and newspaper controversy'.[191] '[I]nspired by the Poor People's March to Washington,' a NICRA committee member remembered in April 1969, the 'Association...decided to carry out a programme of marches.'[192] The DHAC pledged its support to the first march from Coalisland and Dungannon and offered to transport to Tyrone anyone who wished to take part.[193] Dungannon was different from Derry: NICRA had ties in this rural area and the Nationalist MP Austin Currie was working with the Brantry Republican Club in a local non-violent campaign.[194] As the march was to show, they were experimenting with a more basic and less volatile formula than the second city's non-violent activists. Indeed, without knowing it, the organizers went against all the advice that King had publicly given during the Selma marches about how to stage a successful protest. King stated that 'the goal of the demonstration' should be to bring about a 'confrontation with injustice' which would 'reveal...the continued presence of violence'.[195] Confrontation and violence, though, were not what most of the 2,000 or so people marching from Coalisland to Dungannon wanted. The first civil rights march instead resembled a traditional nationalist parade – with five bands, Nationalist MPs in the front ranks, IRA stewards and renditions of 'The Soldier's Song'. At the rally held afterwards, Sinclair praised the crowd for making the march a 'peaceful one'. Currie and Gerry Fitt, the Republican Labour MP for West Belfast, gave more confrontational speeches, using sectarian insults such as 'Orange bigots' and 'black bastards', yet their actions did not match this rhetoric. Fitt claimed that he would have led the people into the police lines which were blocking them from reaching the town centre, 'if it weren't for the presence of women and children'.[196] King, in contrast, had actually sent children into the arms of policemen, the teeth of German Shepherds, the water hoses of fireman and the cells of the local jail to save his Birmingham campaign.[197] Although Republicans were more comfortable with confrontation than constitutional politicians, the stewards were still under orders to keep the crowd away from the police. A confidential document acquired by the RUC Special Branch stressed that they were to 'march peacefully', 'sit down', 'if stopped' and offer 'no resistance'.[198] Leftists from Derry and Belfast tried to resist by throwing 'stones, broken placards and poles' at officers, but, as Currie remembered, they were 'prevented by the stewards from engaging in confrontation with the police'.[199] When the marchers finally began to disperse, some of the radicals clashed with loyalist counter-demonstrators before being cleared off the streets by the RUC – who made only two arrests on the day and were made to appear the neutral guardians of law and order. The next week, St Patrick's hall in Coalisland was filled with parishioners waiting to hear the senior curate's verdict. The police reported that the priest 'expressed the view that the march was a failure' and that the 'meeting endorsed these views'.[200] As King's 'long years of experience' had taught him, it was 'ineffective' to stage 'token marches avoiding direct confrontation'.[201] Despite claims to the contrary, NICRA and Dungannon's non-violent activists had not borrowed and adapted King's tactics to Northern Ireland.

In Dungannon, the Derry radicals were just one part of a coalition

made up of almost all the country's opposition groups as well as individuals who were not caught up in the politics of the politicians. Most
marchers were there for a peaceful protest, not confrontation and
violence; most marchers were there to call for reform rather than
revolution. But, with their colourful language and behaviour, the leftists
were able to attract a disproportionate level of attention. A similar
argument could also be made about their place in the mass movement
that emerged in Derry after 5 October 1968. However, what happened
in between simply cannot be characterized in this way, as the second
civil rights march – the event which transformed the situation – was
wholly planned by the Derry radicals. The DHAC secured NICRA
sponsorship, and then exploited the Belfast-based body's ignorance of
the second city to get complete control of the organizing committee
and to get a route agreed which ended within the walls.[202] A comparison with narratives of West Germany's 'red decade', 1967–77, is
useful here. Stories about the passage from protest through resistance
to armed struggle in the Federal Republic disagree about the particu-
lars and the politics, yet they all tend to agree that it is a German story
– a story about the unmastered Nazi past. While the national context
is clearly important, failing to look beyond it has distorted representations; 'Hitler's children' were also the children of the (global)
revolution, and the Achtundsechzigers, as this chapter has argued,
drew upon a transnational discourse and protest repertoire.[203] The
Derry radicals did the same. This, though, is obscured in narratives
which assume that the Northern Irish past can only be understood in
terms of Protestant and Catholic, unionist and nationalist. When the
march's fortieth anniversary came round, McCann objected to how
the 'international dimension [had] virtually been written out of
history': 'in Derry at least, the activists who triggered the civil rights
campaign didn't see themselves as Orange or Green, but of a hue [i.e.
Red] which, we believed, would…obliterate the colour-coding'.[204]
The march was much more a break with the past than a logical
continuation of it.

CONCLUSION

In late August 1968, the local Labour Party moaned that 'there were not people in Derry prepared to fight for their rights as the blacks in America were fighting'.[205] However, just as there was no such thing as a single Derry Catholic life experience, there was no such thing as a single Derry Catholic protest agenda. People in the city were actually fighting for a wide range of rights, often using strategies that were similar to those employed by African Americans – they were just not backing the radical left's attempts to engineer a confrontation. The previous twelve months alone had seen campaigns to do with poor television reception, rent increases, resettlement grants, vandalism, new water charges, road safety, policing and inadequate midwifery.[206] Contending against marginalization, people in Derry had fought for welfare rights and better standards of living, and in the process they had fought to play an active role as citizens in the decisions that the state was making about their lives. They had shown stamina, courage and flexibility over tactics; they had shown that it was possible to win reform (there was no such thing as a single unionist reaction, either). People in Derry were 'neither passive, disciplined dupes nor heroic agents of antidiscipline, but "co-producers" of systems of provision'.[207] These campaigns, then, were not on straight roads or indeed twisting paths to Duke Street and the civil rights movement (this metaphor leads down a dead end): the strategies and goals that these groups and individuals chose to pursue were limited by Derry's existing, albeit shifting, political, social, economic and cultural contexts. The radicals escaped from these constraints by taking an international perspective, one which held that reform was not enough and that a revolutionary transformation was possible. As a result, they reconfigured the constellation of power in Northern Ireland as well as in Derry, and, when power changed dramatically, so did protest. Life in the city was going to evolve rapidly.

NOTES

1. J. Steinbeck, 'I Go Back to Ireland', in J. Steinbeck, *America and Americans, and Selected Non-fiction* (London: Penguin, 2003 edn.), pp. 262–9, pp. 262–5.
2. D. McClenaghan, 'Abandonment, Civil Rights and Socialism', in P. McClenaghan (ed.), *Spirit of '68: Beyond the Barricades* (Derry: Guildhall Press, 2009), pp. 27–46, pp. 27 and 38.

3. Z. Kövecses, *Metaphor: A Practical Introduction* (Oxford: Oxford University Press, 2002), p. viii.
4. N. McCafferty, *Nell* (London: Penguin, 2004), p. 13.
5. R. Foster, 'Selling Irish Childhoods: Frank McCourt and Gerry Adams', in R. Foster, *The Irish Story* (London: Penguin, 2001), pp. 164–86, pp. 185–6.
6. McCafferty, *Nell*, pp. 10–71.
7. U. Neisser and L. Libby, 'Remembering Life Experiences', in E. Tulving and F. Craik (eds), *The Oxford Handbook of Memory* (Oxford: Oxford University Press, 2000 edn.), pp. 315–32, pp. 318–19.
8. Derry Youth and Community Workshop, *Springtown Camp* (Derry: Derry Youth and Community Workshop, 1980), p. 27.
9. N. McCafferty, *Peggy Deery: A Derry Family at War* (Dublin: Attic Press, 1988), pp. 9 and 22.
10. James Munce Partnership, *Londonderry Area Plan*, April 1968, Belfast, McClay Library.
11. B. Harrison, *Seeking a Role: The United Kingdom, 1951-1970* (Oxford: Oxford University Press, 2009), pp. 249–50; A. Finlay, 'The Cutting Edge: Derry Shirtmakers', in C. Curtin, P. Jackson and B. O'Connor (eds), *Gender in Irish Society* (Galway: Galway University Press, 1987), pp. 87–107, p. 87; *Londonderry Area Plan*.
12. McCafferty, *Peggy Deery*, p. 9.
13. For a general history of the city, see B. Lacy, *Siege City: The Story of Derry and Londonderry* (Belfast: Blackstaff Press, 1990).
14. I. McBride, *The Siege of Derry in Ulster Protestant Mythology* (Dublin: Four Courts Press, 1997), pp. 12–20.
15. R. Lynch, *The Northern IRA and the Early Years of Partition, 1920–1922* (Dublin: Irish Academic Press, 2006), pp. 21 and 54–8.
16. E. Warnock to T. O'Neill, 13 November 1968, Belfast, Public Record Office of Northern Ireland (PRONI), CAB/4/1414.
17. *Derry Journal*, 8 September 1961.
18. Minutes of Executive Committee, 20 June 1958, PRONI, D/1327/6/72, quoted in H. Patterson, 'In the Land of King Canute: the Influence of Border Unionism on Ulster Unionist Politics, 1945–63', *Contemporary British History*, 20, 4 (December 2006), pp. 511–32, p. 528.
19. McCafferty, *Nell*, p. 33.
20. McCafferty, *Peggy Deery*, p. 20.
21. Cabinet conclusions, 29 August 1946, PRONI, CAB/4/683.
22. McCafferty, *Peggy Deery*, p. 21. Between 1951 and 1961, there were high levels of emigration, with the annual rate reaching 1.3 per cent. *Londonderry Area Plan*.
23. *Derry Journal*, 6 November 2009.
24. *Derry Journal*, 31 January 1963.
25. R. Williams, *The Politics of Public Housing: Black Women's Struggles against Urban Inequality* (Oxford: Oxford University Press, 2004), pp. 10 and 85.
26. M. Countryman, *Up South: Civil Rights and Black Power in Philadelphia* (Philadelphia, PA: University of Pennsylvania Press, 2006), p. 183.
27. *Derry Journal*, 27 November 1959.
28. M. Chappell, J. Hutchinson and B. Ward, '"Dress Modestly, Neatly…As If You Were Going to Church": Respectability, Class and Gender in the Montgomery Bus Boycott and the Early Civil Rights Movement' in P. Ling and S. Monteith (eds), *Gender in the Civil Rights Movement* (London: Garland, 1999), pp. 69–100, pp. 72–3 and 88.
29. E. Herdman to W. Douglas, 23 June 1950, PRONI, D/1327/15/14, quoted in Patterson, 'In the Land of King Canute', p. 520.
30. J. Tomlinson, Re-inventing the "Moral Economy" in Post-war Britain', *Historical Research* (early view, 2010).
31. J. Vernon, *Hunger: A Modern History* (Cambridge, MA: Harvard University Press, 2007), p. 15.
32. *Derry Journal*, 14 October 1960.
33. Harrison, *Seeking a Role*, p. 250.
34. *Derry Journal*, 14 October 1960; *Derry Journal*, 31 July 1964; *Derry Journal*, 3 June 1960;

Derry Journal, 3 February 1967; *Derry Journal*, 31 January 1964; *Derry Journal*, 23 October 1964; *Derry Journal*, 24 April 1964; *Derry Journal*, 2 June 1964; *Derry Journal*, 14 July 1964; *Derry Journal*, 9 June 1967.

35. *Derry Journal*, 24 January 1964; *Derry Journal*, 25 July 1967; *Derry Journal*, 6 October 1967.
36. *Derry Journal*, 15 November 1963.
37. *Derry Journal*, 30 June 1967; *Derry Journal*, 8 December 1967; *Derry Journal*, 10 October 1967; *Derry Journal*, 21 November 1967.
38. B. Lynn, *Holding the Ground: The Nationalist Party in Northern Ireland, 1945–72* (Aldershot: Ashgate, 1997), pp. 26–8, 33, 48, 52 and 61.
39. E. McAteer, *Irish Action: New Thoughts on an Old Subject* (Belfast: Athol Books, 1979 edn.), pp. 52–3.
40. *Derry Journal*, 14 February 1961.
41. *Derry Journal*, 21 October 1966.
42. F. Polletta, 'Contending Stories: Narrative in Social Movements', *Qualitative Sociology*, 21, 4 (December 1998), pp. 419–46, pp. 428–9.
43. Non-violence here is defined as actions that occur outside of normal institutional channels. See K. Schock, 'Nonviolent Action and its Misconceptions: Insights for Social Scientists', *PS: Political Science and Politics*, 36, 4 (October 2003), pp. 705–12.
44. McAteer, *Irish Action*, pp. 52–3.
45. B. Lynn, 'Nationalist Politics in Derry 1945-1969', in G. O'Brien (ed.), *Derry and Londonderry – History and society: Interdisciplinary Essays on the History of an Irish County* (Dublin: Geography Publications, 1999), pp. 601–624, p. 607.
46. Lynn, *Holding the Ground*, p. 55.
47. McAteer, *Irish Action*, p. 53. On what it took to win the great non-violent victory at Birmingham, Alabama, see A. Manis, *A Fire You Can't Put Out: The Civil Rights Life of Birmingham's Reverend Fred Shuttlesworth* (London: The University of Alabama Press, 1999).
48. M. Gandhi, *Essential Writings* (Oxford: Oxford University Press, 2008 edn.), p. 94.
49. S. Chabot and J. Duyvendak, 'Globalization and the Transnational Diffusion between Social Movements: Reconceptualizing the Dissemination of the Gandhian Repertoire and the "Coming Out" Routine', *Theory and Society*, 31, 6 (December 2002), pp. 697–740, pp. 699, 701, 706 and 727–8.
50. R. Niebuhr, *Moral Man and Immoral Society: A Study in Ethics and Politics* (London: Charles Scribner's Sons, 1932), pp. 241–4 and 252–3.
51. Gandhi, *Essential Writings*, p. 314.
52. Niebuhr, *Moral Man and Immoral Society*, p. 250. Other intellectuals doubted whether nonviolence would be suitable for American conditions. B. Plummer, *Rising Wind: Black Americans and US Foreign Affairs, 1935–1960* (Chapel Hill, NC: University of North Carolina Press, 1996), pp. 91–2.
53. Branch, *Parting the Waters: America in the King Years 1954–63* (London: Simon & Schuster, 1988), p. 87; N. Schlueter, *One Dream or Two? Justice in America and the Thought of Martin Luther King Jr.* (Oxford: Lexington Books, 2002), p. 126.
54. R. English, *Armed Struggle: The History of the IRA* (London: Macmillan, 2003), p. 87; *Irish Democrat*, April 1965.
55. *Derry Journal*, 2 June 1964.
56. *Derry Journal*, 2 June 1964.
57. *Derry Journal*, 26 January 1965.
58. *Derry Journal*, 29 January 1965.
59. *Irish Democrat*, February 1966.
60. *Derry Journal*, 12 March 1965; *Derry Journal*, 13 April 1965; *Derry Journal*, 15 February 1966; *Derry Journal*, 29 March 1966.
61. *Derry Journal*, 19 January 1965.
62. *Derry Journal*, 26 January 1968; *Derry Journal*, 22 November 1960; *Derry Journal*, 18 January 1963.
63. *Derry Journal*, 14 February 1961.
64. *Derry Journal*, 6 December 1968.

65. *Derry Journal*, 19 May 1964; *Derry Journal*, 19 August 1966.
66. *Derry Journal*, 21 October 1966.
67. *Derry Journal*, 17 February 1967.
68. Memorandum to the Cabinet Submitted by the Minister of Development, 23 April 1970, PRONI, CAB/4/1514; Cabinet conclusions, 4 June 1970, PRONI, CAB/4/1523.
69. *Derry Journal*, 3 November 1967.
70. E. Daly, *Mister, Are you a Priest?* (Dublin: Four Courts, 2000), p. 104.
71. *Derry Journal*, 5 March 1968.
72. Viscount Brookeborough, Diaries, 23 September 1958, quoted in H. Patterson, *Ireland since 1939: The Persistence of Conflict* (Dublin: Penguin, 2006), p. 129.
73. Minute prepared for the purpose of some definite ideas and suggestions before the meeting with the prime minister on 13 September 1956, [September 1956], PRONI, PM/5/95/10, quoted in Patterson, 'In the Land of King Canute', p. 514.
74. R. Harris, *Regional Economic Policy in Northern Ireland, 1945–88* (Aldershot: Avebury, 1991), p. 19; *Derry Journal*, 1 January 1960; *Derry Journal*, 18 October 1960; *Derry Journal*, 22 May 1962; *Derry Journal*, 24 January 1967.
75. *Derry Journal*, 29 December 1964.
76. N. Ó Dochartaigh, 'Housing and Conflict: Social Change and Collective Action in Derry in the 1960s', in G. O'Brien (ed.), *Derry and Londonderry – History and Society: Interdisciplinary Essays on the History of an Irish County* (Dublin: Geography Publications, 1999), pp. 625–45, pp. 625–7.
77. NIHT, *Annual Report of the Northern Ireland Housing Trust* (Belfast: NIHT, 1966), pp. 12–13.
78. *Derry Journal*, 20 September 1966. The official figures were that 1,800 were on the waiting list in 1966. Housing in Londonderry, 9 December 1966, PRONI, CAB/9N/4/20.
79. This paragraph draws upon G. O'Brien, '"Our Magee Problem": Stormont and the Second University', in O'Brien (ed.), *Derry and Londonderry*, pp. 647–96, pp. 647–8, 661–8 and 683–5.
80. A second university for Northern Ireland, February 1964, PRONI, CAB/9D/31/2.
81. Memorandum by the Minister of Education, 11 December 1964, PRONI, CAB/4/1286.
82. E. Jones to H. Kirk, 2 April 1965, PRONI, CAB/9D/31/2. In May 1969, a different Minister of Education reached the same conclusion: 'Such reasons as are in favour of its survival are political not educational'. W. Long, Memorandum – Magee University College, 22 May 1969, PRONI, CAB/4/1445.
83. Handwritten Note of Discussion between the Prime Minister, Education Minister and Representatives of Londonderry Unionism, 19 February 1965, PRONI, CAB/9D/31/2.
84. *Derry Journal*, 19 February 1965.
85. E. Jones to C. Bateman, 11 February 1965, PRONI CAB/9D/31/2.
86. *Derry Journal*, 19 February 1965.
87. *Derry Journal*, 1 January 1965; *Derry Journal*, 29 January 1965.
88. *Derry Journal*, 2 February 1965.
89. *Londonderry Sentinel*, 17 February 1965.
90. *Derry Journal*, 16 February 1965.
91. *Derry Journal*, 19 February 1965.
92. Jones to Bateman, 11 February 1965.
93. *Derry Journal*, 2 February 1965.
94. *Belfast Telegraph*, 26 February 1965.
95. *Derry Journal*, 5 March 1965.
96. *Londonderry Sentinel*, 12 May 1965.
97. *Derry Journal*, 11 May 1965.
98. *Derry Journal*, 7 February 1964.
99. *Derry Journal*, 18 August 1964; *Times*, 24 April 1967.
100. *Derry Journal*, 21 August 1964.
101. *Londonderry Sentinel*, 31 March 1965.
102. E. Jones to H. Black, 2 April 1965, PRONI, CAB/9D/31/3.
103. *Derry Journal*, 10 December 1965.

104. *Derry Journal*, 26 November 1965.
105. *Derry Journal*, 26 November 1965.
106. *Derry Journal*, 19 October 1965; *Londonderry Sentinel*, 27 October 1965.
107. T. Wilson, *Economic Development in Northern Ireland* (Belfast: HMSO, 1965), p. 135; S. Gunn, 'The Rise and Fall of British Urban Modernism: Planning Bradford, circa 1945–1970', *Journal of British Studies*, 49, 4 (October 2010), pp. 849–69, p. 852; Memorandum from J. Oliver to C. Bateman, 17 February 1965, PRONI, CAB/9D/31/2. As late as August 1965, when the initiative still technically lay with it, the corporation remained opposed to an area plan. K. Bloomfield to F. Evans, 26 August 1965, PRONI, CAB/9B/163/10.
108. *Derry Journal*, 11 June 1968; T. O'Neill, *The Autobiography of Terence O'Neill* (London: Hart-Davies, 1972), p. 101; T. O'Neill interview, *Yearbook of the Conservative Unionist Association of Queen's University Belfast 1967–1968*, PRONI, D/3297/3.
109. *Belfast Telegraph*, 10 May 1969.
110. F. Trentmann, 'Materiality in the Future of History: Things, Practices, and Politics', *Journal of British Studies*, 48, 2 (April 2009), pp. 283–307, pp. 293–4.
111. Minute, September 1956, Patterson, 'In the Land of King Canute', p. 514.
112. Housing in Londonderry, 9 December 1966.
113. G. McSheffrey, *Planning Derry: Planning and Politics in Northern Ireland* (Liverpool: Liverpool University Press, 2000), pp. 19–22 and 47–9.
114. *Derry Journal*, 5 March 1968.
115. J. Gold, *The Practice of Modernism: Modern Architects and Urban Transformation, 1954–1972* (London: Routledge, 2007), p. 10.
116. *Londonderry Area Plan*.
117. Housing in Londonderry, 9 December 1966.
118. *Londonderry Area Plan*.
119. *Derry Journal*, 26 March 1968; *Londonderry Sentinel*, 27 March 1968.
120. *Derry Journal*, 10 October 1967.
121. *Derry Journal*, 13 October 1967.
122. *Londonderry Sentinel*, 19 May 1965.
123. *Derry Journal*, 9 March 1965; *Derry Journal*, 25 June 1965; *Derry Journal*, 6 August 1965.
124. *Londonderry Sentinel*, 1 December 1965.
125. M. King, *Letter from Birmingham Jail*, http://www.stanford.edu/group/King/frequentdocs/birmingham.pdf (last accessed 15 March 2011).
126. Hume came to understand that the 'development plan for Derry was wrested from the Government': *Derry Journal*, 6 May 1969.
127. McCafferty, *Nell*, p. 115.
128. *Irish Militant*, October 1967; M. Backus, '"Not Quite Philadelphia, Is It?": An Interview with Eamonn McCann', *Éire-Ireland*, 36, 3&4 (Fall/Winter 2001), pp. 178–91, p. 185; Transcript of BBC interview with E. McCann, [summer 2008] (personal notes); *Derry Journal*, 26 March 1968; *Derry Journal*, 7 May 1968; *Derry Journal*, 17 May 1968.
129. McCafferty, *Nell*, pp. 81 and 116–17.
130. Transcript of BBC interview with D. McClenaghan, [Summer 2008] (personal notes); Transcript of BBC interview with E. Melaugh, [Summer 2008] (personal notes).
131. *Derry Journal*, 3 October 2008.
132. CIA, 'Restless Youth', September 1968, Lyndon B. Johnson Library, Austin, Texas, D/613/68, quoted in M. Klimke, *The Other Alliance: Student Protest in West Germany and the United States in the Global Sixties* (Princeton, NJ: Princeton University Press, 2010), p. 1.
133. P. Gassert and M. Klimke, 'Introduction', in P. Gassert and M. Klimke (eds), *1968: Memories and Legacies of a Global Revolt* (Washington, DC: German Historical Institute, 2009), pp. 5–24, pp. 6–7.
134. Transcript of McCann interview. The interaction between the global and the local in Northern Ireland during the 'long '68' is considered at length in S. Prince, *Northern Ireland's '68: Civil Rights, Global Revolt and the Origins of The Troubles* (Dublin: Irish Academic Press, 2007). This section will focus on direct action, which is almost entirely overlooked in *Northern Ireland's '68*.

135. T. Sugrue, *Sweet Land of Liberty: The Forgotten Struggle for Civil Rights in the North* (New York, NY: Random House, 2008), pp. 354–5.
136. P. Joseph, *Waiting 'Til the Midnight Hour: A Narrative History of Black Power in America* (New York, NY: Henry Holt, 2006), pp. xvii, 1–8, 139, 142–61 and 193.
137. Special Branch report on American political activity in London, 24 November 1967, London, National Archives (NA), HO/325/104.
138. D. Cooper, 'Beyond Words', in D. Cooper (ed.), *The Dialectics of Liberation* (London: Penguin, 1967), pp. 193–202, pp. 201–2.
139. Transcript of McCann interview; B. Dooley, *Black and Green: The Fight for Civil Rights in Northern Ireland and Black America* (London: Pluto Press, 1998), p. 46.
140. S. Carmichael, 'Black Power', in D. Cooper (ed.), *The Dialectics of Liberation* (London: Penguin, 1967), pp. 150–74, p. 168.
141. *Irish Militant*, September 1967; *Irish Militant*, October 1967.
142. W. Mausbach, 'Auschwitz and Vietnam: West Germany's Protest against America's War During the 1960s', in A. Daum, L. Gardner and W. Mausbach (eds), *America, the Vietnam War, and the World: Comparative and International Perspectives* (Cambridge: Cambridge University Press, 2003), pp. 279–98, p. 297.
143. J. Varon, *Bringing the War Home: The Weather Underground, the Red Army Faction, and Revolutionary Violence in the Sixties and Seventies* (London: University of California Press, 2004), p. 41.
144. Klimke, *Other Alliance*, pp. 35–8.
145. J. Varon, 'Refusing to be "Good Germans": New Left Violence as a Global Phenomenon', *German Historical Institute Bulletin*, 43 (Fall 2008), pp. 21–43, p. 32.
146. *Avant-Garde Jeunesse*, Special No. 10–11 (February–March 1968).
147. M. Seidman, *The Imaginary Revolution: Parisian Students and Workers in 1968* (Oxford: Berghahn, 2004), pp. 72 and 73.
148. F. Crouzet, 'A University Besieged: Nanterre, 1967–69', *Political Science Quarterly*, 84, 2 (June 1969), pp. 328–350, pp. 342–9; R. Merritt, 'The Student Protest Movement in West Berlin', *Comparative Politics*, 1, 4 (July 1969), pp. 516–33, pp. 526–7.
149. Seidman, *Imaginary Revolution*, pp. 73 and 75–85.
150. R. Aron, 'Student Rebellion: Vision of the Future or Echo from the Past?', *Political Science Quarterly*, 84, 2 (June 1969), pp. 289–310, p. 292.
151. *Guardian*, 31 May 2000; T. Ali, *Street Fighting Years: An Autobiography of the Sixties* (Glasgow: Fontana, 1987), p. 171; Transcript of McCann interview; Backus, '"Not Quite Philadelphia, Is It?"', p. 185.
152. Special Branch report on American political activity in London, 24 November 1967.
153. *Irish Militant*, October 1967.
154. Special Branch report on American political activity in London, 24 November 1967.
155. Special Branch report on American political activity in London, 26 February 1968, NA, HO/325/104.
156. *Guardian*, 18 March 1968.
157. N. Thomas, 'Protests against the Vietnam War in 1960s Britain: The Relationship between Protesters and the Press', *Contemporary British History*, 22, 3 (September 2008), pp. 335–54, pp. 341–5.
158. *Guardian*, 31 May 2000.
159. Copy of report provided to the BBC under the Freedom of Information Act. For further details, see http://news.bbc.co.uk/1/hi/programmes/newsnight/7424867.stm (last accessed 19 November 2010).
160. E. McCann, 'Civil Rights in an International Context', in P. McClenaghan (ed.), *Spirit of '68: Beyond the Barricades* (Derry: Guildhall Press, 2009), pp. 16–26, p. 21; Transcript of McCann interview.
161. See, for instance, *Derry Journal*, 4 October 2008 and A. Edwards, *A History of the Northern Ireland Labour Party: Democratic Socialism and Sectarianism* (Manchester: Manchester University Press, 2009), p. 138.
162. Transcript of McCann interview.
163. *Irish Democrat*, April 1965.

164. F. Gogarty to George, 18 February 1969, PRONI, D/3253/1.
165. M. Milotte, *Communism in Modern Ireland: The Pursuit of the Workers' Republic since 1916* (Dublin: Gill & Macmillan, 1984), pp. 136 and 164; Patterson, *Ireland since 1939*, pp. 10 and 13.
166. Edwards, *History of the Northern Ireland Labour Party*, p. 138.
167. Transcript of interview with McClenaghan.
168. *Derry Journal*, 7 May 1968; *Derry Journal*, 14 May 1968.
169. *Derry Journal*, 14 May 1968; *Derry Journal*, 3 October 2008. On the Dublin Housing Action Committee, which was formed before the DHAC but resorted to direct action after it, see E. Hanna, 'Dublin's North Inner City, Preservationism, and Irish Modernity in the 1960s', *Historical Journal*, 53, 4 (December 2010), pp. 1015–35, pp. 1030–33.
170. *Londonderry Sentinel*, 3 April 1968.
171. *Derry Journal*, 2 April 1968.
172. *Derry Journal*, 3 May 1968.
173. *Derry Journal*, 25 June 1968.
174. *Derry Journal*, 2 July 1968. The family were eventually given a home at 417 Bishop Street. *Reality*, Anniversary Edition 1968–9, Derry, Derry City Council's Archives (DCCA), Bridget Bond Civil Rights Collection.
175. *Derry Journal*, 5 July 1968.
176. E. McCann, *War and an Irish Town* (London: Pluto, 1993 edn.), p. 91.
177. *Peace News*, September 1967; Varon, *Bringing the War Home*, p. 44; D. Triesman, 'Essex', *New Left Review*, July-August 1968.
178. King, *Letter from Birmingham Jail*.
179. L. Sobel and J. Fickes, *Welfare & the Poor* (New York, NY: Facts on File, 1977), pp. 28–9. See, also, Bernadette Devlin's speech at the Sorbonne in the autumn of 1970: 'the people of Ireland...were born into a system in which there was violence – violence that kills the children of the working class because of the conditions they live in'. *Irish Times*, 13 November 1970.
180. *Derry Journal*, 23 July 1968.
181. *Derry Journal*, 6 September 1968.
182. McCann, *War and an Irish Town*, p. 91.
183. *Derry Journal*, 23 July 1968.
184. L. Donohue, 'Regulating Northern Ireland: The Special Powers Acts, 1922–1972', *Historical Journal*, 41, 4 (December 1998), pp. 1089–1120, pp. 1119–20.
185. J. Earl, S. Soule and J. McCarthy, 'Protest under Fire? Explaining the Policing of Protest', *American Sociological Review*, 68, 4 (August 2003), pp. 581–606, p. 582.
186. J. Habermas, *Toward a Rational Society: Student Protest, Science, and Politics* trans. J. Shapiro (London: Beacon Press; 1971), p. 41.
187. *Derry Journal*, 19 July 1968.
188. *Derry Journal*, 23 July 1968; W. Meharg to Ministry of Home Affairs, 24 July 1968, PRONI, HA/32/2/28; G. Fitt's evidence to the Cameron Commission, 25 July 1969, PRONI, GOV/2/1/140. 'F. Ó Dochartaigh, 'Derry Salutes Connolly', DCCA, Bridget Bond Civil Rights Collection.
189. *Derry Journal*, 23 July 1968.
190. *Derry Journal*, 29 March 1966; *Irish Democrat*, February 1968.
191. *Dungannon Observer*, 3 August 1968.
192. F. Gogarty, 'The Development of the Civil Rights Movement and its Future Course', [May 1969], PRONI, D/3253/3.
193. *Derry Journal*, 16 August 1968.
194. Civil Rights March from Coalisland to Dungannon, 29 August 1968, Belfast, Public Record Office of Northern Ireland, PRONI, CAB/9B/205/7.
195. M. King, 'Behind the Selma March', *Saturday Review*, 3 April 1965.
196. Civil Rights March from Coalisland to Dungannon.
197. Manis, *A Fire You Can't Put Out*, p. 368.
198. D. Johnston to J. Hill, 7 July 1969, PRONI, HA/32/2/28.

199. *Derry Journal*, 27 August 1968; A. Currie, *All Hell Will Break Loose* (Dublin: O'Brien, 2004), p. 106.
200. Civil Rights March from Coalisland to Dungannon.
201. King, 'Behind the Selma March'.
202. *Derry Journal*, 27 August 1968; *Derry Journal*, 10 September 1968; Gogarty to George, 18 February 1969; McCann, *War and an Irish Town*, p. 94; Transcript of Melaugh interview.
203. See, for example, J. Becker, *Hitler's Children: Story of the Baader-Meinhof Terrorist Gang* (Philadelphia, PA: J.B. Lippincott, 1977). The best account of how the global context has been ignored is Varon, 'Refusing to be "Good Germans"'.
204. McCann, 'Civil Rights in an International Context', pp. 16 and 17.
205. *Derry Journal*, 30 August 1968.
206. *Derry Journal*, 27 February 1968; *Derry Journal*, 16 July 1968; *Derry Journal*, 18 June 1968; *Derry Journal*, 28 August 1967; *Derry Journal*, 28 June 1968; *Derry Journal*, 17 May 1968; *Derry Journal*, 28 June 1968; *Derry Journal*, 23 April 1968.
207. Trentmann, 'Materiality in the Future of History', p. 305.

2

The Divis Street Riots of 1964

Just after 3 pm on 7 October 1964, Terence O'Neill rose from his seat in the House of Commons of the Northern Ireland Parliament to make a statement on the civil disturbances which had occurred in Belfast during the course of the previous week. Since becoming Prime Minister in March 1963, he said, he had 'had two principal aims in view': firstly, 'to make Northern Ireland economically stronger and more prosperous, so that all our people may enjoy a fuller and richer life' and secondly, 'to build bridges between the two traditions within our community'. It was clear that he believed the two objectives went hand in hand, for he expressed concern that the disturbances might hinder his government's efforts to attract new industry to Northern Ireland. Although O'Neill recognized that 'only a tiny minority of the citizens of Belfast either provoked or took part' in them, he emphasized that:

> '[w]e cannot go back to the 1920s and 1930s, when 100,000 unemployed were the order of the day and misery and privation stalked the streets of Belfast. I pray God that as we advance in wealth and education and maturity the dreadful scenes which we witnessed will never be repeated, and I trust that men of good will throughout our Province will work to that end.'[1]

Less than five years later, and after he had been forced out of office, O'Neill's vision of a peaceful and prosperous, but Unionist-controlled, province had been shattered. The Troubles had started. The Divis riots of 1964 are a good point of departure for the study of what happened, particularly in so far as the city of Belfast was concerned.

I

When O'Neill referred to 'the two traditions in our community', he meant Protestants (a term which included members of the Anglican Church of Ireland, Presbyterians, Methodists and other, smaller Christian denominations) and Catholics, or unionists and nationalists. These two divisions – the communal and the political – overlapped, but there was no complete correspondence between them. As O'Neill's reference to building bridges between traditions implies, there had been a long history of intimate hatreds which, in Belfast, had begun in the early nineteenth century when large numbers of Catholics began to move into what had previously been an overwhelmingly Protestant town. They had come in search of work in the industries which were to make it the eighth biggest in the United Kingdom by 1911 and the home of 'the largest weaving and tobacco factories, ropeworks and output of shipping in the world'.[2] From less than 10 per cent in 1784, the proportion of Catholics in Belfast rose to 34 per cent in 1861. It fell to 23 per cent by 1926, but then slowly began to rise once more so that by 1961 it stood at 26 per cent.[3]

There were fifteen major riots in Belfast between 1813 and 1909.[4] If Protestants fought with, and sometimes killed, Catholics in Belfast, and vice-versa, it was not, essentially, because of religious disputes and nor was it, essentially, because of ethnic rivalry (although there often were religious and communal dimensions to rioting). Instead, it was, essentially, because of political conflict, with serious rioting usually coming at times of political upheaval, specifically during election campaigns. Indeed, riots involving Irish Catholics in Scottish and English cities as well as in Belfast were rare until the electoral reforms of the 1820s and 1830s. Liverpool, for example, witnessed sectarian rioting after the Whigs took control of local government in 1835 and the Tories chose to use anti-Catholicism to take it back. The pattern of rioting in Belfast, though, changed somewhat after the decision in 1865 to take the responsibility of policing away from the town council and give it to the Royal Irish Constabulary (RIC). So, while in 1864 Protestants and many police officers had battled against Catholics, in 1886 the clashes were largely fought out between Protestants, on one side, and the RIC and the British army on the other.[5]

Unsurprisingly, then, during the years 1920–22, political upheaval and the return of security powers to local politicians worked together to lead to the worst violence in the city's whole history. However, we should be careful not to subsume everything within the Irish Revolutionary narrative because the start of the Belfast 'Troubles' came not with a shooting war between the IRA and the Crown forces but with expulsions from the city's shipyards. This fitted in with a pattern of shipyard expulsions across the United Kingdom, as the post-war economic downturn and the return of servicemen led to 'outsiders' being pushed out in the battle for work. Beginning in July 1920, at Belfast shipyards, thousands of Catholics and left-wing Protestants were ejected from their jobs for being 'Sinn Féin workers'.[6] It was telling that these expulsions came after the annual commemoration of the Battle of the Boyne, on 12 July, where speeches had dwelt on 'loyal' Protestants being unemployed while 'disloyal' Catholics were in work. Trouble was not limited to the shipyards. Loyalist crowd violence was aimed at Catholic churches, convents, houses and businesses; more organized campaigns of intimidation, too, worked to drive Catholics out of Protestant areas. On a smaller scale, members of the Protestant community were also victims of the other side of this struggle for space and security.[7] 'The reciprocity of northern violence', according to Peter Hart, 'does not fit the pogrom model.' The 'battle for Belfast' was 'more like a miniature civil war', one in which the wider war between the British empire and Irish republicanism allowed all manner of communal, social, economic and personal grudges and interests to be pursued.[8]

The end of the Civil War in the South and the survival of the Northern state in some ways marked a return in Belfast to an earlier pattern of politicized communal violence. During the Great Depression, for example, efforts by Marxist-Leninist groups to organize across the communal divide had some successes (in 1932, unemployed Protestants and Catholics rioted together in protest against the low levels of welfare payments), but were thwarted when the Orange card was played. In the 1935 marching season, sectarian riots left ten dead and hundreds forced from their homes – and also resulted in a sharp decline in Communism.[9] One consequence of the regular outbreaks of violence was the residential segregation which prevails in Belfast to this day. A natural tendency on the part of the Catholic minority to cluster in certain parts of the city where they would not only benefit from living near others who shared their values and from the many social outreach activities of their Church was reinforced by a heightened desire for security in the event of trouble. Indeed, people were often forced to move into more 'friendly' areas during or after rioting, a phenomenon which also affected Protestants.

By 1969, this process had produced a situation in which two-thirds of Belfast's households lived in streets in which 91 per cent or more of the households were of the same religion.[10] Catholics were concentrated in five main areas. By far the biggest was the Falls in the west of the city, which contained 70 per cent of the households in streets which were 91 per cent or more Catholic. The next largest was Ardoyne, which was just off the Crumlin Road in the north-west of the city, with 11 per cent of the households in question. Then there was an area to the north-west of the city centre which stretched from the Unity Flats along North Queen Street to the New Lodge Road (8 per cent); another, the Markets, which was to the south of the city centre on either side of Cromac Street (4 per cent); and, finally, Ballymacarrett (or the Short Strand), which was sandwiched between the Newtownards and Albertbridge Roads just across the River Lagan in east Belfast (4 per cent).[11] The division between Protestant and Catholic areas could occur within the width of a single street and much of the inter-communal violence of the nineteenth and twentieth centuries took place along these dividing lines, or interfaces as they are often called.

Patterns of behaviour also varied sharply between those living in these segregated districts. A survey carried out between December 1967 and January 1968 in the Catholic Clonard district, just north of the Falls Road, and an adjacent Protestant district just south of the Shankill Road, showed huge differences between the people in each area in terms of their marital ties, their circle of friends, where they shopped, where they caught a bus into the city centre, which football team they supported and which newspaper they read.[12] Children's education was not included, but presumably only because everyone knew that Catholic parents sent their children to Church schools while Protestant parents sent theirs to state schools. Segregation was widely seen as a simple fact of life. Violence, however, was not.

II

The riots of September–October 1964 were the worst in Belfast since 1935. No-one was killed and no-one has calculated the total of those injured, but speaking in the Northern Ireland Parliament on 7 October 1964 the Minister of Home Affairs, Brian McConnell, stated that seventy-two people were arrested, forty-six police were injured, and fifty-three business premises, fifty private houses, fourteen police vehicles, seven private vehicles and twenty public transport vehicles were damaged.[13] What happened and why? The answers to these questions enable us more fully to understand the political situation in Belfast in the 1960s.

Although Northern Ireland had its own devolved government, complete with Governor, Cabinet, House of Commons and Senate, it also returned twelve MPs to the United Kingdom Parliament in London and the riots occurred during the run up to the General Election of 15 October 1964. All twelve of Westminster's Northern Irish MPs were Unionists – that is, members of the party which had ruled the province without interruption since the devolved government was established in 1921. The Unionists at Westminster took the Conservative Party whip – much to the irritation of the Labour Party. But, while their outlook was similar to that of the Conservatives on many issues, the principal plank in their policy, and that of their colleagues at Stormont, was to defend the integrity of Northern Ireland and its membership of the United Kingdom. Neither the Conservative Party nor the Labour Party existed in Northern Ireland itself, although there was a separate Northern Ireland Labour Party (NILP) which had links with the British Labour Party. Since 1949, it too had been in favour of the Union with Britain, but it was not nearly as strident about it as the Unionists, the latter portraying the NILP as a half-way house on the rocky road to Dublin. It also had more sympathy with the grievances of the Catholic minority over such issues as discrimination in housing and employment.[14] In the late 1950s the NILP had begun to gain support in Belfast, a largely working-class city suffering from high unemployment,[15] and in the 1962 Stormont elections it gained over 40 per cent of the vote in the city and won four seats.[16]

Those in the North who opposed the Union with Britain and who favoured a united Ireland of some kind were broadly divided into two political groupings: those who adhered to the constitutionalist tradition, which had (usually) characterized the old Irish Parliamentary Party, and those who favoured a revolutionary approach (usually) involving armed struggle, the republican tradition which was now embodied in Sinn Féin and the IRA. It was the IRA, of course, which had played a central role in winning independence for the bulk of Ireland back in the early 1920s, but its descendants of the 1960s, the children of numerous splits, were very different. For one thing, they now represented only a minority of nationalists; for another, they were illegal in both Northern Ireland and the Republic of Ireland, and although Sinn Féin was permitted in the latter, its political influence was negligible.[17]

The IRA had not seriously embarrassed the authorities in Northern Ireland since the early 1920s, thanks largely to the powers the government possessed under the notorious Special Powers Acts, to suppress it,[18] although it played a part in the wider campaign against the United Kingdom which was launched in 1939.[19] Another IRA campaign, this time specifically directed against Northern Ireland, was launched in December 1956. Codenamed 'Operation Harvest', it is also known as 'the Border Campaign', since most of the action was carried out close to the frontier areas of the province. Some claim that Belfast was deliberately excluded from the border campaign in order to avoid a repetition of the bloodshed of the 1920–2 fighting, but it has also been pointed out that the Belfast IRA had drawn up plans for attacks on targets in the city which ranged from RUC stations and the homes of policemen to contractors working for the security forces.[20] In any event, the campaign failed. Internment, on both sides of the border, undoubtedly contributed to its defeat, but the main reason, as the IRA frankly admitted in its statement of 26 February 1962 which called a halt to hostilities, was 'the attitude of the general public whose minds have been deliberately distracted from the supreme issue facing the Irish people – the unity and freedom of Ireland'.[21]

Among the Northern Irish candidates presenting themselves for election to Westminster in October 1964 were twelve 'Republicans', a pseudonym for Sinn Féin, a disguise which fooled no one, but which was sufficient to get around the government ban on the party. The Republican candidate in the constituency of West Belfast, which included the solidly Catholic Falls district, was William (Billy)

McMillen, a 35-year-old scaffolder, described as 'stocky and short, a fluent Irish-speaker who was active in the Gaelic League (where he was generally referred to as Liam)...'[22] More important than all of this, he was the Officer Commanding of the Belfast IRA.

Although the other three Belfast seats were safe for Unionism, West Belfast promised to be a more interesting contest. Apart from the Catholic Falls, it included solidly Protestant districts too. Indeed, it had been a Unionist seat prior to the election, although there was a new Unionist candidate, James Kilfedder, a London barrister, albeit one with Irish roots. In addition, there were two other strong, local candidates: Harry Diamond, a left-wing nationalist standing under the rubric of Republican Labour and the sitting Stormont MP for the Falls constituency; and Billy Boyd (NILP), who also sat at Stormont for the Protestant Woodvale constituency.

As his campaign headquarters McMillen had chosen an unoccupied shop at 145 Divis Street, a thoroughfare which ran from the edge of the city centre to the Falls Road. McMillen displayed an Irish Tricolour in the window. The Tricolour was like a red rag to unionist bulls and, indeed, the Northern Ireland Government had passed a Flags and Emblems Act in 1954 which prohibited displays that were likely to cause a breach of the peace. McMillen had already fallen foul of this legislation the previous year when he was involved in one of the commemorative parades which were a feature of political life in Northern Ireland: a celebration of the anniversary of the birth of Wolfe Tone, one of the leaders of the United Irishmen rising in 1798. The organizers asked the IRA to provide a colour party for the parade, but the government invoked the Flags and Emblems Act to prevent it. McMillen was all for defying the ban, but the then Officer Commanding in Belfast, Billy McKee, argued for acceptance. This led to a blazing row inside the IRA which eventually led to McKee quitting as Belfast commander and to his leaving the organization altogether. Nevertheless, the Tricolour was not carried in the parade and McMillen later noted that 'the IRA colour party marched up the Falls minus the colours!'[23]

Whether McMillen chose to display the Tricolour in his campaign office in 1964 as a deliberate act of defiance is not clear. He remarked in 1972 that the government had made no attempt to ban its display in the 1964 Belfast parade commemorating the Easter Rising of 1916, although an IRA member was arrested and jailed for three months for carrying it elsewhere in the province. Moreover, one of his electoral opponents, Diamond, pointed out that it was on display in Divis Street – a solidly Catholic area – for almost three weeks in September 1964 without anyone taking exception to it.[24] It was at this point, however, that following 'a number of complaints', the RUC intervened. According to McConnell, 'the police had an interview with some of the occupants of the premises at No. 145. They expressed to them their fears that trouble might be caused by continuing to display the Tricolour in the window, but at that interview no duress was used by the police. It was entirely a friendly approach...'[25]

Whence did these 'complaints' originate and how many were there? We do not know the whole story, but it is clear that McMillen's Unionist opponent, Kilfedder, was involved as he sent a telegram to O'Connell urging him to 'remove [the] Tricolour in Divis Street which is aimed to provoke and insult loyalists of West Belfast'.[26] So, too, was a fundamentalist Protestant preacher, the burly, 38-year-old, six-foot-three-inches tall Reverend Ian Paisley, who announced that since representations made to both the Hastings Street RUC barracks – which was responsible for policing Divis Street – and Unionist Party headquarters had not resulted in any action, he would organize a march on Divis Street.[27]

Paisley had plenty of predecessors in the province, notably perhaps Reverend ('Roaring') Hugh Hanna, the Presbyterian minister whose fiery speeches and sermons were alleged to have played a part in more than one of the nineteenth-century Belfast riots.[28] Like Hanna, Paisley wove together religion and politics. In 1951, he founded his own Free Presbyterian Church and soon acquired a reputation for intemperate attacks on Catholicism and any form of ecumenism, which he regarded as selling out to the Vatican. He was politically involved as early as January 1949, when he campaigned on behalf of the successful Unionist candidate in the marginal Dock ward in central Belfast during the elections to the Stormont Parliament. In the late 1950s, he was a leading member of Ulster Protestant Action, a militant unionist ginger group, but broke with it in 1961.[29] Although he had supported the Unionist candidate in Dock ward in 1949 and was now supporting Kilfedder in West Belfast, Paisley was deeply suspicious of the Unionist leadership, and particularly of O'Neill. Here he was resurrecting a dormant dissenting discourse which doubted the motives of all elites, be they political or religious. As Paisley's *Protestant Telegraph* put it in May 1967, 'the hoards of Romanism and the compromise of O'Neillism' had placed 'our Protestant heritage' in danger.[30] Paisleyism, its supporters claimed, was offering new vehicles in which to pursue traditional religious and political beliefs and practices. Although the 1961 Census counted only 344 declared members of Paisley's Free Presbyterian Church in Belfast out of a total of 416,000 religious believers,[31] his political influence was much greater than these figures suggest. People who were not particularly religious were giving their support to this fundamentalist preacher because he represented the Protestant tradition that had historically defined their community. At a time when some felt that Unionism was under threat, Paisley appeared to be a reliable and relentless defender.[32]

III

Paisley's intervention galvanized the Northern Ireland Government into action. The march was banned, but on the evening of 28 September 1964, policemen broke into 145 Divis Street and removed the Tricolour. There was no resistance from McMillen and his election agent, the only two people in the building, at the time, but as the then senior officer at the Hasting Street police station, Head Constable John Hermon, subsequently recorded:

> Tension inevitably mounted. The ban on Paisley's march did not prevent him holding a rally at the City Hall. Crowds gathered in the vicinity of the Republican Party's office, and police patrols reported an uneasiness and growing hostility amongst local residents, especially the younger ones. The situation was becoming very ugly. Although no serious incidents occurred in Divis Street that particular evening, it was well after midnight before the crowd disappeared, leaving me apprehensive about the rest of the week.[33]

Hermon's apprehension was justified. In the small hours of 29 September, an emergency meeting of the Republican Election Directorate upped the ante by announcing that unless the RUC replaced the Tricolour it had removed within two days, McMillen would put up another in its place.[34] That evening a second vigil was staged outside 145 Divis Street. According to the *Belfast Telegraph,* about 100 children gathered opposite the Republican headquarters around 7:30 pm singing rebel songs. By 9 pm they were joined by a number of adults and 'there was loud cheering when a group of boys ran along Divis Street flaunting the ... Tricolour and an anti-Paisley banner'. The flag was placed beside the election headquarters and garbage and stones were thrown at police officers who were trying to persuade the crowd to disperse. It finally did so around midnight and a disgruntled Divis Street shopkeeper remarked the following morning that the whole business had been started by teenagers and that 'if there had been a heavy shower of rain...the whole thing would have been over in ten minutes'.[35]

At the same time as these incidents in Divis Street, Paisley was holding his rally in Donegall Square, brandishing a message from the hardline Ulster Loyalist Association that congratulated him on his 'stand against the Tricolour'. He called for the prosecution of Republicans and criticized the RUC for its handling of the matter. Although he had appealed for order, about 100 of his followers had to be dissuaded by a sizeable police presence from proceeding to the Shankill via the Falls.[36]

Serious trouble broke out on the following night. As on the previous day a crowd began to gather in Divis Street at about 7:30 pm. Two hours later, bottles were being hurled at passing vehicles. By 10 pm the road was covered in broken glass. The appearance of a police Land Rover prompted a shower of bottles and four vans, containing fifty policemen, were rushed in as reinforcements. The police marched up Divis Street and the crowd scattered into the side streets whence they continued to bombard the police with missiles. The crowd was estimated at about 1,500 when the violence reached its peak at around 11:30 pm. The demonstrators began to chant 'Burn, Burn, Burn the Bastards!' while cursing Paisley. The police drew their batons. According to one report, 'women screamed, and children scattered and policemen clashed with the demonstrators. Several were knocked underfoot and hundreds ran for the shelter of nearby Percy Street and other adjoining streets ...One young girl ran into a side street with blood streaming from her head'.[37] McMillen blamed the Minister of Home Affairs. 'To appease mob law', he said, 'he ordered armed police into a 100 [per cent] nationalist area and created a situation the consequence of which has been to destroy respect for the civil law and set a deplorable example to the more unruly elements.'[38]

McMillen duly replaced the Tricolour on 1 October 1964, as he had threatened to do. The police promptly broke in to remove it. This precipitated further mayhem which escalated into what the nationalist *Irish News* called 'a night of fear' during which petrol bombs exploded around police vehicles, a Belfast Corporation trolleybus was set on fire, plate-glass windows in shops were smashed and blood flowed from more than thirty injured heads as iron gratings, bottles and stones showered down from the side streets.[39] Across the Lagan in east Belfast, the author of the parish chronicle of the Catholic St Matthew's Church wrote in an entry dated 2 October 1964, 'it looked as if serious trouble might develop and partisan strife be again violently enkindled [sic] in the City. Also alarming – to the police [–] was their helplessness against and the devastation that could be caused by the "Molotov cocktail"…used for the first time in Belfast against the hithertofore invincible police tenders'. A local milkman, he claimed, could not lay his hands on many empty milk bottles for his Saturday morning delivery.[40]

Paisley stirred the pot still further by issuing a statement in which he and one of his colleagues demonized all Catholics. 'The disgraceful acts on the Falls Road', it declared, 'which have been instigated by the Republican associates of the murderous IRA demonstrate the real character of the Catholic population'. No responsible spokesman of the Catholic community, it claimed, had condemned the violence, but had instead slandered Protestants and loyalists who, despite provocation, had remained orderly and law-abiding. The replacement of the Tricolour, it thundered, was 'a challenge which cannot be ignored, and the Catholic community better know that the loyalist and Protestant people will not capitulate to this illegal and riotous behaviour'.[41] As the peak number of rioters was estimated at 1,500 and the entire Catholic population of Belfast was over 114,000 in 1961,[42] this blanket condemnation of the latter was absurd. Indeed, it was even claimed subsequently that some of the rioters were Protestant agents provocateurs.[43]

As it happened, both Protestant and Catholic Church leaders did appeal for calm on Friday, 2 October 1964, as did O'Neill. Even the Republicans seemed to realize the danger posed by what they had helped produce when they issued a statement which said: 'We wish to avoid injury to innocent people and do not intend to allow the issue of flying the Tricolour to overshadow other issues. The flag is merely a symbol of freedom'.[44] But there was further rioting on the night of 2/3 October 1964 in which petrol bombs were again thrown and shops looted, although a police spokesman was quoted as saying, 'We don't think it has been as severe as last night.'[45]

There was no serious trouble after that; even though there was a 5,000-strong march through Catholic west Belfast on 4 October 1964 in the course of which people waved miniature Tricolours and sang Irish songs. The march ended in a rally at which seven out of the twelve Republican candidates in the election were present on the platform, together with Ena Connolly, daughter of James Connolly, who presented McMillen with a 'lucky Tricolour horseshoe'. The proceedings concluded with the singing of 'The Soldier's Song', in Irish.[46] None of this had much effect on the results of the election, which took place eleven days later. As a Metropolitan Police Special Branch report of 16 November 1964 pointed out, they brought 'little joy' to the Republicans. They obtained 101,619 votes out of a total of 633,263 throughout the province and although this was an improvement upon their position in 1959, it was almost 50,000 votes fewer than they had polled in 1955.[47] McMillen came bottom of the poll in West Belfast and lost his deposit. Kilfedder won the seat with a majority of 6,659 over Diamond, with Billy Boyd in third place. The new Unionist MP reportedly stated that he owed his victory to Paisley.[48]

IV

A 'Top Secret' report of February 1966 by the RUC Special Branch claimed that the Divis riots 'were not casual riots but an organised attempt to incite sectarian troubles. While firearms were not used, incendiary bombs were thrown at police vehicles...It was noticed that important members of the IRA who presumably thought they were unknown to the police, worked secretly in the background playing a major part in creating troubles during the elections.'[49] But this was not what the police were saying at the time. On 3 October 1964 the RUC's City Commissioner for Belfast, Graham Shillington, said of the rioting,

'It is not controlled by anyone, but is entirely undisciplined, a lot of young hooligans running wild'.[50] Nor was there any hint of deliberate IRA orchestration of the riots in government statements during the parliamentary debate on the subject. If there was 'an organised attempt to incite sectarian troubles', it was singularly badly planned, as there was no attempt to confront Protestants, but only the police, and all the rioting took place in a Catholic area. If there was any sectarian threat, it came not from the Catholics but from Paisley and his supporters. As for the presence of 'important members of the IRA', this was no surprise. They *were* the Republican candidates in Belfast and their principal helpers. As we shall see, the organization was not particularly thick on the ground.

A private post-mortem on the Divis riots was carried out after the election by O'Neill at two meetings held at Stormont on 2 November 1964: the first with the Cabinet and a Unionist Party official; the second with the Minister of Home Affairs and senior police officers. He was 'anxious', he told the first meeting, 'to clarify certain details of the West Belfast election', both in response to speeches made in Stormont and because he thought the matter might come up in his forthcoming meeting with the newly elected Labour Prime Minister of the United Kingdom, Harold Wilson. The reference to 'speeches at Stormont' is obscure, but it may have included the somewhat fanciful accusation by the two Republican Labour MPs, Diamond, and Gerry Fitt, the loquacious and pugnacious former merchant seaman who had won the Dock constituency from the Unionists in 1962, that the riots had been the consequence of a plot hatched by the Unionist Party, the government and Paisley to ensure the victory of Kilfedder in West Belfast.[51] O'Neill wanted to know about the contents of the election leaflets circulated during the campaign and was told that the one issued by the Ulster Loyalist Association, which was sympathetic to Paisley, was 'hard-hitting but not politically objectionable', whereas 'the really objectionable leaflet', which asked 'do you want Catholics in your street?' was published by his erstwhile associates in Ulster Protestant Action. It was further emphasized that although Paisley had supported Kilfedder, he and his followers 'were in no sense part of the official Unionist organization'. Indeed, Paisleyite candidates had stood against official Unionists in previous elections and might well do so again.[52]

At the second meeting, O'Neill enquired what could be done to forestall a repeat performance of the rioting. The answers were disappointing. There were no powers to ban the establishment of a Republican headquarters in any particular place. A curfew could only be imposed under emergency powers and was almost impossible to enforce. Little advance preparation could be done with the Catholic Church, as it would only be willing to take a line when it thought it would be followed, and in any case, 'some of the people who fomented trouble were beyond Church influence'. The prevailing view in the police was that 'the only way of avoiding trouble was prompt, informal and friendly contact with those who might foment it'.[53]

The document in question clearly equated 'those who might foment' trouble with the Republicans on this occasion. But was this altogether fair? It was, after all, Paisley and his associates who turned the display of the Tricolour into a political issue in the first place. If they had not done so, it is unlikely that its display, occurring as it did in a Catholic and nationalist area, would have given rise to any trouble. It could also be argued that the government was to blame for rising to the bait, although the Unionist leadership had few other options, especially as one of their own candidates had linked himself with Paisley on the issue and they clearly wished to prevent a possible sectarian confrontation on the streets. The police, moreover, did not go in mob-handed in the first instance, but tried to employ a tactic of persuasion. Where McMillen and his supporters contributed to the problem, and in so doing played into the Paisleyites' hands, was when they issued their own ultimatum demanding the replacement of the Tricolour which had been removed. They must have realized that such an ultimatum would not be accepted and the two days' breathing space given to the police to comply, far from lowering tension, gave more time for it to build up.

It is more difficult to evaluate the consequences of the riots. George Clarke, a beat policeman in the area at the time, has recently claimed that, ever since the violence of the early 1920s, the RUC 'had been slowly but surely building up trust with the Catholic population' only to see it shattered by 'one idiot policeman who smashed a shop window and removed a small Tricolour on display'. He goes on to say that '[t]he two communities in the North started to move apart again', and that he 'firmly believed that the Divis Street riots lit the fuse for the Civil Rights movement...[which] in turn led to the involvement of the IRA, and out of this rose the Provos and thirty years of death and misery'.[54] But this is surely overstated. Clarke suggests that his relations with the Catholics on his beat in the Falls were excellent, but while this may have been true, it would be misleading to equate his personal experience with relations between Catholics and the police in general. The RUC, in the words of a senior British policeman, was 'not a police force in the English sense. It is a para-military organisation accountable to a Minister'.[55] Along with the Unionist Party and the Orange Order, it was one of the pillars upon which the Northern Ireland state rested. It was hardly surprising, therefore, that it had a negative image amongst the Catholic population, an attitude which probably accounts as much for the fact that the proportion of Catholics in the RUC was a mere 10.5 percent in 1966 as the alleged discrimination against those Catholics who applied to join the force.[56]

In so far as the overall relationship between Catholics and the Unionist regime was affected by the Divis riots, the judgement of a moderate nationalist who had experienced and strongly disapproved of the RUC's handling of them is probably nearer the mark. 'Divis Street', he subsequently wrote, 'marked the end of the honeymoon period for Terence O'Neill. As nationalists saw it he had had a chance to tell Ian Paisley to get lost but instead had capitulated to his huffing and puffing.'[57]

As for the direct link between the Divis riots, the civil rights movement and the rise of the Provisional IRA, it needs to be emphasized that Dr Conn and Patricia McCluskey had already set up their Campaign for Social Justice in Dungannon earlier in the year, that NICRA was not launched until January 1967, that marches did not start for another year and that the IRA split and military campaigns lay far ahead. Eight years later, McMillen was to claim that the riots 'embittered the nationalist population against the Stormont regime, revived all their frustrations and resentment against the Government repression, and set the stage for future confrontation between the youth of the nationalist areas and the RUC' and that 'a couple of dozen new recruits' joined the Belfast IRA in their wake. The same source stated that there were only twenty-four members at the end of the Border Campaign, so that even if we accept that the organization had begun to revive in 1964, it was still very small beer in a city of over 415,000 people, which included 114,000 Catholics.[58]

McMillen also observed that the 'trail of lost Republican deposits' in the 1964 election was 'a costly demonstration that people with the vote were not willing to vote for abstentionist candidates – that abstentionism was dead, and that it was time to bury the corpse'.[59] This strategy, which meant that even a victorious Republican candidate would not take his or her seat in the parliament of a state the legitimacy of which it refused to recognize – and this included the Dáil, too – was not exactly an inducement to voters to turn out.

All we can conclude with some assurance is that the Divis riots showed that O'Neill's bounded reforms could easily be undermined by Republicans and loyalists. The events of the next few years saw this perplexing partnership undermine many other attempts at reform.

NOTES

1. *Northern Ireland House of Commons Debates*, vol. 57, 7 October 1964, cols. 2835–86.
2. S. Gribbon, *Edwardian Belfast: A Social Profile* (Belfast: Appletree Press, 1982), p. 13.
3. See Table 1.1 in A. Hepburn, *A Past Apart: Studies in the History of Catholic Belfast 1850–1950* (Belfast: Ulster Historical Foundation, 1996), p. 4.
4. In 1813, 1832, 1835, 1841, 1843, 1852, 1857, 1864, 1872, 1880, 1884, 1886, 1898, 1907 and 1909. The list is taken from I. Budge and C. O'Leary, *Belfast: Approach to Crisis. A Study of Belfast Politics, 1613–1970* (London: Macmillan, 1973), p. 89. For further details, see A. Boyd, *Holy War in Belfast* (Belfast: Pretani Press, 1987 edn.); S. Baker, 'Orange and Green: Belfast 1832–1912', in H. Dyos and M. Wolff (eds), *The Victorian City: Images and Reality* (London: Routledge, 1973), pp. 789–814; C. Hirst, *Religion, Politics and Violence in 19th Century Belfast: The Pound and Sandy Row* (Dublin: Four Courts Press, 2002); M. Doyle, *Fighting like the Devil for the Sake of God: Protestants, Catholics and the Origins of Violence in Victorian Belfast* (Manchester, Manchester University Press, 2009).
5. S. Wilkinson, *Votes and Violence: Electoral Competition and Ethnic Riots in India* (Cambridge: Cambridge University Press, 2004), pp. 204–35.
6. *Manchester Guardian*, 22 July 1920.
7. A. Parker, *Belfast's Holy War: The Troubles of the 1920s* (Dublin: Four Courts Press, 2004), p. 12.
8. P. Hart, *The IRA at War 1916–1923* (Oxford: Oxford University Press, 2005 edn.), p. 251. For further discussion of 'the pogrom model', see pp.210–11 below.
9. Hepburn, *A Past Apart*, p. 183.
10. M. Poole and F. Boal, 'Religious Residential Segregation in Belfast in mid-1969: a Multi-Level Analysis', *Social Patterns in Cities* (London: Institute of Geographers, 1973), p. 13.
11. Ibid., p. 14.
12. F. Boal, 'Territoriality on the Shankill-Falls Divide', *Irish Geography*, 6, 1 (1969), pp. 30–50.
13. *Northern Ireland House of Commons Debates*, vol. 57, 7 October 1964, col. 2896.
14. For the extent of and the rationale for anti-Catholic discrimination, see J. Whyte, 'How Much Discrimination Was There under the Unionist Regime, 1921–68?', in T. Gallagher and J. O'Connell (eds), *Contemporary Irish Studies* (Manchester: Manchester University Press, 1983), pp. 1–35; M. Mulholland, 'Why Did Unionists Discriminate?', in S. Wichert (ed.), *From the United Irishmen to Twentieth-Century Unionism: A Festschrift for A.T.Q. Stewart* (Dublin: Four Courts Press, 2004), pp. 187–206.

15. In the 1961 Census seven out of ten adult males in Belfast were classified as manual workers. See Government of Northern Ireland, *Census of Population 1961: Belfast County Borough* (Belfast: HMSO, 1963), p. xxxiv.
16. On the NILP, see A. Edwards, *A History of the Northern Ireland Labour Party: Democratic Socialism and Sectarianism* (Manchester: Manchester University Press, 2009).
17. It won 5 per cent of the vote in the general election of 1957 and 3 per cent in that of 1961. C. O'Leary, *Irish Elections 1918–1977: Parties, Voters and Proportional Representation* (Dublin: Gill & Macmillan, 1979), p. 104.
18. L. Donohue, 'Regulating Northern Ireland: The Special Powers Acts, 1922–1972', *Historical Journal*, 41, 4 (December 1998), pp. 1089–1120.
19. This campaign involved bombings in England as well as actions in Northern Ireland. R. English, *Armed Struggle: A History of the IRA* (London: Macmillan, 2003), pp. 53–71.
20. S. Cronin, *Irish Nationalism: A History of its Roots and Ideology* (The Academy Press, 1980), p. 171; *Belfast Newsletter*, 16 March 1957. Cronin was Chief of Staff of the IRA during much of the campaign and was responsible for planning it. Another explanation for the failure to undertake operations in Belfast is that there were suspicions that there was an informer in the ranks of the IRA in the city who might betray them. See B. Anderson, *Joe Cahill: A Life in the IRA* (Dublin: O'Brien Press, 2002). p. 137.
21. B. Flynn, *Soldiers of Folly: The IRA Border Campaign 1956–1962* (Doughcloyne: Collins Press, 2009), p. 197; B. Hanley and S. Millar, *The Lost Revolution: The Story of the Official IRA and the Workers' Party* (Dublin, Penguin Ireland, 2009), pp. 7–21; English, *Armed Struggle*, pp. 72–76; *United Irishman*, March 1962.
22. Hanley and Millar, *Lost Revolution*, p. 33. It was as Liam McMillen that he stood in West Belfast.
23. L. McMillen, 'The Role of the IRA in the North from 1962 to 1969', in *Liam McMillen: Separatist, Socialist, Republican, Respol Pamphlet, No. 21* (Dublin: Sinn Féin, n.d.), pp. 2–3. (This was a lecture which McMillen gave in Dublin in June 1972.) See also Hanley and Millar, *Lost Revolution*, p. 35; P. Bishop and E. Mallie, *The Provisional IRA* (London: Corgi Books, 1988), p. 56; M. McKeown, *The Greening of a Nationalist* (Dublin: Murlough Press, 1986), pp. 32–33.
24. McMillen, 'The Role of the IRA', p. 3; *Northern Ireland House of Commons Debates*, vol. 57, 7 October 1964, col. 2837.
25. Ibid., col. 2892.
26. *Belfast Telegraph*, 28 September 1964.
27. Idem. The conventional wisdom is that Paisley threatened that he and his supporters would remove the Tricolour themselves, but neither the press nor the Minister of Home Affairs said this at the time.
28. See Doyle, *Fighting like the Devil*, p. 292. I am greatly indebted to Dr James Greer of Queen's University Belfast for allowing me to read his unpublished work on Paisley.
29. E. Moloney, *Paisley: From Demagogue to Democrat?* (Dublin: Poolbeg Press, 2008), pp. 25–26 and 73–96.
30. *Protestant Telegraph*, May 1967.
31. *Census of Population 1961: Belfast County Borough*, Table 18, p. 33.
32. S. Bruce, *Conservative Protestant Politics* (Oxford: Oxford University Press, 1998), p. 72.
33. J. Hermon, *Holding the Line: An Autobiography* (Dublin: Gill & Macmillan, 1997), p. 58.
34. *Belfast News Letter*, 29 September 1964.
35. *Belfast Telegraph*, 30 September 1964; *Irish News*, 30 September 1964.
36. *Belfast Telegraph*, 30 September 1964.
37. *Belfast News Letter*, 1 October 1964.
38. *Irish News*, 1 October 1964.
39. *Irish News*, 2 October 1964.
40. St Matthew's Parish Chronicon, 2 October 1964.
41. *Belfast Telegraph*, 1 October 1964.
42. *Census of Population 1961: Belfast County Borough*, Table 18, p. 33.
43. See Diamond's speech at Stormont. *Northern Ireland House of Commons Debates*, vol. 57, 7 October 1964, col. 2839.

44. *Belfast Telegraph*, 2 October 1964. The St Matthew's Parish Chronicon of 2 October 1964 gives details of the Bishop's appeal for calm which was to be read out in all churches.
45. *Irish News*, 3 October 1964; *Belfast News Letter*, 3 October 1964.
46. *Irish News*, 5 October 1964.
47. Special Branch Report, 16 November 1964, Belfast, Public Record Office of Northern Ireland (PRONI), HA/32/1/1394.
48. Moloney, *Paisley*, p. 112.
49. Enclosure to Hopkins letter, 18 February 1966, PRONI, HA/32/1/1378A.
50. *Belfast Telegraph*, 3 October 1964.
51. *Northern Ireland House of Commons Debates*, vol. 57, 7 October 1964, cols. 2838 (Diamond) and 2874 (Fitt).
52. Unsigned minutes of meetings on 2 November 1964, PRONI, CAB/9B/294/1A.
53. Ibid.
54. G. Clarke, *Border Crossing: True Stories of the RUC Special Branch, the Garda Special Branch and the IRA Moles* (Dublin: Gill & Macmillan, 2009), pp. 56–8.
55. Mark report, 18 August 1969, London, National Archives (NA), CJ/3/71.
56. *Northern Ireland House of Commons Debates*, vol. 64, 9 June 1966, cols. 163–4.
57. McKeown, *Greening of a Nationalist*, p. 29.
58. McMillen, 'Role of the IRA in the North', pp. 2 and 4–5.
59. Ibid., p. 5.

3

Between the IRA and the UVF

There appeared, in June 1973, a booklet by 'P. Ó Néill', the nom-de-plume which adorns authorized statements from the Provisional IRA. It gives a version of the origins of the Provisionals which the latter have cultivated ever since the split of 1969. Referring to the riots of August 1969, the author states that although it must have been clear from 1966 onwards 'to anyone with a modicum of sense that major violence on the nationalist areas was at hand', when it actually occurred, 'the victims to their horror found themselves without protection from the one source they hitherto trusted – the Irish Republican Army'.[1] But was Belfast in these years caught between aggressive loyalists and ineffectual Republicans?

I

'P. Ó Néill' blamed 'the policy pursued by the then leadership [of the IRA], or a majority of them, throughout the mid-sixties' for leaving the 'nationalist areas', supposedly, without defenders. '[F]ormer members of the Communist Party of Great Britain who came back to Ireland with the intention of setting up an ultra-left wing front based on the Republican Movement' had, it was alleged, 'diverted the movement to political and social agitation to the almost total exclusion of the traditional military role'.[2] There is something to this account: the Republican movement did move to the left. As the new IRA Chief-of-Staff, Cathal Goulding, recalled in an interview with an Irish journalist in early 1972, if the Border Campaign had failed due to the lack of popular support, the reason for that lack of support was because people did not understand what the IRA meant by its ultimate objective of 'freedom'. 'Freedom', he explained, had to relate to the needs of ordinary people. 'To do this we had to involve ourselves in their everyday struggles for existence. In housing, land, trade unions, unemployment...' It might take ten years of agitation along these lines before there was even the basis of a revolutionary movement and the IRA 'wasn't geared to this type of action at that time. Most of the people in the Movement were geared to a physical force campaign...[P]olitical agitation wasn't as exciting I suppose.'[3] (Goulding's last comment is a useful reminder that people participated in the IRA for social as well as political reasons.)[4]

This did not mean that the IRA was opposed to the use of physical force. Goulding himself declared on 15 August 1965: 'There will be a fight, there must be a fight. It will have to be a fight on many fronts. We have only to look around us to see that we will have to fight on the military front, the economic front and the cultural front.' The IRA's Adjutant-General, Séamus Costello, was even more explicit in a speech on 19 June 1966: 'to imagine that we can establish a Republic solely by constitutional means', he said:

> is utter folly. The lesson of history shows that in the final analysis the Robber Baron must be disestablished by the same methods that he used to enrich himself and retain his ill gotten gains, namely force of arms. To this end we must organise, train. And maintain a disciplined armed force which will always be available to strike at the opportune moment.[5]

The Irish police report from which these quotations are taken identified twelve different training camps in 1965 and eleven in 1966 at which IRA members received instruction in the use of various weapons. Six of those in 1965 and seven in 1966 were attended by members from Northern Ireland and in six of them the training officer was identified as coming from Belfast. These camps were in addition to other meetings and exercises conducted by the organization.[6]

As Goulding implied in his interview, there was opposition to the new, more political approach of the IRA after the end of the Border Campaign. One of the leading opponents was Seán Mac Stíofáin, a London-born member of the Army Council who had been in jail with Goulding following an arms raid on a British public school in 1953, and who later became the first Chief-of-Staff of the Provisional IRA. In his memoirs, Mac Stíofáin complained about the excessive attention paid by the Republican movement to 'agitation on social and economic issues' when 'the main objective [was] to free Ireland from British rule'. 'Some of the older Republicans', Mac Stíofáin wrote, 'who had been with the movement for years and still had years of service to contribute to it, began to drop away in disgust and protest'. If the Irish police report cited above is to be believed, however, this did not prevent a year-on-year increase in the strength of the IRA from 657 at the end of December 1962 to 1,039 at the end of October 1966.[7]

Meanwhile, in Northern Ireland, Terence O'Neill caused a sensation in January 1965 by welcoming his opposite number in the Republic of Ireland, Seán Lemass, on an official visit to Stormont. No such visit had occurred since partition, more than forty years before. Lemass, who had been a member of the IRA during the War of Independence and the Civil War, reportedly told O'Neill, 'I shall get into terrible trouble for this', whereupon O'Neill replied, 'No, Mr Lemass,...it is I who will get into trouble for this'.[8] The Ulsterman was right.

Although public opinion in Northern Ireland generally welcomed his effort to improve relations with the Republic of Ireland, there were rumblings of discontent within his own party and also the powerful Orange Order, the body to which virtually all Unionist politicians belonged, which enjoyed a statutory role in the counsels of the Unionist Party and which organized regular marches commemorating Ulster's Protestant heritage. This discontent was due not only to the Prime Minister's failure to consult his Cabinet colleagues before issuing the invitation to Lemass, but also to the very fact that the meeting took place at all. Ian Paisley, unsurprisingly, was full of righteous indignation and it was in this context that he uttered his famous remarks equating O'Neill's bridge building with treachery.[9]

Ten months later, on 21 October 1965, the IRA made a dramatic reappearance in Belfast. A group of men wearing masks and carrying hurley sticks broke up a British Army Kinema Corporation film show at Saint Gabriel's Intermediate Boys' School on the Crumlin Road in the north-west of the city, injuring two members of the unit involved and damaging their screen and projector. The IRA admitted responsibility in a statement issued four days later, explaining that 'the Belfast unit of the IRA now give notice that this immoral proselytism of Irish youths will be stamped out by whatever means deemed necessary'.[10]

Two days after this statement, O'Neill called a Stormont election for 25 November 1965, although there is no reason to suppose there was any connection between the two events. His principal objective seems to have been to undermine support for the NILP, particularly in Belfast. If this was so, the tactic worked. Even though the Unionist vote in Belfast fell from 67,350 in 1962 to 62,646 in 1965, the NILP vote fell even further, from 60,170 to 43,363. More importantly, the Unionists gained two seats at the expense of the NILP, reducing the latter's representation at Stormont to two.[11]

This was a heavy blow to the one party which enjoyed a degree of cross-community support. The parish chronicle of St Matthew's church in the Catholic enclave of the Short Strand in east Belfast describes how one of the two remaining NILP MPs only held on to his seat as a result of Catholic votes. The Unionists, the author wrote, 'tried their utmost' to win the Pottinger constituency in which the Short Strand was located. The party selected a popular milkman and supposedly liberal candidate in the shape of Jack Bannister, who had contributed to Catholic charities and who, together with his Unionist councillor wife, had been photographed alongside the two parish priests for the nationalist *Irish News*. But the priests did not wish it to seem as though they had been 'bought over by Bannister's largesse' and therefore 'felt compelled to vote Labour', as did 'all the Catholics who cared to vote at all'. There was therefore 'no truth in the Unionist assertion that they got Catholic votes in this election – certainly not in Pottinger. History was made in that the Unionists sought Catholic votes'.[12]

In the meantime, the O'Neill Government had been informed on 9 November 1965 that the IRA was plotting a new campaign in Northern Ireland, 'the most sinister aspect of which was a threat to the lives of members of the Cabinet and...Special Branch'. Ministers were 'painfully conscious' that if the news leaked out it would be represented as an election stunt. Some fifty members of the Ulster Special Constabulary (USC) – the notorious B-Specials, the all-Protestant police reserve – had been mobilized in order to support the RUC in providing adequate protection for ministers as well as for the former Prime Minister, Viscount Brookeborough, and for the Speaker. The placing of guards at ministers' homes came to the attention of the media and the government was forced to issue a statement.[13]

On 17 November 1965, five young men in a parked car close to the official residence of the General Officer Commanding (GOC) British troops in Northern Ireland on the outskirts of Belfast were arrested. They were wearing 'semi-military dress' and a bayonet and a pair of handcuffs were discovered in the car. Although they initially gave their names and addresses to the police, 'on a command being given in Irish by the person who appeared to be the leader they ceased to answer any further questions'. They were later charged under the Special Powers Acts of being in possession of an offensive weapon and records of police movements and of being members of an illegal organization. On 3 December all five were sentenced to a year in jail. They refused to utter a word during the run-up to and throughout the course of their trial.[14]

A public statement by the Minister of Home Affairs, Brian McConnell, on 7 December 1965 referred to 'information which has been received', indicating that the IRA was about to resume its subversive activities and that attacks would be made against selected persons as well as against property and public services. It concluded that the arrest and conviction of the five young men, together with the incident at St Gabriel's School, 'were the first overt activities by the I.R.A. for some years'.[15]

An even more alarming message was delivered by the Inspector-General of the RUC, Sir Arthur Kennedy, to the GOC Northern Ireland, Lieutenant-General Sir Desmond Fitzpatrick, on 4 February 1966. He told Fitzpatrick 'that he had received information from two sources within the last 24 hours that the IRA intend forthwith to initiate incidents on a gradually increasing scale'. These incidents would be modelled on those carried out by EOKA in Cyprus in the 1950s and would consist of attacks on individuals rather than the sabotage of installations. The RUC was forming 'special mobile squads armed with light automatic weapons' to meet the threat. The GOC admitted that 'all this may sound alarmist', but there was no doubt that the Inspector-General was taking the threat 'very seriously' and MI5 was being kept informed.[16]

Kennedy continued to sound the tocsin. On 22 February 1966, he gave a top secret update of his earlier warning to the GOC. The IRA's intention, he argued, was 'to set extremists on both sides at each other's throats and thus bring about a situation in which sectarian riots will precede other acts of violence and sabotage in Northern Ireland'. There was good reason to believe that the campaign would begin in Belfast. Indeed, a number of recent petrol bombings and slogan paintings in the city (which he listed) suggested that the first shots had been figuratively fired already. Such provocative incidents, he believed, would continue until Easter when it was hoped that a Protestant extremist backlash against the commemoration of the fiftieth anniversary of the Easter Rising of 1916 would in turn necessitate intervention by the RUC and the British army.

At this point, the Inspector-General continued, 'members of the IRA will close with the police and military in hand to hand combat and will shoot and also seize any weapons they can'. As the situation developed, further IRA units would infiltrate across the border in order to exploit the situation to the full. Power supplies might be interfered with and while only small arms and petrol bombs would be used in Belfast, heavier weapons would be employed to attack military and police installations elsewhere. The RUC would be 'stretched to full capacity' and it was therefore essential that 'strong military forces be available to come to the aid of the civil power', if this proved necessary.[17]

Another anxiety was the Republican movement's plan for a so-called 'Freedom Train' which would transport 'a large number of Republicans and sympathisers' from south of the border to attend the Easter Rising commemorations in Belfast on 17 April 1966. 'The influx of these supporters of the Irish Republican Army into Northern Ireland at this time', the RUC felt, 'will no doubt create a great deal of tension'. Indeed, it had been intimated by 'various sources' that these people were coming to Belfast 'with the express purpose of causing disturbances by roaming through various parts of the City flaunting Tricolours' and that efforts would be made 'to create incidents in which retaliatory action can be taken against the police'. Unless 'wiser counsels' prevailed, it was claimed, all the signs were that the IRA were 'poised to open a campaign of violence within the next month or two and that every effort will be made to create major trouble in Belfast, which fortunately remained quiet during the last [IRA] campaign'.[18]

The Northern Irish Government's anxieties were communicated to Whitehall. The Vice-Chief of the General Staff, General Sir Geoffrey Baker, decided to visit Northern Ireland himself on 30–31 March 1966 to assess the situation at first hand. He reported on his return that there was 'a very real likelihood of trouble, of two main kinds'. The first consisted of IRA violence on the EOKA model, with attacks on key individuals, the police and the military, together with action against police stations and military establishments, especially armouries. The second was sectarian violence, 'most probably in Belfast', which could lead to 'communal rioting of a particularly virulent sort'. The most likely date for the outbreak of trouble was the weekend of 16–17 April and the Inspector-General intended to take precautionary measures on 14 April, which would include searches and the arrest and interrogation of known IRA leaders. The Inspector-General had made it clear that any trouble over the weekend in question would not be 'a one-shot affair', but would mark the beginning of an indefinite campaign. Baker noted that, throughout his discussions, he was impressed 'by the Inspector-General's sober, balanced and "down-to-earth" approach' and that 'his conclusions had obviously been formed on a basis of reliable information, cross-checked and carefully weighed against a background of wide experience of the IRA problem over a number of years'.[19] Prompt action was taken as a result of the VCGS's visit. An extra battalion of troops (the 3rd Royal Green Jackets) was sent to Northern Ireland to reinforce the existing garrison 'ostensibly for training purposes', but in reality to come to the aid of the civil power if necessary. A special communications link was established between Northern Ireland and Britain and a senior MI5 officer was sent to Belfast for the period 15–20 April.[20]

Depending on which way one looks at it the outcome was either a damp squib or a triumph of foresight and preparation, for there was no serious trouble over the weekend of 16–17 April. Indeed, the RUC's 'Security Intelligence Review' for the month recorded only seventeen 'minor incidents' during the entire month. The MI5 officer who had been in Belfast over the weekend in question wrote in his report that, as late as 15 April, the RUC had believed it was the IRA's intention to exploit the celebrations 'in order to shoot members of the Crown forces' and that it was only thwarted by three factors. The first was the restraint of the authorities themselves, who assisted rather than obstructed the nationalist parade and who decided – contrary to the Inspector-General's previously stated intention[21] – not to make precautionary arrests. The second was the closing of the border on the night of 16–17 April. The third was 'the high order of police work' embodied in their 'courteous firmness' and skill in handling rival demonstrations, their deployment of reserves, their excellent communications and 'the individual efficiency and high morale of officers and men', all of which 'combined...to frustrate the IRA plan'.[22]

But was there an 'IRA plan' in the first place? It seems unlikely. The

Republican Publicity Bureau in Dublin had issued a denial on 22 February 1966.[23] At the end of the previous year, Roy Johnston, the IRA's Education Officer, told C. Desmond Greaves, the Communist Party of Great Britain's Irish expert, that 'there is no truth in the six-county rumour that a further disturbance is to be expected', adding that 'if the IRA didn't exist, the six-county government would have to invent it'.[24] If these denials may be discounted as self-serving, it is also worth noting that two leading southern members of the IRA's Army Council, Mac Stíofáin and Ruarí Ó Brádaigh, were publicly advertised as speaking at rallies in Northern Ireland on 17 April 1966.[25] Unless this was part of some elaborate deception, it would surely have been unwise to have these two men away from headquarters and within the grasp of the RUC on the very day on which a military campaign was to be launched. Finally, none of the scholarly studies of the Republican movement during this period provide any evidence to support a claim that the IRA was planning major military action at this time.[26]

The most that the IRA probably hoped for was what actually happened. Billy McMillen later claimed that the Belfast IRA saw the 1966 Easter Rising commemorations 'as a golden opportunity to drive a coach and four horses through the notorious flags and emblems Act. From January until April the whole resources and energy of the Belfast movement were devoted to preparations for the celebrations.' Although he argued that 'no great material benefit accrued to the IRA' as a result of the parade, it must have been gratifying to be able to claim that 12,000 took part in it and 400,000 had watched,[27] while even O'Neill conceded in his memoirs that 'the Catholic streets in Belfast became and remained a forest of Irish Republican flags for the duration of the celebrations'.[28]

II

If anyone was planning a campaign of violence in 1966 it was loyalists. According to Augustus ('Gusty') Spence, then a 32-year-old former regimental policeman and stager in the Harland and Wolff shipyards, he was approached in the autumn of 1965 by 'two people…one of them being a Unionist Party politician', who told him that the Ulster Volunteer Force (UVF), the paramilitary Protestant force which had been formed to fight against Home Rule on the eve of the First World

War and whose members were to distinguish themselves in that conflict, was being reconstituted and that he (Spence) was to be responsible for it in the Shankill district. 'The way the story was put to me', Spence explained, 'was that there was incipient rebellion and I had taken an oath to Her Majesty the Queen to defend her...against enemies foreign and domestic. I saw my service in the UVF as a continuation of my British army service'. Spence and three other men travelled to a rural location in Tyrone in November where they were formally sworn in, along with others whom he did not know, by an ex-army colonel. The group acquired weapons and, again according to Spence, at the time of the Easter commemoration '[t]he UVF was stood to...and on duty at interface areas' in Belfast.[29]

On 21 May 1966 the unionist *Belfast Telegraph* published a statement issued in the name of 'Captain William Johnston', the UVF's equivalent of 'P. Ó'Néill', which struck an ominous note. 'From this day on', it announced, 'we declare war against the IRA and its splinter groups. Known IRA men will be executed mercilessly and without hesitation'. Although those who simply helped the IRA would attract 'less extreme measures' in the first instance, 'more extreme measures' would follow if they failed to mend their ways and property would not be exempt from attack. Finally, 'Johnston' concluded, 'We will not tolerate any interference from any source and we solemnly warn the authorities to make no more speeches of appeasement. We are heavily-armed Protestants and dedicated to this cause.'[30]

In fact, a campaign of violent intimidation against Catholics living in Protestant areas and their property had already begun. Shots were fired at the home of Patrick Darling in Hopewell Street in the small hours of 23 April 1966 and a petrol bomb thrown at O'Hara's Catholic grocer's on the Shankill Road the following night. On the evening of 7 May a petrol bomb was thrown through the window of a house in Upper Charleville Street. The latter was occupied by a disabled elderly widow, Mrs Matilda Gould. She was badly burned in the ensuing fire and died some seven weeks later. Mrs Gould was a Protestant, but she lived next door to a Catholic-owned off-licence and the bombers evidently assumed her home was part of it.[31]

Just six days after the publication of 'Captain Johnston's' statement in the *Belfast Telegraph*, on the night of 27 May 1966, a 28-year-old Catholic storeman, John Patrick Scullion, was attacked after leaving a bar in Milford Street off the Falls Road. He managed to stagger to his nearby home, but then collapsed and was taken to hospital, where he died on 11 June. Anonymous telephone calls to the *Belfast Telegraph* claimed that he had been shot by an extreme Protestant organization, but the police insisted that he had been stabbed, that is, until his body was exhumed on 22 June 1966 and an autopsy showed that he had indeed been shot.[32] Both Gould and Scullion were victims of a UVF murder gang and on 26 June 1966 it struck again.

On the evening of 25 June 1966, Spence convened a meeting of Shankill UVF members to arrange the assassination of Leo Martin, a member of the Belfast IRA's brigade staff. Martin, however, was not at home when the hit squad arrived at his house so they contented themselves with breaking in and starting a fire. Later that night, however, four young men in the Malvern Street bar where Spence and his colleagues were drinking were identified as IRA men, solely it would seem by eavesdropping on their conversation, and they, too, were marked down for assassination. This is significant, as it shows that in what is often described as a random sectarian murder there were still elements of choice and politics. Spence and others lay in wait for the men and they were shot at as they left the bar. One of the victims, an 18-year-old barman called Peter Ward, was killed in the fusillade.[33] Spence has always denied that he was involved in Ward's murder and his biographer agrees with him.[34] It is also true that charges against him in respect of the killing of Scullion were dropped.[35] Nevertheless, he was convicted of Ward's murder on 15 October 1966, along with Hugh McLean and a third man, Robert Williamson, and sentenced to life imprisonment.[36]

These murderous events brought O'Neill back from France, where, by a terrible coincidence, he had been commemorating the fiftieth anniversary of the original UVF's role in the Battle of the Somme in 1916. He told the Northern Ireland Parliament on 28 June 1966 that 'information which has come to hand' in recent days had made it clear that 'the safety of law-abiding citizens is threatened by a very dangerous conspiracy prepared at any time to use murder as a weapon'. He therefore invoked the Special Powers Act 'to declare an organization which has misappropriated the title "Ulster Volunteer Force" an unlawful association'. As O'Neill subsequently recalled in his memoirs, 'This was a traumatic experience for Ulster Protestants who had always regarded the Special Powers Act as something which was for use only against the IRA'.[37]

What was the information which had recently come into the Prime Minister's hands and which had prompted his dramatic decision to ban the UVF? We cannot be entirely certain, for the main Government file on the UVF remains closed, but there is an interesting letter from the Inspector-General to the senior official in the Ministry of Home Affairs which throws some light on the matter. Dated 22 June 1966, it stated that 'a serious situation' appeared to be developing in the province which was 'reminiscent of the mid-1930s'. 'While there is always the I.R.A. and its splinter groups in the background ready to seize any opportunity to disturb the peace', it went on, 'the fact is that an equal or even greater threat is posed at present by extremist Protestant groups'. This alarming opinion was based upon a detailed list of political incidents since mid-April and a lengthy report of 20 June 1966 on the Paisleyite movement, made the sensational claim that Paisleyism was virtually coterminous with the UVF.[38]

According to the report, the link was personified by a 25-year-old printer, Noel Doherty, who was both secretary of the UVF and of Paisley's recently formed Ulster Constitution Defence Committee (UCDC). Doherty was certainly a man with a taste for both organization and intrigue. According to a statement which he gave to the police, he 'visualised a[n] alternative voice to the Unionist Party emerging' and accordingly set up not only the UCDC but also a local network of Ulster Protestant Volunteers (UPV).[39] Many years later Doherty told the British journalist, Peter Taylor, that he set about arming the UPV so that 'Paisley would have his own private army'. However, Paisley was not told about this aspect of the enterprise as 'he had to be protected', presumably from any suspicion of acting illegally.[40]

Doherty's police statement referred to clandestine meetings involving members of Spence's UVF and others in which the provision of gelignite and other weapons was discussed and there was talk of blowing up IRA monuments and reprisal killings of IRA members. At one of these meetings, one of Spence's associates produced a handgun and Doherty allegedly took fright. 'This was the start of my breaking away from this group', he told the police, 'as I believe that when men start handling arms their intention is to kill. These men were intent on killing IRA leaders as reprisals. This was the last contact that I had with this group as I did not agree with taking life',[41] in which case one wonders why he wished to arm the UPV.

Further evidence of Doherty's alleged links with the UVF came with the bizarre episode of the anonymous telegrams sent on 9 June 1966 to O'Neill and Nathaniel Minford, a Unionist MP at Stormont who was a vociferous critic of Paisley, in the name of 'the officers and members of the First Shankill Division of the UVF'. Minford's telegram was duly referred to an ad-hoc Parliamentary Committee of Privileges which reported on 23 June 1966 that both telegrams had come from a char-lady, Mrs Wilhelmina ('Mina') Browne, a member of the UPV and a keen supporter of Paisley. She claimed that the reference to the Shankill UVF was a mistake and that it should have been the UPV. She also added that she had invited 'a young man' whom she had met on Royal Avenue to accompany her into the post office from which she sent the telegrams. The 'young man' turned out to be Doherty, who subsequently confessed to drafting the telegrams.[42]

In the circumstances it is not surprising that the RUC suspected that there was a connection between the Paisleyite UCDC/UPV and the UVF. During his interrogation following the Ward murder, Spence was asked what connection he had with Paisley and replied that he did not agree with him and had no connection with him.[43] His co-defendant, Hugh McLean, on the other hand, was said to have stated, in answer to a question on why he joined the UVF, 'I was asked did I agree with Paisley, and was I prepared to follow him. I said that I was.' He then added, 'I'm terribly sorry about this. I am ashamed of myself. I am sorry that I ever heard of that man Paisley, or decided to follow him. I am definitely ashamed of myself to be such a position.' However, he later insisted that he had never made any such remark.[44]

In a speech on 28 June 1966 Paisley hotly denied any connection between the UCDC, the UPV and the UVF. 'I don't know what the UVF is', he declared. 'I don't know who its leaders are. I don't know what its intents and purposes are...We have nothing whatsoever to do with the so-called UVF.' As a Christian and a Protestant minister, he went on, he deplored and condemned anyone who dared take the law into their own hands and shoot down their fellows, regardless of their class or creed. As for McLean's alleged statement to the police, Paisley said, 'I don't know him...[H]e is not a Free Presbyterian...and I go further. Mr McLean never, never was a member of the Ulster Constitution Defence

Committee [and] never a member of the Ulster Protestant Volunteer Divisions'. McLean, Paisley concluded, either made his statement under duress or never made it at all.[45]

When Doherty was arrested in connection with explosives offences – for which he was sentenced to two years in jail – he was immediately disowned by Paisley and expelled from the UCDC and the UPV, actions which clearly still rankled thirty years later.[46] This, of course, could have been no more than a sensible precaution, but Ed Moloney writes that the Attorney-General's office advised against prosecuting Paisley for his involvement in Doherty's activities on the grounds that the evidence was too tenuous.[47]

To acquit Paisley of direct involvement with the UVF, however, does not mean that he does not share a good deal of the blame for exacerbating tensions in the summer of 1966. On the evening of 6 June 1966, he led a march from his church in east Belfast to the Presbyterian Assembly building in the city centre in order to protest against the 'back-sliding' of the Presbyterian Church in Northern Ireland in such matters as ecumenism. According to a police report, when the protesters reached Cromac Square, which was on the edge of the Catholic Markets district, 'Republican supporters...using stones, bottles and other missiles attacked the police who were on duty for the passing of the Paisleyite protest march...Four police were injured and removed to hospital. Two were detained for some days. Thirteen persons were arrested for disorderly behaviour and assault on police'.[48]

Paisley's legal adviser, the Unionist MP Desmond Boal, argued in a Stormont debate on the episode on 15 June 1966 that the Free Presbyterian leader had been punctilious in observing the procedures for marches set out in the Public Order Act of 1951 by giving the required forty-eight hours notice, that the RUC had not suggested any change in the route and that local Catholics had 'taken great trouble to be offended, and not only...be offended but...to throw missiles, stones and other weapons'.[49] But feeling in the House of Commons was heavily against Boal. While O'Neill conceded that the IRA might have been involved in the counter-demonstration,[50] he laid most of the blame fairly and squarely at the door of Paisley and his associates. 'They call themselves "loyalists",' he declaimed, 'but to what are they loyal? To the Queen whose personal representative they revile? To the United Kingdom in which their fellow citizens view their conduct with a mixture of ridicule and contempt? To Protestantism, many of whose leaders they have personally abused?' The Prime Minister went on to liken Paisley-ism to Nazism and declared that '[h]istory must not be allowed to repeat itself in this small corner of the British Commonwealth'.[51]

This was why, when Paisley was brought before the courts for his be-haviour on 6 June, it was not because of what happened in Cromac Square, but what took place outside the Presbyterian Assembly. He, two of his fellow Free Presbyterian ministers and two others were charged with public order offences. All were found guilty and fined. Anony-mous donors could and did pay the fines, but the magistrates also bound the guilty parties over to keep the peace. Arguing that this would prevent them from taking part in any further public protests, they refused and on 20 July were incarcerated in Belfast's Crumlin Road jail.[52]

Paisley's imprisonment prompted serious rioting outside the prison in which he was held on 22–23 July. Enclosing a list of those arrested, the Inspector-General pointed out in a letter to the Cabinet Secretary that the majority were in their teens or twenties and that thirty-two (out of a total of forty-one) had previous convictions. Kennedy thought it followed from this that 'these people would exploit any situation which gave them an opportunity to commit acts of aggression' and that '[i]n the main they are of the hooligan type who have no respect for law and order'.[53]

In fact, the detailed list enables us to make a few more generalizations: those arrested were overwhelmingly male – only three were women – and working class. Nineteen were listed simply as 'labourer' and only one, de-scribed as a 'costing clerk', can be unhesitatingly classified as a white-col-lar employee. In addition, it seems that the recruiting ground for the rioters expanded geographically between the first and second riots. Thus, ten out of the sixteen arrested on the first night had addresses in the immediate Shankill area, whereas only eight of the twenty-two arrested on the second day did so. Indeed, two of those arrested on 23 July came from Lisburn, eight miles south-west of Belfast.[54]

It is hard to imagine the rioters as representative of the respectable upstanding members of his Free Presbyterian Church who turned out every Sunday in their best clothes to listen to his lengthy sermons. Inspector-General Kennedy referred to them as hooligans without respect for law and order and Marx would no doubt have described them as members of the *lumpenproletariat*.[55] But they were also people who had just experienced the 'Twelfth', with its Orange Order marches, bands, bonfires complete with burning effigies and tub-thumping orators more than capable of stirring up resentment (not to say hatred) of a community which only three months earlier, had commemorated the fiftieth anniversary of a rebellion against the Crown and army towards which, for all kinds of reasons, they felt an instinctive sense of loyalty. Nevertheless, these men were not mindlessly following a script laid down by their culture. The Crumlin Road riots were a form of political action, one which was directed against the unionist elite as much as it was against Irish Republicanism.

A revealing insight into the mindset of the more 'respectable' Paisleyites is provided by the record of a conversation between O'Neill and four Free Presbyterian ministers on 10 August 1966. Their chief spokesperson and acting moderator of the Church, Reverend Cooke, claimed that Paisley's trial had been 'a political conspiracy' in which 'certain ecclesiastical leaders' – i.e. from the main Presbyterian Church – had been involved, an accusation which the Prime Minister hotly denied. O'Neill, in turn, referred to the bad impression which Paisleyite demonstrations had had in London (from whence he had just returned). Harold Wilson's Cabinet, he pointed out, 'was under pressure from its back-benchers. If the situation in Northern Ireland were to deteriorate to the point where the United Kingdom Government said "We won't have this in the United Kingdom", then there could be a very great threat to our constitutional heritage and to all the economic benefits which were at stake'. Cooke's response was that 'the whole background, position and history of Northern Ireland was such that we were committed to receiving an adverse press around the world'. What he and his people believed was that 'it was the Protestants of Northern Ireland who would keep it free'.[56]

The conversation later turned to relations between the two communities in Northern Ireland. 'What if Roman Catholic organisations chose to march night after night, and their supporters did the same?' the Prime Minister asked. 'Tempers would become very frayed', he continued, answering his own question and reminding his audience that, so far, 'the minority had remained fairly quiet, despite the shootings'. However, 'if offensive statements were made against their religion, the Catholics became angry and might retaliate'. It was the government's job, he said, to keep people from each other's throats. By its actions, on the other hand, Paisley's movement 'set people at each other's throats'. Cooke replied that Northern Ireland 'would be sustained by Protestant votes' and that '[t]heir [i.e. the Paisleyites'] main enemy was the attitude, and the departure from the Protestant faith, of leading denominations...They felt bound to warn the Protestant people where their leaders were taking them'. It was a classic example of what the French call 'a dialogue of the deaf' and O'Neill concluded by saying that 'they must obviously agree to differ'.[57]

How did the Catholic community see the events of the summer of 1966? An answer can be found in the chronicles of two churches: the Clonard Monastery in the Lower Falls, which was situated on the interface between the Catholic Falls and Protestant Shankill districts and the parish church of St Matthew's in east Belfast. Both referred to the Malvern Street killings. The Clonard chronicler wrote of how they 'spread fear among Catholic border areas in the city', while the St Matthew's chronicler described them as 'wanton killings'. Both were critical of Paisley's march through Cromac Square, the Clonard chronicler condemning the way in which the RUC 'brutally attacked' the Roman Catholics who displayed 'just resentment' at the anti-Catholic sentiments displayed on the marchers' placards and banners, and his St Matthew's counterpart observing that 'there had been no Prot[estant] procession through [the] Markets attempted since 1920'.[58]

Writing about the run-up to the parades of 12 July, the Clonard chronicler highlighted three Paisley meetings at which the preacher uttered 'the same string of blasphemies against the Mass, the Catholic Church, the Pope, etc.' An American reporter, on hearing one of the speeches, was heard to remark, 'My God, this is worse than Saigon'. On the 'Twelfth' itself, moderates who spoke at the open-air rally at Finaghy following the parades 'were heckled and jeered', while the Orange Order's Grand Master and some others 'attacked the Romanizing tendencies of the Churches and, especially of the World Council of Churches'.[59]

The St Matthew's chronicler dealt with matters closer to home. 'Because of [the] appeal by [the] Bishop for restraint', he wrote, 'the 12th passed without incident. One drunken parishioner, 'when thwarted in his efforts to get at Orangemen at the end of Seaforde St, made his way through the School and Church grounds to attempt to hammer with a stick, through the locked front gate of the Church [as] the Orange Processions [were] returning from the field'. He was led away by another parishioner and two policemen. The appeal for peace had not reached him, but then he had not attended Mass for years and his brother had been in Borstal: just 'the type who makes trouble', the chronicler ruefully observed.[60]

Both churches had been the target of Protestant vandalism, although in the case of the Clonard monastery, 'the police surprised the would-be perpetrators and they fled, leaving their paint and brushes behind them'. At St Matthew's, on the other hand, 'the letters UVF and F*** the Pope and such inscriptions were written on 3 front doors of the church plus [the] Sacristy door' on the opening day of Paisley's trial, 18 July 1966. The police erased the writing before 7 am and two men were subsequently arrested and fined £10 apiece and ordered to apologize to the parish priest.[61]

One sees in these accounts the genuine alarm felt by the Catholic community in Belfast during and after the events described in the second half of this chapter, although a critical commentator might draw attention to the odd error and omission. O'Neill, for example, was not compelled by the British Government to ban the UVF and to condemn Paisley, as the Clonard chronicler maintained. He was genuinely horrified by the former and heartily loathed the latter. Neither document even mentions the Easter Rising celebrations, let alone their effect upon the Protestant population. With the increase of violence and, even more so, the fear of violence, people in Belfast were finding it harder to think themselves out of conservative positions, let alone into the position of someone with an opposing worldview. Simple stories were gaining in strength.

NOTES

1. 'P. Ó Néill', *Freedom Struggle by the Provisional IRA* (Dublin: Irish Republican Publicity Bureau, 1973), pp. 18–19.
2. Ibid.
3. R. Sweetman, *'On Our Knees': Ireland in 1972* (London: Pan Books, 1972), pp. 141–2.
4. See M. Abrahms, 'What Terrorists Really Want: Terrorist Motives and Counterterrorism Strategy', *International Security*, 32, 4 (spring 2008), pp. 78–105.
5. An Garda Síochána, Review of Unlawful and Allied Organisations: December 1, 1964, to November 21, 1966, Dublin, National Archives of Ireland, 96/6/495. I am greatly indebted to Dr Tom Hennessey of Canterbury Christ Church University for a copy of this document.
6. An Garda Síochána, Review of Unlawful and Allied Organisations'. Billy McMillen confirms

the attendance of Belfast IRA members at training camps during this period. See L. McMillen, 'The Role of the IRA in the North from 1962 to 1969', in *Liam McMillen: Separatist, Socialist, Republican, Respol Pamphlet, No. 21* (Dublin: Sinn Féin, n.d.), p. 7.

7. S. Mac Stíofáin, *Memoirs of a Revolutionary* (Edinburgh: Gordon Cremonesi, 1975), pp. 92–3; An Garda Síochána, 'Review of Unlawful and Allied Organisations'. See also R. English, *Armed Struggle: A History of the IRA* (London: Macmillan, 2003), pp. 84–94.

8. T. O'Neill, *The Autobiography of Terence O'Neill* (London: Rupert Hart-Davis, 1972), p. 72.

9. For the opposition which the Lemass visit provoked, see H. Patterson and E. Kaufmann, *Unionism and Orangeism in Northern Ireland since 1945: The Decline of the Loyal Family* (Manchester: Manchester University Press, 2007), pp. 67–71.

10. IRA Incidents in Northern Ireland from 1st September, 1965, Belfast, Public Record Office of Northern Ireland (PRONI), HA/321/1/1378A.

11. M. Mulholland, *Northern Ireland at the Crossroads: Unionism in the O'Neill Years 1960–9* (London: Macmillan, 2000), pp. 42–8.

12. St Matthew's Parish Chronicon, 25 November 1965.

13. Note on the Activities of the IRA and the Consequent Necessity to Guard Northern Ireland Ministers, [n.d.], PRONI, HA/32/1/1378A. There was no direct reference to the IRA in the statement issued by the Northern Irish Government on 10 November 1965.

14. J. Greeves letter, 3 December 1965, PRONI, HA/32/1/1378A; IRA incidents in Northern Ireland. The leader of the group was apparently Joseph McCann, an 18-year-old bricklayer, who later became well known as an Official IRA volunteer in Belfast during the early Troubles. He was killed by British troops in the Markets district on 15 April 1972. B. Hanley and S. Millar, *The Lost Revolution: The Story of the Official IRA and the Workers' Party* (Dublin, Penguin Ireland, 2009), pp. 46 and 178.

15. B. McConnell statement, 7 December 1965, PRONI, HA/32/1/1378A.

16. D. Fitzpatrick letter, 4 February 1966, London, National Archives (NA), DEFE/25/301.

17. A. Kennedy, memorandum attached to an unsigned letter of 25 February 1966, [n.d.], PRONI, HA/32/1/1378A.

18. RUC Security Intelligence Review – February 1966, 2 March 1966, PRONI, HA/32/1/1378A.

19. G. Baker memorandum, 1 April 1966, NA, DEFE/25/301.

20. G. Baker telegram, 1 April 1966, NA, DEFE/25/301; E. Ashmore minute, 22 April 1966; MI5 report, 20 April 1966, NA, DEFE/25/301.

21. Baker memorandum.

22. MI5 report.

23. RUC Security Intelligence Review – February 1966. The statement denounced claims of impending IRA action as part of 'a deliberate policy on the part of the Unionist Party designed to create a situation in which the observance of the 1916 Jubilee in the occupied area [Northern Ireland] will become impossible'. It denied all responsibility for 'any of the recent actions in the Belfast area which would appear to have added substance to the totally unreal stories purveyed by Mr. McConnell...and his accomplices in rumour'.

24. D. Greaves journal, 10 December 1965, cited in R. Johnston, *A Century of Endeavour: A Biographical and Autobiographical View of the Twentieth Century in Ireland* (Carlow: Tyndall Publications, 2003), p. 191. Johnston retrospectively endorses this statement. The British Government, he points out, had no separate intelligence of its own and had to rely on that provided by the RUC. 'The motivation of the RUC and the Unionist establishment for promoting this deception was of course to keep in existence the excuse for their repressive regime'.

25. *Belfast Telegraph*, 7 April 1966.

26. See R. English, *Armed Struggle*, pp. 81–92; Hanley and Millar, *The Lost Revolution*, pp. 50–64.

27. Even granted the influx of visitors from outside, these figures, which amount to more than the total population of Belfast in 1966, are almost certainly exaggerated. The RUC more conservatively estimated that 5,000 'Republicans and supporters' took part in the parade. RUC Security Intelligence Review – April 1966, 5 May 1966, PRONI, HA /32/1/1378A.

28. McMillen, 'The Role of the IRA', p. 6; O'Neill, *Autobiography*, p. 79.

29. R. Garland, *Gusty Spence* (Belfast: Blackstaff Press, 2001), pp. 48–51. Spence has never disclosed the names of the 'two people' who recruited him.

30. *Belfast Telegraph*, 21 May 1966.

31. RUC Security Intelligence Review – April 1966; List of political incidents attached to A. Kennedy letter, 22 June 1966, PRONI, CAB/9B/300/1; D. Boulton, *The UVF 1966–73: An Anatomy of Loyalist Rebellion* (Dublin: Torc Books, 1973), pp. 39-40; J. Cusack and H. McDonald, *UVF* (Dublin, Poolbeg, 1997), pp. 5–6; D. McKittrick, S. Kelters, B. Feeney, C. Thornton and D. McVea, *Lost Lives: The Stories of the Men, Women and Children who died as a result of the Northern Ireland Troubles* (Edinburgh: Mainstream Publishing, 2004 edn.), pp. 28–9.

32. McKittrick et al., *Lost Lives*, pp. 25–26; Boulton, *The UVF*, pp. 40–41; Garland, *Gusty Spence*, pp. 56–57.

33. H. McLean's statement, 27 June 1966, and statement of H. Johnston, 1 July 1966, PRONI, BELF/1/1/2/214/3. For other accounts of this episode see McKittrick et al., *Lost Lives*, p. 26; Boulton, *The UVF*, pp. 48–50; Garland, *Gusty Spence*, pp. 57–58. Two of the other young men were wounded in the attack, but one escaped unhurt.

34. Garland, *Gusty Spence*, pp. 65–77.

35. Ibid., p. 72; Mc Kittrick et al., *Lost Lives*, p. 25.

36. Garland, *Gusty Spence*, p. 78.

37. *Northern Ireland House of Commons Debates*, vol. 64, 28 June 1966, cols. 777–78; O'Neill, *Autobiography*, p. 82.

38. A. Kennedy letter and enclosures, 22 June 1966, PRONI CAB/9B/300/1.

39. N. Doherty's statement, 6 July 1966, PRONI, BELF/1/1/2/214/28.

40. P. Taylor, *Loyalists* (London, Bloomsbury, 2000 edn.), pp. 35–7.

41. Doherty's statement; Boulton, *The UVF*, p. 36.

42. Parliament of Northern Ireland, Report from the Committee of Privileges, 23 June 1966, H.C.1726; Doherty's statement.

43. Garland, *Gusty Spence*, p. 62.

44. L. McBrien's statement, 19 August 1966, PRONI, BELF/1/1/2/214/23; S. Bruce, *Paisley: Religion and Politics in Northern Ireland* (Oxford: Oxford University Press, 2007), pp. 219–20. The police, it should be noted, did not record interviews at that time.

45. I. Paisley speech, 28 June 1966, PRONI, CAB/9B/300/2.

46. Taylor, *Loyalists*, p. 39.

47. E. Moloney, *Paisley: From Demagogue to Democrat?* (Dublin: Poolbeg Press, 2008), pp. 133–4.

48. RUC Security Intelligence Review – June 1966, 7 July 1966, PRONI, HA/32/1/1378A.

49. *Northern Ireland House of Commons Debates*, vol. 64, 15 June 1966, cols. 360–62.

50. Whether this was true or not, the IRA was responsible for a grenade attack on an RUC Land Rover in the vicinity of Cromac Square on 7 June 1966. See the list of incidents enclosed with A. Kennedy letter, 22 June 1966, PRONI, CAB/9B/300/1, and McMillen, 'Role of the IRA', p. 7.

51. *Northern Ireland House of Commons Debates*, vol. 64, 15 June 1966, cols. 309 and 311.

52. Bruce, *Paisley*, p. 86.

53. A. Kennedy letter and enclosure, 4 August 1966, PRONI, CAB/9B/300/1

54. Kennedy letter and enclosure, 4 August 1966. In his letter Kennedy wrongly gave the number of those arrested as thirty-seven.

55. For two vivid descriptions of the *lumpenproletariat* see K. Marx, 'The Class Struggles in France' and 'The Eighteenth Brumaire of Louis Bonaparte', in K. Marx and F. Engels, *Selected Works – Volume I* (Moscow: Progress Publishers, 1969), pp. 219–20 and 442.

56. K. Bloomfield memorandum, 10 August 1966, PRONI, CAB/9B/300/1.

57. Ibid. For a brief summary of O'Neill's conversations in London on 8 August 1966, during which he asked to be allowed a brief pause in his attempts to bring about better relations between the two communities in Northern Ireland because of the tense political situation, see G. Warner, 'Putting Pressure on O'Neill: the Wilson Government and Northern Ireland 1964–69,' *Irish Studies Review*, 13, 1, (February 2005), pp. 13–1, p. 15.

58. Clonard Monastery, Domestic Chronicle, July 1966; St Matthew's Parish Chronicon, 6 June, 12 and 18 July 1966.
59. Ibid.
60. Ibid.
61. Ibid.

4

The Day the Troubles Began

INTRODUCTION

The fifth of October 1968 has a strong claim to being the second most significant date in twentieth-century Irish history. However, while the scholarly work published on Easter week 1916 would fill a library, the first Derry civil rights march and its violent aftermath has not even had a full chapter or article written about it. The fullest account is still to be found in *Politics in the Streets*. Bob Purdie concludes that 'the whole affair was a series of blunders': the march was not part of a Republican/Communist conspiracy to sweep away Stormont; Stormont was not conspiring to sweep the marchers and their politics off the streets.[1] When the choice is between conspiracy and cock-up, the historian is wise to opt for the latter. Except, of course, for those occasions when it is possible to choose not to choose. Human agency mattered here: individuals and groups did have plans, albeit vague ones that they were not able to put completely into effect. Whenever an individual did something, his or her acts – whatever had been intended – were reinterpreted by other individuals, who then reacted in often unanticipated ways and changed the contexts within which the first individual now thought and acted.[2] As the day passed, and the running battles between policemen and working-class Catholic youths continued, the contexts in which everyone in Derry and in Northern Ireland, too, thought and acted had been transformed. The fifth October 1968 did not just mark the shift from one era of history to another, it was essential to bringing about that shift.

The chapter's first section addresses the build-up to the day, especially the difficulties that the Derry radicals had to overcome to get the route banned and then to get the march to go ahead anyway. The second section examines how the march led to violence and draws upon the 'Flashpoints Model of Public Disorder', which has been tested and refined by being applied to numerous cases over the last two decades.[3] According to this model, public disorder is best – but still imperfectly – understood in terms of interdependent, and occasionally overlapping, levels of analysis: structural, political, cultural, contextual, situational, interactional and institutional. If nothing else, the model serves as a constant reminder that crowd events are complicated and ephemeral, with many of their details left unrecorded and few of their details left uncontested. The third section explores the three days of rioting that followed the march – and which are almost ignored in the existing literature.[4] The rioters were not indulging in mindless violence, but rather were taking part in a form of political action. The conclusion describes how television carried the impact of 5 October 1968 beyond Derry and notes that the drama was not interpreted in the same way by everyone.

STAGE FRIGHT

In a private letter exchanged between friends, Frank Gogarty, a NICRA committee member, looked back to before the march and admitted that 'Derry was deserted', 'due especially to Betty Sinclair'. 'The people were left without leaders.'[5] In fact, the people were left with the Derry radicals: Eamonn McCann, Eamon Melaugh and Fionnbarra Ó Dochartaigh took responsibility for selecting the route and planning the march.[6] The DHAC promoted the event as part of its wider campaign, appealing to 'every working-class person in the city both Protestant and Catholic' to turn up at the station. The leftists yet again insisted upon 'the falseness of the religious division': 'By no means all the people living in the slum hovels are Catholics. By no means all the Rachman landlords are Protestants'.[7] The local Nationalist Party, unsurprisingly, and other opposition groups kept their distance from the preparations.[8] Eddie McAteer even contacted NICRA members to warn them about, as one of the executive later put it, 'the company we were keeping'.[9] Although McCann has consistently claimed that the NICRA committee was 'so ignorant…of the realities in Derry [that] they didn't know what we were up to', the Belfast-based body seems to have been aware that it was taking a risk in the second city – but believed that this risk was one that could be managed.[10] Some figures inside NICRA appear to have deluded themselves about this right up until the confrontation started.

The RUC, in contrast, knew Derry well, knew what the radicals were up to in the city and knew the risks. At one of the trials arising out of what happened on 5 October 1968, District Inspector Ross McGimpsey gave evidence that he was 'satisfied that if the route had been followed by the civil rights marchers there would have been breaches of the peace'.[11] The leftists were mounting a three-pronged attack on the spatial order of the city: they were challenging the Unionist monopoly on marches within the walls; they intended to bring Nationalists, Republicans and Communists to the war memorial; and they were going to gather Catholics in a Protestant district, the Waterside.[12] While the organizers maintained that they were staging 'no sectarian march' and the local Nationalist Party explained that it would not be 'involved officially', most Protestant citizens read things differently.[13] Stormont told Whitehall ahead of the march that 'the police have received numerous complaints from law-abiding residents'.[14] Civil servants at the Ministry of Home Affairs also stressed to their colleagues in London that this was not just a parochial matter, that there was an international dimension, too; they sent a clipping of a *Times* editorial entitled 'No Right to Riot', which ran through events in Grosvenor Square, Paris and Chicago before thundering that 'violence is being deployed as a weapon of protest in an entirely new way'.[15] The march therefore would have been banned from 'several areas on the route', where McGimpsey 'anticipated...a confrontation between the marchers and those opposed to the march', even if there had not been what Stormont referred to as the 'other complication' of an Apprentice Boys parade.[16] (The RUC later maintained that this decision had been justified because the 'Protestant opposition' to the march had 'in fact' been next to Railway Square in their hundreds.)[17] The commission of inquiry was 'quite satisfied' that this 'proposed procession was not a genuine "annual" event [and] merely a threat to counter demonstrate by political opponents of the Civil Rights march'.[18] This is a slight exaggeration, as the Murray Club had been travelling over from Liverpool to Derry for the initiation of new candidates since 1962 and was to continue doing so after 5 October 1968. But, this event was then exploited to try to push the authorities into banning all marches on that date.[19] When McGimpsey met with Bill Craig, the Minister of Home Affairs, in Belfast to discuss how the day should be policed, the idea of imposing a ban on marches in the county borough and on meetings within the walls was rejected.[20] Instead, Craig made an order banning the civil rights marchers only from the Waterside and the walled city – it was 'made clear to the organisers [that] they are free to hold processions and meetings anywhere in the City apart from the two parts mentioned'.[21]

The details of the ban were not important; the ban itself was. 'We are not asking for our rights we are taking them', responded Labour, 'and we ask the people of Derry to come with us'.[22] The march was now about government repression as well as the other injustices Unionism had inflicted upon the second city. McCann therefore remembered feeling 'very positive' when the policeman arrived on 3 October 1968 at his parent's house to deliver the ministerial order.[23] The ban forced local Nationalist politicians and key figures in the self-help movement to commit themselves to the march.[24] McAteer, though, was careful to highlight that this was simply the least worst option, telling the *Derry Journal* that it was 'another example of the Nationalist Party being wrong no matter what it does'.[25] Within NICRA, however, the pressure brought to bear by the ban led to open division rather than an uneasy unity; the committee was split over whether to abandon the march altogether or to repeat what had been done in Dungannon.[26] On 4 October 1968, Gogarty and three other NICRA members were sent to Derry for what they thought would be private discussions with the local organizers over how they should proceed but which instead turned into a meeting packed with leftists from as far away as Belfast and Cork that was determined for the march to go ahead. Near the end of around two hours of heated debate, Gogarty came out for the radicals, which, in turn, required the rest of the delegates to compromise, too, rather than chance breaking up the NICRA coalition.[27] 'We welcome the unanimous decision of the meeting to adhere to the original plan', ran the Labour press statement. All the actors needed to put on the drama were going to take to the stage. That said, as a NICRA spokesman pointed out, the moderates were 'preparing for a peaceful march', not a direct confrontation.[28] The commission of inquiry concluded that the outcome of this meeting showed again that the 'local militants...made the running for the march' – they did, but there were further hurdles for them to leap as 5 October 1968 began.[29]

5 OCTOBER 1968

At lunchtime on the day of the march, McCann was touring Derry in a car. 'We the Labour Party will defy the ban of the Minister of Home Affairs', he said over a loud-speaker system. 'Citizens come out in your thousands to the railway station this afternoon at 3:30 pm'.[30] The radicals had told the media that they were expecting 'massive support in the region of 5,000 people' – at least double the number which took part in the Coalisland-Dungannon march.[31] However, only about 400 marchers were there at the start; a figure which shows that there was not yet a civil rights movement and that the leftists remained on the margins.[32] While the radicals could not deliver on the advance publicity's promises that there would be a cast of thousands, they had nonetheless managed to sign up some big stars for their Saturday matinee. 'Those who gathered at the Waterside Railway Station', noted the commission of inquiry, 'represented most of the elements in opposition to the Northern Ireland Government and the Unionist regime in Londonderry'.[33] The radicals were looking to make their names; others were just hoping to make it through to the curtain call with their reputations intact; some were intending to steal scenes from their fellow actors. Among the last group was Gerry Fitt, the Republican Labour MP for West Belfast, who had used the British Labour Party conference in Blackpool as a press junket, promising politicians and reporters that 'trouble might break out'.[34] Fitt helped to get three Labour MPs to agree to make cameos, Fleet Street to send over journalists to write reviews and the television networks to film the performance.[35] The stage was set.

Stormont was on the whole indifferent and on occasion hostile to expressions of disaffection. Shortly after the Coalisland-Dungannon march, McAteer advised 'the Cabinet [to] take a good hard look at the apparent policy of needlessly restricting...anti-Government opinion' because '[i]t is important that the democratic safety valve be used'.[36] By sticking with this strategy, Stormont was encouraging its opponents to view the police as repressive. Although the Foyle Hill II tenants' association was campaigning for the RUC to make routine patrols of the Creggan, Catholics made a distinction between the police's law-and-order functions and its political role.[37] The *Derry Journal*, for example, argued that 'recogniz[ing] the extreme efficiency of the RUC in carrying out the normal duties of a police force' was 'in no way inconsistent with' criticism that officers 'had been used in Nationalist areas, on the one hand, to protect coat-trailing Unionist processions...and, on the other, to assist in the suppression of Nationalist activities'.[38] The objections to the route raised by local Unionist politicians, the Middle Liberties Young Unionists and the Apprentice Boys yet again proved to Derry's majority community that it was the minority which dictated what did and did not happen in the city. The Minister of Home Affairs's remarks about the march being simply 'a Nationalist-Republican parade' added to the impression that the Unionist Party saw its small world in fixed, binary terms.[39] Craig, though, was courting his party's hardliners in his ongoing struggle to take the leadership, making up the ground he had lost when the RUC allowed Republicans to defy a ban on an Easter parade in Armagh, rather than hinting at a plan to clean civil rights activists off the streets.[40] Still, policemen were given a signal that the marchers could be treated severely.

The radicals rejected 'the desperate efforts of Craig'.[41] Restricting civil rights protest to Catholic and Irish nationalist spaces was 'an obvious attempt by the authorities to give it a sectarian basis', claimed the DHAC, 'which had been a weapon for generations to divide the common people in their fight for justice'.[42] Space had symbolic significance and the march was challenging the way it was ordered in the city.[43] This was not something unique to Northern Ireland in 1968: for example, Parisian students and the French authorities each transgressed the other's boundaries during May and June, working to transform protest into revolt.[44] The Derry radicals were also trying to bring the confrontational tactics used on the boulevards of Paris to the city's streets – which represented another important break with traditions of collective action. There was no breakdown in communication, however. As McGimpsey had hauled in McCann, Melaugh and Ó Dochartaigh for talks in his office so often that he even knew what snacks to offer them (Jaffa Cakes), the RUC broadly understood what the radicals wanted to do and the radicals broadly understood how the RUC would react.[45] Both sides were prepared for a confrontation.

'The police', acknowledged the commission of inquiry, 'expected trouble'. 'Only sixty police were normally available, but altogether about 130 men were assembled on the morning of 5th October [including] two platoons of the Reserve Force [and] two water wagons'.[46] This was substantially below the number of officers that had been drafted into Armagh at Easter, when the RUC had been policing a loyalist counter-demonstration and Republican parade. However, this was still a show of force and was without doubt a provocation to those marchers who had come for a peaceful protest – and, indeed, to the city's Catholic community.[47] County Inspector Bill Meharg, who was the officer in charge that day, added to this effect by twice announcing over a loudhailer that 'the police would see that the Order was enforced' and that 'women and children [should] leave the area and... go home'.[48] Some members of the crowd shouted back 'Gestapo'.[49]

In contrast to the Coalisland-Dungannon march, the start of the proposed route through Derry was banned, so the RUC had placed a cordon close to the railway station across Distillery Brae.[50] With nearby Duke Street left open, the chief marshal, IRA volunteer Sean Gallagher, led the march off – a little late – into the traffic still coming down from Craigavon Bridge.[51] The local organizers had ensured that the front ranks were made up of MPs from Stormont and Westminster; when the marchers came into contact with the small group of policemen who had been rushed to Duke Street, these politicians were consequently caught up in the initial scuffles.[52] Fitt, for example, remembered that he was 'propelled forward' by 'a big surge' into the RUC lines, where he was 'batoned twice on the head', arrested and taken to hospital.[53] (The Derry radicals and the Republicans from outside the city who were in the rows behind may well have been the people pushing.)[54] Some of the placards carried by the leftists, which had slogans such as 'Class not Creed' and 'The Proper Place for Politics is in the Streets', were hurled at the police – allowing the RUC to argue afterwards that a pole rather than a baton had cut Fitt's head open.[55] The official explanation for the injuries sustained by McAteer at this time was even more outlandish: in response to claims made by one of the Westminster MPs on BBC network radio and elsewhere that an officer had struck the Nationalist leader in 'the groin region', the Inspector-General went into huge medical detail to present the bruise as having an unknown origin.[56] Few people in Derry on 5 October 1968, however, had any doubt about how the two most important Catholic elected representatives had been hurt. John Hume testified at the petty sessions in December 1968 that as the news of Fitt's injury spread there was 'resentment in the crowd'.[57]

And yet, even at this late stage, conflict was not inevitable. The marshals – though they were lacking in numbers and in training – were able to move the marchers back from the police and efforts to start a sit-down protest in the street failed.[58] The Derry radicals had improvised a violent confrontation; senior figures in both NICRA and the RUC now took their chance to begin improvising a peaceful compromise, with each side making reparations to the other one. Sinclair, who had arrived late from Belfast, tried to repeat the tactics that had been used in Dungannon and had again taken upon herself the role of chairing a meeting.[59] In the 'middle of every riot', McCann sardonically recalled, 'there's always somebody ... waiting for a meeting to happen, and this was no exception'.[60] The RUC responded to Sinclair's initiative by allowing this illegal meeting to take place and by providing her with a chair and a loudhailer.[61] Speaking first to a crowd that had grown to around 1,000 people by 4 pm and seeking to set the tone for the whole meeting, Sinclair stressed that they were not there to overthrow the constitution, that the RUC had been co-operative, that Craig was the real villain and that violence would only serve to transform what was a clear defeat for the Minister into an undeserved victory for him.[62] McAteer picked up on the basic theme in his speech, asking his audience to '[j]oin me in wishing that no-one should be exposed to hurt here today'.[63] Although other speakers were to make similar pleas, McCann took a different line when he had his turn on the chair. According to the evidence he himself gave at the petty sessions, McCann said that he was 'not advising anyone to rush the police cordon' nor was he as 'a private individual' going to 'stop anyone'. A plainclothes police officer who took notes on all the speeches informed the court that McCann had been less circumspect than this: 'If you wish to charge the police cordon it is not my problem'.[64] What is certain is that one of the main organizers of the march did not tell the crowd to disperse peacefully when the meeting had finished and that Sinclair afterwards told a friend that 'she would walk off' rather than speak on the same platform as McCann again.[65]

Ivan Cooper negotiated a deal with a senior police officer whereby people would be allowed to filter through the cordon provided no attempt was made to reform the march or carry banners.[66] However, the leftists – from Belfast as well as from Derry – had no intention of walking off the stage; when Sinclair used her 4:40 pm curtain call to ask people one last time to go home quietly, they jeered her words, taunted officers with 'Sieg Heil' chants and hurled broken placards and stones at the police lines.[67] The RUC believed that the situation was slipping out of control, and this determined what was to happen next.[68] While Craig and other Unionist leaders were concerned with the broad range of threats that the groups on the march were seen to represent, the police were concerned with what they saw as an immediate threat to public order. In a study of over 15,000 demonstrations that took place in America between 1960 and 1990, the sociologists Christian Davenport and Sarah Soule found that the 'approach of the police' was 'proportional to the level of threat posed by the behaviors of protesters'. There was a 'near-perfect correspondence': verbal threats led to verbal warnings, physical threats led to physical responses and lethal threats led to lethal force. The ways in which protesters behaved at each event essentially shaped how many arrests were made and what degree of violence was used by officers; changes to institutions and strategies over this period had far less of an impact on the policing of demonstrations.[69] In Northern Ireland, the RUC's response was not proportional (Davenport and Soule's 'even hand' was unevenly applied to unionist and opposition marches), but there was still a clear relationship with the perceived level of threat. Indeed, when Stormont's opponents took to the streets, they were rarely beaten off them by the police. Two years earlier, as the fiftieth anniversary of the Easter Rising loomed, the Northern Irish authorities 'fear[ed]' that 'attempts will be made to foment sectarian troubles'.[70] But, reported the senior MI5 officer sent over as an observer, the commemorations passed off peacefully except for a few minor incidents and the RUC helped rather than hindered the marches.[71] The Easter parades may have been seen as representing a diffuse challenge to Unionist control, yet they did not at any point present the police with such a threat to public order that officers thought they needed to respond with mass arrests and baton charges.[72] Although the issue of civil rights offered a subtler and, in some aspects, more dangerous way of attacking the dominant party, the Coalisland-Dungannon march was not a direct confrontation and so it did not bring a violent reaction. On 5 October 1968 itself, as has been described above, the relationship between the behaviour of the protesters and the response of the police was obvious once again. When protesters had gathered at the railway station with the intention of marching, the County Inspector had warned that the ban would be enforced; when the front ranks had been pushed forward into the RUC lines, some policemen had reacted by striking protesters; when marchers had been pushed back and a meeting had been started, officers had allowed this peaceful protest to take place. Now, after being subject to a barrage of abuse and broken banners for around five minutes, the policemen on Duke Street were ordered by Meharg to draw their batons and 'clear the mob'.[73]

'They broke a bit rough', a senior police officer told journalists a few hours later, 'but they broke'.[74] The careless callousness of this statement reflected what had just happened: there had been no organized baton charge, rather, policemen had lost their discipline and swung out indiscriminately; groups of officers had chased after individual protesters who had been trying to leave the area; the water wagon had been called in and had sprayed jets at people looking out of first-floor windows on Duke Street and at shoppers in the city centre as well as at fleeing marchers.[75] Many protesters and spectators were driven to the other end of the street, where they found themselves trapped by another police cordon. These officers had been moved here shortly after 3:30 pm to guard a building site, which 'contain[ed] more than ample ammunition for violent demonstration', but they had not been informed that the marchers were dispersing nor had they been ordered to let pass this rush of people (RUC headquarters would later excuse these failings as a 'tactical error on the field').[76] Hume gave evidence that this 'line of policemen', 'with looks on their faces I have never seen before in my life', 'moved in on the crowd'. Turning back up Duke Street, Hume met 'a young man with blood on his face and two young girls stiff with hysteria'.[77] By about 5 pm, the 'mob' had been cleared.[78] The RUC's poor crowd-control strategy and mainly Protestant membership may have played only minor roles in the decision to meet violence with violence, yet they had then helped to produce a reaction which was out of all proportion to the provocation. (That said, it should be acknowledged that not all policemen behaved in the same way: for example, the *Irish Times*'s correspondent wrote that 'many of the officers, probably local men, went no further than duty required'.) [79]

The marchers had come to the Waterside with different intentions; while only the leftists had wanted a violent confrontation, the RUC had treated everybody harshly and had pushed all of them into the same antagonistic relationship. Eyewitness accounts from civilians of what took place on Duke Street returned again and again to iconic moments:

ones where the police – usually portrayed in general terms – brutally attacked vulnerable victims, such as the elderly, the disabled and girls.[80] The RUC was presented as a partisan police force that used excessive violence to defend an unjust system. A new context and a new relationship had therefore been created in which people were much more willing to act and much more willing to oppose the authorities than they had previously been.[81] Polarization was a product of violence rather than a cause of it.[82] This identity shift was not just limited to those who had been trapped in Duke Street because news and clashes spread rapidly throughout the city. For instance, a small crowd waiting for the march to arrive in the Diamond listened to rumours that a girl had been killed, watched policemen arresting a group of leftists who were trying to unfurl a Campaign for Nuclear Disarmament banner near the war memorial – and then intervened.[83] This was a variation upon what had become a familiar theme during the 'long 1960s', on both sides of the Atlantic: the 'children's crusade' in Birmingham, Alabama, led to bystanders joining the movement and joining battle with law-enforcement officers; after Parisian police raided the sacred space of the Sorbonne, passers-by blocked the buses that were carrying the student radicals to the cells.[84] This drama was now being played out in Derry and the radicals were finding that they had produced a runaway smash hit. McClenaghan remembered making his way into the city centre to watch 'the first riot'. 'McCann and I sort of looked at one another ... and he said: "God, Dermie, the revolution has started"'.[85]

RATIONAL RIOTERS

At Stormont, in the debate on the disturbances, Craig denounced the young Derrymen who had fought against the RUC as 'hooligans'.[86] Officials throughout the western world during the 1960s delivered similar lines: the Los Angeles chief of police branded the people taking part in the August 1965 Watts ghetto uprising 'monkeys in the zoo'; Parisian police reports from May 1968 used the term 'hooligans' to describe the youths on the city's streets.[87] The implied adjective modifying these nouns is 'mindless', but are rioters irrational? While there were no leaders, no demands and no negotiations, the three days of rioting in Derry that began on 5 October 1968 was nonetheless still a form of political action. It was not, though, the political action that McCann ultimately wanted; his revolution was already being devoured by its children.

Derry was anxious in its sleeplessness on the night of 5/6 October 1968. As the gloom had gathered, the crowd on the streets had grown larger and more homogenous. What had started in Duke Street with a crowd made up of people who differed in their ages, social positions, genders, national identities and politics had developed into a crowd almost entirely composed of young, working-class Catholic men from the Bogside and Creggan. It has to be emphasized here that 'crowd' is a concise, convenient way of referring to a collection of individuals each of whom felt varying degrees of solidarity with the group. Given that there was such a close correspondence between their group and individual identities, the members of the late-night crowd found it relatively easy to agree common goals and then to work together in pursuit of them. These Derry youths were not looking beyond the city to McCann's global struggle but were instead looking after their own small world, after their streets. The RUC's strategy, such as it was, had been to drive them out of the city centre and into the Bogside; this was seen by Catholics as an enemy incursion into their territory and taken as a further provocation. The basic pattern for the riots was set: the crowd tried to expel the police officers from its space and to challenge their control of the space within the walls. As well as fighting with the RUC over space, the crowd targeted state property – throwing stones at a fire engine brought out by a false alarm and setting a B-Special hut ablaze.[88] This was not mindless violence.

On the afternoon of 6 October 1968, a slightly different crowd with a slightly different agenda invaded the Diamond. The crowd was still drawn from the city's Catholic working-class youth, yet there were now many more women and children on the streets than there had been in the early hours of the morning. (The night's rioting had led to few arrests or injuries, so the likely personal cost of getting involved in further violence had been shown to be low.) A new set of targets had been selected: the windows of Protestant-owned shops in the city centre were smashed.[89] This was an attack on some of the most significant figures inside the local Unionist association and on businesses that were exploiting the impoverished Bogside and Creggan. However, the vandalism and looting that took place were also sectarian and criminal acts – political grievances, communal grudges and private greed were not mutually exclusive motivations.[90] Press interviews with rioters suggest that there were yet more reasons for their actions, including boredom and peer pressure.[91] Of course, some motives, though, will always remain unknown. And, policemen were there, too, in public and private roles: trying to restore order but also shouting sectarian insults, smashing windows in the Bogside and beating up Catholic couples on the way back from the cinema.[92]

The RUC put McCann, Melaugh and Ó Dochartaigh under arrest that afternoon for breaching the ban. After the dispositions had been taken, Melaugh addressed the special court about 'the happenings of Saturday night and said that these were the actions of hooligans and asked if he could be facilitated in going to...talk to these irresponsible people' (these are most likely not the terms Melaugh himself used). McGimpsey consented; the RUC was conceding that it needed help in keeping order in Derry.[93] The organizers of the march, however, were not able to stop the violence that had followed it from continuing into a second and later a third night, during which barricades were put up and the offices of the NIHT was almost burnt down.[94] Eight years earlier, at Queen's University, McCann had written and put on a satirical revue about Irish history in which the character played by Nell McCafferty had praised 'the real uprising' of Easter 1916, that staged by 'the people who looted profitably'.[95] Now, when the radicals had looters in their own city, they began to recognize that this was not the uprising that they had wanted. Derry Labour, in the first statement that they issued after the weekend's disturbances, argued that 'political militancy' should 'not [be] measured by one's willingness to take on the police'.[96] Looking back in early August 1969, McCann noted that the march had produced 'a ready-made mass movement'; instead of growing a movement from the grass roots up, a short cut had been taken to bring politics onto the streets.[97] At the time, he was confident that he and his comrades could 'divert the aroused militancy of Derry people away from sectarian channels'.[98] Nonetheless, barely six months later, McCann was telling the *New Left Review* that hopes that they would be able to 'educate and radicalize' the young people who were out throwing stones were 'a lot of pompous nonsense'. He cheered himself up by adding that other civil rights activists had also 'failed so far to channel the thing in a safe direction'.[99]

The contrast with what happened in Birmingham is in some ways marked. When the city's black schoolchildren took over the downtown area, they staged sit-ins, pickets and marches through segregated stores – just as they had been trained to do.[100] The young people had been inspired to take part in the movement by local disc jockeys, had attended non-violent workshops, had been repeatedly shown a film about the successful 1960 Nashville student protests, had been made to hand over their knives and had chosen their own leaders. These 'kids' also achieved something that had eluded adult activists for decades: they fulfilled the Gandhian goal of filling the jails.[101] Making this comparison is not about raising up the American civil rights movement as peaceful and organized so as to knock down the Northern Irish civil rights movement as violent and chaotic (in fact, as will be discussed later in the book, the Birmingham campaign was often far more violent and chaotic). Nor, is it about showing that non-violent action was fated to fail across the Atlantic (this form of political action, as the next chapter will lay out, actually proved to be very successful). Rather, drawing attention to the different ways in which some of the youth of Derry and Birmingham behaved serves to highlight the degree to which previous planning and experience mattered. The Derry movement's rival would-be generals and their ill-disciplined foot soldiers were all mobilized *after* 5 October 1968 and found themselves going through boot camp, going about putting in place the logistics and going into battle for civil rights all at the same time. As a result, there were mutinies and desertions right from the start. So, when the rioting died down on the third night, it was not only obvious that Unionist control over the second city had been broken, but also that no-one at all was now in control there.[102] During the weekend, eight police officers, one fireman and sixty-one civilians (seven women and eight children aged fourteen years and under) had been treated for minor injuries at Altnagelvin hospital; other people had been hurt, too, but either had not needed to go to accident and emergency or had been afraid (not without cause) that the doctors would pass on details to the police.[103] More violence was to follow – much more.

CONCLUSION

A fortnight later, one of the Unionist MPs at Westminster stood up during Prime Minister's Questions to praise the RUC as 'probably the finest police force in the world'. Harold Wilson replied by acknowledging that 'Up to now we have perhaps had to rely on the statement of himself and others on these matters', before reminding the honourable member that 'since then we have had British television'.[104] More accurately, they had had Irish television. At Duke Street, the Ulster Television camera had been hit by a jet from the water wagon and the BBC unit had also had their filming impaired in the melee; the Telefís Éireann crew was the only news team that had gotten footage of the march and its aftermath.[105] However, thanks to the close relationship built up between the two national broadcasters over the years, a former BBC employee living in Derry was able to get a deal agreed in which the Telefís Éireann film could be shown on Northern Irish and British television.[106] The revolution was televised. As was the case with the Birmingham campaign – 'television's finest hour' according to a leading civil rights activist – the coverage brought further publicity, brought people onto the streets in other cities and brought pressure to bear on the authorities.[107] That said, television viewers were not passively absorbing a simple drama. 'Audiences are in fact complex amalgams of cultures, tastes, and ideologies', Lawrence Devine explains. 'They come to popular culture with a past, with ideas, with values, with expectations, with a sense of how things are and should be.'[108] The consensus that has grown up around 5 October 1968 should not therefore be allowed to obscure the extent to which the event was contested by contemporaries in Northern Ireland and beyond. McCann remembered his march as 'a plot point in the narrative of Northern Ireland history'; it was, but part of what was to drive the story forward were the different readings of what had just happened.[109]

NOTES

1. B. Purdie, *Politics in the Streets: The Origins of the Civil Rights Movement in Northern Ireland* (Belfast: Blackstaff Press, 1990), p. 146.
2. J. Drury and S. Reicher, 'Collective Action and Psychological Change: The Emergence of New Social Identities', *British Journal of Social Psychology*, 4, 39 (December 2000), pp. 579–604, p. 582.

3. D. Waddington, K. Jones and C. Critchter, *Flashpoints: Studies in Public Disorder* (London: Routledge, 1989). For a recent critique, see P. Bagguley and Y. Hussain, *Riotous Citizens: Ethnic Conflict in Multicultural Britain* (Aldershot: Ashgate, 2008), pp. 29–33. The latest gloss on the model is D. Waddington, 'Applying the Flashpoints Model of Public Disorder to the 2001 Bradford Riot', *British Journal of Criminology*, 50, 2 (March 2010), pp. 342–59.
4. See, for example, Purdie, *Politics in the Streets*, p. 143.
5. F. Gogarty to 'George', 18 February 1969, Belfast, Public Record Office of Northern Ireland (PRONI), D/3253/1.
6. T. O'Neill to E. McAteer, 8 October 1968, PRONI, CAB/9B/205/7; E. McCann, *War and an Irish Town* (London: Pluto, 1993 edn.), p. 94; Transcript of BBC interview with E. Melaugh, [summer 2008] (personal notes); Transcript of BBC interview with F. Ó Dochartaigh, [summer 2008] (personal notes).
7. *Derry Journal*, 27 September 1968.
8. The Government of Northern Ireland, *Disturbances in Northern Ireland (Cameron Report)* (Belfast: HMSO, 1969), p. 27.
9. *Derry Journal*, 27 September 1968; F. Heatley, 'The Early Marches', *Fortnight*, 5 April 1974.
10. The quote is taken from Transcript of BBC interview with E. McCann, [summer 2008] (personal notes). McCann has been making the same point since his 1974 memoir, *War and an Irish Town*.
11. *Derry Journal*, 13 December 1968.
12. *Cameron Report*, p. 25.
13. *Derry Journal*, 4 October 1968; *Derry Journal*, 27 September 1968.
14. J. Greeves to I. Woods, [before 5 October 1968], PRONI, CAB/9B/205/7.
15. Ministry of Home Affairs to R. North, 6 September 1968, PRONI, CAB/9B/205/7.
16. *Derry Journal*, 13 December 1968; Greeves to Woods, [before 5 October 1968].
17. J. Hill to H. Black, 20 February 1969, PRONI, CAB/9B/205/8; *Londonderry Sentinel*, 9 October 1968.
18. *Cameron Report*, p. 26.
19. *Londonderry Sentinel*, 23 September 1970; *Derry Journal*, 4 October 1968.
20. *Derry Journal*, 13 December 1968; *Londonderry Sentinel*, 11 December 1968.
21. Greeves to Woods, [before 5 October 1968].
22. *Derry Journal*, 8 October 1968.
23. Transcript of McCann interview. Melaugh and Ó Dochartaigh also recall feeling elated when they heard about the ban. Transcript of Melaugh interview; Transcript of Ó Dochartaigh interview.
24. B. White, *John Hume: Statesman of the Troubles* (Belfast: Blackstaff Press, 1984), pp. 62–3; F. Curran, *Derry: Countdown to Disaster* (Dublin: Gill & Macmillan, 1986), pp. 79–80; P. Doherty, *Paddy Bogside* (Cork: Mercier Press, 2001), p. 53.
25. *Derry Journal*, 4 October 1968.
26. Purdie, *Politics in the Streets*, p. 140.
27. Heatley, 'Early Marches'; C. McCluskey, *Up Off Their Knees: A Commentary on the Civil Rights Movement in Northern Ireland* (Dublin: Conn McCluskey and Associates, 1989), pp. 110-11; McCann, *War and an Irish Town*, pp. 96–7.
28. *Derry Journal*, 8 October 1968.
29. *Cameron Report*, p. 26.
30. *Derry Journal*, 13 December 1968.
31. *Derry Journal*, 1 October 1968.
32. *Derry Journal*, 8 October 1968.
33. *Cameron Report*, p. 27.
34. *Belfast Telegraph*, 3 October 1968; C. Ryder, *Fighting Fitt* (Belfast: Brehon Press, 2006), pp. 120-1.
35. *Observer*, 6 October 1968; Three eyewitnesses report on Londonderry, 8 October 1968, London, National Archives (NA), PREM/13/2841; G. Fitt's evidence to the Cameron Commission, 25 July 1969, PRONI, GOV/2/1/140.
36. E. McAteer to T. O'Neill, 26 August 1968, PRONI, CAB/9B/205/7.
37. *Derry Journal*, 28 June 1968.
38. *Derry Journal*, 18 January 1963.

39. *Derry Journal*, 4 October 1968.
40. *Derry Journal*, 16 April 1968.
41. *Derry Journal*, 4 October 1968.
42. *Derry Journal*, 27 August 1968.
43. N. Jarman and D. Bryan, 'Green Parades in an Orange State: Nationalist and Republican Commemorations and Demonstration from Partition to the Troubles, 1920–70', in T. Fraser (ed.), *The Irish Parading Tradition: Following the Drum* (London: Macmillan, 2000), pp. 95–114, p. 107.
44. L. Mathieu, 'The Spatial Dynamics of the May 1968 French Demonstrations', *Mobilization*, 18, 3 (September 2008), pp. 83–97.
45. F Ó Dochartaigh, *Ulster's White Negroes: From Civil Rights to Insurrection* (Edinburgh: AK Press, 1994), p. 49; Transcript of Ó Dochartaigh interview; Transcript of McCann interview.
46. *Cameron Report*, p. 28.
47. *Derry Journal*, 16 April 1968.
48. W. Meharg, Northern Ireland Civil Rights Parade and Meeting in Londonderry, on Saturday, 5th October 1968, 7 October 1968, PRONI, HA/32/2/26.
49. *Londonderry Sentinel*, 9 October 1968.
50. Northern Ireland Civil Rights Parade.
51. J. McAnerney to R. McGimpsey, 30 September 1968, PRONI, HA/32/2/28; Transcript of Ó Dochartaigh interview; *Derry Journal*, 8 October 1968.
52. *Cameron Report*, p. 28; *Irish Times*, 7 October 1968; W. Meharg to J. Hill, 19 December 1968, PRONI, HA/32/2/30.
53. Fitt's evidence.
54. *Derry Journal*, 6 December 1968; B. Hanley and S. Millar, *The Lost Revolution: The Story of the Official IRA and the Workers' Party* (Dublin: Penguin Ireland, 2009), p. 104.
55. *Derry Journal*, 8 October 1968; *Londonderry Sentinel*, 11 December 1968; Transcript of Ó Dochartaigh interview.
56. Transcript of World at One, 17 October 1968, PRONI, CAB/9B/205/7; A. Peacocke to J. Hill, 19 December 1968, PRONI, CAB/9B/205/8.
57. *Derry Journal*, 6 December 1968.
58. *Derry Journal*, 1 October 1968; *Cameron Report*, p. 31; Transcript of Ó Dochartaigh interview.
59. *Irish Times*, 7 October 1968.
60. Transcript of McCann interview.
61. Northern Ireland Civil Rights Parade.
62. *Irish News*, 7 October 1968.
63. *Derry Journal*, 8 October 1968.
64. *Derry Journal*, 6 December 1968.
65. D. Greaves, *Journals*, 19 October 1968, extract from the Century of Endeavour electronic archive (contact R. Johnston at www.rjtechne@iol.ie about access).
66. *Londonderry Sentinel*, 9 October 1968.
67. *Derry Journal*, 6 December 1968; *Cameron Report*, p. 29.
68. Northern Ireland Civil Rights Parade.
69. S. Soule and C. Davenport, 'Velvet Glove, Iron Fist or Even Hand? Protest Policing in the United States, 1960–1990', *Mobilization* 14, 1 (March 2009), pp. 1–22. See also J. Earl and S. Soule, 'Seeing Blue: A Police-Centered Explanation of Protest Policing', *Mobilization* 11, 2 (June 2006), pp. 145–164.
70. F. Soskice, Preparations Being Made to Meet the Threat of IRA Violence, 4 April 1966, NA, PREM/13/980.
71. MI5 Report, 20 April 1966, NA, DEFE/25/301.
72. See M. O'Callaghan, '"From Casement Park to Toomebridge" – The Commemoration of the Easter Rising in Northern Ireland', in M. Daly and M. Callaghan (eds), *1916 in 1966: Commemorating the Easter Rising* (Dublin: Royal Irish Academy, 2007), pp. 86–147.
73. *Derry Journal*, 6 December 1968; Northern Ireland Civil Rights Parade.
74. *Irish Times*, 7 October 1968.

75. *Irish News*, 7 October 1968; *Derry Journal*, 8 October 1968; Peacocke to Hill.
76. Hill to Black.
77. *Derry Journal*, 6 December 1968.
78. *Cameron Report*, p. 30.
79. *Irish Times*, 7 October 1968.
80. See, for example, *Irish News*, 7 October 1968; *Derry Journal*, 8 October 1968; *Derry Journal*, 6 December 1968.
81. Drury and Reicher, 'Collective Action and Psychological Change', pp. 594–600.
82. S. Kalyvas, *The Logic of Violence in Civil War* (Cambridge: Cambridge University Press, 2006), pp. 64–6.
83. *Londonderry Sentinel*, 9 October 1968; Three eyewitnesses report on Londonderry.
84. T. Branch, *Parting the Waters: America in the King Years 1954–63* (London: Simon & Schuster, 1988), p. 763; M. Seidman, *The Imaginary Revolution: Parisian Students and Workers in 1968* (Oxford: Berghahn, 2006), pp. 94–5
85. Transcript of BBC interview with D. McClenaghan, [summer 2008] (personal notes).
86. *Northern Ireland House of Commons Debates*, vol. 170, 16 October 1968, col. 1022.
87. A. Oberschall, 'The Los Angeles Riot of August 1965', *Social Problems*, 15, 3 (Winter 1968) pp. 322–41, p. 324; Seidman, *Imaginary Revolution*, p. 216.
88. *Derry Journal*, 8 October 1968.
89. *Derry Journal*, 8 October 1968; *Londonderry Sentinel*, 9 October 1968.
90. S. Kalyvas, 'The Ontology of "Political Violence": Action and Identity in Civil Wars', *Perspective on Politics*, 1, 3 (September 2003), pp 475–494, pp. 475–6.
91. *Irish Times*, 7 October 1968.
92. See the court proceedings reported in *Derry Journal*, 17 December 1968.
93. Note of telephone message from C. Inspector Meharg, 6 October 1968, PRONI, HA/32/2/26.
94. *Londonderry Sentinel*, 9 October 1968.
95. N. McCafferty, *Nell* (London: Penguin, 2004), pp. 77–8.
96. *Derry Journal*, 8 October 1968.
97. E. McCann, 'Who's Wrecking Civil Rights?', August 1969, PRONI, HA/32/2/28.
98. *Derry Journal*, 8 October 1968.
99. A. Barnett, 'Discussion on the Strategy of People's Democracy', *New Left Review*, May–June 1969.
100. Branch, *Parting the Waters*, p. 777.
101. D. McWhorter, *Carry Me Home: The Climactic Battle of the Civil Rights Revolution* (London: Simon & Schuster, 2001), pp. 360–1, p. 368.
102. D. Corbett's evidence to the Scarman inquiry, 30 September 1969, London, Institute of Advanced Legal Study, Scarman minutes of evidence, days 9–13.
103. E. Watson to R. McGimpsey, 7 October 1968, PRONI, HA/32/2/26.
104. *House of Commons Debates*, vol. 770, 22 October 1968, cols. 1088–90.
105. *Derry Journal*, 6 December 1968; W. Meharg to J. Greeves, 17 January 1969, PRONI, CAB/9B/205/8; J. Bardon, *Beyond the Studio: A History of BBC Northern Ireland* (Belfast: Blackstaff Press, 2000), p. 29.
106. R. Cathcart, *The Most Contrary Region: The BBC in Northern Ireland, 1924–84* (Belfast: Blackstaff Press, 1984), pp. 207–8.
107. McWhorter, *Carry Me Home*, pp. 374 and 378.
108. L. Levine, 'The Folklore of Industrial Society: Popular Culture and Its Audiences', *American Historical Review*, 97, 5 (December, 1992), pp. 1369–99, p. 1381.
109. Transcript of McCann interview.

5

The Civil Rights Movement

INTRODUCTION

Nell McCafferty played with her pills. She was in the Guildhall on 4 October 2008, and the men who had already spoken at the commemoration had made her feel 'like reaching for my pills'. Where they had talked about constitutional nationalism and militant republicanism, McCafferty chose (finally) to talk about illegal, direct action. She got everyone who had broken the law in those months to put up their hands, although John Hume needed some gentle bullying first.[1] McCafferty was and remains 'a disorderly woman' because 'I find the social order under which people live globally to be intrinsically out of tune'; the civil rights movement in Derry was about maintaining disorder, about creating a 'crisis to bargain with'.[2] This needs to be understood if the movement and its impact are to be understood.

Research on the effects of repression has produced mixed findings: sometimes it leads to an increase in dissent, sometimes it leads to a decrease in dissent and sometimes it leads to no change in dissent. This is the 'Punishment Puzzle'.[3] A solution to the version of the puzzle set by Derry is that the repression experienced over the weekend of 5–6 October 1968 mobilized thousands of people while also pushing them away from both non-violent confrontation and rioting (at least in the beginning).[4] The chapter's first section describes the early attempts to take over leadership of the new movement and the limits that existed on what leadership could be exercised. In this and most of the other sections, comparisons are briefly made with contemporary American campaigns: not because they are ideal models that should have been followed, but because they help to illuminate what happened in Derry. The next section explores how unionism reacted to the crisis by falling out over what reforms should be conceded and, as a result, by failing to offer the movement a deal. Neither unionism nor the movement were unitary actors; they were composite actors and their different parts interacted with each other to shape strategy.[5] The inconsistent responses of the authorities together with divisions inside the movement encouraged some individuals and groups to turn towards confrontational and indeed violent acts.[6] The third section sets out how the movement brought such disorder to Derry that the police and business community were forced into asking Stormont to find a political settlement. The final two sections examine how a temporary deal was reached, only to then break down soon afterwards. The civil rights movement had ended, yet the struggle was to continue.

CITIZENS ACT

Three days after the civil rights march, the local organizers met in the City Hotel to discuss their next moves. Eamonn McCann briefed the press that they had decided to call for a token one-hour strike and to try again to march into the walled city to 'defend the fundamental human rights [of] all our citizens'. This attempt to revive the hit drama of 5 October 1968 – indeed, to also get productions staged in Belfast and other parts of Northern Ireland – was boosted by Bill Craig signing on, as expected, to play the villain once more. Within hours of McCann's announcement, the Minister of Home Affairs was telling the media that he 'would not allow the march to go on'. However, this did not ensure that the show would go on: the city's other public figures were not willing to reprise the cameo roles in which the Derry radicals had previously cast them. In the wake of the long weekend of violence, they not only wanted to prevent further trouble breaking out but to exploit the instability as well – in the best interests of the city and of themselves, too. So, the next day, the moderates held a meeting in the City Hotel to select a more broad-based organizing committee.[7] As Fionnbarra Ó Dochartaigh later remembered, the 'origin' of the meeting 'is still shrouded in some mystery'.[8] Perhaps the best approach, then, to picking a way through conflicting memories is to recognize that there was no orchestrated plot so much as a network of people edging towards what was for them an obvious solution. The initial efforts to organize the civil rights movement were disorganized.

The second meeting was, according to the *Derry Journal*, 'attended

GREEN APPLE BOOKS
506 CLEMENT ST
SAN FRANCISCO CA 94118
415-387-2272

Terminal ID: *****718   ***8
12/21/17   1:41 PM
MASTERCARD - INSERT
AID: A0000000041010
ACCT #: ************1299

CREDIT SALE

UID: 735516050167   REF #: 2778

BATCH #: 105   AUTH #: 036182

AMOUNT $75.89

APPROVED

ARQC - A5E1322FA6A2141B
CUSTOMER COPY

:ople representative of the business, profes-
union life of the city'. As with the University
: moderates wanted to portray themselves as
novement that was seeking to make things
imunity – 'to achieve a united city where all
:r, just like the radicals, the moderates were
) restage their earlier success. Campbell Austin,
nan and retailer, had backed the university
e corporation for 'murdering the city'.[10] And
away from the civil rights movement because
) be connected in any way with civil disobedi-
forces of order'.[11] The contemporary labels,
thus hinder as well as help efforts to under-
lace; these were not parties, but rather loose
who agreed on very little. So, when the radi-
sizing each other up at the City Hotel, in what
tense meeting lasting for several hours, they
ıeir comrades. For example, the radicals, inside
ıeeting, clashed over how widely they should
at was the risk of becoming marginalized and
g out by inviting people who had been watching
centre stage.[12] The outcome of the meeting
was as a result not so much a hostile takeover of the leadership of the
movement than a forced merger: the five radicals who had officially
organized the civil rights march joined together with the eleven
moderates who had been elected from the floor to form the Derry
Citizens Action Committee (DCAC). Among those who had been voted
onto the committee were three people from the self-help movement:
Hume, Michael Canavan and Paddy Doherty. Paul Grace, area organ-
izer for the Post Office Workers' Union, had come on board as chief
steward. The local parties were represented on the committee by Austin
(briefly), James Doherty, Claude Wilton and Ivan Cooper – who had
been appointed chair (with Hume vice-chair) to advertise that the
DCAC was non-sectarian.[13] This, though, was not how McCann chose
to present the new committee. Explaining to the press his decision not
to become part of the DCAC, McCann branded it 'the old politics
of old men'. 'Only an open appeal to the working class over respectable
trade-union bureaucrats, middle-class do-gooders and practiced [sic]

band-wagon jumpers gives any hope for the future.'[14] These criticisms, which were splashed across the local newspapers, were an acrid first taste of what it meant to have McCann outside the DCAC's big tent.

The would-be leaders of the movement were divided – and that qualifying adjective is important. While McCann may have boasted to the media that the radicals had 'given birth' to the 'movement' 'last Saturday', his wilful child did not always recognize the parental author-ity of either its fathers or its step-fathers.[15] The DCAC, playing up its continuity with the organizing committee, had cancelled the strike and the march announced by McCann. However, on 11 October 1968, about a hundred female employees at the Brookehaven shirt factory walked out on strike, paraded over to the Guildhall, staged a picket in protest against police brutality and then returned to work. Their spokeswoman used her interviews with journalists to attack trade unionists, in particular, for failing to support the call for a token strike.[16] The Northern Ireland Officer of the Irish Congress of Trade Unions had been privately encouraged by Stormont to 'condemn' the strike; he afterwards warned the government that 'he was afraid that there was very little he could do' about what was occurring 'down the line'.[17] Deference was in decline. Indeed, although men had monopo-lized the two planning meetings held that week, it was women who had actually acted, defying the DCAC as well as Unionist control by march-ing within the city walls. Politics in Derry was no longer an elite pursuit, but instead a game open for all to play.

Four decades on from the start of the civil rights movement, the Bogside Artists paid tribute to Hume and Martin Luther King, both then Nobel laureates, by painting a mural of the giants standing shoulder-to-shoulder.[18] Before they became icons, though, they were young men working with friends and rivals to co-ordinate movements that other people had begun and that seethed with possibilities and problems. Admittedly, many differences can be found between Montgomery, Alabama, in 1955 and Derry in 1968, yet even a cursory comparison is worth making because it puts into perspective the size of the challenge faced by the DCAC. The Montgomery bus boycott lasted for over a year; the community organized a car pool made up of hundreds of volunteers; many people nonetheless still had to walk to their work; police officers harassed the car-pool drivers; white vigilantes also tried to intimidate their black neighbours by bombing their homes and churches; negotiations with the city broke down and the movement was pushed into taking a federal law suit against bus segregation all the way to the Supreme Court; the city successful prosecuted King under an old law banning boycotts; everyone involved in the boycott had to learn about the theory and practice of non-violent direct action; African-American youths came close to rioting; and victory, when it was finally won, was somewhat of an anti-climax, as the Supreme Court's ruling that bus segregation was unconstitutional took time to implement.[19] The month after the boycott ended, with the bombs, backsliding and bickering all weighing down upon him, King showed the strain of the last year or so, and stood silent and still at the pulpit until he was led away.[20] Based on this American experience, DCAC moderates could reasonably expect to find themselves having to experiment with the 'science of non-violence', build up the machinery needed to maintain the movement, master public relations, stand firm against repression, earn the respect of the people whom they aspired to lead and fight a long struggle that would deliver only ambiguous results. Except, of course, it could not go on for too long: they could not hope to restrain indefinitely those who wanted to use violence. So, to a certain extent, DCAC moderates were fortunate that their knowledge was based on the media narrative of the 'classical' phase of the American civil rights movement (1954–65), as they may well have been overwhelmed by thoughts of what lay ahead of them.

UNIONISM REACTS

On 7 October 1968, at a press conference in Leicester, Terence O'Neill explained that the 'Ulster police' 'had no alternative but to ban the march in Londonderry' because it was 'an act of pure provocation' which would have led to a 'fight' and to 'fatalities'. 'I hope nothing of this kind will happen again'.[21] In fact, the Prime Minister privately despaired that surely something much worse was slouching its way closer: 'If we take the wrong turning now', he confided to his Cabinet a week later, 'we may well risk rising disorder' and 'a period when we govern Ulster by police power alone'. The Unionist leader acknowledged that 'the first reaction of our people to the antics of anti-partition agitators…and the abuse of the world's Press is to retreat into hardline attitudes'; but, he insisted, the government had a 'duty' to recognize that 'Londonderry has drastically altered [the] situation to our great disadvantage'. 'Whether the…coverage was fair is immaterial', O'Neill told his ministers – what mattered was that the dominant narrative in the British news had been changed. 'Ulster Weeks', such as the one in the English Midlands at which the premier had been spinning while Derry was burning, had been part of a wider strategy to promote a positive image of Northern Ireland. So long as it seemed that the country was 'calm' and that 'slow but steady progress was underway', the British Prime Minister, Harold Wilson, had 'fobbed off' calls from the Labour backbenches to deal with accusations of discrimination himself, choosing instead to focus upon his government's 'many other headaches'. Now, the old narrative had been usurped by a new one in which Northern Ireland was in disorder and in need of major reform. And this story was not just being told in Britain: 'We have become a focus of world opinion', lamented O'Neill. '[T]he Embassy and BIS [British Information Service] in America,' he noted with concern, 'have been under intense pressure from the American press.' With its Cold War masters following the story, Westminster would certainly 'no longer be able to stand aloof' and this would 'bring nearer a dreadfully dangerous review our whole constitutional position'. Stormont would not be able to defy the 'imperial parliament', especially given that a 'UDI [Unilateral Declaration of Independence] attitude [was] wholly absurd in view of Ulster's geographical, military and economic position'. (The reference to Rhodesia is a reminder that one of the wider British narratives at this time was of imperial retreat.) O'Neill thus argued that the Cabinet should turn to 'fairness' as well as to 'firmness' – 'can any of us truly say in the confines of this room that the minority has no grievances calling for a remedy?' This emotional admission gave way to cold political calculation as the Unionist leader sketched out what he was willing to concede and what was 'essential to maintain our position'. His party's control over Derry fell into the former category. As it was going to be a 'very hard job to sell' such 'bitter choice[s]' to 'our people', O'Neill needed a united Cabinet, 'every one of us', to 'undertake [this] difficult task'.[22] The problem was that he did not have one.

Craig and Brian Faulkner, thinking as usual that one step higher would set them highest, kept the Cabinet discussions deadlocked, questioning each strand of O'Neill's argument. From the first Cabinet meeting after the Derry riots, the Minister of Home Affairs had been demanding 'an attitude of considerable firmness' and the Minister of Commerce had been 'indicat[ing]' his 'support for the...police'.[23] Even when the British Government set down a date and agenda for a summit at Downing Street, the pair continued to think it 'unlikely that Mr. Wilson would proceed to any extreme course which would be wholly unacceptable to majority opinion in Northern Ireland'. Craig believed that the decision about whether or not to grant universal suffrage for local elections should be put off until the restructuring of local government, which was currently under way, had been finished. Faulkner, playing a cagier game, claimed to hold 'no dogmatic views on the franchise', but was nonetheless against introducing changes 'under a threat of duress'.[24] Despite all these positions, however, categorizing Craig and Faulkner as 'right wing' does not capture the complexity of their responses to the crisis. They were speaking broadly the same 'language of conflict' as that which was used by O'Neill, the British Home Secretary, Jim Callaghan, and, indeed, other western politicians; they were telling a story which depicted the upheaval as having its origins in social and economic issues.[25] Craig, as early as four days before the DCAC laid out its demands, was criticizing the 'lack of any sense of urgency in tackling the housing problem on the part of the local authorities' and proposing to the rest of the Cabinet that 'a New Town Commission should be established' to push the 'Area Plan' forward.[26] The following week, Faulkner singled out 'jobs and houses' as being the 'basic issues'; he agreed with Craig that a development commission would 'create problems', but that the government should still 'hold to it firmly even if it was not acceptable to all local opinion'.[27] The civil rights movement, though, was not a rerun of the crisis over the second university. The socio-economic language of conflict was therefore distorting how politicians understood developments, and adversely affecting the shape which their reactions took.[28]

With the Cabinet deadlocked, critical editorials were soon being published in the unionist press.[29] On 23 October 1968, the *Belfast Telegraph* blasted the 'divided' leadership for 'failing the greatest test of statesmanship on the highest level that Northern Ireland has yet faced'.[30] This newspaper had long been pushing for O'Neill to take a more liberal line and had responded to the crisis by calling for the pace of reform to be picked up – 'Otherwise Northern Ireland will be faced with more disturbance'.[31] While the *Belfast Telegraph* feared that the government's relative silence was a way of 'sounding the retreat to the old trenches', the Orange Order was, by contrast, hearing hints of betrayal.[32] A delegation from the Order told the party hierarchy that the Fivemiletown District had passed a resolution attacking Stormont for failing to 'repudiate in the strongest possible terms the unfounded allegations of discrimination'. The Chief Whip, Roy Bradford, tried to reassure the Orangemen that 'they were not going to give in on basic principles…but on housing and other social problems'.[33] The marching feet of the civil rights movement had encouraged unionists to grope and grovel with their fingers inside their existing wounds.

WE SHALL OVERCOME

On 19 October 1968, the DCAC held a sit-down rally, which Hume presented as 'the first step in a campaign of non-violent protest'. The DCAC members had to teach most of the 4,000 to 5,000 people who had come to Guildhall Square on a rainy Saturday afternoon what they actually meant by non-violent protest. Grace instructed the crowd to sit down and Cooper had everyone sing the as-yet-unfamiliar American civil rights anthem 'We shall overcome'. Paddy Doherty later played the part of an African-American pastor, using call and response to get the 'people of this city' to deny Craig's claims that they were 'irresponsible', 'Communists' and risking 'bloodshed'.[34] McCafferty remembered sitting in Paddy Doherty's vast congregation and hearing McCann start to sing 'Fly me to the moon' softly to himself.[35] McCann, who had tried to keep up to date with the American civil rights movement, found himself watching a loose remake of the 'classical' phase. A section of the audience chanted '[w]e want McCann', but he had embraced passive resistance that day – even when Hume claimed that '[t]his movement has no political ends', that, in other words, 'its purpose is [not] to unite Ireland [nor] to unite the working class'.[36] Although the DCAC's vice-chair may only have wanted Derry to be 'united as a people in our demands', the speeches showed that there were still divisions within the committee. Ó Dochartaigh asked 'the representatives of the international Press' to let 'Wilson' know that 'the white Negroes of Derry' 'demand the same thing here that [he is] demanding for the blacks in Rhodesia'. (The Rhodesia parallel occurred to most parties to the conflict at this time, and is being used here to call for political control.)

James Doherty asked for an 'end [to] the political travesty which was at the root of [the] social and economic evils'. However, these were just personal opinions; Hume made clear that the DCAC's official demands were merely for a 'crash programme' of house building, a 'fair points system in the allocation of houses' and the 'Stormont Government to bring in some form of legal control in the renting of furnished accommodation'. As had often happened in the United States, a civil rights campaign had opened with local concerns, infighting among the organizers, people uncertain about what they were supposed to do, disappointing numbers (the DCAC had briefed the media that they were expecting at least 5,000) and the limited aim of securing change 'within the existing system'. Yet, it had also opened up greater possibilities. 'We shall channel the spirit of the people', said Hume in an echo of King, 'and we shall overcome'.[37]

What did not happen that afternoon was more significant than what did: there was no violence. The *Londonderry Sentinel* afterwards 'admitted that the arrangements were well made'.[38] Hume had warned before the protest that 'Anyone who causes trouble will be regarded by the committee as an enemy of the civil rights movement' – and these words had been backed up by actions.[39] Stewarding, which had been treated as an afterthought by the Derry radicals, was at the front of the minds of the DCAC moderates, who had recruited and trained up hundreds of volunteers.[40] At the conclusion of the sit-down rally, around twenty of the new marshals had surrounded a small group of people singing 'God save the Queen', successfully neutralizing a potential flashpoint. Although the organized loyalist counter-demonstration which had been threatened by Ronald Bunting, Ian Paisley's lieutenant, had not taken place, the RUC had still sealed off the section of the walls overlooking Guildhall Square. The police had otherwise kept their distance and thus earned for themselves the 'congratulations' of the *Derry Journal*.[41] As the city was in disorder and yet violence was in abeyance, the DCAC members agreed at the next committee meeting that 'we do not at this juncture open negotiations with the authorities'.[42] Canavan later told the commission of inquiry that the 'majority thought we would need something stronger in the line of pressure'.[43]

Sitting was followed by walking; four weeks after 5 October 1968, the fifteen committee members (in an order chosen by lot) set out to walk the route of the first civil rights march.[44] While they had put in place plans to hold a sit-down protest if they were attacked by the police, the RUC had informed them on the day of the walk that Bunting's counter-demonstration had been postponed and that officers had orders to keep the peace.[45] At about 2:35 pm, a white Ford Cortina, displaying both the Union Jack and the Northern Irish flag, pulled up opposite the Waterside railway station and Bunting, in a British army battle-dress blouse, flannel trousers and a tweed hat, climbed out on to the pavement. He explained to the District Inspector on duty that he was not going to lead a march at all now but instead hold a 'Teach-Out' inside the city walls.[46] As 3 pm drew nearer, the crowd swelled to around 1,000 spectators and Hume, who was in the front rank alongside Canavan and Cooper, looked at his watch and said, 'Thirty seconds to go'.[47] The fifteen men strolled down the road, with police officers at their flanks and rear and with stewards making sure that supporters stayed on the pavements and stayed away from the scattered groups of loyalist protesters.[48] A token effort was made by Bunting to stop the 'Rebels' by blocking off Ferryquay Gate, but the marshals and the police were able to push a way through into the walled city.[49] After the walkers reached the Diamond, Eamon Melaugh's 11-year-old son read the Universal Declaration of Human Rights, Cooper praised the crowd's 'discipline' and the stewards got the vast majority of people to disperse peacefully. Those who chose to reject the DCAC's authority remained behind for Bunting's meeting and the police found themselves having to separate rival crowds of teenagers who were shouting abuse and hurling fireworks at each other.[50] Finally, after about an hour, the youths drifted away – although thirty or so Protestant boys and girls retreated back to the Fountain 'in procession form' behind a Union Jack.[51]

The DCAC then announced that they were going to stage a full-scale march from the station to Guildhall Square a fortnight later.[52] Craig, in response, opted on 13 November 1968 to ban marches and meetings from taking place within the walls for a period of one month. Senior RUC officers from Derry had advised the Minister that 'the march should be permitted to proceed along the full route' and had been 'somewhat hesitant' about whether a ban 'could be enforced'; but, Craig had bullied them into accepting his decision.[53] Once again, the organizers of a civil rights march called upon 'all the people of Derry to resist the Minister' and, once again, Craig warned that 'the police will enforce the law'.[54] However, this is where the repetition became a farce. The

DCAC members agreed to mount just a 'symbolic confrontation' and to 'appoint delegates in case of our arrest'.[55] The Inspector-General issued 'very strict' instructions that 'Batons and other forcible methods ...will not be used merely to stop marchers' and that 'Police will accompany the marchers, even in a banned route, in available strength and endeavour to afford them protection against attack'.[56] With the DCAC and RUC in fairly regular contact, they soon became aware that each side wanted a compromise and a pantomime was duly scripted for that Saturday afternoon.[57]

Over 15,000 people (for the first time, attendance at a civil rights demonstration had far outstripped the estimates of the organizers) watched as Hume asked the County Inspector, 'in the name of peace and non-violence', to 'let our people through'; as the County Inspector replied to Hume that the 'order had to be complied with insofar as the police were able to do it'; and as the four nominated members – Canavan, Johnny White, Willie Breslin and Dermie McClenaghan – threw themselves harmlessly into the RUC lines on Carlisle Square.[58] There are parallels here with the second Selma, Alabama, march, in which King had 'disengaged', 'having made our point, revealing the continued presence of violence and showing clearly who are the oppressed and who the oppressors'.[59] As the press and the people were already there in such large numbers, King and Hume were satisfied with symbolic confrontation. 'We have broken the ban', the DCAC Vice-Chair told the marchers. This did not satisfy some people. While Hume was speaking, the loyalist counter-demonstrators behind the police waved the Union Jack and provoked a surge from the crowd which was checked by the stewards. Although most marchers were content to follow the DCAC away from the walls, the RUC and the counter-demonstrators, a large section chose instead to charge towards Ferryquay Gate (in the banned area but not on the route), passing by loyalist stone-throwers and passing through police tenders. The leaderless movement took the unionist citadel; the DCAC members arrived after the battle was lost and won.[60]

Thousands of people had spent the night praying for peace in Derry's two cathedrals and now some started referring to 'the miracle of Carlisle Square'.[61] Decisions taken by the DCAC and the RUC, the discipline shown by stewards and policemen and the wide disparity between the numbers of marchers and loyalists on the streets had all played a part in preventing a serious incident – but so had chance. On 18 November 1968, the Monday after the march, the DCAC moderates found that their luck was beginning to run out. The opening of the first trials arising from the city's long weekend of violence attracted a crowd of about 100 people outside the courthouse, half of whom tried to force their way past the police into the building. Grace calmed the situation by negotiating a deal with the RUC in which a dozen or so people, relatives of some of the defendants, were allowed inside to watch. After the resident magistrate adjourned the cases until the following month, the crowd, which had roughly trebled in size, carried Cooper and Gerry Fitt to the Guildhall, where panicked policemen shut the gates and swung out with their batons. The crowd, though, listened to Cooper's calls not to be provoked, but the majority of people in the square still insisted on parading back up to the Diamond before dispersing. This was not the end, however. Rumours of violence outside the Guildhall reached Derry harbour, inspiring 400 or so Catholic dockers to march to their union headquarters in the city centre to send telegrams of protest to both O'Neill and Wilson. Hume congratulated the dockers and urged them to return to work, which they did – through the banned area, singing 'We shall overcome' and shouting 'SS RUC'. This chant was taken up soon afterwards by the hundreds of workers, mainly women, who poured out of six factories, including the one managed by Cooper, to embark upon a short march to the Diamond. McCann met them there (the radicals were encouraging the spontaneous marches, while the moderates were trying to stop them) and praised the 'factory girls of Derry' for having 'walked all over Craig's ban'.[62] They walked over the ban again by parading back to their work by way of the RUC's Victoria barracks; at this point, the 150 teenagers that had been trailing after the adult marchers broke off to stage a sit-down protest, before then heading off on a mile-long circuit of the walls. Hume, a former teacher, was reduced to pleading with schoolchildren to go home to their mammies.[63]

   That day, the DCAC had not held any of the marches which had taken place; that night, it did not hold back the violence which took place. At 11 pm, outside Cooper's factory, between thirty and forty teenage boys from the Protestant area of the city lobbed bottles at the female workers coming off their shift.[64] The following afternoon, just over 100 factory girls from the Maydown industrial estate marched the five miles into Derry to protest about the attack on their fellow workers, but they were blocked at Ferryquay Gate by the RUC. While four of the women began bargaining with the police, the rest sat down and started chanting 'SS RUC'. Although DCAC moderates and marshals soon took control of the march, they got there just moments before the dockers and policemen who were also hurrying to the reported flashpoint. In Ferryquay Street, the dockers were almost run over by the water wagon – which had been brought into action against the instructions of the Inspector-General – and a number of them reacted by hurling bottles from a brewers' lorry. Hume and the marshals intervened and the police withdrew, restoring order and allowing the dockers and the factory girls to march peacefully back through the banned area to the port for a meeting. When news of what was happening reached Cooper's factory and the neighbouring ones as well, 400 female workers resolved to set off for the harbour, too; yet they only got as far as the walls before being ambushed by stone-throwing teenagers from the Fountain and so cut short their march. Men from James Doherty's abattoir joined up with the women and escorted them safely back to their factories. In the half-light, the city centre once again belonged wholly to the movement: schoolchildren hammered on the closed gates of Victoria barracks and thousands of workers paraded unhindered through the streets. However, after the light had yielded completely to the mournful gloom, civil rights supporters, who had come to defend the evening-shift workers at Cooper's factory, and loyalists, who had come to attack the factory girls, clashed in Carlisle Square. (As had happened in the American civil rights movement, popular notions of what it meant to be a man made it too difficult for some males to embrace non-violence.)[65] When the DCAC and RUC arrived on the scene, they did not work together to keep the peace, rather the riot squad baton charged the stewards as well as the people fighting in the streets. Twenty-four luckless individuals ended up in hospital, twelve policemen and twelve civilians; another casualty that night was Hume's claim, made the day before, that 'We can control our own people'.[66]

The movement's ownership of Derry's city centre, symbolic and physical, was not just contested by loyalist stone-throwers. Paisley, as he had since his movement's beginnings in Ballymena, County Antrim, also chose to politicize public space.[67] On 9 November 1968, Paisley and about 1,000 of his supporters, who had come from as far away as Liverpool and Glasgow, paraded into the walled city behind a man carrying a crown on a Bible (a well-known Orange symbol of a Protestant state). Paisley told the meeting staged afterwards in the Diamond that 'Londonderry is part of Ulster'. Meanwhile, Melaugh and the revived DUAC were holding a 'teach-in' (another American import) that was attended at its peak by around 500 people. After both events had ended, policemen, DCAC stewards and Paisleyite marshals were called upon to keep apart rival crowds of teenagers, one waving the Union flag and the other the Irish Tricolour. Watching this all take place were the poppy sellers near the war memorial; the president of the Londonderry branch of the British Legion had first appealed to Paisley not to come to his city and then had refused to withdraw his men from the Diamond. The following day, Remembrance Sunday, the war memorial, which had been profaned by the Paisleyites as well as the civil rights protesters, was reconsecrated, as the unionist establishment oversaw a ceremony in which flags, uniforms, medals, music, words and, above all, silence linked them across time and space with the rest of the British world and with its virtues.[68] Order was (briefly) restored.

The DUAC's 9 November 1968 teach-in was one of a series of protests that the radicals had been mounting. At Londonderry Corporation's October 1968 meeting, the DHAC had taken their usual places in the public gallery and taken up the new chant of 'civil rights'. When the Unionist councillors refused to receive a Labour delegation and adjourned for a short break, Melaugh led an occupation of the chamber, ensconcing himself in the empty mayoral chair. He was at the heart of the action again later that week, inspiring twenty young men to burn their signing-on cards at a teach-in he was chairing outside the city's employment exchange.[69] From these flames rose the re-born DUAC, which raged to the press that '[o]ther committees have failed in their attempts to find a solution to Derry's unemployment problem because they have tried to work within the rotten system. We are out to destroy it'.[70] McCann, playing the king across the water, was not so oblique when he criticized the moderates and, indeed, his own comrades: 'From the radical socialist point of view', he informed students at the new university, 'civil rights has inherent disadvantages as...it can, in Northern Ireland, serve as cloak for objectively reactionary groupings, [and] this is disastrous'.[71] As Canavan explained to the commission of inquiry, although the DCAC was repeatedly urged to co-opt McCann, the moderates did not want him to become a member because he 'would split the unity that existed among the different groupings'.[72] They could keep him out of the committee, but they could not keep him off the stage. When the DCAC held a mass meeting at the Guildhall on 19 November 1968 to renew its mandate, the audience demanded a speech from McCann – and, after thanking the committee, he went on to outline his 'many sharp disagreements' with the moderates.[73]

The DCAC moderates were still not masters of the movement; in fact, no-one was. At the Guildhall meeting, Cooper, who had been forced out of his home by a stream of threatening telephone calls and letters, had appealed for an end to the spontaneous marches, especially as Hume was 'dead on his feet'.[74] Even before the clashes that night in Carlisle Square, the moderates had decided to try to take politics off the streets, to take the pressure of Stormont. It was the movement – not the DCAC or anyone else for that matter – that therefore went on to create a situation so crisis packed it pushed opened the door to negotiations. And, the threat of increasing violence was not the only weapon which was wielded by the movement against the wishes of the DCAC: an unofficial boycott of the city's Protestant-owned shops was also in place. By early November 1968, it was already starting to bite, with shopkeepers inside the walls complaining to the *Londonderry Sentinel* that their trade was down by as much as half.[75] Hume was 'totally and completely against this sort of action because it was unjust' and the DCAC instructed the stewards to 'help to undo the boycott' – but a boycott of segregated stores had been at the centre of King's Birmingham, Alabama, campaign.[76] Money mattered more than morality. In both of these cities, it was people from the private sector rather than public officials who first looked to cut a deal.[77] On 20 November 1968, the *Londonderry Sentinel* reported that the newspaper had 'learned' that the 'top flights of industry and business' were 'discussing the problem with a view to making approaches to the Government for a discussion on the working out of a solution as quickly as possible'.[78] The movement had overcome.

CONCESSIONS

At the Downing Street summit, on 4 November 1968, Wilson warned O'Neill, Craig and Faulkner that 'my government cannot tolerate a situation in which the liberalizing trend was being retarded rather than accelerated and if this were to arise they would feel compelled to propose a radical course involving the complete liquidation of all financial agreements with Northern Ireland'. The Labour leader also muttered darkly about 'weakened...standing abroad', the 'role' the 'Ulster Members...play in British affairs' and how Belfast's Short and Harland aircraft factory 'had become a kind of 'soup-kitchen'. However, both what was at issue and what was at risk were of less consequence than Wilson's performance suggested. The two sides were speaking the same language of conflict: the Junior Minister present felt that 'jobs and social improvement were the things dominating most people's thoughts' and Faulkner concurred that 'jobs and houses were generally accepted as the really important matters on which progress was required'. Wilson even had some sympathy for the claim that leftists had set out to exploit genuine material grievances, as '[r]iots could be regarded as a major industry these days' and 'the Grosvenor Square affair had also been premeditated'. But, while the British and, to a certain extent, O'Neill believed that ground had to be given, too, on the Special Powers Act, independent scrutiny and the local government franchise, Craig and Faulkner, as they explained to colleagues afterwards, would only 'support changes they believed to be justifiable in themselves'.[79] The pair, furthermore, remained unconvinced that Westminster would freely wander into the Irish bog. So, at the next Cabinet meeting, when O'Neill insisted that it 'could be discounted' that the 'United Kingdom government was bluffing', Craig and Faulkner countered that they were still 'unwilling to accept dictation'.[80] They were gambling that Stormont was in control of the crisis.

The 'principal dilemma', James Chichester-Clark, the Minister of Agriculture, stressed to his colleagues on 14 November 1968, 'lay in the fact that Mr Wilson...placed [the] main emphasis upon the local-government franchise, while it was precisely in this area that it was most difficult to move'. Bradford noted that the 'Government accepted universal adult suffrage in principle'; however, in practice, they had to take into account their previous commitments and the opposition of many within their party. They needed 'farther time to educate the people in the realities of the situation'. Bradford suggested that they should try to buy time from the British by putting together a 'package deal', 'not a grudging instalment of reform but the maximum possible concessions compatible with their vital political interests'. According to Chichester-Clark, these were the establishment of a 'Commission to investigate and report upon grievances'; the 'Abolition of the company vote...at an early date'; a commitment to reach a settlement with the Catholic Church's Mater hospital; '[m]easures to ensure fair allocation of public housing'; the '[a]ppointment of an Ombudsman'; and a 'democratic decision' (a referendum or a general election) on the local-government franchise. Some were accepted, others were rejected and most were the starting points for more debate.[81] As had so often happened in American civil rights struggles, the details that were in dispute ahead of doing the deal were relatively trivial, yet they were enough to drag out discussions.

Developments in Derry did away with the deadlock. Relations between the RUC and the Minister of Home Affairs broke down over how to address the escalating disorder. During the second day of spontaneous marches, Craig told the Cabinet that 'the rank-and-file police had been deterred by their officers from dealing effectively with militants'.[82] The Inspector-General, in contrast, was days away from sending his political master a letter – to which he had given 'considerable thought' – that attacked almost everything Craig was saying and doing: 'people holding important public positions should carefully refrain from making public statements which are ... calculated to inflame passions'; 'the loyalist side are confused and are not making any distinction between the IRA and Civil Rights marchers'; 'the constitution is not in danger from those who are protesting'; 'many professing Unionists support the protesters'; 'the unrest...seems likely to continue until electoral reform is introduced'; and 'the small police force we have in Ulster...may find [it] quite impossible to cope'.[83] On 20 November 1968, the Cabinet as a whole became involved in this on-going disagreement. Ministers listened to the Inspector-General and two other senior officers argue that the ban was 'logistically impossible' to uphold, that it would be 'prudent' to lift it and that 'further really firm police action could lead to the most serious and prolonged disorder in Londonderry and elsewhere'. The 'police view' was the 'heat' needed to be 'taken out of events by political means'. Although Craig 'expressed great concern', the 'general view of Ministers' was that the 'police advice...could not be ignored'.[84] And, nor could the government dismiss the 'anxieties' that had been expressed to O'Neill and Faulkner the following morning by 'an influential group of Londonderry businessmen', who wanted not only 'the ban [to] be lifted' but also the corporation 'to be replaced'. With the city fathers pushing Stormont to 'take the political decisions which would restore normal conditions', the Cabinet finally agreed the package deal that day. Local authorities were to adopt a points system for public housing allocations, a British-style Ombudsman was be appointed, the emergency powers that offended against the European Convention on Human Rights were to be withdrawn 'as soon as the security conditions permitted', a commission was to replace the Londonderry council and to put the area plan speedily into effect, and the company vote was to be abolished 'at an early date'.[85] These modest reforms were more than the Unionists had ever before conceded.

O'Neill 'congratulated his colleagues', yet he 'wondered whether the package...would be sufficient in the absence of a commitment to alter the local government franchise, to satisfy the United Kingdom Government or to restrain the Civil Rights marchers'.[86] That said, two days earlier, Wilson had sent a letter to O'Neill that, while using 'plain language', had actually shifted Westminster's position from expecting that 'by next Spring...the franchise [would be] in the process of being changed' to instead requiring, within six months, a public pledge to pass universal adult suffrage into law.[87] Now, after news of the reforms was released, the British released even more of the pressure. 'A split in the Unionist Party and the downfall of [the O'Neill] government would be very serious at the present moment', reasoned a Home Office memorandum, 'and renewed pressure in public on the local government franchise at this point in time carries the risk of provoking this'. So, while sticking with the six-month deadline, the officials advised that 'more [of] the initiative on timing...be left to Captain O'Neill'.[88] When Wilson composed his next letter, which was dispatched on 23 December 1968, he therefore limited himself to expressing his 'disappoint[ment] that you have not so far felt able to announce a policy of early introduction'.[89] Westminster was not going to intervene in the short term. In fact, the contingency planning that was taking place in Whitehall departments at the end of the year was geared much more towards keeping British troops off Northern Irish streets than about keeping the Northern Irish Government on track to deliver British rights.[90]

The DCAC's reaction followed the same basic pattern as the British one: say it was not enough, but take some of the pressure off. The committee, meeting exactly a month before Wilson's letter was sent, 'welcome[d]' four of the five reforms (Craig's public comments about how the Special Powers Act would be required for the foreseeable future had made 'it difficult to place confidence in the Government's intentions'). Nonetheless, the DCAC still 'Resent[ed] the total failure of the Government to face up to what is the central & crucial issue – democra[tic] rule in this city, because this is the root cause of the present unrest'. The 'struggle' therefore had to 'continue...until this was achieved'; yet, the moderates also decided that the break from street protests had to continue and 'the people of Derry' had to be asked 'to continue to exercise restraint'.[91] At the subsequent press conference, journalists asked: 'Are you considering a fresh campaign?', 'Have you a plan of campaign?' and 'Will you call a meeting of the people of Derry?' – the DCAC had no answers.[92]

While the moderates may have hoped to restrain the civil rights marchers, the DCAC were not in control of the Derry movement let alone the other local movements that it had inspired. The Armagh civil-rights committee decided to go ahead with their planned march on 30 November 1968; Paisley went ahead with what he considered 'appropriate' action to prevent Armagh becoming 'another Londonderry'. The two sides, the lawful march and the illegal counter-demonstration, were kept apart by the RUC throughout a tense day, until the evening when a small riot had to be cleared by a baton charge.[93] After what the *Belfast Telegraph* called 'one of the blackest days in the history of Northern Ireland', O'Neill slowly spotted that 'decent and moderate people' felt that the country was 'on the brink of chaos' and that this supposed majority, who had so far been 'silent', could now be persuaded to 'make [their] voice heard'.[94] These phrases featured in his televised address on 9 December 1968: the Prime Minister told the viewing publics a story where the protests of 'noisy minorities' (he bundled civil rights activists and loyalists together) were producing violence and risking 'bloodshed', yet 'moderates on both sides' could still choose to 'come with us into a new era of co-operation, and leave the extremists to the law'.[95] Within a week, close to 150,000 people had let O'Neill know that they had made that choice.[96] Their voices silenced his opponents: Craig was sacked, not one of O'Neill's critics on the backbenches dared vote against a motion backing his leadership, civil rights groups everywhere suspended their marches and the Derry shopping boycott ended.[97] 'The superior hero wins again,' trumpeted the *Sunday Times*.[98] But, this was not the end of the story. As *Time* recorded after the Birmingham campaign, this was 'a fragile truce based on pallid promises'.[99] Mary Holland, writing in the *Observer*, put the praise in perspective: 'Captain O'Neill has not saved Ulster, he has merely given her a breathing space'.[100]

FREEDOM OF THE CITY

'One night as we all sat in the City Hotel', remembered McCafferty, 'Mary silenced the older men who sat round her in a circle...by asking one of them to shift slightly as he was obscuring her view of Eamonn.'[101] Holland, through her relationships with the Derry radicals, had a clearer view than most foreign journalists of McCann – she knew that he would not let O'Neill rest. Looking back on 1968, McCann mocked how 'the end result of the Civil Rights campaign has been to install...O'Neill as [our] unchallenged father-figure'. 'He has not given us anything,' argued McCann. 'What we have got so far we have had to tear from his hands.'[102] So, the radicals chose to lend their support to the spontaneous marches which took place on the day McCann's court case resumed, to the Creggan mothers who picketed the corporation's housing manager, to the homeless families who were occupying part of the Guildhall and to the hunger strike undertaken by some of these squatters.[103] They also chose to support the Belfast-based People's Democracy, who were going to begin 1969 by marching from the capital to the second city. As for the moderates, they had no choice except to promise to 'gladly receive and refresh' their uninvited guests – they were not masters in their own house.[104] And this left the back door open for the local Nationalist party, which was secretly working with the Unionist Government 'towards a lowering of the temperature'.[105] A former Nationalist alderman, claiming he was only 'say[ing] publicly what many civil-rights supporters are saying in private', wrote to the *Derry Journal* that the march was 'ill advised' and that the 'truce...should be extended'.[106] The response to the letter was sufficiently encouraging for McAteer to tell the press a few days later that 'it was not good marching weather in more senses than one'. McCann, though, was marching against 'Tories of Green and Orange variety' and to make the political weather. 'We are conscious of the class nature of the issues that we are attempting to dramatize,' he spat back.[107] McCann had helped start the movement and now he wanted to help restart it; the Christmas break was over.

From the first morning, as NICRA's Frank Gogarty witnessed, the marchers were 'surrounded' by 'howling hostile' loyalists, usually led by the 'brazen lout' Bunting.[108] The young people's unearned suffering changed things. On the night before the final leg of the march, Paisley held a prayer meeting in the Guildhall, bringing his supporters into the city and bringing out his opponents in the city. A crowd of about 800 Derrymen and women gathered in the square, and idled away the time until the end of the service by throwing stones and burning Bunting's car. Cooper, Hume and even McCann exhorted them to disperse, without success – causing the District Inspector in charge to conclude that the would-be leaders had 'lost control of the crowd'. The RUC cleared people away from the entrance to the Guildhall, but many of the Pais-leyites did not want to be escorted to safety and burst out of the building brandishing broken chair legs. The two sides clashed for a couple of minutes and then broke off, allowing police officers to drive them out of the city centre. Nonetheless, the District Inspector still reported that 'this was the most explosive situation I had yet to contend with'.[109] The next day would be even more explosive.

On the road between Claudy and Derry, at Burntollet Bridge, local loyalists, including off-duty B-Specials, ambushed the People's Democracy march, now numbering several hundred people – and its leaders hesitated.[110] They had been pushed through the 'danger area' and the police 'endeavoured to keep them moving', but some 'showed an inclination to come back and assist those following', who were being 'sharply attacked by the loyalists with sticks and stones'. The police report suggests that the RUC then restored order: the 'loyalists were attacked and baton charged', and 'with the aid of some cover provided by police tenders the remainder of the marchers got past this point'.[111] Accounts given by the marchers, in contrast, describe chaos, cruelty and collusion. Gogarty, who had made the choice to take part rather than watch, was 'bludgeoned' until he let go of the civil rights banner, and the primary-school teacher who had been trying to help him was 'hustl[ed]' away by a constable 'with the aid of a shield against my chest'.[112] 'The police did not lack the power to prevent the Burntollet ambush,' concluded Derry Labour, 'they lacked the will.'[113] Judging by the three further assaults on the march before it reached Guildhall Square, the reverse is a more appropriate verdict; riot police on each of these occasions drew batons and tried to disperse the loyalist stone-throwers, yet they always found themselves outnumbered. Although Burntollet has attracted much more memory work (probably because of the later collusion between the security forces and loyalist paramilitaries), many more working-class Catholics and Protestants were involved in these incidents on the edge of the city. Indeed, the small People's Democracy march that had traipsed across the country had been transformed into one of the Derry movement's biggest marches, as over 2,000 local men and women traversed the familiar route over Craigavon Bridge and into Guildhall Square, where thousands more were waiting to welcome them.[114] Holland was there, too, and she 'listened to civil-rights leaders begging the people to go home, to refrain from violence and to think of world opinion. The crowd said what they thought of world opinion in no uncertain terms, asked what it had ever done for the poor of Derry and told their leaders that they were too late'.[115] The DCAC moderates could not control their 'own people'. There had been a succession of flashpoints that day; the riot that developed after the meeting was predictable.

Once again, the RUC and working-class Catholic youths battled over space. During the initial stages of the fighting, Hume 'approached the police who were carrying batons and shields and asked them to withdraw the water canon which, in our opinion, had been the major cause of the incitement to the people'. The peacemaker, though, was cursed, not blessed. 'One of the policemen replied: "If you take a step closer I'll beat your – head in."'[116] Six weeks before, the Inspector-General had given 'instructions' that officers should employ the 'minimum degree of force...to prevent or quell rioting' and 'must be well disciplined and restrained in their actions no matter how great the provocation may be'.[117] That night, they did not and they were not. Over half the officers who had set out from Belfast with the People's Democracy march had been injured on the road to Derry and seventy-four policemen were also hurt in the disturbances after it reached the city; many members of the mobile units wanted a revenge that went much further than their orders permitted. After the clock had struck midnight, a sizeable number even turned into rioters themselves – smashing windows, battering at doors and using sectarian insults. In an editorial on the 'weekend that brought matters to a head', the *Derry Journal* 'spel[t] out publicly what is being said over and over again in homes and wherever people gather' about the 'relations between the RUC and the vast Catholic majority'. The police were not 'a peace-keeping organization', but rather 'the chief ingredient of violence in the city streets'.[118]

When a *Derry Journal* reporter toured the Bogside on the morning of 5 January 1969, he found that an 'ugly mood had developed 'among the men': 'Many of them had armed themselves with cudgels and iron bars'.[119] DCAC moderates had previously had to talk teenagers out of violence; now, they had to address their older brothers and fathers. Hume had persuaded a reluctant Fitt to speak to the people, too, as he was 'terribly worried' that they 'are are going to march on the police station and there is going to be bloodshed'.[120] The West Belfast MP added his voice to those who were calling for 'caution' at a meeting in the Bogside, and the crowd was convinced that the women from the area should march in silent protest to Victoria barracks instead. Amid the faintly falling snow, with the truce now dead, the 'mammies' staged their 'funeral march' and then delivered a sermon to the city's top policemen, warning them that 'Our men have made up their minds to defend us if you can't'.[121] This was not yet the decisive break with non-violence, even though it may appear to be: throughout the 'classical' phase of the American civil rights movement, local defence bodies protected organizers, provided armed escorts and patrolled black neighbourhoods at night. For example, the Deacons for Defense and Justice, equipped with rifles and walkie-talkies, frightened the Ku Klux Klan out of the black districts of Bogalusa, Louisiana – and frightened the state's Governor into enforcing the 1964 Civil Rights Act.[122] Nonetheless, Hume was reluctant to move still further away from constitutional politics and closer towards the politics of the gun. 'Let us show that we are capable of policing our own area,' he told a meeting held after the women's march; but, he did not feel able to become a vigilante himself. Other DCAC moderates, some stewards and a few veteran Republicans were prepared to put themselves forward to lead the self-defence groups that were starting to form. Seán Keenan, who had been interned during each of the IRA's last two campaigns, announced at the day's first meeting that 'we have only two cheeks and we have turned the other for the last time'.[123] As an American civil rights activist had observed two years earlier, most people mistakenly believed that non-violence stood for 'turning the other cheek, submitting instead of resisting'.[124] Many men in both Bogalusa and the Bogside regarded this as degrading and wanted to defend their women and children, to meet violence with violence.

'Keenan, who is in charge of the St Columb's Wells area, ... said that disciplinary action would take the form of taking those responsible for offenses home and asking them to stay off the streets.' McCann's show on 'Radio Free Derry', a pirate station broadcasting from Rossville flats, was made up of news reports like this one – as well as music from Elvis Presley, The Beatles and local show bands; interviews with People's Democracy marchers and Bogsiders; satire, including a skit about Paisley, 'the Mao Tse Tung' flu' and 'Protestant vaccine'; and propaganda demanding 'Tories Out, North and South'. The radicals were revelling in 'the liberated area'.[125] What pleased McCann most was that O'Neill's '"liberal" views' had been exposed as 'lies': 'The attackers of innocent people in Northern Ireland are not the police or the Paisleyites, but...their political master' – and 'The mask has [finally] slipped'.[126] Once again, McCann was speaking the language of global revolt (for example, the American New Left aimed at 'unmasking corporate liberalism' and West Berlin's student activists set out to 'unmask our state as a police state').[127] A year after he had come home convinced that he could sweep up the old parochial politics by introducing a new international dimension, McCann now hoped that it was becoming obvious that the struggle was between the working class and capitalism. 'Come and help us,' he asked 'the Protestants and policemen who are listening', 'we are fighting for jobs and houses and a decent standard of living for all, we are fighting...the system'.[128] He also delivered this message in person. 'With some trepidation,' as he remembered half a year later, McCann left behind the barricades and went right into the front rooms of the Fountain. 'I gave out the usual CR line about wanting justice for all sections of the community...A middle-aged woman told me immediately: "But if you Catholics were in control there would be no life for us here. We would have to leave our homes and get out." It was clear that every one of them actually believed that.' McCann was starting to fear that his hosts were not 'brainwashed', that unionism was 'the political philosophy which happens to be accepted by the overwhelming majority of Protestants'.[129] As another Irishman wrote of another revolution, 'Every fear, every hope will forward it' – and they were carrying the Derry revolution away from what its father had expected.[130]

On 6 January 1969, senior RUC officers outlined to the Cabinet 'the circumstances in which the police had temporarily withdrawn from an area of Londonderry, which was being controlled by an organized and armed force'. Their assessment was that 'considerable force', 'possibly ... even firearms', would be required to 're-enter the area', and so they instead recommended holding back and holding talks with the moderates. The Minister of Home Affairs therefore arranged to meet Hume. A crackdown, though, also came with these concessions, as the government agreed that the 'regular force would have to be further supplemented...by mobilization of Special Constables'.[131] Derry Labour warned that 'this could lead directly to civil war'; but, the radicals were not the only leftists in the city issuing statements, something which allowed the immediate crisis to be brought to a peaceful resolution.[132] The Socialist Labour League, two or three Trotskyists who had joined this British sect in the mid-1960s, distributed a leaflet calling for 'Armed workers defence guards' and a 'ONE DAY STRIKE'.[133] With the backing of bishops and trade-union bureaucrats, the whole of the DCAC stepped in to stop the proposed strike taking place.[134] Most people in 'Free Derry' may not have wanted the RUC, yet they still wanted law and order – and they were worried about where things were heading. Indeed, the Bogside was awash with rumours, including one about Keenan presiding over 'secret courts', which suggested that fears of social breakdown were widespread.[135] So, after five days, the moderates were able to bring the barricades down and the patrols off the streets; the *Derry Journal* thundered that 'Only those inimical to, or lacking any understanding of, the true objectives of the civil rights movement in Derry will quarrel with the Citizens Action Committee's decision'.[136] This was a contested claim. As the next chapter on Derry will demonstrate, the months that followed would be dominated by quarrels over how the movement should be understood, what were its objectives and who was betraying it.

CONCLUSION

Hume still believed 'beyond a shadow of a doubt that non-violent protest is the only effective protest'. '[C]ivil rights,' he continued, 'can only be obtained by attracting publicity to the injustices and by getting more public sympathy on our side. This sympathy is the more easily won to our cause if we are seen to be...accepting provocation, injury and damage to our homes...If, however, we are seen to burn, loot and attack, we lose all sympathy.'[137] McCann agreed with his rival that non-violence worked, while disagreeing with him over how it worked. 'In so far as the Government has moved,' he reminded the Belfast Young Socialists at the end of 1968, 'it has moved in the face of direct action.'[138] Pressure was applied to the authorities through publicity and from the streets, but it was also applied by the threat and the fact of violence – violence inflicted by supporters of the movement as well as by its opponents. Although O'Neill felt that 'some extremely sinister elements' had been behind the People's Democracy march and 'Free Derry', he nonetheless advised his Cabinet colleagues that 'political as well as law-and-order solutions' were needed. For the Prime Minister, the 'concept of an inquiry' offered 'a very late, if not last chance to deal with events before they dispose of us'.[139] The success of non-violence in Northern Ireland was thus in some ways parasitic on violence. Again, this is not an attempt to blacken the Derry movement's name by contrasting it with the 'pure' non-violent campaigns conducted on the other side of the Atlantic: violence gave the black struggle leverage, too. Birmingham inspired more than 700 sit-ins, mass meetings and marches in almost 200 cities, and President John F. Kennedy was 'concerned about those demonstrations'. 'I think they go beyond...protest,' he said at a press conference in July 1963, 'and they get into a very bad situation where you get violence'. He therefore told 'those people who have responsible positions in Government and in business and in labor [to] do something about the problem which leads to the demonstration[s]'.[140]

Derry was not Birmingham; Northern Ireland was not the United States. Birmingham's local civil rights groups had been organizing for years before King turned up to reinforce them with his international profile, a million-dollar budget, hundreds of full-time staff members and a plan of campaign. The Birmingham movement had discipline and strategy. The Derry movement, however, was less a hierarchy and more a network, one in which everyone was equal (though some were more equal than others), so leaving it much weaker on discipline and strategy. From early January 1969 onwards, with all the would-be leaders fumbling towards new strategies, such discipline as there was went into deep decline. (This is not to ignore Westminster's failure to intervene, Stormont's limited concessions, police brutality and loyalist violence; but, it should also be noted that Washington DC had to be forced to act, reform came slowly, law enforcement defended injustice and racists maimed and murdered.) Rival gangs roamed Derry at night seemingly targeting individuals who had taken part in marches or counter-demonstrations.[141] While some of the motives behind these acts will, of course, remain unknown, the violence was clearly driven by politics and sectarianism. Politics, in particular, matters here. The American civil rights movement can be seen, among other things, as part of a long struggle to deliver the promises of the American Revolution to all Americans. The Northern Irish civil rights movement, in contrast, can be seen, among other things, as another phase in the long struggle within Ireland over who ruled and by what right. The Irish revolution was not over.

NOTES

1. International Civil & Human Rights Conference, 4–5 October 2008, Derry (personal notes).
2. N. McCafferty, *Nell* (London: Penguin, 2004), p. 422; the last quote is from one of Martin Luther King's lieutenants in *Time*, 3 January 1964.
3. C. Davenport, 'State Repression and Political Order', *Annual Review of Political Science*, 10, 1 (June 2007), pp. 1–23.
4. W. Moore, 'Repression and Dissent: Substitution, Context and Timing', *American Journal of Political Science*, 42, 3 (July 1998), pp. 851–3.
5. On composite actors, see W. Pearlman, 'A Composite-Actor Approach to Conflict Behavior', in E. Chenoweth and A. Lawrence (eds), *Rethinking Violence: States and Non-State Actors in Conflict* (Cambridge, MA: MIT Press, 2010), pp. 197–219.
6. K. Gallagher Cunningham and E. Beaulieu, 'Dissent, Repression and Inconsistency', in Chenoweth and Lawrence (eds), *Rethinking Violence*, pp. 173–95.
7. *Derry Journal*, 11 October 1968.
8. F. Ó Dochartaigh, *Ulster's White Negroes: From Civil Rights to Insurrection* (Edinburgh: AK Press, 1994), p. 58.
9. *Derry Journal*, 11 October 1968.
10. *Derry Journal*, 16 May 1967.
11. *Derry Journal*, 15 October 1968.
12. D. McClenaghan, 'Abandonment, Civil Rights and Socialism', in P. McClenaghan (ed.), *Spirit of '68: Beyond the Barricades* (Derry: Guildhall Press, 2009), pp. 27–46, pp. 39–40; P. Doherty, *Paddy Bogside* (Cork: Mercier Press, 2001), pp. 60-1; E. McCann, *War and an Irish Town* (London: Pluto Press, 1993 edn.), pp. 100–1.
13. *Derry Journal*, 11 October 1968.
14. *Londonderry Sentinel*, 16 October 1968.
15. Ibid.

16. *Derry Journal*, 15 October 1968.
17. A. Murdoch, Note for the Record, 14 October 1968, Belfast, Public Record Office of Northern Ireland (PRONI), HA/32/2/26.
18. *Derry Journal*, 20 June 2008.
19. D. Garrow, *Bearing the Cross: Martin Luther King, Jr., and the Southern Christian Leadership Conference* (New York, NY: William Morrow, 1986), pp. 11–82.
20. T. Branch, *Parting the Waters: America in the King Years 1954–63* (London: Simon & Schuster, 1988), p. 201.
21. Report from Leicester of the Prime Minister's News Conference, PRONI, CAB/9B/205/7.
22. Memorandum by the Prime Minister, 14 October 1968, PRONI, CAB/4/1406.
23. Cabinet conclusions, 8 October 1968, PRONI, CAB/4/1405.
24. Cabinet conclusions, 23 October 1968, PRONI, CAB/4/1409.
25. R. Bourke, 'Languages of Conflict and the Northern Ireland Troubles', *Journal of Modern History* (forthcoming). Post-war politicians in the west generally believed that the 'polarizations of the last inter-war decade were born directly of economic depression and its social costs'. T. Judt, *Postwar: A History of Europe since 1945* (London: William Heinemann, 2005), p. 72.
26. Cabinet conclusions, 15 October 1968, PRONI, CAB/4/1407.
27. Cabinet conclusions, 23 October 1968, PRONI, CAB/4/1409. It was not acceptable to all local opinion. See, for example, Deputation to Stormont, 25 November 1968, Derry, Derry City Council's Archives (DCCA), Londonderry Rural District Council Minutes, June 1967 to March 1969.
28. Bourke, 'Languages of Conflict'.
29. See, for example, *Londonderry Sentinel*, 16 October 1968: 'The Unionist Party...has not uttered a word'.
30. *Belfast Telegraph*, 23 October 1968.
31. A. Gailey (ed.), *Crying in the Wilderness – Jack Sayers: A Liberal Editor in Ulster, 1939–69* (Belfast: Institute of Irish Studies, 1995), pp. 92–3; *Belfast Telegraph*, 7 October 1968.
32. *Belfast Telegraph*, 23 October 1968.
33. H. Patterson and E. Kaufman, *Unionism and Orangeism in Northern Ireland since 1945: The Decline of the Loyal Family* (Manchester: Manchester University Press, 2007), pp. 80–1.
34. *Derry Journal*, 22 October 1968.
35. McCafferty, *Nell*, p. 127.
36. *Londonderry Sentinel*, 23 October 1968.
37. *Derry Journal*, 22 October 1968.
38. *Londonderry Sentinel*, 23 October 1968.
39. *Derry Journal*, 15 October 1968.
40. *Derry Journal*, 18 October 1968; M. Canavan's evidence to the Cameron Commission, PRONI, GOV/2/1/186.
41. *Derry Journal*, 22 October 1968.
42. Photocopy of DCAC minutes, 21 October 1968, PRONI, GOV/2/1/186.
43. Canavan's evidence.
44. Photocopy of DCAC minutes, 29 October 1968.
45. Photocopy of DCAC minutes, 1 November 1968.
46. W. Hood, Civil rights march and counter demonstrations in Londonderry, [November 1968], PRONI, HA/32/2/26.
47. R. McGimpsey, Parades at Londonderry, [November 1968], PRONI, HA/32/2/26.
48. Hood, Civil rights march.
49. Statement of District Inspector E. Woods, [November 1968], PRONI, HA/32/2/26.
50. *Derry Journal*, 5 November 1968; *Londonderry Sentinel*, 6 November 1968.
51. W. Harrison, Civil rights march at Londonderry, [November 1968], PRONI, HA/32/2/26.
52. *Derry Journal*, 8 November 1968.
53. A. Kennedy to B. Craig, 22 November 1968, PRONI, HA/32/2/26.
54. *Derry Journal*, 15 November 1968.
55. Photocopy of DCAC minutes, 15 November 1968; Photocopy of DCAC minutes, 13 November 1968.
56. A. Kennedy to P. Kerr, [November 1968], PRONI, HA/32/2/26. See, also, R. McGimpsey to Head Constables, Sergeants, 16 November 1968, PRONI, HA/32/2/26.
57. McCafferty, *Nell*, p. 134.

58. *Derry Journal*, 19 November 1968.
59. M. King, 'Behind the Selma March', *Saturday Review*, 3 April 1965.
60. *Derry Journal*, 19 November 1968.
61. *Londonderry Sentinel*, 20 November 1968.
62. Ó Dochartaigh, *Ulster's White Negroes*, pp. 69–70.
63. *Derry Journal*, 19 November 1968; *Londonderry Sentinel*, 20 November 1968.
64. *Derry Journal*, 19 November 1968.
65. See, S. Wendt, '"They Finally Found Out that We Really Are Men": Violence, Non-Violence and Black Manhood in the Civil Rights Era', *Gender & History*, 19, 3 (November 2007), pp. 543–564.
66. *Londonderry Sentinel*, 20 November 1968; *Derry Journal*, 22 November 1968; *Derry Journal*, 19 November 1968.
67. I am greatly indebted to Dr James Greer of Queen's University Belfast for this information.
68. *Londonderry Sentinel*, 13 November 1968; *Derry Journal*, 12 November 1968.
69. *Derry Journal*, 1 November 1968.
70. *Derry Journal*, 8 November 1968.
71. *Londonderry Sentinel*, 6 November 1968.
72. Canavan's evidence.
73. Public Meeting, Derry Guildhall, 19 November 1968, PRONI, D/2560/4; *Derry Journal*, 22 November 1968.
74. *Derry Journal*, 22 November 1968.
75. *Londonderry Sentinel*, 6 November 1968.
76. *Derry Journal*, 28 January 1969; Photocopy of DCAC minutes, 27 November 1968.
77. A. Morris, 'Birmingham Confrontation Reconsidered: An Analysis of the Dynamics and Tactics of Mobilization', *American Sociological Review*, 58, 5 (October 1993), pp. 621–636, pp. 631 and 636.
78. *Londonderry Sentinel*, 20 November 1968.
79. Meeting at 10 Downing Street on 4th November 1968, PRONI, CAB/4/1413; Extract from a Meeting Held at 10 Downing Street on 4th November 1968, London, National Archives (NA), PREM/13/2841; Meeting on 4th November 1968, NA, CAB/164/334.
80. Cabinet conclusions, 7 November 1968, PRONI, CAB/4/1413.
81. Cabinet conclusions, 14 November 1968, PRONI, CAB/4/1414.
82. Cabinet conclusions, 19 November 1968, PRONI, CAB/4/1417.
83. A. Kennedy to B. Craig, 25 November 1968, PRONI, HA/32/2/26.
84. Cabinet conclusions, 20 November 1968, PRONI, CAB/4/1418. At this time, police headquarters was also warning the army that 'things are now at flashpoint in Londonderry'. I. Harris to V. Fitzgeorge-Balfour, 20 November 1968, NA, DEFE/25/257.
85. Cabinet conclusions, 21 November 1968, PRONI, CAB/4/1419.
86. Ibid.
87. H. Wilson to T. O'Neill, 19 November 1968, NA, PREM/13/2841; Meeting at 10 Downing Street on 4th November 1968.
88. Memorandum by the Home Secretary, [13 December 1968], NA, CJ/3/30. See also B. Cubbon to P. Gregson, 20 December 1968, NA, PREM/13/2841: 'Excessive pressure from here at the present moment would not, we think, bring about the best results'.
89. H. Wilson to T. O'Neill, 23 December 1968, NA, PREM/13/2841.
90. See, for instance, Military Aid to the Civil Authority in Northern Ireland, 13 December 1968, NA, PREM/13/2841.
91. Photocopy of DCAC minutes, 23 November 1968.
92. *Derry Journal*, 26 November 1968.
93. Cabinet conclusions, 2 December 1968, PRONI, CAB/4/1422; *Irish News*, 2 December 1968. On the People's Democracy's planning ahead of the march, see 'note by Nick', PRONI, D/3297/7.
94. *Belfast Telegraph*, 2 December 1968.
95. T. O'Neill, 'Crossroads' speech, 9 December 1968, in T. O'Neill, *The Autobiography of Terence O'Neill* (London: Hart-Davis, 1972), pp.145–8.
96. *Belfast Telegraph*, 16 December 1968.
97. *Derry Journal*, 13 December 1968; *Londonderry Sentinel*, 24 December 1968.
98. *Sunday Times*, 15 December 1968.

99. *Time*, 24 May 1963.
100. *Observer*, 15 December 1968.
101. McCafferty, *Nell*, p. 132.
102. *Derry Journal*, 20 December 1968.
103. Ibid.; P. Kerr, Derry Situation, 4 December 1968, PRONI, HA/32/2/26; *Derry Journal*, 10 December 1968; *Reality*, January 1969, DCCA, Bridget Bond Civil Rights Collection.
104. Photocopy of DCAC minutes, 12 December 1968.
105. Cabinet conclusions, 15 November 1968, PRONI, CAB/4/1415.
106. *Derry Journal*, 27 December 1968.
107. *Derry Journal*, 31 December 1968. Compare McCann's statement here with one of King's: 'The goal of the demonstrations in Selma...is to dramatize the existence of injustice'. King, 'Behind the Selma march'.
108. F. Gogarty, Notes on the PD march, [January 1969], PRONI, D/3253/3/8/1.
109. R. McGimpsey, Incidents at Guildhall Square, 14 January 1969, PRONI, HA/32/2/26; A. Kennedy to J. Hill, 22 January 1969, PRONI, HA/32/2/11.
110. C. Bateman, Note of a meeting with Lord Cameron, 20 August 1969, PRONI, CAB/9B/308/1.
111. W. Harrison, Report on events of 4 January 1969, 6 January 1969, PRONI, CAB/9B/312/5.
112. See, for instance, F. Gogarty to M. Farrell, 6 January 1969, PRONI, D/3253/3.
113. *Ramparts*, vol. 1, no. 2, PRONI, D/2464.
114. *Derry Journal*, 7 January 1969.
115. *Observer*, 5 January 1969.
116. *Londonderry Sentinel*, 8 January 1969.
117. Kennedy to Kerr, [November 1968].
118. *Derry Journal*, 7 January 1969.
119. *Ibid.*
120. G. Fitt's evidence to the Cameron Commission, 25 July 1969, PRONI, GOV/2/1/140.
121. *Derry Journal*, 7 January 1969.
122. L. Hill, *The Deacons for Defense: Armed Resistance and the Civil Rights Movement* (Chapel Hill, NC: University of North Carolina Press, 2004).
123. *Londonderry Sentinel*, 8 January 1969.
124. Wendt, '"They Finally Found Out"', p. 548.
125. Transcripts of 'Radio Free Derry', 10 and 11 January 1969, PRONI, HA/32/2/26.
126. *Derry Journal*, 7 January 1969.
127. S. Lynd, 'The New Left', *Annals of the American Academy of Political and Social Science*, 382, 1 (March 1969), pp. 64–72, p. 72; U. Meinhof, *Everybody Talks About the Weather...We Don't: The Writings of Ulrike Meinhof* trans. K. Bauer (New York, NY: Seven Stories Press, 2008), p. 42.
128. Transcripts of 'Radio Free Derry', 10 and 11 January 1969.
129. E. McCann, 'Who's Wrecking Civil Rights?' August 1969, PRONI, HA/32/2/28.
130. E. Burke, *The Works of the Right Honourable Edmund Burke, Volume 7*(London: F. and C. Rivington, 1803), p. 85.
131. Cabinet conclusions, 10 January 1969, PRONI, CAB/4/1426.
132. *Derry Journal*, 7 January 1969.
133. Strike call, 8 January 1969, PRONI, HA/32/2/26.
134. Statement regarding proposed strike, 8 January 1969, PRONI, HA/32/2/26; P. Kerr to J. Hill, 10 January 1969, PRONI, HA/32/2/26.
135. Transcript of 'Radio Free Derry', 11 January 1969; G. Fine, 'Rumor, Trust and Civil Society: Collective Memory and Cultures of Judgment', *Diogenes*, 54, 1 (February, 2007), pp. 5–18.
136. Photocopy of DCAC minutes, 10 January 1969; *Derry Journal*, 14 January 1969.
137. *Derry Journal*, 14 January 1969. Hume by this time had met with foreign pacifists such as Bob Overy. B. Overy to K. Boyle, 16 January 1969, PRONI, D/3297/7.
138. *Londonderry Sentinel*, 4 December 1968.
139. Memorandum by the Prime Minister, 14 January 1969, PRONI, CAB/4/1427.
140. Presidential news conference, 17 July 1963, http://www.jfklibrary.org/Research/Ready-Reference/Press-Conferences/News-Conference-58.aspx (last accessed 14 February 2011).
141. B. Meharg to J. Greeves, 27 January 1969, 28 January 1969, 31 January 1969 and 3 February 1969, PRONI.

6

To the Brink in Belfast

Nineteen sixty-seven was a quiet year in Belfast after the turmoil of 1966. RUC intelligence reports in July 1967 and January 1968 both stated that there was 'no immediate indication' of the IRA resuming militant action against Northern Ireland.[1] This was a reflection of the state of the organization. At a meeting on 29–30 August 1967, a gloomy picture was painted of the current situation: although there were 614 volunteers on the rolls, only 274 were effective; the army was broke, owing its staff members £274 and another £334 to individuals; and it appeared that it only had 'enough ammo. for one good job [and] a very limited amount of arms and explosives'.[2]

What was the reason for this disarray? The ongoing dispute between what may be called the traditionalists and modernizers in the Republican movement had something to do with it. Seán Mac Stíofáin was temporarily suspended from membership in the second half of 1966 because he had refused to distribute copies of the Sinn Féin newspaper, *The United Irishman*, in his command area. The offending issue contained a letter from Roy Johnston which criticized the saying of the rosary at Republican commemorations on the grounds that it was sectarian. Mac Stíofáin, like many IRA members a devout Catholic, believed that the Marxist Johnston's 'real target…was not sectarianism, but religion as such'.[3]

These events inevitably had their repercussions in Northern Ireland, including Belfast. Billy McMillen stated that 'strenuous efforts were being made to radicalize our membership who were still very reluctant to adapt to the unfamiliar role of political activists' and '[t]he Belfast Battalion Staff impressed on Headquarters the necessity for a happy blend of political agitation and military activity'.[4] McMillen's task was probably not made any easier by the fact that, as the IRA's Intelligence Officer, Mac Stíofáin decided to 'concentrate personally on the North', where he found Belfast 'on its toes' and seeing 'eye-to-eye on policy matters' with him.[5]

Paisleyism, on the other hand, was faring relatively well. While only thirteen congregations of the Free Presbyterian Church had been founded between 1951 and 1966, twelve more were added in the eighteen months that followed July 1966, a rate of one every six weeks. On the political front, Ian Paisley's wife, Eileen, topped the poll in a municipal election for the St George's Ward in Belfast in May 1967, although the two other candidates on her Protestant Unionist ticket were beaten by supporters of Terence O'Neill. A *Belfast Telegraph* poll published in December 1967 showed that 34 per cent of all Unionists 'usually' agreed with what Paisley said, while 44 per cent did not believe that he had deliberately tried to stir up bad feeling between Catholics and Protestants.[6]

A new ingredient was added to Northern Ireland's politics in 1967, however, which was to have an enormous influence on both Republicanism and Paisleyism and other loyalist groups. This was NICRA, which was set up in January 1967. Its aim was to campaign against what were seen as the worst abuses in Northern Ireland's political system: the gerrymandering of local authority boundaries, the restriction of the local government franchise to property owners and their spouses, discrimination in the allocation of council housing and public sector jobs and the Special Powers Act.[7] These were mainly, but not exclusively, Catholic grievances. Many Protestants, for example, were affected by the restriction of the local government franchise. Thus, while 31 per cent of Catholics in Belfast did not have a vote, neither did 22 per cent of Presbyterians, 18 per cent of Church of Ireland members and 13 per cent of members of other Protestant denominations.[8] Those in the NICRA coalition who wished to build bridges between the Catholic and Protestant working classes could take comfort from this and those who did not could use the fact to counter the charge that it was a purely Catholic/Nationalist/Republican pressure group.

I

Over twenty years later, William Craig, who had been Minister for Home Affairs in 1967, was still convinced that NICRA was a Republican front. 'To me', he told Peter Taylor, 'it was the beginning of a republican

campaign organized entirely by the IRA and it was much more significant than any previous campaign. It was a deliberate effort by the IRA
to play a bigger part in the politics of Northern Ireland and the Irish
Republic. Of course, it would exploit and use local figureheads where
it could, but I would have said quite categorically that it was the guiding
hand.'[9]

Although there is some evidence to support the claim that the
Republican movement in general and the IRA in particular were instru-
mental in forming NICRA,[10] this does not mean that it was, in Craig's
words, 'organized entirely by the IRA' which was its 'guiding hand'.
From its beginnings in 1967, NICRA was a coalition and its executive
consisted of Communists, Nationalists and people of no particular
political persuasion as well as Republicans.[11] With the passage of time,
moreover, other political groupings made their influence felt, notably
the People's Democracy. The Republicans certainly exploited NICRA,
but they did not control it even if, as McMillen claimed, they could
have done so.[12]

For the first eighteen months of its existence, NICRA was little more
than a pressure group and it only achieved salience in Northern
Ireland's politics when it moved into the streets.[13] Its iconic moment
came with the Derry march of 5 October 1968, and, as has been
explained elsewhere in this book, NICRA was nevertheless a minor
player in someone else's political theatre. The ensuing violence, in
McMillen's opinion, 'did more in a few hours to rock the tribal
Orange/Unionist Establishment, and did more for the minority in the
Six Counties than the IRA physical force campaigns had been able to do
in fifty years'.[14] In so doing, however, it confirmed the view among
many Protestants that the demand for 'civil rights' was little more than
a pretext for Catholics, and especially Republicans, to try and overthrow 'their' government by force. 'The situation is explosive', a brief
for British ministers warned, 'civil war is not impossible.'[15]

In Belfast, the most immediate consequence of the 5 October 1968
march was the emergence at Queen's University of what became the
People's Democracy. After the violence in Derry, the poet Seamus
Heaney detected 'embarrassed, indignant young Ulstermen and women
whose deep-grained conservatism of behaviour was outweighed by
a reluctant recognition of injustice'.[16] On 7 October 1968, the Joint
Action Committee, which had been created the year before to protest

against the ban on the university's Republican Club, was brought back to organize a march from Queen's to Belfast City Hall to take place two days later.[17] Paisley and his wife called upon the RUC Commissioner for Belfast on 8 October to draw his attention to the resentment which they claimed was felt by a number of citizens, and particularly those of Mrs Paisley's municipal constituents who lived in loyalist Sandy Row, near which the students' march was scheduled to pass. The Commissioner impressed upon the Paisleys that 'it was their duty as responsible citizens to do everything in their power to preserve the peace' and they promised to do so. Instead, Paisley promptly set about organizing a counter-demonstration. The police, fearing a violent clash between the two groups of protesters, chose to re-route the students' march.[18]

Having reluctantly accepted the police re-routing of their own march, the students discovered as they were approaching Donegall Square that the Paisleyites had switched the venue for their counter-demonstration to this space. Once again concerned about a possible violent clash between the two groups, the RUC refused to allow the students into the square. The angry students sat down in Linenhall Street and did not start leaving until the early evening, whereupon the Paisleyites also dispersed.[19] Not all the students went home. A group of fifty or so met in MacMordie Hall and set up a permanent protest group to campaign for social and political change. As Paul Arthur, a participant-observer, has written, 'What began as a small gathering of disenchanted students intent on voicing their criticisms of the organizers [of the march], the police and the counter-demonstrators grew into an emotional and intense mass meeting concerned with solving the fundamental problems of the divided community'.[20] 'Student Power', the university newspaper declared, 'had come to Belfast'.[21]

The meeting produced a six-point policy programme which closely mirrored that of NICRA. It also elected what Arthur describes as a 'faceless committee' of ten people with no known political affiliations. The title of the movement was deliberately chosen so as not to exclude those without connection to the university.[22] Kevin Boyle, a young lecturer popular with the students, subsequently admitted to an American interviewer in 1972 that its 'faceless committee' was in fact manipulated by political activists, something which is confirmed by notes in his private papers.[23] Leftists, such as Eamonn McCann's close comrade

Michael Farrell, had been looking for an issue that would serve as a 'bridge to involvement' for university students: civil rights had now given them it.[24] Farrell, who was teaching at a local college, was present at the first meeting and came to play an increasing role in People's Democracy.[25] Indeed, although he was not on the 'faceless committee', he was to become the face of People's Democracy.

Following the original clash between the student demonstrators and the Paisleyites, repeat performances regularly occurred over the next few weeks and months, with the police often in the unenviable position of trying to keep the two apart. On 16 October 1968, the People's Democracy belatedly made it to Donegall Square. 'Let me tell you', declared Boyle at the meeting which followed, 'there are many people in this city who feel that [now that] the students have got to the City Hall our marching is finished for Civil Rights. I would like to say from the platform today that they are very, very wrong'. Bernadette Devlin, a psychology undergraduate who had been elected on to the 'faceless committee', reached out to the Paisleyite counter-demonstrators in her speech. She called on 'the people across the street' 'to support us in demanding, not a political issue, not a sectarian issue, but a human issue'.[26] They did not. On 4 November 1968, after the police enforced a ban on another march to City Hall and People's Democracy responded with a sit-down protest, some Paisleyites assaulted several students. A group of Paisleyites then headed over to Queen's University and occupied Hamilton Hall – 'claiming' it 'as part of the Empire' – for several hours, before leaving under police escort. This, together with the aggressive behaviour of many police officers earlier in the day, had such an impact upon students that even an undergraduate who was a 'staunch believer in the principles of Unionism' had his 'faith in the RUC' brought to a 'rather low ebb'.[27]

Stormont did not at this stage regard the People's Democracy as being as much of a threat as the Derry movement. On 24 October 1968, when People's Democracy activists had occupied the Northern Irish House of Commons, the Speaker did not call in the police, the Minister of Education spoke to the students and a Unionist MP added his name to a declaration of civil rights.[28] This changed during December. Although a sizeable number of students wanted to give O'Neill the breathing space that he asked for in his televised address to Northern Ireland, Farrell was able to exploit participatory democracy and the

Christmas vacation to secure a vote in favour of marching from Belfast to Derry in the New Year.[29] The march was consciously modelled on the Selma-Montgomery marches which had in the basic narrative presented in the mass media restarted the stalled American civil rights movement.[30]

After the Burntollet ambush, the marchers complained bitterly that, when attacked, the police failed adequately to protect them, an opinion shared by a junior minister at the British Home Office.[31] The obvious answer to these charges – which, of course, the police strenuously denied – was that the marchers should have followed the proposed alternative route in the first place. Indeed, the independent inquiry which looked into this and other disturbances during the period concluded that the leaders of the march, the most prominent of whom was Farrell, saw it 'as a calculated martyrdom'.[32]

Distinguishing 'turning points' in history is a perilous task. However, Burntollet is a better candidate than many where the start of the Troubles is concerned. People's Democracy justly claimed to be non-sectarian, but Boyle, who was on the march, said later that he could still remember the depression he felt at one point on 'seeing the Catholic school children out all waving to us and the Protestant school not waving and how that, in effect, was the end of my innocence in the Northern Ireland conflict, and the real worries about sectarianism that I had kept down becoming clear'.[33] An anonymous welder from the shipyards of east Belfast, someone to whom People's Democracy wanted to reach out, wrote a letter to the *Belfast Telegraph* in which he explained that, although he had voted Labour for the past twenty years, 'the Kevins, the Michaels, the Eamonns, the Bernadettes, etc.' had converted him 'from a very moderate, tolerant "live and let live" Protestant into a near Paisleyite'. This was a view which, he claimed, was shared by all his moderate, Protestant friends in the shipyards.[34]

This created something of a dilemma for the IRA. Seán Garland, one of the heroes of the border campaign, told his Belfast audience at the annual Easter Rising commemoration on 6 April 1969,

> Unless and until the NICRA is able to re-create that unity of purpose and discipline of action as the Protestant working-classes of this city...showed in the early part of this century and as they again showed in 1932 when Orangemen and Republicans fought shoulder to shoulder against their common enemy [i.e. the Outdoor Relief riots] there can be no hope of success.

Yet soon after Burntollet, on 19 January 1969, the Coiste Seasta, a powerful sub-committee of Sinn Féin dominated by the IRA, had agreed that 'it was vital that 15 radical marchers be elected to the Executive of NICRA at its AGM', thereby encouraging the very phenomenon which working class Protestants like the anonymous welder found so objectionable.[35] The dilemma was never resolved.

II

Throughout January 1969, O'Neill's position was becoming increasingly insecure. He opted to respond to the renewed violence in Derry with concessions and a crackdown: a commission of inquiry and a 'firmer use of police power'. Most of his Cabinet colleagues saw the commission as a 'breathing-space' that should be used to press on with the existing policy on local government restructuring and franchise reform. But Brian Faulkner, the Minister of Commerce, argued that it would be 'regarded as an abdication by the Government' and that 'a more direct approach would be to agree as a Cabinet to universal adult suffrage'.[36] Away from the Cabinet table, Craig also took the line that setting up the inquiry showed a 'lack of confidence', and he put down a motion asking the government to resist outside interference. With his main rival making ground, Faulkner decided the moment had come to move against O'Neill, and so he too left the Cabinet and made his criticisms public. Another Cabinet minister also resigned and O'Neill stumbled into another backbench revolt.[37] The Prime Minister claimed that the rebels had gone to the country by issuing a manifesto in Portadown, so he chose to follow them by calling an election.[38] O'Neill once more sought to mobilize popular support in order to strengthen his political position.[39]

The election, which took place on 24 February 1969, was therefore in large part a plebiscite for or against O'Neill. Thanks to the decentralized nature of the Unionist Party, pro- and anti-O'Neill Unionists stood against one another in some constituencies. There were six such contests in the sixteen Belfast seats and the pro- and anti-O'Neill candidates won three each. The three won by the Prime Minister's opponents (St Anne's, Shankill and Woodvale) were all in west Belfast and, significantly perhaps, they all abutted on to overwhelmingly Catholic areas and were predominantly working class.[40]

O'Neill hoped to win some Catholic votes and thus we find him campaigning in Oldpark, a seat which was 40 per cent Catholic and where the sitting member for the previous eleven years had been Vivian Simpson of the NILP. On 20 February 1969, the *Belfast Newsletter* carried a story under the headline: 'He made her house seem like a castle', which referred to a statement by Mrs Mary McNulty of Jamaica Street, whose home O'Neill and the local Unionist candidate, Alderman Joseph Cairns, had visited on the previous day. 'As long as there are men like Captain Terence O'Neill and Alderman Cairns in the Unionist Party', Mrs McNulty told the newspaper, '…then I'll vote Unionist.'[41]

Jamaica Street was in Ardoyne, a predominantly Catholic district bordering on the Crumlin Road, and its population included a number of Republican supporters and activists who were put out by Mrs McNulty's remarks. According to Joe Graham, who was an IRA volunteer with connections in the area, 'some irate neighbours who didn't seem to share Mary's fondness for Unionist ass kissing, redecorated her "palace" with tar and feathers and increased the ventilation by breaking all the windows'. A petition condemning the visit, which seems to have been the idea of Graham and another IRA volunteer who lived in the area, Martin Meehan, was circulated and attracted 106 signatures out of the 131 residents of the street. In view of what had happened to Mrs McNulty's house, it is noteworthy that as many as twenty-five people refused to sign precisely because they disapproved of it.[42] Such independence would become rare in the years that followed.

Paisley's newly-created Protestant Unionist Party only contested two seats in Belfast, both in the mainly Protestant east of the city. Its candidate came second in Bloomfield, beating the NILP into third place, but the positions were reversed in Victoria, where Major Bunting ended up bottom of the poll. Bunting and Paisley had been sentenced to three months in jail on 27 January 1969 for their conduct in Armagh the previous November, but the latter chose to sign a bail bond pending his appeal and was quickly released (although not before a riot similar to that which had occurred when he was previously incarcerated in 1966). Bunting, who was fasting in protest against his sentence, chose to remain in jail until he too was released to fight the election. On 25 March 1969, however, both men returned to prison after dropping their appeals.[43]

Five days later, at 3:53 am on 30 March 1969, an explosion occurred at the Lisnabreny sub-power station at Castlereagh in the eastern suburbs of Belfast causing £500,000 worth of damage.[44] This was followed, during the course of the next month, by four other major attacks on public utilities, including the Belfast water-supply pipes from the Silent Valley reservoir in the Mourne Mountains to the south-east and Lough Neagh to the north-west. Paisley's newspaper, the *Protestant Telegraph*, had no doubts as to the identity of those responsible. 'This is the first act of sabotage perpetrated by the IRA since the murderous campaign of 1956', it declared.[45] Although 1,000 B-Specials were mobilized to guard key installations, the Northern Ireland Government felt this was not enough and asked for British troops, too. This request was granted and Home Secretary James Callaghan told the Labour Cabinet on 24 April 1969 that although it was not yet possible to say who was behind the explosions, it was known that 'the Irish Republican Army was now dominated by a Communist element and that the civil rights organization contained a mischievous fringe of extremists'.[46]

From the outset, however, it was suggested that suspects other than the usual ones were responsible. On 31 March 1969, for example, the *Belfast Newsletter* received an anonymous telephone call blaming the UVF. The RUC received a similar call two days later.[47] Unfortunately, we know next to nothing about the size and state of the UVF in 1969 other than that it was commanded by a man named Samuel 'Bo' McClelland, who took over from 'Gusty' Spence when the latter was jailed in 1966.[48] Spence himself told Taylor that UVF men were involved in the explosions. One of them, Thomas McDowell, figures on the UVF Roll of Honour as a result of his subsequent death in October 1969 when he was accidentally electrocuted while attempting to blow up another electricity sub-station in the Republic of Ireland. But McDowell was not only a member of the UVF; he was also a member of Paisley's UPV and a Free Presbyterian. Indeed, according to the key witness in the subsequent trials, Samuel Stevenson who turned Queen's evidence, others involved in the explosions were also members of the UPV, including Robert Murdock, one of those charged with Noel Doherty in 1966 for attempting to obtain explosives. Referring to the attacks on public utilities in March and April 1969, Stevenson told the police: 'These jobs were done to cause confusion and get rid of O'Neill'.[49] As in 1966, there was no firm evidence linking Paisley himself with these events, but once more some of those who followed him were clearly prepared to use violent methods in order to obtain their objectives.

The explosions were not the only contribution to the deterioration of the situation in April 1969. Serious violence broke out once more in Derry on 19 April 1969, and for the first time since the civil rights movement had emerged, it spread to Belfast. The IRA fire-bombed ten post offices in the city on the night of 20/21 April 1969 in an attempt to draw the RUC away from Derry[50] and on the following two nights there was rioting on the Falls Road. On 21 April there was a march from the recently built Divis Tower block to the Springfield Road RUC barracks, where a petition against police brutality in Derry was delivered. After the marchers had returned to the Divis Tower for an open-air meeting, a section of the crowd broke away and attacked the nearby Hastings Street police station with stones and bottles. During the course of the rioting the local police commander, District Inspector Frank Lagan, one of the few Catholics who had attained a high rank in the RUC, was beaten up by a group of youths and had to seek refuge in a private house.[51]

Both the march and the meeting were organized by NICRA and People's Democracy. But there was also another participant in the shape of the Belfast Housing Action Committee (BHAC). This organization was, in fact, a Republican front, although this was hotly denied at the time.[52] Its main purpose was to agitate for improvement in the undeniably poor housing conditions in west Belfast and it had recently installed a family, whose own house had been seriously damaged by fire, as squatters in an empty flat in the Divis Tower while campaigning for them to be properly re-housed. Such action was in accordance with what headquarters in Dublin was then advocating, but, in the words of one member of the BHAC, events in Derry enabled it to extend its efforts as 'part of a larger strategy to help alleviate the struggle against [the] RUC in Derry who were attacking and oppressing the nationalist people on a daily basis'.[53] Hence the BHAC's involvement in the protest march on 21 April 1969. This tactic of relieving the situation in Derry by creating a diversion in Belfast was tried again by Republicans, among others, in August 1969 with fatal consequences.

Republicans also took advantage of an outbreak of violence in Ardoyne the following month. This revolved around the Edenderry

Inn, a public house with a somewhat unsavoury reputation on the corner of Hooker Street and the Crumlin Road. Trouble erupted between the police and patrons of the establishment on the night of 16 May 1969 and continued over the following two nights. These clashes, which drew in other residents of the area, involved baton charges and the throwing of stones, bottles, pieces of iron grating and the occasional petrol bomb. The RUC originally played down these incidents as being 'in the nature of "pub brawls"', but they soon developed into something more than that.[54] Following a further violent confrontation between the police and rioters on the night of 23 May 1969, considerable anger was expressed by some residents over what they regarded as the heavy-handed conduct of the police. One even thought the area could become another Bogside, in the sense that the police would be excluded and replaced by local vigilantes.[55] Feelings were such that two meetings were held in nearby Butler Street on 24 and 25 May 1969 and a Citizens Action Committee was formed. Republicans spoke at the meetings and two IRA volunteers, Joe Graham and Tony Cosgrove, were elected to the committee. A number of men, mainly youths, began to patrol the area, and it seemed that the police were adopting a lower profile.[56]

On 29 May 1969, members of the committee went to see the RUC City Commissioner and his deputy. According to one of them, Father Marcellus Gillespie, a priest from the neighbouring Holy Cross Church, Cosgrove and Graham tried to get the police 'to admit that they were guilty to some extent in the trouble'. Graham admits that he wanted to provoke a dispute which 'would result in the representatives of the committee walking out in feigned disgust', but goes on to say that 'the RUC beat us to the punch' by inviting Father Marcellus to a private tête-à-tête after which he left the meeting in a hurry, telling Graham and his companion later, 'look lads, you are all IRA men and I am not going to be used. I am resigning my membership of the committee as of this moment'. Father Marcellus's own account does not mention this incident, but it is clear that he did not approve of Graham and Cosgrove who, he claimed, were later told by the locals 'to get out of the district and stay out'.[57]

Graham eventually admitted that '[t]here was an element of political agitation involved' in setting up the Action Committee, but some Ardoyne residents had worked this out for themselves at the time. A 'Peaceful Citizen' complained in the *Irish News* of 26 May 1969 that it was unrepresentative and concluded, '[i]t is time that the people banded together to tell this new committee of people who seem to be running things in the vicinity, to mind their own business and let us get back to normal lives'. This prompted a reply from Rebecca McGlade, a Republican on the NICRA executive, criticizing 'Peaceful Citizen' for concealing his or her identity. To which the latter retorted that Mrs McGlade 'knows very well that in an area such as Ardoyne that anyone who speaks out against an element such as that which caused all the damage to property in the area is classed as a "traitor" and "RUC tout" and is a marked person'.[58]

There were signs of increasing loyalist militancy in these days, too. Between 21 April and the end of May 1969 the RUC recorded some dozen incidents of intimidation against Catholics either living or working in mainly Protestant areas. Two families actually left their homes on the night of 21/22 April after threats that they would be burned out and letters were sent to three residents of two neighbouring streets, each containing a live 9 mm round and containing an order to leave their homes or face the prospect of being shot dead.[59] Many of these threats purported to come from the UVF, although whether that organization was responsible or whether its name was appropriated for greater effect is not known.

On 1 May 1969, it was announced that a Shankill Defence Association (SDA) had been set up 'to secure better conditions for Protestants scheduled for rehousing...and to defend loyalist lives and property after the threats last week of Falls Road rioters'.[60] Its chair was to be a 39-year-old 'manager's agent', John McKeague, a member of the UPV who had been arrested in a fracas when the police came to take Paisley to jail on 28 January 1969. The following month, McKeague had stood, unsuccessfully, as the Protestant Unionist Party candidate for the Victoria Ward in a council by-election. By the time he was elected chairman of the SDA, however, his relationship with Paisley seems to have been under some strain.[61]

While these developments were taking place, there had been a change of government in Northern Ireland. The February election had not produced the decisive outcome which O'Neill had hoped for and his party was still riven with dissension, notably over the early introduction of one-man-one-vote in local elections. His cousin, James Chichester-Clark, resigned over the issue on 23 April 1969 and five days later O'Neill, unable to guarantee the passage of the reform, followed suit. Bonfires were lit on the Shankill Road and the Union Jack was flown over Paisley's church in the Ravenhill Road.[62]

Joe Cahill, a veteran Republican who had narrowly escaped the fate of his young commanding officer, Tom Williams, who was hanged for the killing of a policeman in 1942, later made a revealing comment to his biographer. 'The one person who realised that the nationalist people could be won over with a few reforms', he said, 'was Terence O'Neill... I suppose we should be thankful to people like Paisley and the others who did not want to see any reforms implemented. They were responsible for O'Neill being ousted'.[63] Even if one disagrees with Cahill's assessment, his view was typical of those Republicans who feared that reform would mean the end of their preferred revolution.

O'Neill was succeeded by Chichester-Clark, who appointed Faulkner, but not Craig or any of the more outspoken opponents of the former Prime Minister, to his Cabinet.[64] On 6 May 1969, an amnesty was announced for all those charged or convicted as a result of political protests. Paisley and Bunting were released from jail, and pending prosecutions of leading figures in the civil rights movement such as Gerry Fitt, Bernadette Devlin and Austin Currie, the young Nationalist MP for East Tyrone, were dropped.[65] There was a temporary easing of the situation, but it did not last for long.

III

On 18 May 1969, NICRA issued an 'ultimatum' to the Unionist Government stating that unless the latter announced an acceptable timetable of reform within six weeks it would continue with its civil disobedience campaign. Since the timetable was expected to include the abandonment of the Public Order (Amendment) Bill, which was designed to deal with the disruptive tactics previously used by civil rights activists and which was then slowly and painfully proceeding through Stormont, together with the abolition of the B-Specials, the outlook was not particularly hopeful.[66] It therefore came as no surprise when, as from 28 June 1969 onwards, marches were again staged in many parts of the province.

Just over a week later the head of the RUC's Special Branch, County Inspector Douglas Johnston, sent a special assessment of the civil rights movement to the Inspector-General. His was a rather more sophisticated analysis than that of those who, like Craig and Paisley, equated NICRA with the IRA. Johnston felt that recent attendance figures at marches suggested that they had 'lost their steam', and if it was not to wane or founder it must necessarily become more militant, with 'a new crop of impossible demands'. (He could have added that the harsh treatment meted out to some demonstrators by the police and the courts were also giving activists plenty of additional grievances.) Although there had been 'a Protestant sprinkling of idealists and do-gooders' in the movement at the beginning, it had now 'crystallized into the familiar "green" composed of Republicans and Nationalists but still...containing a vociferous minority grouping of Trotskyites or Revolutionary Socialists' and it was against this background that the present struggle for power could be seen.[67]

As far as the Republican movement was concerned, Johnston did not think that it approved of People's Democracy, despite the latter's support for a thirty-two county socialist republic. Basing himself on an internal strategy document, he said that the Republican movement emphasized the importance of short-term agitation in favour of democracy, civil rights, job discrimination and security, the aim being to obtain maximum concessions while Harold Wilson was still in 10 Downing Street. Demonstrations should have no party political content and be non-violent. In the medium term, it was hoped to build a six-county movement based on workers, farmers, the self-employed and professionals, irrespective of religion, in order to undermine the popular basis of Unionist rule. No long-term objective was cited, but Johnston did say that, under the influence of his namesake, Roy Johnston, the Republican movement had become a Connollyite socialist movement using infiltration, manipulation and any alliance which served its purpose for the time being in order to undermine and destroy the existing system of government.[68]

One of the more revealing comments in Johnston's assessment concerned Paisley and the symbiotic relationship that he had with the civil rights movement. 'If the Reverend gentleman could only be persuaded to leave it to the Government and police...', Johnston complained, 'the Civil Rights attendances would probably continue to fall away' as the movement fed and thrived on such opposition. So, of course, did Paisleyism, which meant that 'the Reverend gentleman' was unlikely to oblige. What is clearly missing from this assessment is any recognition that the police themselves were part of the production of violence and not merely caught between the extremists.[69]

Sectarian tension was heightened as a result of the 'Twelfth'. This was not an automatic outcome, but rather the product of conscious efforts on the part of certain individuals and groups. The almost entirely Catholic Unity Flats complex at the bottom of the Shankill Road was surrounded by police after the residents had showered the passing Orangemen with bottles and stones. In Ardoyne, an Irish Tricolour was displayed in a window of the Edenderry Inn as Orange marchers were returning from their rally in south Belfast up the Crumlin Road. According to a policeman present, the loyalist crowd on the southern side of the road 'became incensed and began to shout and point in the direction of [the Edenderry Inn]'. Members of the marching lodge tried to break ranks, but the stewards kept them moving and the police prevented the loyalists from crossing over the Crumlin Road to the Catholic side. The police, who had earlier requested the manager to lock the doors to prevent any trouble, had to break into the premises in order to arrest the alleged miscreants.[70]

Both District Inspector Shaw Montgomery, the policeman in charge of Belfast District C (which included Ardoyne), and Father Marcellus thought they detected a change in the atmosphere after 12 July 1969. Beforehand, they felt, the trouble in the area had been mainly between some of the Catholics in the Hooker Street area and the police, but afterwards it became much more between people from the two communities.[71]

Just how acute tensions had become in Belfast was shown by the events of the weekend of 2-3 August 1969. As the name suggests, the marching season in Northern Ireland is not confined to 12 July, and on 2 August 1969 the Junior Orange Lodge of No. 1 District marched down the Shankill Road towards the railway station, on their way to an outing in nearby Carrickfergus. This took them past the Unity Flats. The SDA had provided an 'escort' for the young marchers in case there was an attack by the residents. There was no disorder while the procession was passing, but shortly afterwards some 200 Protestants tried to enter the flats and there was stone-throwing and some fighting in the courtyard.[72]

Real trouble broke out during the late afternoon and early evening, when the marchers were returning from their outing. A large crowd came down from the Shankill inflamed by inaccurate rumours that the children had been attacked on their way to the station in the morning. Prevailing notions of manliness meant that men were required to protect children. The police sought to cordon off the flats and some entered the courtyards. This move backfired, however, and fighting broke out between the residents and the police. During the course of the fracas a 61-year-old man, Patrick Corry, was batoned by the police; he subsequently died some four months later of his injuries.[73]

The Junior Orange Lodge returned at about 7 pm. Once again there was no violence against them, but after the parents had collected their children, a hard core of would-be vigilantes – described by one policeman as 'hooligans, agitators and criminals' – remained behind. They launched a full-scale attack on the Unity Flats, which was repulsed by the police, who then drove them back up the Shankill Road. The fighting went on in this area until midnight. Little thanks was shown to the RUC by the residents of the Unity Flats, who continued to throw stones at the police and the fighting there went on until 3 or 3:30 am.[74]

Deprived of their prey in the Unity Flats, the crowd on the Shankill Road resorted to widespread looting and vandalism. The *Irish Times* described the scene on the morning of 3 August 1969: the Shankill 'looked...as though it had been blitzed. Hundreds of windows in shops and private houses were smashed and the contents of shop windows looted. The roadway was covered with broken glass, stones, bricks, fragments of paving stones and pieces of iron which had been thrown during the riots'.[75]

There was also rioting on the Crumlin Road on the night of 2 August 1969. Following a report that a crowd was moving up Hooker Street to the Crumlin Road, a small group of police was sent to the area. After dark a rival crowd appeared, led by two men carrying Union Jacks and shouting 'let's wreck the fucking pope heads'. Although there were only six policemen and despite a shower of stones, bottles and sticks, they managed to force the Protestants up the Crumlin Road and into the side streets on the south side. After reinforcements had arrived, the police were able to persuade a larger Protestant crowd to disperse. By then, however, a Catholic crowd had gathered and a barricade was erected across Hooker Street. At about 11:30 pm people emerged from behind this barricade and began hurling petrol bombs and other missiles at the police. The latter, led by an armoured car and followed by Land Rovers, made baton charges into Hooker Street to break up the crowd.[76]

Following further rioting on both the Shankill and the Crumlin Road on the night of 3 August 1969, the SDA issued a statement in which it said that, while it deplored looting, the police had shown partiality towards the Catholics and, as a result: '[w]e make it clear that the police are no longer friends of Ulster Loyalists and can never expect our help again'. Indeed, McKeague asked the authorities to send B-Specials to keep order on the Shankill Road, which they did.[77]

The *Irish News* described the disturbances in Belfast over the weekend of 2-3 August 1969 as the 'first major clashes between Protestants and Catholics since...1935'.[78] This was no exaggeration and, in addition, the police were becoming more aggressive. During the course of rioting in Ardoyne on the night of 4 August 1969, for example, a young man, Neil Somers, was knocked down and badly injured by a police Land Rover. Former Constable Spenser Cusack told the Scarman Tribunal that it was the vehicle in which he was riding which struck Somers. Moreover, it had been done deliberately and one of his colleagues had screamed 'Run the bastards down' as they turned into the street where the incident occurred. This was denied by other police witnesses and the accident was attributed to another Land Rover altogether,[79] but it is significant that when Martin Meehan was arrested on the same night, he was so badly beaten up that he had to remain in hospital for a week and came out still walking with the aid of a stick, although the police claimed that he had fallen and that his injuries were 'a result of hitting his head on the kerb'.[80]

An increase in intimidation came with the rioting, and many families living in the 'wrong' neighbourhoods were forced to leave their homes. The *Belfast Telegraph* reported on 5 August 1969 that over two dozen Catholic families had been forced out of Protestant areas and that seven out of seventeen Protestant families in Hooker Street alone had signed up for new houses. There even appears to have been some semi-formal arrangement between bodies on either side of the communal divide to 'swap' houses, although this can only have provided limited consolation to those driven out of homes in which some of them had lived in peace alongside their neighbours for years.[81]

IV

To what extent was there any organization behind this rioting? It is interesting that the *Irish News* routinely referred to the Protestants who attacked Unity Flats on 2 August 1969 as 'Paisleyites'.[82] Although those involved may well have been influenced by his anti-Catholic, anti-Republican and anti-Communist rhetoric, there is no evidence that Paisley had anything to do with organizing the rioting. Indeed, he held an open-air service close to the Lower Shankill during the afternoon of Sunday, 3 August 1969, in which he asked people to go home. His appeal had little effect, however. Moreover, the same *Irish News* reported that Major Bunting was on the Crumlin Road that night, appealing to the Protestant crowd to go home. He was booed and stoned for his pains.[83]

On the other hand, it is clear that McKeague and the SDA were active on the Shankill Road. His attentions then switched to the Crumlin Road. When asked why at the Scarman Tribunal, he replied that he had SDA members living in the area 'and they requested us to come up because over a long period of time they had been subject to abuse verbally and otherwise coming from the Hooker Street/Herbert Street area'. He admitted that there was 'some hostility against us' at the beginning, 'but as time wore on and people realised what was materializing, what was building up, they later came and apologized to me and thanked us for being there'. McKeague added that the membership of the SDA rose to 2,000 during this period.[84] As for UVF involvement, we know nothing.

When it comes to what was happening in the Catholic areas, we return to the IRA. It seems that IRA volunteers were placed on defensive duty in Ardoyne and the Unity Flats in July 1969.[85] Jim Sullivan, the Belfast IRA's second-in-command, was spotted by the police in the flats on 2 August 1969 and he evidently arranged for the delivery of a vanload of pick handles later in the day, rather to the disappointment of the future Provisional, Gerry Bradley, then only 15 years old, who had hoped for guns.[86] In Ardoyne, Meehan and Graham were active and Gerry Adams has recorded that '[w]hen a defence committee was set up in Ardoyne, I and other activists from outside the area went there regularly in solidarity with local activists'.[87]

McMillen later admitted that 'heavy pressure was being exerted on the Belfast Battalion Staff to introduce weapons into the situation'.

They were reluctant to do so, however, because 'we realized that the meagre armaments at our disposal were hopelessly inadequate to meet the requirements of the situation and that the use of firearms by us would only serve to justify the use of greater force against the people by the forces of the Establishment and increase the danger of sectarian pogroms'.[88]

One of the principal complaints against the then IRA leadership by those who set up the Provisional IRA was precisely that it did nothing to remedy this situation. According to Ruairí Ó Brádaigh, one of the founders of the Provisionals, there had been a meeting in Dublin in May 1969 at which he had suggested setting up vigilante groups to keep 'pro-British elements out of the Catholic areas', on the grounds that it was the 'height of irresponsibility and madness to have the pressure continue from the civil rights movement knowing where it was going to lead and being unable to meet the logical consequences'. Cathal Goulding allegedly replied that 'it was up to the official forces of the British Army and the RUC to defend the people'.[89] It is hard to believe that Goulding would have made such a remark. As another account of what is probably the same meeting implies, it is more likely that he had not given the matter much thought.[90] Perhaps he should have done so, as it was the Belfast IRA which took the fateful decision which produced the Belfast riots of August 1969 and not some loyalist conspiracy.

NOTES

1. RUC Security Intelligence Review, 14 July 1967, Belfast, Public Record Office of Northern Ireland (PRONI), HA/32/1/1378B; RUC Security Intelligence Appreciation, 3 January 1968, PRONI, HA/32/1/1378B.
2. B. Hanley, *The IRA: A Documentary History 1916–2005* (Dublin: Gill & Macmillan, 2010), p. 150; B. Hanley and S. Millar, *The Lost Revolution: The Story of the Official IRA and the Workers' Party* (Dublin, Penguin Ireland, 2009), p. 622.
3. S. Mac Stíofáin, *Memoirs of a Revolutionary* (Edinburgh: Gordon Cremonesi, 1975), p. 96; R. Johnston, *A Century of Endeavour: A Biographical and Autobiographical View of the Twentieth Century in Ireland* (Carlow: Tyndall Publications, 2003), p. 196.
4. L. McMillen, 'The Role of the IRA in the North from 1962 to 1969', in *Liam McMillen: Separatist, Socialist, Republican, Respol Pamphlet*, No. 21 (Dublin: Sinn Féin, n.d.), pp. 7–8.
5. Mac Stíofáin, *Memoirs*, p. 101.
6. S. Bruce, *Paisley: Religion and Politics in Northern Ireland* (Oxford: Oxford University Press, 2007), p. 89; *Belfast Telegraph*, 3 May 1967; *Belfast Telegraph*, 16 May 1967; *Belfast Telegraph*, 18 May 1967; *Belfast Telegraph*, 12 December 1967; *Belfast Telegraph*, 15 December 1967.

7. *Irish Democrat*, March 1967.
8. I. Budge and C. O'Leary, *Belfast: Approach to Crisis: A Study of Belfast Politics, 1613–1970* (London: Macmillan, 1973), p. 178.
9. P. Taylor, *Loyalists* (London, Bloomsbury, 2000 edn.), p. 52.
10. *Tuairisc*, August 1966; *Irish Democrat*, January 1967; Johnston, *Century of Endeavour*, pp. 197–201 and 231; C. McCluskey, *Up Off Their Knees: A Commentary on the Civil Rights Movement in Northern Ireland* (Dublin: Conn McCluskey and Associates, 1989), p. 104; McMillen, 'The Role of the IRA', p. 8.
11. There was even a Unionist for a while, but he did not last long. McCluskey, *Up Off Their Knees*, p. 106.
12. McMillen, 'The Role of the IRA', p. 8.
13. NICRA, *We Shall Overcome... The History of the Struggle for Civil Rights in Northern Ireland, 1968-78* (Belfast: NICRA, 1978), p. 11; E. Stewart, 'What Is NICRA?', Belfast, Linen Hall Library, NICRA Archive Box 2.
14. McMillen, 'The Role of the IRA', pp. 9–10.
15. Northern Ireland: Note by Officials, October 1968, London, National Archives (NA), PREM/13/2847.
16. *The Listener*, 24 October 1968.
17. *Belfast Telegraph*, 9 October 1968.
18. List of principal meetings and other events connected with the Paisleyite movement during the month of October 1968, 2 December 1968, PRONI, CAB/9/B/300/3.
19. Ibid.
20. P. Arthur, *The People's Democracy 1968-73* (Belfast: Blackstaff Press, 1974), pp. 30–1.
21. *Gown*, 22 October 1968.
22. Arthur, *People's Democracy*, pp. 30–1.
23. W. Van Voris, *Violence in Ulster: An Oral Documentary* (Amherst, MA: University of Massachusetts Press, 1975), p. 74; Untitled draft speech to swing People's Democracy behind contesting the February 1969 Stormont elections, [n.d.], PRONI, D/3297/1.
24. *Irish Militant*, October 1967; *Black Dwarf*, 27 January 1969.
25. Security Service memorandum, 18 February 1969, NA, PREM 13/2842; A. Barnett, 'Discussion on the Strategy of People's Democracy', *New Left Review*, May–June 1969.
26. Speeches made at meeting of People's Democracy at Belfast City Hall, 16 October 1968, PRONI, HA/32/2/28; *Gown*, 22 October 1968.
27. *Gown – March Supplement*, 5 November 1968.
28. *Belfast Telegraph*, 25 October 1968.
29. 'A former supporter of PD' to K. Boyle, 10 December 1968, PRONI, D/3297/1; *QUBIST*, 12 December 1968, PRONI, D/3297/3; Arthur, *People's Democracy*, pp. 36–9.
30. K. Boyle to J. Heaney, [n.d.], PRONI, D/3297/1.
31. Egan and McCormack, *Burntollet*, pp. 26–7 and 41–4; Lord Stonham minute, 5 January 1969, NA, CJ/3/74.
32. Government of Northern Ireland, *Disturbances in Northern Ireland: Report of the Commission Appointed by the Governor of Northern Ireland (Cameron Report)* (Belfast, HMSO, 1969), p. 47.
33. Van Voris, *Violence in Ulster*, p. 85.
34. *Belfast Telegraph*, 14 January 1969. Kevin Boyle was warned by a friend that for 'the average liberal Prod' 'PD is exclusively QUB, is mainly Catholic [and] republican'. J. Teasey to K. Boyle, [January 1969], PRONI, D/3297/7.
35. S. Swann, *Official Irish Republicanism 1962 to 1972* (Raleigh, NC: Lulu, 2007), pp. 269 and 271.
36. Cabinet conclusions, 15 January 1969, PRONI, CAB/4/1427.
37. *Belfast Telegraph*, 27 January 1969; *Belfast Telegraph*, 29 January 1969.
38. *Belfast Telegraph*, 4 February 1969.
39. *Belfast Newsletter*, 4 February 1969
40. Detailed election results for the Belfast area can be found in S. Elliott, *Northern Ireland Parliamentary Election Results 1921–1972* (Chichester: Political Reference Publications, 1973), pp. 36–50. See also F. W. Boal and R. H. Buchanan, 'The 1969 Northern Ireland election', *Irish Geography*, 6, 1, 1969, pp. 78–84.
41. *Belfast Newsletter*, 20 February 1969.

42. J. Graham, *'Show Me the Man': The Authorised Biography of Martin Meehan* (Belfast: Rushlight Publications, 2008), pp. 32–3; *Irish News*, 21 February 1969; *Irish News*, 22 February 1969.
43. *Irish News*, 26 January 1969; *Irish News*, 30 January 1969; *Irish News*, 31 January 1969; E. Moloney, *Paisley: From Demagogue to Democrat?* (Dublin: Poolbeg Press, 2008), pp. 163 and 169.
44. *Belfast Newsletter*, 31 March 1969.
45. D. Boulton, *The UVF 1966–73: An Anatomy of Loyalist Rebellion* (Dublin: Torc Books, 1973), p. 92.
46. *Belfast Newsletter*, 1 April 1969; Cabinet conclusions, 20 April 1969, PRONI, CAB/4/1435; Cabinet conclusions, 24 April 1969, NA, CAB/128/44.
47. *Belfast Newsletter*, 1 April 1969; Belfast No. 24 B, Belfast, McClay Library, Scarman Belfast exhibits, Schedule 1 (Belfast B). 'Belfast B' refers to one of the six police districts (A–F) into which Belfast was divided at this time.
48. R. Garland, *Gusty Spence* (Belfast: Blackstaff Press, 2001), p. 108; J. Cusack and H. McDonald, *UVF* (Dublin, Poolbeg, 1997), p. 21. McClelland is not even mentioned in other histories of the UVF or loyalist paramilitarism in general, such as Boulton, *The UVF*, and Taylor, *Loyalists*.
49. Taylor, *Loyalists*, p. 61; Cusack and McDonald, *UVF*, pp. 28–30; http:www.bebo.com/Profile.jsp?MemberID=7657546648&ShowSims=Y (last accessed 23 March 2011); Statement of S. Stevenson, 1 November 1969, PRONI, BELF/1/1/2/230/2, Statement of S. Stevenson, [n.d.], PRONI, BELF/1//1/2/229/21; Statement of R. Murdock, 6 July 1966, PRONI, BELF/1/1/2/214/28.
50. McMillen, 'The Role of the IRA', p. 10; *Irish News*, 22 April 1969.
51. *Belfast Telegraph*, 22 April 1969; *Irish News*, 22 April 1969.
52. Both Gerry Adams and Joe Graham name Republicans involved in the BHAC: G. Adams, *Before the Dawn: An Autobiography* (London: Heinemann, 1996), p. 83; J. Graham, *'Show Me The Man'*, p. 16. A. Doran's letter in the *Irish News*, 18 April 1969.
53. Graham, *'Show Me The Man'*, p. 28.
54. JIC(A)(69)(UWG), 20 May 1969, NA, PREM/13/2843; RUC report, 27 May 1969, PRONI, HA/32/2/7.
55. *Belfast Telegraph*, 23 May 1969.
56. RUC report, 27 May 1969; *Sunday News*, 25 May 1969; *Irish News*, 28 May 1969.
57. *Irish News*, 30 May 1969; M. Gillespie's evidence to the Scarman Tribunal, 27 April 1970, Belfast, McClay Library, Scarman minutes of evidence, pp. 33–5; M. Gillespie's evidence to the Scarman Tribunal, 28 April 1970, p. 23; Graham, *'Show Me The Man'*, pp. 35–6.
58. *Irish News*, 26 May 1969; *Irish News*, 29 May 1969; *Irish News*, 1 June 1969. Slogans threatening RUC informers had already appeared on Ardoyne walls and gables along with exhortations to join the IRA. *Belfast Telegraph*, 24 May 1969.
59. Belfast No. 24 B, Scarman Belfast exhibits, Schedule 1 (Belfast B).
60. *Belfast Telegraph*, 1 May 1969.
61. *Belfast News Letter*, 29 March 1969; *Belfast Telegraph*, 13 February 1969; J, McKeague's evidence to the Scarman Tribunal, 18 May 1971, p. 37; J. McKeague's evidence to the Scarman Tribunal, 21 May 1971, pp. 5–6 and 11–12.
62. *Irish News*, 29 April 1969.
63. B. Anderson, *Joe Cahill: A Life in the IRA* (Dublin: O'Brien Press, 2002), p. 166.
64. Cabinet conclusions, 5 May 1969, PRONI, CAB/4/1440.
65. *Belfast Telegraph*, 7 May 1969.
66. NICRA Ultimatum to Stormont, [June 1969], PRONI, D/3297/4.
67. RUC report, 7 July 1969, PRONI, HA/32/2/28.
68. Ibid.
69. Ibid.
70. *Belfast Telegraph*, 14 July 1969; T. Gracey's evidence to the Scarman Tribunal, 2 March 1970, pp. 1–2; J. Murray's evidence to the Scarman Tribunal, 4 March 1970, pp. 31–3. The IRA was behind this episode, although, as I have been confidentially told by someone who was involved, the original intention had been to display the Tricolour from a private dwelling further up the Crumlin Road. The man charged with the task became fed up with waiting and wandered down to the Edenderry Inn for a drink, taking the Tricolour with him.

71. S. Montgomery's evidence to the Scarman Tribunal, 26 May 1970, p. 3; Gillespie's evidence, 27 April 1970, p. 38.
72. Government of Northern Ireland, *Violence and Civil Disturbances in Northern Ireland in 1969 (Scarman Report)* (Belfast: HMSO, 1972), pp. 48–9.
73. *Scarman Report*; pp. 52–4; D. McKittrick, S. Kelters, B. Feeney, C. Thornton and D. McVea, *Lost Lives: The Stories of the Men, Women and Children who Died as a Result of the Northern Ireland Troubles* (Edinburgh: Mainstream Publishing, 2004 edn.), p. 45.
74. *Scarman Report*, pp. 55–6; *Irish Times*, 5 August 1969.
75. *Irish Times*, 4 August 1969.
76. *Scarman Report*, pp. 59–60.
77. *Irish Times*, 4 August 1969; McKeague's evidence, 18 May 1971, pp. 43–4.
78. *Irish Times*, 4 August 1969.
79. S. Cusack's evidence to the Scarman Tribunal, 13 May 1970, p. 11; R. Catterton's evidence to the Scarman Tribunal, 15 May 1970, p. 30; J. Gilchrist's evidence to the Scarman Tribunal, 27 May 1970, pp. 61–2; *Scarman Report*, p. 61.
80. Catterton's evidence, pp. 15 and 25; Gillespie's evidence, 17 April 1970, p. 48; J. Graham, 'Show me the Man', p. 41.
81. *Belfast Telegraph*, 4 August 1969; *Belfast Telegraph*, 5 August 1969; C. Entwistle's evidence to the Scarman Tribunal, 27 February 1970, p. 5; McKeague's evidence, 18 May 1971, p. 56. Both the evidence to the Scarman Tribunal and the contemporary press reports contain poignant accounts of these enforced migrations.
82. *Irish News*, 4 August 1969.
83. *Belfast Telegraph*, 4 August 1969; *Irish News*, 5 August 1969. Paisley later claimed that his presence in the Shankill Road had been requested by the RUC's Belfast Commissioner. I. Paisley's evidence to the Scarman Tribunal, 17 June 1971, p. 15.
84. McKeague's evidence, 18 May 1971, pp. 45 and 48.
85. Hanley and Millar, *Lost Revolution*, p. 124.
86. *Scarman Report*, p. 48; G. Bradley with B. Feeney, *Insider: Gerry Bradley's Life in The IRA* (Dublin: O'Brien Press, 2009), p. 31.
87. Graham, 'Show Me the Man', pp. 39–41; Adams, *Before the Dawn*, pp. 94–5.
88. McMillen, 'The Role of the IRA', p. 11.
89. P. Bishop and E. Mallie, *The Provisional IRA* (London: Corgi Books, 1988), p. 93. See also R. White, *Ruairí Ó Brádaigh: The Life and Politics of an Irish Revolutionary* (Bloomington, IN: Indiana University Press, 2006), pp. 143–4.
90. In 2001, another member of the IRA's Army Council, Mick Ryan, told Roy Johnston of a meeting in July 1969 at which which Ó Brádaigh asked Goulding whether he had 'a plan to defend the people [of Belfast] in the event of a pogrom, of which he had picked up early warning signals'. Goulding replied in the affirmative, 'but not very convincingly'. Johnston, *Century of Endeavour*, p. 262.

7

Narrating the Civil Rights Movement

INTRODUCTION

'Once upon a time' was how Eamonn McCann began an August 1969 pamphlet that told the story of the civil rights movement.[1] During the start of the Troubles, especially in the period between the People's Democracy march and the Battle of the Bogside, almost everyone had a story to tell about what had recently taken place in Derry. Indeed, the civil rights movement was being remembered and commemorated from the moment it came into being. Memorabilia was created, songs were composed, records were produced, special anniversary issues were published and documentary films were made.[2] McCann and the other radicals tried to restage the 5 October 1968 march just a week later and the DCAC marches all followed a similar route.[3] Commissions of inquiry, private investigations and criminal and coroners' courts took written and oral evidence from a wide range of individuals and groups.[4] However, these attempts to engage with the past have been overlooked in the existing literature on the start of the Troubles. 'Memory work' is a subject that has instead been left to 'memory studies', which is not so much concerned with what happened at the time but rather with the trajectory of how it was remembered and commemorated across the decades.[5] Such a division is unhelpful here. The struggle to shape how an event is described and interpreted – to control the narrative – is an integral part of the event itself. Definitions are imposed and rejected, blame is assigned and displaced, responsibility is claimed and contested and past causes and future courses are suggested and debated.[6] The events of the conflict matter, but so do the languages of conflict – the words which were the contexts for the actions.[7] This is not to dismiss other accounts at all; rather, the chapter sets out to bring into focus important aspects of the period that have previously appeared fuzzy.

This chapter argues that narratives mapped out the contours of the conflict. It requires an interdisciplinary approach because narrative bridges the arts and the sciences, the individual and the collective and the past, the present and the future. The chapter's first section sets out how human memory is thought to operate, especially the ways in which false memories are constructed. The next section examines how group narratives bias personal memories and how they are weaved into the identities of individuals. In the third section, the Stormont General Election campaign of February 1969 is used to explore the narrative forms of constitutional nationalism, republicanism, socialism and unionism. The final section pulls together research which shows that human memory and group narratives are both focused on the future to explain how people in Derry tended to act in line with what was plotted out by their own stories. Writing a narrative about the start of the Troubles has to involve writing about the many competing narratives of the start of the Troubles.

FALSE MEMORY

In one of the trials arising out of the events of 5 October 1968, a policeman gave evidence that at the beginning of the march he had heard Ivan Cooper shout 'For God's sake stewards, come to the front'. When Cooper took to the stand, however, he said that the marshals had been called to the head of the march by someone else. Cooper went on to maintain that the protest had been 'non-violent' and that there had 'not [been] physical contact with the police'. McCann, though, told the court that 'there was physical contact between the marchers at the front and the police'.[8] The Troubles was being misremembered almost from the moment it had begun. By the spring of 1970, McCann was 'sick and tired' of people falsely identifying him as being at 'every outbreak of trouble': 'one lady from the Bogside informed myself and numerous others that she had seen me urging youths to attack British soldiers – not that she had heard I was there, or had been given to believe that I was there, but that she had SEEN me there'. On that date, McCann had in fact been in the Canadian province of Manitoba.[9] A few months later, the *Derry Journal* chose to highlight the case of a 19-year-old Derry man who had been charged with having taken part in a recent riot. Two military witnesses had stated in court that they could not possibly be mistaken about the identity of the culprit; the defendant's boss had given evidence that he had been working the night shift at the time, the defendant's time card had been produced and the defendant's colleagues had testified that they had seen him on the factory floor.[10]

How significant is the part played by false eyewitness identifications in miscarriages of justice? In 1972, the English Criminal Law Revision Committee suspected that 'mistaken identification [is] by far the greatest cause of actual or possible wrong convictions'.[11] Almost three decades later, the first forty cases in the United States in which DNA evidence was used to exonerate convicted criminals proved that it matters more than all other causes combined. In 90 per cent of these cases, one or more eyewitnesses gave evidence that mistakenly identified the accused as the culprit.[12] With so much at stake, criminal lawyers and cognitive psychologists specializing in false memory have been encouraged to go into a profitable partnership.

The unreliability of eyewitness memories may have been interesting psychologists since the turn of the twentieth century, but it was in the 1970s that Elizabeth Loftus transformed how it was both studied and applied.[13] When Loftus was completing her postgraduate studies at Stanford University, most laypeople thought of memory as akin to a replay of the past. Memory stored imprints of what had been experienced, which could then be retrieved when prompted. Loftus helped to show that these prompts could in fact alter memories. She began by researching the ways in which post-event information could distort memories of traffic accidents: for example, she found that using a suggestive word such as 'smashed' led subjects to remember seeing broken glass at the scene when none was there. Still, this was just a laboratory experiment. In 1973, however, she assisted the Seattle, Washington, public defender's office on a murder case that came down to conflicting eyewitness accounts over how much time had elapsed for pre-meditation; the defendant was acquitted. Other attorneys soon spotted that she could help them to win cases, too.[14] Incriminating evidence could be undermined and yet neither the witness nor the police had to be branded liars. Loftus has since given evidence in over 250 hearings and trials.[15]

Loftus's monograph, *Eyewitness Testimony*, was first published in 1979; across the Atlantic, Pierre Nora was trying out his lieu de mémoire concept for the first time at a seminar at the École des Hautes Études en Sciences Sociales.[16] Here were the early stages of two distinct 'memory booms', which have continued to run parallel to each other, almost never coming into contact.[17] The humanities and social sciences have produced an ever expanding number of articles, books, specialist journals, conferences and internet discussion groups on memory.[18] Success, though, also has its failures. Memory is much written about, yet rarely is it employed in the same way by different scholars – or, for that matter, in a way which accords with either general or scientific usages.[19] On the other side of the academy, the vast body of psychological research on false memory is also marked by variety and disputes. One of the most important differences within this field relates to the complexity of the material that is being used, from simple word lists and narratives through detailed personal experiences to intricate mathematical and scientific problems. Other key divisions exist between work on events charged with emotion and that which deals with more mundane memories, between studies that implant false memories and those that focus upon ones which are already there and between researchers who are open about their aims and others who hide them. However, there is something that is common to the entire field: the false memories reported are consistent with the gist of the test subjects' experiences. The gist of a narrative used in one experiment is that it is a description of washing clothes, and participants reported false memories for actions related to their understanding of washing clothes. The gist of a culprit's appearance is that he or she has a certain gender, age and ethnicity, which can lead to eyewitnesses mistakenly identifying someone who shares those features. The gist of a class-inclusion task done by schoolchildren is a numerical relationship between two sets (for instance, the different numbers of horses, cows, pigs and chickens add up to the total number of farm animals), so subjects falsely remembered values that fitted in with how they made sense of that relationship. Memory is an effort after meaning; the false memories seemed familiar to the participants in the studies because they preserved their personal understanding of the meaning of their particular experiences.[20]

There is also something that both brings together and divides the field of false-memory research, the continuum of relative suggestibility.[21]

As Loftus had found in her original studies, suggestive questions distort the contents of eyewitness memory.[22] Such strong and direct suggestion lies at one end of the continuum, along with cases where acceptance of a false memory has been coerced, such as in a police interview. Weaker and less direct forms of suggestion include inferences or associations that came to mind at the time, events that occurred afterwards and previous experiences. At the other end of the continuum, only suggestion very broadly defined is involved: the false memories seem familiar because they are consistent with the gist of an individual's experience as it relates to the things that are to be remembered. These two unifying threads run through the labyrinth of research and lead towards a single explanation for the origins of different types of false memories.[23]

Fuzzy-trace theory has been developed in the last two decades or so as, among other things, an elegant explanation for false memory. Most experiences leave memory traces, but there is no single part of the brain where literal traces are stored; instead, different facets of an experience are encoded in different locations. Remembering involves solving the problem of how to piece together all the elements, and mistakes are therefore often made.[24] Traces can be divided into verbatim and gist traces, which are stored in parallel. Verbatim traces are integrated representations of the experience's surface content and other information that is specific to it. As the surface content is being encoded, the mind is also accessing episodic interpretations of concepts – meanings, relations and patterns – and generating elaborations. The resulting representations are gist traces. Put simply, if a person heard the word 'army', a verbatim trace would consist of remembering this word, while a gist trace would be the things that he or she knew about armies. Gist traces vary in the degree to which they relate to the experience, so hearing 'army' could lead to accessing concepts such as 'military', 'security forces' and 'state' which are less and less directly connected – that is to say, fuzzy.[25]

Memory is not just of two minds when memory traces are stored but also when they are retrieved, and different cues will help lead to different types of representations being accessed. Cues that match the surface content of the encoded experience will favour verbatim retrieval; cues that match meaning content rather than surface form will favour gist retrieval. When someone remembers a largely accurate memory, the two parallel retrieval processes have worked together –

the meanings overlap and support each other. With false memory, on the other hand, the processes are in opposition: gist retrieval is promoting the error and verbatim retrieval is suppressing it. This, though, is an imperfect mechanism, which does not always succeed in weeding out every false memory and that sometimes weeds out accurate ones as well. The false memory that, for instance, a policeman made the arrest could be suppressed if the verbatim trace of the experience of a soldier making the arrest could still be accessed. This would undermine the familiar feeling produced by the gist-consistent false memory of another member of the security forces performing the act. But, over time, access to verbatim traces declines much more sharply than that to gist traces, and so more and more false memories escape elimination. The passage of time also weakens the other important form of false-memory rejection, what is sometimes called the strong remembering criterion. The retrieval of verbatim traces often brings a vivid form of remembering in which a range of sensory information is re-experienced; when this is absent, doubts are raised about the accuracy of what has been remembered. However, as it becomes more difficult to access a verbatim trace, these doubts will be raised without cause and encourage a memory that is not false to be mistakenly dismissed. In some special circumstances, gist retrieval can induce the illusion of vivid recollection, and things that were not experienced are remembered as if they had physically occurred. This happens when events repeatedly cue certain familiar meanings, which make gist traces of those meanings very strong, and when gist-consistent false memories are particularly good examples of those meanings.[26] (These issues largely account for both why we have tried to use the earliest possible eyewitness reports in this book and why we have used oral history only when it was unavoidable.)

Fuzzy-trace theory fits the findings of decades of research and predicts results that are counter-intuitive. An example of the latter that has particular relevance to the study of the Troubles is the way in which negative emotion impacts upon false memory. Contrary to common sense, experiencing emotional events does not burn memories onto the brain; in fact, remembering such moments can stimulate high levels of false memory. Experiments conducted across different languages and cultures have found that false memories are reported much more often when the test material is changed to induce a negative rather than a positive or neutral emotional association.[27] The reasons behind this increase are that negative associations cause gist-consistent false memories to feel more familiar and verbatim traces to become less effective at suppressing them. This conclusion and others like it have unsurprisingly led to hostile reactions among the wider public. Loftus has had to endure attacks on her professional reputation, the presence of armed guards in her classes and accusations that she molested her own children, even though she has not got any.[28] As Loftus herself recognizes, it is a 'horrifying idea that what we think we know, what we believe with all our hearts, is not necessarily the truth'.[29]

STORYTELLING

Stored not-so-safely in the earth around the city of Derry are traces of neolithic and bronze-age life: broken pottery, flint tools and burnt bones. Archaeologists have retrieved some of these objects and, guided by their training, have used them to make imperfect reconstructions of the past located in the present.[30] Memories, too, are constructed out of the physical and the thought; memories therefore are biased to be consistent with the gist of a person's worldview. But, how is an individual worldview constructed? This is where the two, parallel memory booms can be beneficially brought into contact, as the research that has been carried out in the humanities and social sciences offers ways of understanding what links individuals and societies.

Collective memory, the social representation of the past, tends to take narrative form. This is because narrative is a particularly useful way of conceiving of how individuals and groups relate to each other and how they both relate to time and space. Storytelling is universal: people across the world and across history have communicated, thought, remembered and dreamed in narrative.[31] Individuals make sense of their own personal identities in a fashion that approaches how they come to understand characters in fictional stories.[32] The identities of characters emerge from the plot, which pulls together the events that befall them, their aims, their actions and the contexts in which everything happens. Likewise, individuals try to bring order and meaning to their world and control to their self by telling themselves stories – by helping to create narrative identities for themselves. Constructing these narratives allows individuals to act with purpose and meaning because it lets them organize their memories of experiences into a series of causes and effects. Since these actions change their world, they also change their narratives. An individual's identities are not fixed and can be reworked right up until the end of the story, which makes 'identity' more of a verb than a noun.[33] This is something that stands out in modern Irish life-writing. 'Repeatedly', observes the literary critic Liam Harte, 'we come upon acts of self-portraiture that show...the Irish autobiographical self is most itself in the very process of becoming'.[34]

Narrative is also used to give meaning to collective life over time; as Nancy Partner has noted, 'religion, politics, and the collective life of societies [frequently] take narrative form'.[35] Irish nationalism is among the best examples of a worldview being expressed through narrative. In 'The Story of Ireland', Roy Foster shows how closely the Russian formalist Vladimir Propp's ideas about folktales apply to the nationalist narrative, with its fixed elements, roles assigned in advance and promises of a happy ending.[36] A group's representation of 'our story' gives shape to a long past, a complicated present and possible futures – and therefore to its shifting identities.

Individual and group narratives and individuals and groups are connected to each other. They bleed into each other, especially in the telling of the Irish story: Foster argues that national history often becomes a 'kind of scaled up biography' and autobiography a 'microcosmic history'.[37] Hence, Gerry Adams reacted to the debate on historical 'revisionism' 'like a family trauma'.[38] The stories that individuals tell about themselves necessarily involve other people, and this entwining of personal narratives leads to shared, group identities.[39] All human beings possess such identities; indeed, the individual's stories develop out of an interaction with the situation in which he or she finds his or herself, including its group narratives and the language, values, and beliefs that these impart. As the social psychologist Dan McAdams puts it, '[t]he self comes to terms with society through narrative identity'.[40] The gap between the individual who receives the group narratives and the group that stores these narratives is spanned because all narratives possess a point of view and can evoke empathy. The author or implied author's perspective, which comes from the position taken in time and space relative to the content, influences the way in which the recipient understands and responds to the narrator.[41] The recipient therefore can sympathize with the situation and empathize with the individuals and groups depicted in the narrative. Empathy does not require the recipient to identify completely with the group's narrative nor does it require every member of the group to have an identical interpretation of the narrative. Recipients complete the narrative for themselves, redefining and reinterpreting what is already there in terms of their own narratives to produce individual readings of the group's narratives. Individuals can fail to be moved by even the best told stories, can subvert even the most well constructed ones and can weave together even the most contradictory ones.[42] From the subjective point of view of Matt O'Leary, the first chair of the DHAC, even the narrative forms of Communism and Catholicism, two of the greatest and most antagonistic stories ever told, could cohere.[43] Still, the freedom individuals have to adapt group narratives can vary considerably, given that this process has to take place within a particular time and space. When violent conflict is the context, as was increasingly the case in Derry during these years, then the constraints on contestation grow.[44]

TELLING THE BEST STORY, TELLING THE STORY BEST

The Stormont General Election campaign of February 1969 provides a useful way of exploring the key group narratives. Constitutional nationalism, republicanism, socialism and unionism – the different worldviews and their narrative forms – were intensely promoted, debated and attacked throughout this month. And all this happened at one of the sites where politics comes together: in a campaign, high meets low, elite meets popular and centre meets periphery.[45] Elections also make the diffusion and reception of a narrative easier to assess, as the voting, however imperfectly, offers a guide to their impact upon the public.[46] Narratives were particularly important in the fights to win the City and Foyle seats because party machinery was generally absent, still being built up or falling apart, and because the policy differences between the main candidates in each contest were so small. Narratives played the leading role in mobilizing voters, turning confusing events into a story of overcoming and turning a sense of threat into a story of standing firm.[47] The confusing events and/or sense of threat that loomed largest in people's minds were related to the civil rights movement, which had had its obituary notice printed in the *Derry Journal*.[48] This was partly a period of sustained 'collective remembrance', to use Jay Winter and Emmanuel Sivans' phrase. Adapting their metaphor to Irish conditions, people were gathering in a handful of pubs to play music and sing together – everyone joined in at different times, some displayed more talent and enthusiasm than others, the lyrics and melodies were given personal touches, new songs were tried out and traditional ones were reworked. However, almost everyone there was following an accepted way of performing and was being influenced by what the rest of their pub was doing.[49]

On the day Stormont was dissolved, a caravan sat outside the Guild-hall with a large sign declaring that 'Anderson Must Go'. For the whole afternoon, people queued up to sign a petition calling for Albert Anderson to abandon the backbench revolt and support his leader – eventually, 4,000 people would put their name to it. (Many of these signatories would not have been from the constituency and would not have been Unionist voters.)[50] Anderson, by contrast, always maintained that the 'election is not about policies or anything else; it is and always has been a matter of leadership and the unity of the Unionist Party...I want a strong, united but progressive Unionist Party'.[51] That said, 'progressive' here appears to have stood for policies that increased the prosperity of the 'Ulster' people and the first local associations to give Anderson their backing were among the most hardline, which was reflected in his speeches to them.[52] When he addressed the Waterside Unionist Association, for instance, Anderson presented the civil rights movement as a 'planned campaign [of] revolutionary socialists, anarchists, Communists'. He told a story in which Derry had been enjoying 'immensely improved community relations' and a 'much better get together in the Corporation' – until the 'civil rights people came here'. This was almost the same narrative that opponents of the American civil rights movement had been using for years. George Wallace, Alabama's Governor, had blamed the 'troubles in Birmingham' on 'outside agitation planned and directed by members of the communist party'.[53] The movements in both Derry and Birmingham, according to these readings, were not reactions to injustice but instead revolutionary plots. The implication was that they should have been forcibly put down. Anderson concluded his speech by regretting that Terence O'Neill had not taken the required action: 'I think we ought to have had firmer steps taken at the start and not to allow this sort of thing – I know it is very difficult.' The recipients, some of whom heckled him, probably got the gist of what he was saying.[54]

Anderson was chosen as the official candidate by the City of Londonderry and Foyle Unionist Council – which owed as much to patronage networks and rivalries among the local establishment as to his narrative.[55] The defeated nominee, Peter Campbell, and his supporters were 'jostle[d] and jeer[ed]' by a crowd 'waving Union Jacks' and 'singing "Dolly's Brae"'.[56] Politicians no longer expected to bear such indignities at election time; this was just one of many breaches of the norms of respectability during the campaign, which highlighted how politics was changing.[57] And it was not changing in the ways that Campbell wanted, as this upper-class naval officer sided with 'decent moderate people' and hoped that soon 'the Unionist cause can be openly espoused by all who believe in constitutional links with Great Britain, whatever their religion'.[58] Nonetheless, he was encouraged to go forward by the 'business and professional' people who had supported the University for Derry Committee, been hit by the de-facto boycott, backed the petition and asked Campbell to challenge Anderson. These were the people whose economic interests depended more on keeping Derry peaceful than keeping the city in Unionist hands.[59] Campbell therefore sought and received the backing of the Unionist Central Council. This, in turn, allowed Anderson to project himself as the local candidate, urging his audience at the Apprentice Boys Memorial Hall to 'vote for a Derryman who knows you and your needs'.[60] Campbell, in many ways, was an outsider: he was from outside the city, he had been picked out as the Stormont Government's man, he was looking out to the United Kingdom as a whole and he was reaching out to Catholic voters. At his last rally, Campbell was joined on the platform by a number of Catholics and a pre-recorded message from O'Neill was played. Like the Prime Minister, Campbell was sure that the electorate would identify more with the O'Neillite narrative than the party activists did. However, when his election workers canvassed in an estate that was daubed with slogans such as 'UVF' and 'Fenians Out', they were met with insults, shouts of 'Up Anderson' and 'Up Paisley', bricks, kicks and spit.[61]

Although Campbell did poll higher than the nomination ballot suggested he would against Anderson, he was still easily defeated by 6,480 votes to 4,181 on a turnout of 85.3 per cent (this was a three-way contest because Claude Wilton stood for the Liberals).[62] The result should not be read as evidence that there was an uneven split between, say, liberal and right-wing unionism, British and little-Ulster unionism or assimilatory and segregationist unionism. Putting aside the other reasons for the voting – some of which have been given above, some of which have been overlooked and some of which cannot be known – the stories told by the candidates also point away from binary divides. Anderson and Campbell were together relating a single group narrative, one with which the vast majority of Protestants identified. It ranged from a version where the British link was central, Catholics could be won over and reform was overdue to one where the Protestant people were forever threatened by enemies, traitors and unreliable allies. Anderson benefited from having hinted at so many of these different tellings. An O'Neill supporter could opt for Anderson on the grounds that he was the official candidate, he had signed up to the manifesto and party unity mattered above all else; a Paisleyite could vote for him because of his attacks upon the imaginary Republican/Communist plot. To reprise an earlier metaphor, there was a cacophony inside the unionist pub. However, as outside the sounds of riots grew louder and were joined by the noise of gunfire, the sectarian songs in the repertoire were likely to be taken up by ever more people.[63]

Campbell had been counting on Catholics, who made up over a third of the electorate, to put a cross next to his name: his campaign had placed adverts in the *Derry Journal* with the slogan 'Back O'Neill Vote Campbell'.[64] He does seem to have won as many as a few hundred Catholic votes, which highlights again how ethnic identity fails to predict political behaviour.[65] That said, the figures suggest that the community overwhelmingly went with Wilton.[66] Unofficially, Wilton – a member of the DCAC – had been running as the civil rights candidate, and this is where Catholic loyalties basically lay. In the Foyle constituency, however, voters had three civil rights supporters from which to choose: McAteer, McCann and John Hume. A 'Save the Derry Civil Rights Movement Committee' was formed to protest the schism, but its petition was abandoned when it became obvious that it was being manipulated by some of the campaigns.[67] Smears, dirty tricks and voter fraud marked the election from start to finish.[68] Political strategies now required differences within the movement to be played up rather than down, so competing stories were being told about what had and had not been done in the previous months – and what this meant for the future.

On 7 February 1969, the day after McAteer declared his candidacy, the *Derry Journal* endorsed the Nationalist leader: its editorial praised his 'faithful' service to 'his people's cause' and argued that the city needed him to 'pursue his statesmanlike course through such a testing time'.[69] McAteer, while 'not a Cassius Clay type', took up the theme of his impressive record, one that long pre-dated the civil rights movement.[70] With his election broadcast, McAteer reminded his audience that 'we gave warning that equal rights would have to be given'. Asking them to cast their minds back to 'five months before Derry disaster day', he read a speech from *Hansard* in which he had forecast that 'If this repression continues there may be a reaction which all of us would deplore'. McAteer regretted that 'for some agonising days' it had indeed appeared that 'they might fall into a sectarian battle'; so, while his ultimate goal remained Irish unity, he was therefore working in the short term to bring peace to his city and to the North.[71]

Hume, who had concluded that here was his best chance to challenge McAteer, had to attack his opponent's reading of the Nationalist Party's record.[72] This was not just electioneering: movement activists tend to deny their forebears to construct their own identity, their story of breaking with the recent past. From the first DCAC demonstration, Hume had portrayed the civil rights movement as something that had come from nowhere (it was 'completely outside the control of the people') and yet was also the result of decades of injustice ('the city had been a victim of history'). The DCAC was merely 'channel[ling] the spirit of the people' and civil rights was simply a 'moral issue'.[73] This narrative cut through existing political allegiances and demanded involvement. It had another strategic advantage, too, because it countered unionist tales that the movement masked a Green and Red conspiracy.[74] Hume, though, had now chosen to descend from what a Nationalist councillor called his 'pedestal above and beyond the political arena' – signalling that the civil rights era was over.[75] Justifying his decision, Hume claimed that 'civil rights was only a minimum' and, after they had all come, 'There would remain serious social and economic problems which would require tackling by strong and energetic voices in Parliament'.[76] McAteer's record, in this telling, showed that he would not be able to take on these challenges with the necessary vigour. 'Is there anyone in the community', asked Hume, 'who doubts the emergence of the people on the streets was due in part to...the failure of existing opposition?'[77] This narrative not only relegated the Nationalists – with what Hume described as their 'abuse [of] the flag of Ireland once every five years by using it as a political emblem' – to the past, but also set the party against the 'spirit of the people' and on the wrong side of history. Hume, by contrast, had learned the 'lessons of the past four months', which had 'proved that a lot can be done if we fight, fight and fight again [for] the basic problems of the people – housing, unemployment and emigration'.[78]

The *Derry Journal*, in its last editorial before polling day, systematically attacked Hume's efforts to caricature 'the leader and the party that have never failed their trust'.[79] As a matter of fact, the Nationalists were not singularly focused on partition. In 1964, which was also the year that Hume sketched out his views on 'The Northern Catholic' for the *Irish Times*, a committee of Irish nationalist political groups was writing a comprehensive statement of party policy.[80] The 'Thirty Nine Points' promised that the Nationalists would work for the 'creation of an integrated community based on principles of social justice and mutual respect' and for the 'effective end to discrimination on political or religious grounds'. Indeed, virtually every one of the main demands that the civil rights movement would later make can be found in this manifesto. The party further committed itself to securing 'adequate mortgages at low interest rates', an end to exploitation of tenants and full employment.[81] The Nationalists, admittedly, failed to deliver on these aspirations in any meaningful way, and on hopes of creating a united opposition at Stormont.[82] However, as McAteer had warned the 1968 party conference and Hume would soon discover, these disappointments owed more to structural constraints than to limited ambitions and abilities.[83]

Looking ahead to the end of 'the ugly discrimination era', McAteer asked the Derry party in early November 1968 if it would be 'treasonable to work towards rule from Belfast rather than Dublin' and 'a sort of little United-Nations-type grouping of these islands'?[84] This speech intrigued civil servants at the Home Office enough for them to brief Lord Stonham to press McAteer for further details when he came to London later that month.[85] The Nationalist leader duly confessed to the British that 'he did not see any virtue in, nor did he desire, a unified Ireland'.[86] At London's Irish Club, McAteer backtracked (slightly). On the 'long journey to the Promised Land of a United Ireland', he was leading his tribe 'along the middle of the road' and was stopping at 'the wayside well to refresh ourselves with a draught of...Civil Rights'. The two communities, with the co-operation of Westminster and the Dáil, could then agree upon an 'honourable peace in the North'.[87]

Hume's stance on the national question was not so different. The need to distance himself from the Nationalists therefore explains, in part, why Hume's narrative not only pushed McAteer into the past, but was also vague about its ending, a united Ireland. This was a concern that continued after the election. As Hume told Eamonn Gallagher, an official at the Department of External Affairs, seven months later, he had to 'continue to distinguish [himself] from the Nationalist Party'.[88] And, once again, this move also helped to counter unionist charges that the issue was not the issue, that reform was just a way of bringing down Northern Ireland. Talking to another influential diplomat that autumn, this time the UK Representative Oliver Wright, Hume noted that 'there was no demand at the moment for Irish reunification and the least said about that, the soonest mended'.[89] The sophistication of this strategy should not be overstated. Hume's rhetorical sleight of hand – with its references to the 'constitutional position' and the United Irishmen – was easy to spot, and supporters and opponents could guess how he wanted his unfinished narrative to end.[90] In 'private', Gallagher reported back to Dublin, Hume was firm that 'a normalized society would eventually reconsider the real place of Northern Ireland in Irish society'.[91]

Hume defeated McAteer by 8,920 votes to 3,653 on a record turnout of 84 per cent.[92] Among the Foyle electorate, Hume's version of the constitutional-nationalist group narrative clearly elicited greater empathy than McAteer's one. What was also vital to Hume's win was his skill as a storyteller – which was something both McAteer and McCann conceded. The Derry Nationalist Party's campaign postmortem recognized that Hume had been far more successful in getting his message across to the voters.[93] When Councillor James Doherty resigned shortly afterwards from the DCAC, he remarked upon how Hume had used civil rights slogans, songs, emblems and colours.[94] McCann, at the time and in his memoirs, praised Hume for having 'matched the mood of the moment perfectly' with words and actions that were 'reasonable, respectable, righteous, solid'.[95] However, as McCann reminded his party soon after the election, moments pass – and he intended to make it 'pass...as quickly as possible'.[96] Hume, too, was conscious of how vulnerable his position was. More than one-third of his new constituents had voted against him, politics was still in the streets and further conflict would lead ever more people to decide that 'a normalized society' would come after reunification rather than before.[97] 'Power,' warned McCann, 'lies between the pavement and the pavement'. 'We will be on the streets'.[98]

During the election campaign, McCann had recalled that he had been in the street when it was 'a fairly lonely place to be [and when] respectable gentlemen...were noticeable by their absence'. This interpretation of the socialist group narrative had McCann and Derry Labour as its protagonists, and cast Hume and the Nationalists as bystanders and even antagonists. McCann 'remember[ed]' that at the first DHAC protest, Hume had 'left the public gallery' and Alderman James Hegarty had 'used the "Red" smear'. One of his campaign team took the story forward half a year to when 'McCann had resisted the pressure of moderate leaders in the city...to cancel the October 5 march' and had become 'the driving force behind the civil rights movement'.[99] This allowed accusations that the leftists were splitting the movement and exploiting it to push their own agenda to be thrown back at their critics. 'I asked on October 9 when the Citizens Action Committee was set up and I ask again now', McCann told election workers, 'unity to what, unity for what?' Where his opponents wanted to unite the Catholic community in a struggle for Irish unity, McCann instead wanted to unite the working classes in a struggle for socialism. Civil rights, a term with multiple meanings, was defined here as 'one man, one job' and 'one family, one house'.[100] This was a consistent message: the Duke Street march had been promoted as 'no sectarian march, but ...a working-class march' and a statement issued in July 1969 would attack 'moderates' for 'demanding...equal shares of misery'.[101] It was also a message with which few people identified. McCann won 1,933 votes.[102] When he was interviewed that spring by the *New Left Review*, McCann confessed that the failure was worse than these figures implied. 'All we managed to get across was that we were more extreme', he said. 'We have never made it clear that this difference in militancy stemmed from a political difference'.[103] The leftists were literally

composing new lyrics about civil rights – which often parodied contemporary hits – to be sung to the tune of old rebel songs. At the end
of 1968, *Reality*, the DHAC newssheet, told readers to sing a rework-
ing of Bob Dylan's 'God on Our Side' ('The town that I come from is
in the North West') to the tune of 'The Patriot Game'.[104] For those people in the polling booths and on the streets who had little empathy with
constitutional nationalism and its moderation, there was a more relevant and appealing group narrative than revolutionary socialism. As
McCann explained to his British comrades, 'when one calls for revolution, no matter what one actually demands there is always a link...to
1916 and the armed uprising'.[105]

The debate in the letters page of the *Derry Journal* regarding the
paternity of the civil rights movement placed Fionnbarra Ó Dochartaigh's name alongside those of Hume and McCann.[106] Someone signing
him or herself 'Republican' detailed 'Republican participation' in the
DHAC and in the DCAC, and then he or she warned the candidates to
'stick to the truth'. Ó Dochartaigh was more subtle with his interven-
tions, and told a story that placed republicanism above petty politics.
Ó Dochartaigh defended McCann against the Hume campaign's Red
baiting, but he did so by describing the Labour man as a junior partner.
From 1965 onwards, at Ó Dochartaigh's 'request', McCann had taken
'part' in the struggles for jobs and houses that the Republicans had
started and led.[107] Indeed, Ó Dochartaigh was continuing to lead them:
near the start of the election campaign, he joined the squatters in the
Guildhall and 'occupied the Mayoral Chair'.[108] Ó Dochartaigh pleaded
with 'those who supported the cause not to indulge in verbal battles of
a sectarian nature'; 'converts' were to be gained by 'pointing out that
all sections of the community were deprived'. Above all else, Ó Dochartaigh wanted the 'sticks and stones' of 'our enemies' to be met with
the same 'tolerance and perseverance' which had 'won the respect of
freedom-loving peoples throughout the world' during the past four
months.[109] He remained silent about the Republican movement's
continued commitment to armed struggle.

Violence, however, was explicitly linked with republicanism by other
storytellers. In unionist and constitutional-nationalist narratives, the
shadow of the gunman was conjured up to scare recipients into identifying more closely with the stories. Bill Craig, for instance, cautioned
Londonderry Young Unionists that 'this sort of revolution...could

become a campaign of armed violence'.[110] But, there was no plot and no orchestrators; to a certain extent, there was no need because the story was so simple and well known. The physical-force version of the republican narrative itself was there to be picked up by many of those individuals who were rioting in the streets, clashing with Linfield fans, attacking Protestants late at night and defending the Bogside.[111] It lent both legitimacy and added menace to their actions. It taught them that Northern Ireland was inherently sectarian and incapable of reform, that their community needed their protection and that armed struggle was the only path to a united Ireland. And it was an easy story to remember, as the republican narrative could be expressed in just three letters: IRA.

REMEMBERING THE FUTURE

Human memory is subject to all kinds of mistakes, illusions and biases; these have practical results that range from absent-mindedly forgetting someone's name to falsely identifying someone as a murderer. So, why is personal memory a constructive process of pulling together bits and pieces of information as opposed to something approaching a replay of the past? A predictable answer is that storing memories in gist and verbatim traces protects the system from overload. Another, more surprising explanation is that it also allows individuals to imagine future events. As the future will never be an exact repetition of the past, imagining what may come depends upon a system that can flexibly extract and rework aspects of previous experiences. The 'constructive episodic simulation' hypothesis is supported by a growing body of evidence. Cognitive psychology experiments have highlighted strong similarities between remembering the past and imagining the future: for instance, the effects of emotions and of temporal distance on pre-experiencing are broadly the same as they are on re-experiencing. Neuroimaging studies have demonstrated that the same core network of neural structures is involved in putting together representations of both the future and the past.[112] To a certain extent, individuals remember their futures.

Groups know – that is to say, they think they know – how their narratives will unfold in the future. Narrative and memory were among the things left washed up on the shore when the tide of post-modernism in the humanities and social sciences rolled back. Memory studies, though, has generally taken narrative for granted, skipping over the form in the rush to examine the content. After all, narrative, especially when the synonym story is used, seems so natural and childlike. Why work hard to understand something that is employed every day without difficulty? Because the form does matter, as has been increasingly acknowledged by scholars. What is most relevant about narrative form when it comes to describing and analyzing the early Troubles is that narratives have beginnings, middles *and* endings.[113] As the literary critic Frank Kermode argues, 'to make sense of our lives...we need fictions of beginnings and fictions of ends, fictions which unite beginning and end and endow the interval between them with meaning'.[114] So, the politics of the present shaped the narrative forms of constitutional nationalism, republicanism, socialism and unionism; but, their fixed beginnings and endings also shaped the politics of the present. From the perspectives of contemporaries, the Troubles was not the motor of history, rather it was the result of, say, the endless conflict between unionists and nationalists or the nation's long struggle to achieve the inevitable goal of Irish freedom. The wider nationalist and unionist narratives, in particular, were almost impossible to bridge, spiralling around each other without ever touching.[115] This is not just about a moment in history being read in radically different ways. Even supposing that people could have agreed on a factual account of the civil rights movement, the narratives would have arrived at this shared site from different starting points in the past and would have headed off in different directions towards the future.[116]

Foster's 'own belief is that the most illuminating history is often written to show how people acted in the expectation of a future that never happened'.[117] What futures were the citizens of Derry expecting at the end of the civil rights movement? Verbatim and gist processes of memory, personal and group narratives and remembered pasts and imagined futures loop into each other. Memories are usually constructed to fit with an individual's understanding of the meaning of their own experiences; this personal narrative is formed, in part, from idiosyncratic readings of group narratives; verbatim and gist traces place limits on how stories are received, diffused and developed; the future is imagined in ways that draw upon reworked memories and the plot trajectories of group narratives; these simulations are so vivid that they can later be mistaken for verbatim memories. Derrymen and women therefore tended to expect futures that were related to those which were mapped out by the narrative forms of constitutional nationalism, republicanism, socialism and unionism. There were, of course, individual variations within each of these groups, but, as the conflict grew more violent, it became more difficult for people to contest elements of the narratives. Like a shard from a broken mirror, a group narrative puts into the hand both a distorted reflection and a potential weapon.

CONCLUSION

Setting narratives alongside wars, revolutions, economic changes and social upheavals when trying to understand how the violence of the start of the Troubles was produced may have at first appeared absurd. However, a group narrative, 'our story', can attract a powerful emotional investment from its recipients and can impose constraints and directives upon their actions. This is what the narrative forms of the modern-democratic ideologies discussed in this chapter did. As was again demonstrated during the election campaign, in Northern Ireland the sovereign 'people' were synonymous with the democratic 'majority' – which was defined differently in each narrative. Unionists were the majority within Northern Ireland; constitutional nationalists were the majority in the whole island; socialists represented the working class, which would eventually come to realize that it was the majority class; republicans took their legitimacy from the majority vote of 1918, and the movement would remain the custodian of the people's will until the next time it was expressed in an all-Ireland vote. This was what was driving the Troubles, the conflict over who ruled and by what right.[118] The narratives resisted evidence that contradicted them and they played more of a role than precise, qualitative information did in how people made decisions.[119] Although these group narratives could be described as 'imagined communities', they were constructed out of the memories, thoughts, actions, dreams and loyalties of human beings – they were therefore 'real and persistent over time'.[120] The internalization of the group narratives, making them part of an individual's identity, kept the conflict going.[121] The start of the Troubles cannot be understood without understanding the narratives.

NOTES

1. E. McCann, 'Who's Wrecking Civil Rights?' August 1969, Belfast, Public Record Office of Northern Ireland (PRONI), HA/32/2/28.
2. See, for example, *Derry Journal*, 25 March 1969; *Derry Journal*, 11 February 1969; *Londonderry Sentinel*, 22 October 1969; *Reality*, Anniversary Edition 1968–9, 'Derry, Derry City Council's Archives (DCCA), Bridget Bond Civil Rights Collection; *Londonderry Sentinel*, 12 November 1969.
3. *Derry Journal*, 11 October 1968; *Derry Journal*, 5 November 1968; *Derry Journal*, 19 November 1968.
4. See, for example, M. Canavan's evidence to the Cameron Commission, no date, PRONI, GOV/2/1/186; B. Egan and V. McCormack, *Burntollet* (London: LRS, 1969); *Londonderry Sentinel*, 11 December 1968; *Londonderry Sentinel*, 18 December 1969.
5. Compare the different approaches to exploring 'Bloody Sunday' taken in N. Ó Dochartaigh, *From Civil Rights to Armalites: Derry and the Birth of the Troubles* (Basingstoke: Palgrave Macmillan, 2004 edn.) and B. Conway, *Commemoration and Bloody Sunday: Pathways of Memory* (Basingstoke: Palgrave Macmillan, 2010).
6. This interpretation was pioneered by P. Brass, *Theft of an Idol: Text and Context in the Representation of Collective Violence* (Chichester: Princeton University Press, 1997).
7. R. Bourke, 'Languages of Conflict and the Northern Ireland Troubles', *Journal of Modern History* (forthcoming).
8. *Londonderry Sentinel*, 11 December 1968.
9. *Derry Journal*, 31 March 1970; *Derry Journal*, 27 March 1970.
10. *Derry Journal*, 7 July 1970.
11. Lord Devlin, *Report to the Secretary of State for the Home Department of the Departmental Committee on Evidence of Identification in Criminal Cases* (London: HMSO, 1976), p. 76.
12. G. Wells, M. Small, S. Penrod, R. Malpass, S. Fulero and C. Brimacombe, 'Eyewitness Identification Procedures: Recommendations for Lineups and Photospreads', *Law and Human Behavior*, 22, 6 (December 1998), pp. 603–47, p. 605.
13. C. Brainerd and V. Reyna, *The Science of False Memory* (Oxford: Oxford University Press, 2005), pp. 37 and 286.
14. E. Loftus, 'Reconstructing Memory: The Incredible Eyewitness', *Psychology. Today*, 8 (August 1974), pp. 116–19.
15. N. Zagorski, 'Profile of Elizabeth F. Loftus', *Proceedings of the National Academy of Sciences*, 102, 39 (September 2005), p. 13721–3; W. Saletan, 'The Memory Doctor', *Slate*, May–June 2010, www.slate.com/id/2251882 (last accessed 6 September 2010).
16. E. Loftus, *Eyewitness Testimony* (Cambridge, MA: Harvard University Press, 1996 edn.); P. Anderson, 'Union Sucrée', in *London Review of Books*, 23 September 2004.
17. The most notable exception to this are J. Winter and E. Sivan, 'Setting the Framework', in J. Winter and E. Sivan (eds) *War and Remembrance in the Twentieth Century* (Cambridge: Cambridge University Press, 1999), pp. 6–39 and S. Radstone and B. Schwartz, *Memory: Histories, Theories, Debates* (New York, NY: Fordham University Press, 2010).
18. G. Rosenfeld, 'A Looming Crash or a Soft Landing? Forecasting the Future of the Memory "Industry"', *Journal of Modern History*, 81, 1 (March 2009), pp. 122–58, p. 141.
19. K. Klein, 'On the Emergence of Memory in Historical Discourse', *Representations*, 69 (Winter 2000), pp. 127–150, p. 130.
20. Brainerd and Reyna, *Science of False Memory*, pp. 51–5.
21. This concept was first introduced in V. Reyna and F. Lloyd, 'Theories of False Memory in Children and Adults', *Learning and Individual Differences*, 9, 2 (April 1997), pp. 95–123.
22. E. Loftus, D. Miller and H. Burns, 'Semantic Integration of Verbal Information into a Visual Memory', *Journal of Experimental Psychology*, 4, 1 (January 1978), pp. 19–31.
23. Brainerd and Reyna, *Science of False Memory*, pp. 53–4 and 227.
24. D. Schacter and D. Addis, 'The Cognitive Neuroscience of Constructive Memory: Remembering the Past and Imagining the Future', *Philosophical Transactions of the Royal Society B*, 372 (2007), pp. 773–786, p. 775.

25. Brainerd and Reyna, *Science of False Memory*, pp. 72–84 and 96.
26. Ibid., pp. 85–9.
27. C. Brainerd, L. Stein, R. Silverira, G. Rohenkohl and V. Reyna, 'How Does Negative Emotion Cause False Memories?', *Psychological Science*, 19, 9 (September 2008), pp. 919–25.
28. Saletan, 'Memory Doctor'.
29. J. Neimark, 'The Diva of Disclosure', *Psychology Today* , 29, 1 (January 1996), p. 48.
30. *Derry Journal*, 14 August 2009.
31. J. László, *The Science of Stories: An Introduction to Narrative Psychology* (Hove: Routledge, 2008), p. 2.
32. For a contrary view, see G. Strawson, 'Against Narrativity', *Ratio*, 17, 4 (December 2004), pp. 428–52.
33. P. Ricoeur (trans. K. Blamey), *Oneself as Another* (London: University of Chicago Press, 1992), pp. 141–8.
34. L. Harte, 'Autobiography and the Irish Cultural Moment', in L. Harte (ed.), *Modern Irish Autobiography* (Basingstoke: Palgrave Macmillan, 2007), pp. 1–13, p. 5.
35. N. Partner, 'The Linguistic Turn along Post-Postmodern Borders: Israeli/Palestinian Narrative Conflict', *New Literary History*, 39, 4 (autumn 2008), pp. 823–845, p. 832.
36. R. Foster, 'The Story of Ireland', in R. Foster, *The Irish Story* (London: Penguin, 2001), pp. 1–22, pp. 5–8.
37. R. Foster, 'Introduction', in Foster, *Irish Story*, pp. xi-xx, p. xi.
38. F. O'Connor, *In Search of a State: Catholics in Northern Ireland* (Belfast: Blackstaff Press, 1993), p. 246.
39. Ricoeur, *Oneself as Another*, pp. 147–8.
40. D. McAdams, 'Personal Narratives and the Life Story', in O. John, R. Robbins and L. Pervin (eds), *Handbook of Personality: Theory and Research* (New York, NY: Guildford Press, 2008 edn.), pp. 242–62, p. 243.
41. P. Ricoeur, *Time and Narrative, Volume III* trans. K. McLaughlin and D. Pellauer (Chicago: Chicago University Press, 1988), p. 177.
42. J. Liu and J. László, 'A Narrative Theory of History and Identity: Social Identity, Social Representations, Society and the Individual', in G. Moloney and I. Walker (eds.), *Social Representations and Identity: Content, Processes and Power* (Basingstoke: Palgrave Macmillan, 2007), pp. 85–107, pp. 93–8; B. Schwartz and H. Schuman, 'History, Commemoration and Belief: Abraham Lincoln in American Memory, 1945–2001', *American Sociology Review*, 70, 2 (April 2005), pp. 183–203, p. 197.
43. *Derry Journal*, 19 November 1968; *Derry Journal*, 22 November 1968.
44. P. Hammack, 'Narrative and the Cultural Psychology of Identity', *Personality and Social Psychology Review*, 12, 3 (August 2008), pp. 222–47, pp. 237–9.
45. J. Lawrence, 'Political History', in S. Berger, H. Feldner and K. Pasmore (eds), *Writing History: Theory and Practice* (London: Routledge, 2003), pp. 183–202, pp. 196 and 199.
46. P. Mandler, 'The Problem with Cultural History', *Cultural and Social History*, 1, 1 (January 2004), pp. 94–117, pp. 96–7.
47. F. Polletta, 'Contending Stories: Narrative in Social Movements', *Qualitative Sociology*, 21, 4 (December 1998), pp. 419–46, p. 429.
48. 'RIGHTS – In the Mid-Derry and Foyle constituencies, after a short and fatal illness, lust for power, Derry Civil, aged approx 4 months.' *Derry Journal*, 11 February 1969.
49. Winter and Sivan, 'Setting the Framework', pp. 9 and 28.
50. *Derry Journal*, 4 February 1969; *Londonderry Sentinel*, 12 February 1969.
51. *Londonderry Sentinel*, 19 February 1969.
52. *Londonderry Sentinel*, 26 February 1969.
53. J. Woods, *Black Struggle, Red Scare: Segregation and Anti-Communism in the South, 1948–1968* (Baton Rouge, LA: Louisiana State University Press, 2004), p. 170.
54. *Londonderry Sentinel*, 5 February 1969.
55. M. Mulholland, *Northern Ireland at the Crossroads: Ulster Unionism in the O'Neill Years, 1960–9* (London: MacMillan, 2000), p. 181.
56. *Londonderry Sentinel*, 12 February 1969.

57. J. Lawrence, 'Forging a Peaceable Kingdom: War, Violence, and Fear of Brutalization in Post-First World War Britain', *Journal of Modern History*, 75, 3 (September 2003), pp. 557–89, p. 571.
58. *Londonderry Sentinel*, 19 February 1969.
59. *Derry Journal*, 2 February 1965; *Derry Journal*, 27 November 1968; *Derry Journal*, 21 February 1969.
60. *Londonderry Sentinel*, 19 February 1969.
61. *Derry Journal*, 24 January 1969; *Londonderry Sentinel*, 26 February 1969.
62. *Derry Journal*, 28 February 1969.
63. For a more detailed examination of the unionist worldview and its narrative forms at the start of the Troubles, see G. Walker, 'The Ulster Unionist Party and the Bannside By-election 1970', *Irish Political Studies*, 19, 1, (Summer 2004), pp. 59–73.
64. *Derry Journal*, 28 February 1969.
65. S. Kalyvas, 'Ethnic Defection in Civil War', *Comparative Political Studies*, 41, 8 (August 2008), pp. 1043–68, p. 1051.
66. *Derry Journal*, 28 February 1969.
67. *Derry Journal*, 11 February 1969; *Derry Journal*, 18 February 1969.
68. *Derry Journal*, 25 February 1969; F. Curran, *Derry: Countdown to Disaster* (Dublin: Gill & Macmillan, 1986), p. 117; P. Doherty, *Paddy Bogside* (Cork: Mercier Press, 2001), p. 99; N. McCafferty, *Nell* (London: Penguin, 2004), p. 154.
69. *Derry Journal*, 7 February 1969.
70. *Derry Journal*, 18 February 1969.
71. *Derry Journal*, 18 February 1969.
72. Curran, *Derry*, pp. 115–16; DCAC Minutes, 4 and 7 February 1969, PRONI, GOV/2/1/186.
73. *Derry Journal*, 22 October 1968.
74. Polletta, 'Contending Stories', pp. 426–30.
75. *Derry Journal*, 21 February 1969; *Derry Journal*, 14 February 1969.
76. *Derry Journal*, 14 February 1969.
77. *Derry Journal*, 21 February 1969.
78. *Derry Journal*, 18 February 1969.
79. *Derry Journal*, 21 February 1969.
80. *Irish Times*, 18 and 19 May 1964; E. McAteer to C. Healy, 5 November 1964, PRONI, D/2991/B/21.
81. *Derry Journal*, 24 November 1964.
82. E. McAteer to C. Healy, H. Diamond, C. Stewart, F. Hanna and G. Fitt, 29 October 1964, PRONI, D/2991/B/21; *Derry Journal*, 8 December 1964.
83. *Derry Journal*, 25 June 1968; H. Black to all ministers, 30 June 1969, PRONI, CAB/9J/37/2; E. Gallagher to S. Ronan, 22 September 1969, Dublin, National Archives of Ireland (NAI), DT/2000/6/660.
84. *Derry Journal*, 8 November 1968.
85. Note for the Minister of State, [November 1968]London, National Archives (NA), CJ/3/30.
86. Note for the Record of the Lord Stonham-Eddie McAteer Meeting, [November 1968], NA, CJ/3/30.
87. *Derry Journal*, 15 November 1968.
88. Gallagher to Ronan, 22 September 1969.
89. Record of Conversation with John Hume MP, 24 September 1969, NA, CJ/5/2.
90. *Irish News*, 11 February 1969. Hume consistently claimed that 'Catholic, Protestant, and Dissenter can work together' – and got the order of the words wrong each time. See, for instance, *Derry Journal*, 27 November 1968 and *Fortnight*, 5 February 1971.
91. E. Gallagher to S. Ronan, 13 November 1969, NAI, DFA/2000/5/48.
92. *Derry Journal*, 28 February 1969.
93. Lynn, *Holding the Ground*, p. 220.
94. *Derry Journal*, 25 March 1969.
95. E. McCann, *War and an Irish Town* (London: Pluto Press, 1993 edn.), p. 103.
96. *Derry Journal*, 7 March 1969.
97. Record of Conversation with John Hume MP.

98. *Derry Journal*, 7 March 1969.
99. *Derry Journal*, 21 February 1969.
100. *Derry Journal*, 14 February 1969.
101. *Derry Journal*, 4 October 1968; Where We Stand on Civil Rights, July 1969, PRONI, HA/32/2/26.
102. *Derry Journal*, 28 February 1969. Cooper later joked that McCann 'is more attractive to women than voters'. J. MacAnthony, 'The Political Ecumenist', *This Week*, September 1971.
103. A. Barnett, 'Discussion on the strategy of People's Democracy', *New Left Review*, May–June 1969.
104. *Reality*, [December 1968], PRONI, HA/32/28/2.
105. Barnett, 'People's Democracy'.
106. See, for example, *Derry Journal*, 28 March 1969.
107. *Derry Journal*, 21 February 1969.
108. *Reality*, February 1969, DCCA, Bridget Bond Civil Rights Collection.
109. *Derry Journal*, 7 February 1969.
110. *Londonderry Sentinel*, 12 February 1969.
111. *Londonderry Sentinel*, 29 January 1969; B. Meharg to J. Greeves, 28 January 1969, PRONI, HA/32/2/26; B. Meharg to J. Greeves, 27 March 1969, PRONI, HA/32/2/26; *Derry Journal*, 8 August 1969.
112. Schacter and Addis, 'The Cognitive Neuroscience of Constructive Memory', pp. 774–83.
113. Partner, 'Linguistic Turn along Post-Postmodern Borders', pp. 823–30.
114. F. Kermode, *A Sense of an Ending* (Oxford: Oxford University Press, 2000 edn.), p. 190.
115. For another example of this process, see R. Rotberg (ed.), *Israeli and Palestinian Narratives of Conflict: History's Double Helix* (Bloomington, Ind.: Indiana University Press, 2006).
116. Partner, 'Linguistic Turn along Post-Postmodern Borders', pp. 830–41.
117. R. Foster, 'Theme-parks and Histories', in Foster (ed.), *Irish Story*, pp. 23–36, p. 34.
118. Bourke, 'Languages of Conflict and the Northern Ireland Troubles'.
119. U. Neisser and L. Libby, 'Remembering Life Experiences', in E. Tulving and F. Craik (eds), *The Oxford Handbook of Memory* (Oxford: Oxford University Press, 2000 edn.), pp. 315–32, p. 317; V. Reyna, F. Lloyd and C. Brainerd, 'Memory, Development, and Rationality: An Integrative Theory of Judgment and Decision-Making', in S. Schneider and J. Shanteau (eds), *Emerging Perspectives on Judgment and Decision Research* (Cambridge: Cambridge University Press, 2003), pp. 201–45, pp. 234–9.
120. Partner, 'Linguistic Turn along Post-Postmodern Borders', p. 832.
121. Hammack, 'Narrative and the Cultural Psychology of Identity', p. 223.

8

The Battle of the Bogside

INTRODUCTION

Nell McCafferty listened to the men in the room talking about how the up-coming Apprentice Boys march on 12 August 1969 would impact upon business. Representatives from Derry's political parties, action committees, Churches and Chamber of Commerce had been brought together in mid-July 1969 by the Development Commission to discuss 'proposals for peace'. McCafferty, unhappy at the way the debate had developed, finally interjected that there was a 'real danger of civil war' and that what 'mattered most of all' was the impact on 'people's lives'.[1] Hopes as well as fears, though, were carrying Derry towards the Battle of the Bogside. At the Stardust Ballroom, a week before the march, 'anti-Unionist' political figures gave speeches which confidently predicted victory.[2] Although there were probably 200 guns in the Bogside and the Creggan (120 of which were legally owned), Seán Keenan, a veteran Republican, recognized during this meeting that only 'sticks, stones and the good-old petrol bomb' would be needed to break the RUC – and maybe break Stormont, too.[3] A confrontation had been written into the group narratives; still, when the confrontation came, it nonetheless led people to rewrite their histories of the past year. The *Londonderry Sentinel* noted that 'many' were 'ask[ing] if the disturbances were not planned many, many months ago and, indeed, if the predictions of...William Craig, in the autumn of last year, were, after all, correct'.[4] An unofficial report for the Northern Irish Government prepared by a military history lecturer attached to the British army in West Germany (from where he had been watching as 'student[s]' 'reversed' the 'teachings' of Che Guevara for 'the industrialized setting of Europe') similarly warned that 'the struggle for "national liberation" has begun'.[5] In fact, it had not begun – but the

IRA campaign was coming. Northern Ireland was under attack; Northern Ireland had to be attacked. The simplest stories were becoming ever more popular.

The chapter's first section covers the failed attempt to revive the civil rights movement in Derry. This failure, in part, was brought about by the city's youthful rioters, and their actions and identities are explored in the next section. Violence not only kept the crisis going, but also encouraged other individuals and groups opposed to unionism to move towards violent strategies as they competed with one another for leadership.[6] Non-violent methods, though, were still being used; the third section describes the forms of political and social activism that were flourishing in the new environment which had been created by the civil rights movement. The fourth and fifth sections examine the build up to the Battle of the Bogside and what happened during those three summer days, in London and Dublin as well as in Derry. The conclusion sets out how the struggle was no longer about reforming Stormont, but instead about removing Stormont. The Battle of the Bogside, to quote the *Irish Press*, had 'overtones of the GPO stand'.[7]

SPRING REAWAKENING

On 22 March 1969, around 2,500 people took part in a sit-down protest in Waterloo Place, near to the Guildhall. The gathering was addressed by John Hume, Ivan Cooper, Claude Wilton, James Doherty, Keenan, Fionnbarra Ó Dochartaigh and Eamonn McCann.[8] Here was another attempt to resurrect the civil rights movement, an attempt which directly appealed to the memory of the event that marked the start of the DCAC campaign – except, of course, things were different this time. McCann was not just one of the speakers, he was also chairing the meeting, as Derry Labour had taken the lead in organizing the demonstration against the Unionist Government's Public Order Bill.[9] So, while the *Derry Journal* saw an 'admirable renewal of the spirit of the unified front in the Civil Rights cause', the radicals were, in fact, renewing their struggle with the moderates (although the divisions within these loose groupings were making such labels increasing irrelevant).[10] As well as fighting each other, some of the would-be leaders found themselves at the end of the protest fighting in the streets with some of the 300 youths who were battering against the gates to Victoria barracks.[11] McCann's belief that stewards would not be needed that day had been shown to be wrong from the start, when policemen had to intervene to protect loyalist counter-demonstrators.[12] These incidents would have been shocking five months earlier, but the ordinary conventions of Derry life had been upset by the disturbances; there was no going back.[13]

The tragicomic revival of the civil rights movement was still running the following Saturday, 29 March 1969, when the DCAC staged a march that referenced the walk of the committee members which had come after the first sit-down protest.[14] Hundreds of stewards and policemen went with the 8,000 or so marchers, yet violence nonetheless broke out in the Diamond, where a man was standing next to the war memorial waving a Union flag. A large section of the crowd surged towards him, sucking marshals, RUC officers and loyalists into a minor skirmish.[15] At one of the court cases arising out of this incident, Edward Harrigan, an unemployed teenager, testified that '[p]eople wearing red, white and blue scarves...were being chased by people wearing green, white and yellow scarves'. This artless but evocative statement was quoted by the *Londonderry Sentinel* in an editorial on 'yet another civil rights parade'; the newspaper called upon the DCAC to 'now realise that ... they have followers who are not prepared to accept their lead' and that 'a growing number of businessmen' were reporting that 'shoppers' were reluctant 'to venture out into the streets'.[16] The *Derry Journal*, in contrast, claimed that the clashes merely 'let down' what was 'otherwise [an] unqualified and unsullied triumph for the principle of non-violent protest', one which showed up 'the massive stupidity on the part of...Craig'.[17] The group narratives were spiralling ever further apart. Just how far is suggested by vox pops carried out in the city on 15 April 1969 by the *Belfast Telegraph*: a Protestant professional complained about the 'usual Saturday antagonistic march' and about how 'civil rights' was becoming 'obnoxious', while a Catholic businessman picked up 'a sense of frustration that people are not going to achieve anything and that Protestant militants are going to take over'.[18]

The next act in the restaged civil rights drama was Burntollet, with the role of the People's Democracy taken in this performance by the North Derry Civil Rights Association. The RUC and the Orange Order, though, persuaded Robert Porter, the new Minister of Home Affairs, to ban the association's planned march from the site of the ambush to

Altnagelvin on 19 April 1969. County Inspector Paul Kerr reported that 'persons in the district who normally took a reasonable attitude to these demonstrations were now saying that they had no control whatsoever over the militant extremists'.[19] The deputation from the Grand Lodge backed this assessment, and added that 'confidence [in the RUC] had been broken' 'in recent weeks' after 'Protestants were herded in the Fountain while Civil Rights marchers were allowed to do as they wished'.[20] Although the association accepted the ban, around 100 loyalists still gathered on the day of the march to hold the bridge and, after repulsing a few cars carrying civil rights activists, headed into Derry to celebrate their dubious victory. Within the city walls, these loyalists came across about forty youths who had been taking part in sit-down protests against the ban – and violence ensued. From the start, the RUC's response was heavy handed and provocative: baton charges and water canon brought more people out on to the streets and brought an attack on Victoria barracks.[21] As rioters and policemen moved to the familiar battlefield at the edge of the city centre, Sammy Devenny started to watch what was happening from the door of his home at 69 William Street. A couple of youths ran into his house, but the officers who were pursuing them gave up the chase and instead assaulted Devenny and his family, leaving him lying on the floor with blood seeping out of his head wounds, with his glasses and false teeth smashed and with one of his teenage daughters unconscious next to him. (The policemen involved were protected from facing justice by a 'conspiracy of silence'.) Devenny later suffered a fatal heart attack, which arguably made him the first person to be killed during the Troubles; that night, however, he was just one of 168 people who needed hospital treatment.[22]

While the police eventually succeeded, once again, in containing a crowd inside the Bogside, they broke with the usual script by firing warning shots and, after midnight, by pushing past the barricades to occupy the area. The next morning, as reinforcements arrived, a group of teenagers began throwing stones, before being scattered by a baton charge. With further violence likely to follow, Hume worked to offer alternative forms of political action: he held public meetings, gave the riot police an ultimatum to pull out, helped move women and children away from the Bogside, suggested that the men of the area should march around the city, telephoned Porter and spoke to churchmen, trade unionists and justices of the peace. These efforts brought about an uneasy truce, in which police withdrew to the fringes of the Bogside and DCAC stewards kept youths from going into the city centre.[23] At the end of March 1969, Derry Labour had announced that the 'city is back to the point it was [between] October 5th and November 16th'; after the weekend's violence, the party's executive 'unanimously agreed that the city was once again back to January 4th'.[24] The spring revival was an abridged version of the civil rights movement. So, asked Frank Gogarty, now chair of NICRA, a fortnight later in Dublin, 'just where do we go from here?' 'Many,' he answered, 'are coming round to the belief that reforms can only come not from a Unionist Government, however liberal, but by revolution alone, by the complete destruction of the Stormont regime and direct rule from either London or Dublin'.[25] (Shortly afterwards, the Northern Irish Cabinet agreed to promote legislation providing for universal adult suffrage in local elections.)[26] Craig, addressing Unionists in Derry, foresaw a different future, one in which 'the sensible, sane community' was 'provoked to a stage that may lead them to take action themselves'.[27] The group narratives were taking an ever darker turn.

'HOOLIGANS'

With the riots that had begun on the 12 July 1969 going into their second day, Hume broke off his holiday in Donegal to return to his constituency. 'This sort of vandalism has no place in civil-rights policy,' he told journalists after touring the scene. The DCAC, the Development Commission and the Cabinet Security Committee all followed him in issuing statements that condemned 'hooliganism'; McCann, however, did not.[28] In a Young Socialists pamphlet, he 'blame[d]' the 'Civil Rights leaders' for having first 'lost contact with the people' and for then 'dismiss[ing them] as "hooligans"'.[29] The Labour newssheet, *Ramparts*, mocked Hume for slipping 'home' to 'watch…the riots on Television' with a 'nice cup of cocoa' after giving his press statement. (The Foyle MP had actually been on the streets late into the night trying to end the violence.)[30] The Labour left wanted to show that it was listening rather than lecturing, and so *Ramparts* published an article from 'an eighteen-year-old youth from Creggan who took an active part'. He explained that the 'hooligans' were surviving on 'one pound a week' and that a government was needed which would 'bring industries to employ between three thousand and four thousand'.[31] These different interpretations suggest that the claims made about the identity and actions of the rioters were self-serving; they also imply that there was a shared assumption that the rioters had just one identity and that motives were unchanging. But, depending on the context, they could have been hooligans *and* militants, their actions could have been private *and* political.[32]

Once more, a brief comparison with the Birmingham, Alabama, campaign helps illuminate what happened in Derry. The day after Martin Luther King announced that he had an agreement on desegregation from the city, a bomb exploded at the motel where he had been staying. When policemen arrived at the motel, the crowd that had gathered there hurled bottles and bricks at them, beginning a riot that was marked by looting, arson and knife attacks. King described the rioters as 'Saturday night drinkers' who 'were not under the discipline of the movement' and who had been used by 'segregationist diehards [seeking] to destroy the peace'.[33] This was not an unreasonable position, but nor was rioting an unreasonable action. Although working-class black youths may not have joined civil rights organizations in large numbers, they still had grievances that they wanted redressed and they had seized their opportunity. Politics, for them, was tied up with issues of financial insecurity, fun, personal safety, manliness, freedom of movement and other aspects of their everyday lives. It was therefore far from surprising that when they did make this rare appearance on the political stage they were neither patient, polite nor peaceful.[34] In Derry, too, hundreds of the city's working-class youth had grabbed the chance to push against the many constraints upon them – a number of which were imposed by their would-be political and community leaders. Starting after the April 1969 riots, teachers and churchmen organized committees and meetings with the goal of controlling the city's 'children'; many youths, though, were no longer willing to submit to such control.[35]

In addition to offering a new way of viewing the changing constellation of power, the history of the 'hooligans' highlights how people on the margins were at the centre of politics for this period. Porter informed the Security Committee that the July 1969 riots had 'stretched the resources of the RUC to the limit' and that the working-class youths were 'dictating [the] situation'.[36] For Home Secretary Jim Callaghan, 'the greatest risk at the present time is of further outbreaks of hooliganism' – and he warned his Cabinet colleagues not to 'under-estimate' the 'danger' that the 'police will not be able to control such outbreaks...and that the Northern Ireland Government will have to ask for military assistance'.[37] (The RUC had shared with the army 'their suspicions' that 'a small hard core...were armed'.)[38] While one of the main arguments of this book is that actions and identities changed dramatically over a short space of time, it is nonetheless worth gliding across the months here so as to underscore just what a fundamental part the 'hooligans' played in the story. At the close of January 1970, for instance, Hume and his constituency party contacted the British army to complain, yet again, about the 'uncontrollable hooligan element'.[39] Half a year later, intelligence officers still saw the 'hooligan element' as 'the major threat to stability', with 'reliable sources' reporting that 'all groups in Bogside' were assessing what 'course of action towards the hooligans...would best suit their long-term interests'. McCann, who was trying to 'steer the youths away from sectarianism or hooligan preoccupations towards politics', was the only leader that had 'any strong influence' over them.[40] That said, attempts made by McCann and the other radicals to guide the people they dubbed the 'little Che Guevaras' all ended in relative failure.[41] On 12 October 1970, after McCann's 'peacekeeping efforts' came to be resented by the 'hard core', he was 'beaten up'; in the next issue of the *Derry Journal*, he shared his worries about 'the generation who have been robbed of respect'.[42] Some of the most important political actors, people such as 'Oxo' Hammett and 'Big Ed' Harrigan, were performing without direction.

NEXT TURNS

In early May 1969, Hume talked to the new Prime Minister, James Chichester-Clark, about 'his concern' over the growing divide between 'the reformers, to which he belonged, and the revolutionaries'. 'He said it would be possible for him to split the movement, but in order to achieve this he would need to have certain assurances from the Government': assurances that Stormont 'meant business' regarding franchise reform, that electoral boundaries would be redrawn by an 'impartial body', that '"State of Emergency" powers' would be introduced 'on the Éire example' and that 'grievances at Local Government level' would be addressed.[43] McCann, if he had found out about this conversation, would probably have found it reassuring. 'Hume,' he claimed at a meeting in Glasgow later that month, 'is a liberal man who works with the weapons at his disposal to pressurize the Unionist regime into a more moderate...position.' For McCann, this was as much a 'political stance' as the left-wing 'perspective' that 'social and economic problems ...can only finally be eradicated by waging a consistent campaign against the whole set up'. Rejecting the 'sacred anti-Unionist unity', which merely masked 'manoeuvring within committees and between committees', McCann was trying to get going a 'public debate' on the 'differences underlying the obvious divisions'.[44] Indeed, as he had informed Derry Labour a few weeks earlier, McCann had now concluded that 'Socialists within the movement should not stay united with the ill-named "moderate" leadership'.[45] The bitter political duel fought out by these two rivals in the run up to 12 August 1969 became something of a soap opera, with even British ministers eager to be kept up to date with every twist and turn.[46]

However, the story of how the civil rights movement had been revived, how the 'hooligans' had kicked it off the stage and how Hume and McCann were arguing over future directions was not the only story about political and social activism in Derry during these months. Many old and new forms of protest were flourishing in the changed political environment. The radicals, unsurprisingly, had not forgotten their roots: the DUAC and the DHAC held meetings, staged pickets and sent out deputations.[47] One of the things that *had* changed was that the coalition partners, the Labour left and the younger Republicans, had started to operate separately much more often. Labour, for example, squatted families in the twenty-five houses in the Waterside that had been left vacant by the Royal Navy and put pressure on the commission to buy or lease the estate rather than to evict its new residents.[48] The 'Republican movement,' insisted Johnny White, 'was the only one that could really unite the people and really tackle the social problems' – but, bringing together the two different political generations led the James Connolly Republican Club to go back to traditional street politics.[49] On 6 April 1969, at the Easter parade, over 5,000 people marched to Guildhall Square behind a colour party displaying the Irish Tricolour, the flag of Na Fianna and the Starry Plough, while police officers stood idly by. 'We are Irish,' Keenan told the marchers, 'and...the enemy is still England'.[50] Later, the RUC issued summonses against five men for defying various bans (the charges were ultimately dismissed), which just gave the Republicans an excuse to stage a small protest march through the city centre in which three Tricolours were carried and the national anthem was sung.[51] The police again did nothing, nor did they intervene when Republicans sold copies of the *United Irishman* outside Victoria barracks; power had shifted and the space for Republican politics was growing.[52]

The radicals, though, did not find that the streets were once more a fairly lonely place to be after the April 1969 riots. Indeed, they had even been joined by some Unionists. When the corporation went, so did some more of the party discipline, and the Young Unionists got involved in housing agitation which threatened the economic interests of key figures within the local leadership. The Young Unionist Housing Action Committee (YUHAC) called on landlords to lower rents and do up properties; sent a deputation to the commission to discuss housing allocations; and squatted Protestant families – some of whom had been intimidated out of their homes – in the Fountain area and promised to resist attempts to evict them.[53] Ferville Wright, who was the driving force behind the YUHAC, was soon being described by Albert Anderson as 'the Protestant equivalent of Eamond [sic] McCann'.[54] Wright and McCann, however, were not so much reflections of each other as secret sharers. From the autumn of 1968 onwards, according to McCafferty's later account, contacts were built up between the Labour left and Young Unionist activists.[55] A year later, army intelligence was 'definate [sic]' that Wright and McCann were 'working together along Revolutionary Socialist and non-sectarian lines'.[56] The military intelligence liaison officer for Derry suspected that there may have been a plan to force out Catholic families who had been given homes in the Irish Street estate, so as to 'bring the whole of the BOGSIDE to the Streets'.[57] A more mundane, but also more realistic, reading of Wright's schemes to keep control over Protestant territory is that the politicization of the communal divide was yet again making it hard to pursue class-based politics.

But, working-class people in Derry were still finding ways to make their lives better; the campaigns for welfare rights survived the end of the civil rights movement, although they had been reshaped by it. At the end of March 1969, for example, tenants' associations in the Creggan asked for a police station on the estate to combat the recent rise in vandalism.[58] Co-operation was to continue even after the following month's riots. On 12 June 1969, over 1,000 local residents took part in a sit-down protest against speeding traffic that blocked Creggan Heights for nearly three hours, while their associations met with the police to agree a deal in which more road signs would be put up by the surveyor's department.[59] Street politics had become an everyday strategy.

BEFORE THE BATTLE

A week after the July 1969 riots, Hume arrived in London prophesying doom; but, the oracles he uttered were different for his different audiences. For Labour backbenchers and Irish diplomats, Hume told a story in which the 'powder keg' would explode on 12 August 1969 and Derry would then look across the border for support – unless Westminster suspended the constitution, appointed a commission and sent in the army.[60] When Hume met with Lord Stonham at the Home Office, he again expressed 'the gravest apprehension', as the 'Catholic population...hated both the Royal Ulster Constabulary and the Special Constabulary'. However, Hume added that 'unemployment and poor housing were at the root of recent disturbances' and that 'the situation could be transformed if between 2,000 and 3,000 jobs could be created'.[61] Throughout the crisis, Dublin and London would listen to voices from Derry telling them what they wanted to hear, speaking, respectively, the political and the socio-economic languages of conflict. This distorted how the two governments understood developments and affected how they both reacted.

What was Hume trying to do with words? Among other things, he wanted to work through Dublin and London to bring pressure to bear on Stormont – and he had some limited success here. On 1 August 1969, Patrick Hillery, the new Minister for External Affairs, used 'Humespeak' in a meeting with his British counterpart, describing Derry as a 'powder keg' where people 'no longer [had] any confidence in the police'. The Foreign Secretary may have reminded Hillery that 'Derry was the responsibility of the Northern Ireland Government', yet he and the mandarins next to him had long been making plans for Westminster to take a greater role if soldiers came on to the streets.[62] Hume's conversation with Stonham led Callaghan to conclude that there was a 'serious concern' that this could happen.[63] Just how much greater the British role would be if it did was thrashed out between Westminster and Stormont in a series of urgent telephone calls, letters and meetings at the start of August 1969. Chichester-Clark talked Callaghan out of his position that 'the intervention would be a case of "all or nothing"' by arguing that 'the suspension of the Northern Ireland Parliament' would be viewed 'as a step in the direction of a merger with the Irish Republic' and therefore 'the Protestant reaction would be widespread and might be very violent'.[64] Still, Chichester-Clark nonetheless had to accept that the Westminster would assume 'direct responsibility for law and order' and exercise 'greater influence and control over other aspects of government'.[65] So, when the Northern Irish Cabinet met the day before the Apprentice Boys' march, ministers agreed that 'the overriding consideration was to avoid the use of troops'.[66] (This is probably what the British Government had been trying to do with words, as the Labour leadership did not want to get any further involved unless it was absolutely necessary.)[67]

Outside the Home Office, Chichester-Clark had been pressed by journalists over whether he would ban the march. His answers were vague; nothing about 12 August 1969 was clear.[68] The decision to let the parade go ahead had, in fact, already been taken. The Cabinet had 'accepted that any attempt to ban a demonstration of this kind could have the most undesirable repercussions' (for example, Anderson had reported to Porter that 'an underground loyalist group was ready for action at the first opportunity').[69] Callaghan, in a telephone conversation with Chichester-Clark, had endorsed this reasoning because he had 'taken a similar view last year of…Grosvenor Square'.[70] Unlike the Vietnam Solidarity Campaign, the Apprentice Boys were eager to co-operate with the authorities, and had worked with police and ministers to sort out the stewarding and to alter the original route to miss out some of the obvious flashpoints.[71] They had even discussed arrangements for the day with what Chichester-Clark described to Callaghan as 'the "opposition" in Londonderry'.[72] However, it was not clear to the Apprentice Boys who this opposition were.

On 8 August 1969, representatives of the Apprentice Boys and of the Bogside met. Hume and McCann had not been invited because what was left of the city's unionist establishment suspected that the pair was aiming to be lords of misrule at their annual carnival; the key figures in the new Derry Citizens Defence Association (DCDA), who were actually less concerned about keeping order, had been invited instead.[73] The DCDA was a reconfiguring of the civil rights coalition. Following the July 1969 riots, those people who were still working within the DCAC were divided over how to prepare for the Apprentice Boys march: some thought the body should take the lead, others that it should honour its commitment to non-violence.[74] The Republicans, in contrast, had no doubt that the area had to be defended – although setting up the DCDA was a step up from street and neighbourhood committees. Once again, though, they reached out to 'representatives of Civil Rights bodies, political parties, and tenants' associations', which gave the DCDA greater legitimacy but gave Republicans less influence.[75] For example, Paddy Doherty, 'a pretty big fish' in the now 'ineffective' DCAC, swam over to the DCDA. 'I had my mind made up,' he testified at the Scarman Tribunal, 'that if there was anybody going to make decisions for the people of this city...I was going to be in the middle of it'.[76]

Doherty, along with Keenan, was certainly in the middle of the 'full and frank' discussions at the Apprentice Boys Memorial Hall. The two 'very outspoken men' warned that the parade could have 'serious consequences' and 'indicated that the people felt entitled to use whatever method was at their disposal to defend their homes'. However, proceedings then moved on to the 'brass tacks' of the stewarding for the event – or rather they appeared to move on to the real business, as the figures mentioned were conjured out of smoke.[77] DCAC stewards had been dropping out (largely in response to the decline in official protests and the rise in violence) and most of those remaining had not been enthusiastic about joining the DCDA's Peace Corps.[78] Paul Grace, who had been the DCAC's chief steward, was enthusiastic, but was passed over for a role because he had lost credibility after he had spoken to police just before a baton charge that had left a marshal injured during the previous month's riots; Len Green, Grace's brother-in-law and brother trade unionist, took charge instead, and took the corps nowhere.[79] Contrary to what the Apprentice Boys were told, 'there really were very little stewarding arrangements for 12th August'.[80]

Another matter that was raised, yet not resolved, in these discussions was the problem of rumours. 'We have been subjected to all sorts of rumours,' James Doherty explained to the tribunal, 'some of which reach alarming proportions.'[81] The most alarming was that the Apprentice Boys were not just planning to invade the Bogside, but that they were also going to be supported by Protestant gangs from Glasgow.[82] Rumour here was a form of political language, telling how trust had broken down and how the future was being imagined by many within the local Catholic community.[83] This particular rumour was an expression of rational anxieties rather than irrational fears: the Bogside had come under attack before, the British and Irish media was covering 'the new wave of Glasgow hooliganism' and Scots were travelling over to Derry.[84] People wanted to believe the rumour because it fitted with how they viewed the world – indeed, efforts to counter this and other stories actually helped to build up the rumours. Similarly, more general calls for peace served to draw attention to its absence.[85] The coming clash was advertised by the Junior Chamber of Commerce's 'Progress through Peace' campaign, with its stickers, badges, posters and (bizarrely) pot plants, as much as it was by the slogans daubed around the Bogside which read 'Remember October 5', 'You won't forget the 12th' and 'Up the IRA'.[86] The narrative that this graffiti told about the past ten months and the days ahead in the city was opened out by Eddie McAteer, in the performance that he gave at the DCDA's Celtic Park rally on 10 August 1969, to cover hundreds of years and the whole island. 'If a hand other than ours embarks on the terrible work which we all fear', he said, 'then be sure that this means the raising of the curtain on the last terrible act of the age-old Irish drama'.[87] McAteer was a born-again nationalist who now believed that it was the end of days for Northern Ireland.

The next day, McCann – for whom motley was still the only wear – ridiculed this 'fleeting vision of green pillar-boxes in the streets of Derry'. 'McAteer's "watching brethren" had been watching for fifty years'.[88] (Paddy Doherty and Keenan were in Dublin that very day finding out that republicans, whether they were in Upper Merrion Street or in Gardiner Place, seemed content to keep watching.)[89] But, the conflict had constrained McCann's ability to contest the wider nationalist narrative. As he had earlier conceded, 'we have finished up participating in the "Defence Association" locking ourselves inside the Catholic area'.[90] The future was locked in place.

THE BATTLE OF THE BOGSIDE

So the story goes, 'Big Ed' Harrigan cast the first stone of the battle.[91] He may well have: it was a group of youths behind the barriers in William Street that at about 2:30 pm started throwing missiles towards the police. Hume and McCann, backed by a smattering of DCAC stewards, urged them to stop, just as they had the night before when hundreds of Catholic and Protestant teenagers briefly clashed in the Fountain.[92] They failed, yet they had tried; Green, by his own admission, was at home asleep and his Peace Corps, which numbered 'not more than 100 anyway', seemed to be taking its lead from him. When Green finally got to William Street, he made no attempt to restrain the rioters but instead headed off with Keenan to 'ensure that barricades were erected all around the Bogside' in the positions planned by the DCDA. Some had been up since the previous day, others were put up quickly using the materials that the DCDA had stockpiled (the association was proving to be far more capable in its second role as defenders than its first as peacekeepers).[93] And yet, no-one had, in fact, attacked the Bogside. Nearly 10,000 people had marched through the city or watched the parade, bands had repeatedly played 'The Sash' and 'Dolly's Brae' and spectators had shouted sectarian slogans – but the rumoured invasion had not come.[94] Even when the William Street crowd began to hurl petrol bombs, rival gangs began to fight in Little James Street and buildings began to burn down, the RUC stuck to static defence (although many officers were chucking bricks back).[95] Only after 5 pm, with senior officers worried that the disorder was spreading, did the police launch a baton charge against the 200 or so rioters.[96] This manoeuvre, however, resulted in the policemen involved getting outflanked by petrol-bomb throwers, and the control room now became concerned that the RUC would be 'overwhelmed' and that the rioters would then 'break out' to 'clash [with the] large groups of loyalists...still in the city'. 'I felt', County Inspector Gerald Mahon testified before the tribunal, 'some action should be taken'.[97] Leslie Scarman, though, privately 'doubt[ed] whether there was really any police strategy after the first ten minutes'.[98]

An armoured Humber was sent to crash through the weak barriers on Little James Street. It then made a loop around the Bogside back to William Street, which it reached from the opposite direction by demolishing, at the sixth or seventh attempt, the strong barricade in Rossville

Street. Another Humber, several Land Rovers, and almost 100 police-men on foot pushed through the gap; they were followed by a number of Protestant civilians (encouraged by some officers, turned back by others) and were met by numberless petrol bombs.[99] This was how many people in the Bogside thought the story was supposed to go: Paisleyites, in and out of uniform, would attack their homes, and be driven back. (BBC Northern Ireland was also, mistakenly, reporting that the Apprentice Boys had indeed marched through the area.)[100] Father Anthony Mulvey, who had been alerted by Paddy Doherty to this 'Paisleyite' invasion, raged to the nearest RUC officer that 'Unless something is done about them immediately I will go into the Bogside and lead the people myself'.[101] According to the police radio and Mahon's evidence, a withdrawal was ordered, so as to 'show that we had no intention of remaining in that area in force' and to let 'people with influence...possibly grasp the situation'.[102] But, people with influence, on the whole, had grasped something else. Mulvey 'declined in rather bad form...to call at the Station to speak to...the Officer in Charge'; Michael Canavan 'changed [his] view of the situation radically', deciding to 'cease peacekeeping operations and instead to help the people to do whatever they had to do to defend their homes'.[103] (Even some foreign students who had come to Derry for a Fellowship of Reconciliation summer camp moved from non-violence to defence.)[104] Mulvey saw a large crowd, 'certainly 1,000 people', chase out the retreating police and Protestants: 'the determination was so unanimous that I could only regard it as a community in revolt'.[105] The police, however, were coming to regard it somewhat differently. The RUC's lawyers submitted to the tribunal that the DCDA had 'deliberately planned and engineered the general course of events, and that that planning was...a further step in a campaign to challenge the authority of the Stormont Government, to disrupt the life of the community and to discredit or destroy the police force'.[106] The narratives could not be bridged.

Under cross-examination at the tribunal, Mahon objected to counsel for the DCDA using the word 'stalemate' to describe what happened that night.[107] The RUC may have pulled out to the edge of the city centre, but '[a]ll forces were committed' (about 700 officers), they were still taking 'quite a number of casualties' and 'the men were beginning to tire'.[108] With 'our manpower...stretched to the limit', the police gave up on keeping back what the logs had referred to as 'Loyalist' and 'Paisleyite' throngs and began to let what were now called 'Civilians' 'assist'.[109] The British army intelligence officer's situation report noted that '91 police [had been] treated in hospital' and that 'it was only with the assistance of the loyalist crowd that the rioters were contained'.[110] By about 11 pm, Mahon's two deputies in the field had agreed that 'this was no longer a police operation, that this was a military operation'; but, politicians at Stormont and Westminster feared intervention, and so the only option open at this time was the folly of CS gas.[111] (Part of the deal reached between Callaghan and Chichester-Clark the week before was that the conditions laid down as to when CS gas could be deployed had been relaxed.)[112] Although the Reserve Force Head Constables – who had recently been trained by the army to use 'tearsmoke' – all felt as early as 9 pm that CS gas was needed, another two hours were to pass before Deputy Inspector-General Graham Shillington, having arrived from Belfast, assessed the situation and consulted the Minister, finally gave the order.[113] Around midnight, after the first of the 1,091 cartridges and fourteen grenades that would hit the Bogside and the Creggan had been fired, Shillington toured the walls and formed the 'impression…that the use of tearsmoke had been a complete success in settling the riotous conditions'.[114] Its use, however, had also been a complete failure in settling the Bogside. The Knights of Malta, which would eventually treat 373 people for the effects of CS gas at its first-aid posts, later complained that clouds 'seeped into houses' and 'old people', in particular, 'choked'. CS gas was '[u]sed punitively' against a whole community 'rather than to move crowds'.[115] The Battle of the Bogside would therefore go into a second day, one in which the fighting would be fiercer than the first.

McCann had 'emerged', 'in the manner of a Tory Party leader', as the DCDA's information officer, so he took responsibility for writing and issuing a leaflet on how to cope with CS gas. He was helped by both a journalist from the *Black Dwarf*, who telephoned the London office of his socialist newspaper for advice, and a Derry doctor, who was involved with the DCAC and Hume's constituency party.[116] Later, Ó Dochartaigh and a bus full of Bogsiders went to Donegal to ask the Irish army for medical supplies and to buy swimming goggles.[117] Local residents in the worst affected streets were also improvising their own solutions, such as burning tyres or leaving bowls of water on doorsteps into which people could dip the handkerchiefs they were using to mask their faces.[118] These reactions are revealing. Although witnesses and barristers at the Scarman hearings presented the Battle of the Bogside as either a spontaneous uprising or a planned insurgency, neither of these views captures the complexity of what happened behind the barricades. Alliance does.[119] Alliance is a process whereby different groups compromise in order to work together – and it is therefore a means, not an end. In Derry, politicians allied with each other, local actors allied with outsiders (notably, an IRA flying column from Donegal and foreign leftists) and the would-be leaders allied with the people on the streets.[120] A reporter from the *Times*, Timothy Jones, encountered another example of alliance in operation when he visited Rossville Street junction at midday on 13 August 1969, after the police had moved back into William Street. He found 'a munitions camp', where 'women and children were filling bottles...from bath-tubs filled with petrol' and 'children were ripping up paving stones, breaking them, putting them in wheel barrows and transporting them'. On the front line, Jones spoke to student radicals who had come over from the continent to show the Bogsiders 'how it was done' and to Bernadette Devlin who was 'encouraging people...to defend the barricade'. Devlin was the dominant figure in this area, yet she was not always doing what the DCDA wanted (she argued with Paddy Doherty) and the fighters were not always doing what she wanted (some of them raised the Irish Tricolour over Rossville flats).[121]

Hume, too, had to try to plead with people to follow him. Later that afternoon, he had to spend 'several hours' at the gasworks talking to 'half-a-dozen' armed, local men who were threatening to 'cause explosions', before he 'finally persuaded them to leave'.[122] Hume's next set of negotiations was not so successful. From about 3 pm onwards, the police station in Rosemount, a mixed neighbourhood just outside the Creggan, had been under attack by as many as 600 men. While such an action could be portrayed as a defensive move intended to relieve pressure on the Bogside or to pre-empt an invasion of the Creggan, this would probably expand the definition of self-defence far beyond the point of conceptual precision; indeed, even after the seventy officers at the barracks had been completely surrounded, the assaults still continued. However, when Hume reached Rosemount four hours into this battle, he was able to win support for a negotiated truce at a series of meetings held behind the barricades. So, during a lull in the fighting, Hume and the ten delegates chosen to accompany him went up to the back door of the station and agreed terms with the RUC (there was, though, one further shower of petrol bombs and two IRA volunteers did argue for more). But, Hume failed to get the siege lifted and later received 'quite an amount' of 'abuse' back in the Bogside for this 'most unpopular' 'ceasefire'. 'I reckoned I was wasting my time standing up to try [to] tell people to stop again'.[123]

Hume therefore had his earlier judgment, formed in the morning, confirmed: 'the only thing they would accept was defeat for the police and, if that was to be done without any further violence, it meant the troops coming in and that I tried to have arranged'.[124] (Hume also tried to arrange for 'the suspension of Stormont'.)[125] Shillington, who was 'only too anxious to withdraw the police', attempted throughout the day to 'get an undertaking from any person who had authority over [the] crowd that they had no intentions of...breaking into the city centre'; Hume, among others, helped him to realize that there was no-one who could make this deal.[126] Devlin, too, had concluded that troops had to come in – but she had telephoned Dublin, not London, at 11 am to ask for them. She had been 'manning the barricades since 4 o'clock yester-day' against a 'united force of police and Paisleyites', the Department of Defence was told, and was now 'in desperate need' of 'fresh men, either officially or unofficially,' and 'a supply of teargas and/or gas masks'.[127] Within the fractured Fianna Fáil Cabinet, which met later that day, there were some ministers who were also eager for a military intervention, maybe even one which aimed at capturing Derry, in the hope of causing an international incident that would carry the question of partition to the United Nations.[128] One of them, Kevin Boland, wrote in his memoirs that 'this was...the time for the solution to the final problem'.[129] The Irish Defence Forces, though, probably did not have the capabilities to mount even such a limited operation. Still, the hawks nonetheless pushed the Taoiseach, Jack Lynch, into sending soldiers to the border and into sexing-up the speech that the civil service had prepared for him. The Secretary of the Department of External Affairs had earlier judged that events had rendered a 'tentative draft' 'inappropriate for use' ('it puts the British Government on the spot publicly' and '[Prime Minister Harold] Wilson might manoeuvre the Taoiseach into appearing to have asked for, or approved of, the use of

British troops') and so he had submitted instead a vague one that 'appeal[ed] for restraint on all sides'.[130] However, the politicians now appeared to want to take sides. At 9 pm, on both radio and television, Lynch delivered a tough, clear message: the 'spirit of reform and inter-communal co-operation has given way to the forces of sectarianism and prejudice'; 'the RUC is no longer accepted as an impartial police force'; 'the employment of British troops' would not be 'acceptable'; a 'Peace-keeping Force' was 'urgently' required; this was 'all the inevitable outcome of the policies pursued for decades by successive Stormont governments'; this 'deplorable and distressing situation' would be ended 'firstly by the granting of full equality of citizenship' and 'eventually by the restoration of the historic unity of our country'.[131]

This may have been a clearer statement of Irish policy than the diplomatic drafts – but, during these summer days, nothing was particularly clear. While Lynch had managed, for the moment, to match the mood of his Cabinet and his country, audiences across the border had listened with different pasts, ideas, values, expectations and senses of how things were and should be.[132] Donal McDermott – who had just been at a DCDA press conference which had requested 'troops of any nation at all [to] come on to the streets of Derry' – described the speech to an *Irish Times* correspondent as 'what we have been waiting for' and 'the greatest thing that could have happened'. The journalist then went over to the Rossville Street area and found the fighters in a 'festive mood'.[133] As Paddy Doherty told the tribunal, the broadcast had 'stiff-ened their back'.[134] But, dreams for some were nightmares for others. Although Eamonn Gallagher (fast becoming the Northern expert at the Department of External Affairs) was to claim six weeks later that 'Lynch's statement...helped to prevent' the 'real possibility' of 'a massacre by B Specials', the Taoiseach's talk actually seems to have led to off-duty B-Specials marching on the Bogside.[135] (The police log shows that a loyalist crowd began to gather after 9 pm and a number of eyewitnesses reported people 'wearing police-style helmets' and 'carrying rifles'.)[136] Caught between the 'rival factions' in Great James Street, the RUC, according to the evidence given by district inspectors on the scene, were 'little better than spectators', until reinforcements arrived and went into action against the Bogsiders (the 'Protestant element' were not 'offer[ing]' 'any violence...to the police').[137] An ITN news crew saw a few officers fire their revolvers.[138] In the early hours of the morning, with the 'opposing factions' heading 'home', the RUC was finally able to execute a pincer movement which dispersed the fighters on Great James Street and which also relieved the besieged Rosemount barracks.[139] The loyalist crowd, meanwhile, tried to burn out the foreign press based at the City Hotel, pushed cars with Southern number plates into the river and stoned the Convent of Mercy and the offices of the *Derry Journal*.[140]

The second, long day of the Battle of the Bogside had closed with a Pyrrhic victory for the RUC. 'Every policeman on duty was out continually without proper rest or relief for meals', the head of the Reserve Force recalled. 'Everyone was committed'.[141] And, there was no longer any possibility of further police reinforcements because trouble had broken out in other parts of Northern Ireland. (During the first night, some of the main players, Keenan, McCann and Devlin, had contacted both NICRA and the local defence committees to get them to stage distractions the following day.)[142] '[W]e were left with a very, very short number of men', admitted Mahon.[143] So, on the afternoon of 14 August 1969, Stormont broadcast a call for all B-Specials to mobilize. In Derry, 210 out of a total strength of 582 reported and were sent out to duties in Protestant areas of the city (only officers were issued with guns).[144] The B-Specials kept back loyalists from the Fountain for a while, yet soon rival crowds were fighting in a blazing Bishop Street and some constables were choosing to take sides.[145] As the lead article in the next day's *Derry Journal* noted, 'there were some fears [that] armed police, plus armed Specials, and aided by Paisleyites would embark on a sanguinary sweep of Catholic areas'. There were also some hopes that 'intervention', whether from 'Britain or Ireland', would come before this pogrom.[146] The RUC, however, was not planning to push forward into the Bogside but instead to 'fall back on the police station[s] and possibly defend [them] with firearms', leaving the 'centre of the city [to] a riotous mob'. Stormont now had no option except to ask Westminster for troops.[147] The formal request was made at 'about 4:35 p.m.' when Callaghan was flying back from a meeting with Wilson at a Cornish air force base; he wrote 'Permission granted' on a signal pad and gave it to the navigator.[148] The British were coming.

When intervention had become inevitable, the General Officer Commanding the British army in Northern Ireland, Lieutenant-General Ian Freeland, had set out for the Ministry of Defence how he would use four companies to prevent Victoria barracks and the city centre from being overrun by rioters – and how he would be prepared to order his men to open fire. (The government and the General 'agreed that in no circumstances would British troops be asked to enter Bogside'.)[149] At 5:45 pm, shortly after news of the deployment had spread through the city, a 'Barricade Bulletin' starting circulating which declared 'Derry is in a state of war' and promised '[w]e shall beat the soldiers as we have now beaten the police'.[150] But, there was to be no confrontation. Thirty or so minutes earlier, McAteer and a major had talked across the wire erected by the army in Waterloo Place and had selected the line to be taken: the crowd was to stay behind the barriers and the police were to stay out of sight.[151] This approach was later accepted at talks involving a DCDA deputation, the regiment's Colonel and senior RUC officers – although, as ever, the would-be leaders then had to try to sell this deal to the people in the streets.[152] Paddy Doherty stood on a burnt-out van and told the crowd that they had won because the army was in control and the police and the B-Specials were withdrawing; Devlin, in contrast, told them to keep fighting because Chichester-Clark had just informed her over the telephone that Stormont was still in control and the army was supporting the police and the B-Specials. Once again, nothing was clear. Doherty prevailed in this debate, yet the verdict was far from unanimous and there were shouts from the Rossville flats of 'Traitors'.[153]

The Battle of the Bogside had ended, the struggle was to continue.[154] The next evening, Devlin telephoned 10 Downing Street with a warning that she would 'hoist the socialist flag of James Connolly on the top of the nine-storey block of flats in Bogside' and 'seek assistance from any quarter'.[155] The one-time moderates took an even more radical position in the days that followed. Paddy Doherty's faction assured one of the Republic of Ireland's agents in the Bogside that British troops were not going to be allowed into the area and that 'this Committee is taking its orders from our Government in Dublin'.[156] 'Free Derry', encompassing some 880 acres and 25,000 citizens, had effectively seceded from the United Kingdom.[157] Doherty and Canavan presented the Colonel with a list of 'long-term demands': the abolition of Stormont, the disbandment of the B-Specials and the granting of a legal amnesty. 'We remain at war with Stormont until these demands are met'.[158]

CONCLUSION

After Callaghan's second visit to 'Free Derry', on 11 October 1969, Paddy Doherty softened the language that he used in public. He praised the Home Secretary's understanding of the problems', 'hard work' and 'political brilliance'. 'We have been given the bones of a just society'.[159] According to the official communiqué, the RUC would be 'civilianised'; Arthur Young, 'the Commissioner of the City of London Police', would be the new Inspector-General; he and his successors would be 'account-able' to a 'Police Authority' that would be 'representative of the com-munity as a whole'; a 'system of independent public prosecutors' would be 'adopted'; the B-Specials would be 'replaced' by a 'volunteer reserve' and a 'locally-recruited military force' 'commanded by the General Officer Commanding, Northern Ireland'; Westminster would invest more money, 'some £3 m' per annum over three years, into industrial development and Stormont would 'initiate a programme of works cost-ing up to £2 m for the relief of unemployment'; 'detailed recommen-dations designed to reinforce the safeguards against discrimination in public employment' would be put into effect; an 'anti-discrimination clause' would be added to 'all Government contracts'; an 'expanded housing programme' would be implemented; a 'single purpose, efficient and streamlined central housing authority' would be created; and a 'broadly based' 'review body' would be 'set up' to study 'current proposal for reshaping local administration'. The socio-economic language of conflict had been used to tell a story in which a 'comprehen-sive programme of reform' 'designed' to 'ensure a common standard of citizenship' and to 'stimulate the economy' would lead to an ending in which 'all citizens' lived in 'harmony and prosperity'.[160] This was a fairy tale, as Callaghan himself was coming to realize. A policy appraisal drafted for him by his officials shortly afterwards was not 'so opti-mistic': the 'minority shows no wish to be reconciled' and the 'ability of Stormont to handle [the] situation' was 'doubt[ful]'.[161]

While the British may not be gifted at learning new languages, the servants of the state were at least trying to learn a new language of conflict in Northern Ireland. The army had been instructed by Callaghan to bring about a 'lowering of tension before his...visit in order to set the way towards reforms'; but, 'off the record', senior officers in Derry had doubts about this strategy because 'Trouble can always break out at no notice whatsoever' and 'the Catholics here...

quote a long history of broken promises which have vanished into air'.[162] The Hunt Committee, appointed to look into ways to reform the police, privately concluded that 'fair play for Roman Catholics was not now the aim of the leaders in Bogside'. 'Even if it could be shown that there was no discrimination...the extremists would continue to fight.'[163] Indeed, Paddy Doherty and McCann, among others, were receiving small-arms training from, respectively, the Irish Defence Forces and the IRA.[164] ('Whatever the men were up to,' McCafferty later recalled, 'nobody told us Derry women.')[165] However, they were also secretly informing the army that they were 'anxious to be relieved of all responsibility'.[166] The would-be leaders kept switching between languages, which was not helping any outsiders, Irish or British, to educate themselves. Indeed, Hume, too, was still speaking different languages with different audiences: making 'no call at all for a united Ireland' in his talks with British officials, while assuring Irish ones that the 'victory in Derry was complete' and that in a 'fair Northern Ireland' constitutional change would be 'inevitable' in ten to fifteen years.[167] Hume told Gallagher that at a dinner thrown by the Development Commission's Health Committee, the President of Ireland had been toasted before the Queen and that this 'curious incident' was evidence that the 'inevitability of some sort of arrangement with Dublin has already made considerable headway in moderate Unionist circles'.[168] It had not made any headway with Anderson, though, who was 'very unhappy' about the reforms and who did not trust London let alone Dublin. 'Ordinary Unionist Members', he 'argued rationally' to Oliver Wright, the UK Representative, 'believed that HMG [Her Majesty's Government] had put the screws on...Chichester-Clark.' Anderson now wanted Westminster to put the hammer to the Bogside and use the army to 'restore law and order' – if not, '"his people" might be forced to do so'. Wright described the City MP as an 'extremist' (British bureaucrats were writing opponents of the Westminster line into the margins).[169] Underlying this 'bible-thumping bloody-mindedness', explained Wright in a later dispatch, was the 'fear' that Unionism was 'threatened' with the 'loss of power in its own territory' and with 'its subjection to a regime which it finds repugnant'. For the UK Representative, the drama would end with a marriage between 'Ulster' and 'the Republic', one brought about by 'seduction not rape'.[170] Anderson and the thousands of voters that he represented were not so much afraid of how the story would end, as of what the next chapters would hold: the IRA campaign that they were certain was coming.[171] The Irish revolution was not over, the narratives had not ended.

NOTES

1. A. Mulvey's evidence to the Scarman Tribunal, 25 September 1969, London, Institute of Advanced Legal Study, Scarman minutes of evidence, pp. 56–7; E. McCann's evidence to the Scarman Tribunal, 30 October 1969, p. 42.
2. E. McCann, 'Who's Wrecking Civil Rights?', August 1969, Belfast, Public Record Office of Northern Ireland (PRONI), HA/32/2/28.
3. P. Tarleton's evidence to the Scarman Tribunal, 24 November 1969, p. 5; INTSUM, 26 September to 3 October 1969, London, National Archives (NA), WO/305/3361.
4. Londonderry Sentinel, 20 August 1969.
5. P. Farrell to B. Faulkner, 25 August 1969, PRONI, CAB/9B/312/1.
6. On competitive violence, see A. Lawrence, 'Triggering Nationalist Violence Competition and Conflict in Uprisings against Colonial Rule', International Security, 35, 2 (Fall 2010), pp. 88–122.
7. Irish Press, 14 August 1969.
8. B. Meharg to J. Greeves, 27 March 1969, PRONI, HA/32/2/26.
9. Derry Journal, 18 March 1969.
10. Derry Journal, 25 March 1969.
11. Meharg to Greeves, 27 March 1969.
12. Londonderry Sentinel, 26 March 1969.
13. S. Kalyvas, The Logic of Violence in Civil War (Cambridge: Cambridge University Press, 2006), p. 57.
14. Photocopy of DCAC minutes, 15 March 1969, PRONI, GOV/2/1/186.
15. B. Meharg to J. Greeves, 8 April 1969, PRONI, HA/32/2/26.
16. Londonderry Sentinel, 1 April 1969.
17. Derry Journal, 1 April 1969.
18. Belfast Telegraph, 22 April 1969.
19. J. Greeves, March by the Civil Rights Association from Burntollet to Altnagelvin, 21 April 1969, PRONI, HA/32/2/26.
20. J. Greeves, Note for the Record, 21 April 1969, PRONI, HA/32/2/26.
21. Derry Journal, 22 April 1969; Londonderry Sentinel, 23 April 1969.
22. Police Ombudsman for Northern Ireland, Findings on Devenny Investigation, 4 October 2001.
23. Derry Journal, 22 April 1969; Londonderry Sentinel, 23 April 1969; J. Hume's evidence to the Scarman Tribunal, 14 November 1969, p. 26.
24. Derry Journal, 28 March 1969; Derry Journal, 22 April 1969.
25. F. Gogarty, 'The Development of the Civil Rights Movement and its Future Course', [May 1969], PRONI, D/3253/3/11/5.
26. Cabinet conclusions, 15 May 1969, PRONI, CAB/4/1443.
27. Londonderry Sentinel, 23 April 1969. Around this time, ministers began to worry about 'massive resistance', a direct reference to the opposition to civil rights in the United States. Cabinet conclusions, 22 April 1969, PRONI, CAB/4/1437.
28. Derry Journal, 15 July 1969.
29. E. McCann, untitled pamphlet, 19 July 1969, PRONI, HA/32/2/28.
30. Cabinet Security Committee Minutes, 15 July 1969, PRONI, HA/32/3/1.
31. Ramparts, 1, 4 [late July 1969] Belfast, Linen Hall Library.
32. S. Kalyvas, 'The Ontology of "Political Violence": Action and Identity in Civil Wars', Perspectives on Politics, 1, 3 (September 2003), pp 475–494, p. 475. Kalyvas's argument is prefigured, albeit in a limited way, in N. Ó Dochartaigh, From Civil Rights to Armalites: Derry and the Birth of the Irish Troubles (Basingstoke: Palgrave Macmillan, 2005 edn.), pp. 213–14.

33. C. Carson (ed.), *The Autobiography of Martin Luther King, Jr.* (London: Abbacus, 2000 edn.), pp. 213–16.
34. R. Kelley, *Race Rebels: Culture, Politics and the Black Working Class* (New York, NY: Free Press, 1994), pp. 9 and 88–90.
35. *Derry Journal*, 25 April 1969.
36. Cabinet Security Committee Minutes, 14 and 31 July 1969.
37. Memorandum by the Secretary State for the Home Department, 28 July 1969, NA, CAB/129/144.
38. Warning, 17 July 1969, NA, DEFE/25/302.
39. INTSUM, 27 January to 3 February 1970, NA, WO/305/3350.
40. INTSUM, 5 to 16 August 1970, NA, WO/305/3356.
41. *Derry Journal*, 7 April 1970; INTSUM, 1 to 7 July 1970, NA, WO/305/3355.
42. INTSUM, 14 to 20 October 1970, NA, WO/305/3358; *Derry Journal*, 16 October 1970.
43. Cabinet Security Committee Minutes, 7 May 1969.
44. *Derry Journal*, 13 May 1969.
45. *Derry Journal*, 25 April 1969.
46. Northern Ireland: Political Summaries, 25 June to 2 July 1969, 3 to 9 July 1969 and 15 to 22 July 1969, NA, CJ/3/5.
47. See, for instance, *Derry Journal*, 13 May 1969; *Londonderry Sentinel*, 14 May 1969; Minutes of fifteenth and seventeenth meeting of the Londonderry Development Commission, 3 June and 17 June 1969, PRONI, DC/3/1/1A/1.
48. *Derry Journal*, 13 May 1969; Summary of Events, 18 May 1969, NA, DEFE/25/302.
49. *Derry Journal*, 15 April 1969
50. *Derry Journal*, 8 April 1969.
51. *Derry Journal*, 11 April 1969; *Derry Journal*, 25 April 1969.
52. *Derry Journal*, 11 April 1969; *Derry Journal*, 24 June 1969; *Derry Journal*, 29 July 1969.
53. *Londonderry Sentinel*, 14 May 1969; Minutes of sixteenth meeting of the Londonderry Development Commission, 10 June 1969; *Londonderry Sentinel*, 23 July 1969.
54. INTSUM, 2 to 9 November 1969, NA, WO/305/3362.
55. N. McCafferty, *Nell* (London: Penguin, 2004), pp. 137–8.
56. INTSUM, 8 to 14 December 1969, NA, WO/305/3363.
57. INTSUM, 27 January to 3 February 1970, NA, WO/305/3350.
58. *Derry Journal*, 1 April 1969; A. McCabe's evidence to the Scarman Tribunal, 6 October 1969, p. 42.
59. *Derry Journal*, 13 June 1969. People living on Bridge Street mounted a similar protest a few weeks later. *Derry Journal*, 8 July 1969.
60. Minute by CH, 24 July 1969, Dublin, National Archives of Ireland (NAI), DFA/305/14/386.
61. Memorandum by the Secretary State for the Home Department, 28 July 1969; Northern Ireland: Political Summary, 15–22 July 1969.
62. Note of discussion at the Foreign Office at 12 noon on Friday, 1 August 1969, NAI, DT/2000/6/657; Minutes of discussion at the Foreign Office, 1 August 1969, NAI, DFA/2000/5/38.
63. Memorandum by the Secretary State for the Home Department, 28 July 1969.
64. B. Cubbon, Northern Ireland, 6 August 1969, NA, FCO/33/765.
65. B. Cubbon to P. Gregson, 8 August 1969, NA, FCO/33/765.
66. Cabinet conclusions, 11 August 1969, PRONI, CAB/4/1458.
67. See, for instance, J. Callaghan, Northern Ireland: General Appreciation on Intervention, 1 May 1969, NA, CAB/130/416: 'our best tactics are to continue to encourage Northern Ireland to sort out their own troubles themselves'.
68. *Belfast Telegraph*, 8 August 1969.
69. Cabinet conclusions, 4 August 1969, PRONI, CAB/4/1456; Cabinet Security Committee Minutes, 31 July 1969.
70. Cubbon, Northern Ireland, 6 August 1969.
71. G. Mahon's evidence to the Scarman Tribunal, 1 October 1969, pp. 22–5; Cabinet conclusions, 11 August 1969.

72. Cubbon to Gregson, 8 August 1969.
73. T. Robinson's evidence to the Scarman Tribunal, 26 November 1969, p. 1.
74. D. McDermott's evidence to the Scarman Tribunal, 11 November 1969, pp. 72–3; P. Grace's evidence to the Scarman Tribunal, 12 November 1969, pp. 77–8.
75. *Derry Journal*, 29 July 1969.
76. P. Doherty's evidence to the Scarman Tribunal, 28 November 1969, pp. 23–4.
77. J. Doherty's evidence to the Scarman Tribunal, 26 September 1969, pp. 69–70. Doherty was using notes taken at the meeting.
78. F. O'Doherty's evidence to the Scarman Tribunal, 11 November 1969, pp. 4–8.
79. P. Doherty's evidence to Scarman, pp. 85–6; *Derry Journal*, 22 July 1969; L. Green's evidence to the Scarman Tribunal, 12 November 1969, pp. 26 and 49.
80. McDermott's evidence, p. 48.
81. J. Doherty's evidence, p. 70.
82. Hume's evidence, p. 4; McDermott's evidence, p. 36.
83. See G. Fine, 'Rumor, Trust and Civil Society: Collective Memory and Cultures of Judgment', *Diogenes*, 54, 1 (February 2007), pp. 5–18.
84. A. Bartie, 'Moral Panics and Glasgow Gangs: Exploring "the New Wave of Glasgow Hooliganism", 1965–1970', *Contemporary British History*, 24, 3 (July 2010), pp. 385–408, p. 390; J. Scott to P. Gregson, 31 August 1970, NA, PREM/15/474.
85. P. Donovan, 'How Idle is Idle Talk? One Hundred Years of Rumor Research', *Diogenes*, 54, 1 (February 2007), pp. 59–82, pp. 69–70; INTSUM, 15 to 21 July 1970, NA, WO/305/3355 (an 'assessment...of the disorders in August '69').
86. *Derry Journal*, 8 August 1969.
87. *Derry Journal*, 12 August 1969.
88. *Derry Journal*, 12 August 1969.
89. The *Observer*, 17 August 1969; P. Doherty's evidence, pp. 25 and 100; P. Doherty, *Paddy Bogside* (Cork: Mercier Press, 2001), pp. 119–26.
90. McCann, 'Who's Wrecking Civil Rights?'
91. McCafferty, *Nell*, p. 162.
92. W. Hood's evidence to the Scarman Tribunal, 6 October 1969, p. 19; *Londonderry Sentinel*, 13 August 1969.
93. Green's evidence, pp. 26-32.
94. INTSUM, 15 to 21 July 1970.
95. *Derry Journal*, 15 August 1969.
96. M. Selvin's evidence to the Scarman Tribunal, 3 October 1969, pp. 54–7.
97. Mahon's evidence, 1 October 1969, pp. 37–8.
98. Note of Meeting with Mr Justice Scarman, 28 September 1969, NA, CJ/3/57.
99. F. Fleming's evidence to the Scarman Tribunal, 6 October 1969, pp. 61–4; INTSUM, 15 to 21 July 1970.
100. *Londonderry Sentinel*, 13 August 1969.
101. Mulvey's evidence, p. 61.
102. Mahon's evidence, 1 October 1969, p. 39.
103. Transcript of W. Golden's tape, London, Institute of Advanced Legal Study, Scarman Londonderry exhibits; M. Canavan's evidence to the Scarman Tribunal, 27 October 1969, pp. 14–15. Mulvey later went to Victoria barracks, received assurances from the police and conveyed these to the people in Rossville Street – but 'any hope of moderation' had been 'brushed aside'. Mulvey's evidence, p. 67.
104. Tarleton's evidence, p. 13.
105. Mulvey's evidence, pp. 62 and 67; INTSUM, 15 to 21 July 1970, reasons that this was 'probably not exaggerated'.
106. RUC's submission to the Scarman Tribunal, [Summer 1971], London, Institute of Advanced Legal Study, Scarman submissions, p. 36. A police spokesman at the time told journalists that 'This was not a spontaneous thing' (*Irish Times*, 13 August 1969) and British intelligence focused on the role played by Republicans and leftists (JIC(A)(69)(UWG), 18 August 1969, NA, PREM/13/2844).

107. G. Mahon's evidence to the Scarman Tribunal, 2 October 1969, p. 12.

108. Figures taken from G. Mahon to A. Peacocke, 2 August 1969, Scarman Londonderry Exhibits.

109. Mahon's evidence, 1 October 1969, pp. 39–44; Police Log – Incidents in Londonderry City, 12–16 August 1969, Scarman Londonderry Exhibits.

110. SITREP, 13 August 1969 (5:30 am), Scarman Londonderry Exhibits.

111. F. Armstrong's evidence to the Scarman Tribunal, 3 October 1969, p. 16; Record of a Meeting, 8 August, NA, DEFE/25/302.

112. Notes on a telephone conversation with the Home Secretary, 6 August 1969, PRONI, CAB/4/1458; Cubbon to Gregson, 8 August 1969.

113. T. Hood's evidence to the Scarman Tribunal, 15 October 1969, p. 12; I. Freeland to G. Baker, 15 July 1969, NA, DEFE/25/302; I. Freeland, Notes for Memoirs, London, Imperial War Museum, Freeland Papers, Box 79/34/4.

114. G. Shillington's evidence to the Scarman Tribunal, 2 October 1969, pp. 33–38; Police Log; Expenditure of Cartridges and Grenades, Scarman Londonderry Exhibits.

115. Injuries treated at first aid posts, Scarman Londonderry Exhibits.

116. McCann's evidence, pp. 50–3; *Irish Times*, 5 September 1969.

117. *Derry Journal*, 15 August 1969.

118. R. McClean's evidence to the Scarman Tribunal, 8 December 1969, pp. 1–12.

119. This is a slight adaptation of the concept developed in Kalyvas, *Logic of Violence in Civil War*, pp. 381–6.

120. INTSUM, 15 to 21 July 1970.

121. T. Jones's evidence to the Scarman Tribunal, 25 September 1969, pp. 21–5; B. Devlin's evidence to the Scarman Tribunal, 29 October 1969, pp. 6 and 24; S. Armstrong, Interview with Bernadette Devlin, 28 August 1969, PRONI, D/3253/4/10/3; K. Speed to T. Heath, 24 August 1969, PRONI, CAB/9B/312/1.

122. Hume's evidence, p. 10; Police Log; Mahon's evidence, 1 October 1969, p. 54; *Derry Journal*, 15 August 1969.

123. R. Carwell's evidence to Scarman, 6 October 1969, pp. 25–9; McCabe's evidence, pp. 46–7; Hume's evidence, pp. 11 and 55–9.

124. Hume's evidence, p. 56.

125. *Derry Journal*, 15 August 1969. Hume spoke to Lord Stonham on the telephone. Record of Conversation between Lord Chalfont and Patrick Hillery, 15 August 1969, NA, PREM/13/244.

126. Shillington's evidence, pp. 40–2.

127. Note for the Record, 13 August 1969, NAI, DFA/2000/5/42.

128. The archival record is not particularly helpful; the account offered here draws heavily upon the reconstruction of the meeting in D. Keogh, *Jack Lynch: A Biography* (Dublin: Gill & MacMillan, 2008), pp. 168–70. The British ambassador reported that 'Several Irishmen… have mentioned to me…that to ensure proper ventilation of the Irish problem at the United Nations it might be desirable to create an international threat to peace by seizing some small town'. A. Gilchrist to Foreign and Commonwealth Office (telegram 175), 14 August 1969, NA, PREM/13/2844.

129. K. Boland, *The Rise and Decline of Fianna Fáil* (Dublin: Mercier Press, 1982), p. 67.

130. H. McCann to N. Nolan, 13 August 1969, NAI, DT/2000/6/657.

131. *Derry Journal*, 15 August 1969.

132. A. Gilchrist to Foreign and Commonwealth Office (telegram 174), 14 August 1969, NA, PREM/13/2844.

133. *Irish Times*, 14 August 1969.

134. P. Doherty's evidence, p. 32.

135. E. Gallagher to S. Ronan, 25 September 1969, NAI, DT/2000/6/659. At lunchtime on 13 August 1969, Shillington and the city commandant decided not to put the B-Specials anywhere near the Bogside. Shillington's evidence, p. 41.

136. Police Log; *Derry Journal*, 15 August 1969; O'Doherty's evidence to Scarman, p. 85.

137. N. McAtanney's evidence to the Scarman Tribunal, 8 December 1969, pp. 51–3 and 78.

138. B. Hatfield's evidence to the Scarman Tribunal, 26 November 1969, pp. 20–1.

139. Police Log.
140. *Derry Journal*, 15 August 1969.
141. W. Hood's evidence, p. 24.
142. INTSUM, 15 to 21 July 1970; F. Gogarty, Statement, 2 March 1970, PRONI, D/3253/3/22/1.
143. Mahon's evidence, 1 October 1969, p. 65.
144. E. O'Neill's evidence to the Scarman Tribunal, 16 October 1969, pp. 41–2.
145. D. Black's evidence to the Scarman Tribunal, 16 October 1969, p. 76–7.
146. *Derry Journal*, 15 August 1969.
147. Note for the Record, 14 August, NA, PREM/13/2844.
148. N. Cairncross, Note for the Record, 14 August 1969, NA, CJ/3/11; Note of a meeting held at RAF St Magwan, 14 August 1969, NA, PREM/13/2844; J. Callaghan, *A House Divided: The Dilemma of Northern Ireland* (London: Collins, 1973), pp. 41–2.
149. R. Hattersley to J. Callaghan, 14 August 1969, NA, CJ/3/11.
150. *Barricade Bulletin*, 14 August 1969.
151. D. Hanson's evidence to the Scarman Tribunal, 25 September 1969, pp. 45–7; E. McAteer's evidence to the Scarman Tribunal, 26 September 1969, pp. 22–3; *Derry Journal*, 15 August 1969.
152. Police Log.
153. P. Doherty's evidence, pp. 68–70; Tarleton's evidence, pp. 14–15; Devlin's evidence, pp. 44–5; *Londonderry Sentinel*, 20 August 1969.
154. Derry Young Socialists, 'the struggle continues...', [late August 1969], Derry, Derry City Council's Archives, Bridget Bond Civil Rights Collection. See also M. Farrell, Motion at People's Democracy conference, 12 October, PRONI, D/3297/4.
155. 'David from Roger', 15 August 1969, NA, PREM/13/2844.
156. S. Brady, An eye-witness report from Derry, 19 August 1969, NAI, DT/2000/6/658.
157. *Derry Journal*, 12 September 1969.
158. Canavan's evidence, pp. 80–4; *Derry Journal*, 19 August 1969.
159. *Derry Journal*, 14 October 1969; SITREP, 12 October 1969, NA, WO/305/3361.
160. Communique issued following the Home Secretary's discussions with the Northern Ireland government on 9–10 October, 10 October 1969, NA, CJ/4/5.
161. 'Home Secretary' [R. North], Northern Ireland: A Political Appraisal, 2 December 1969, NA, CJ/3/9.
162. P. Leng to D. Toler, 2 October 1969, NA, WO/305/3361; P. Leng to O. Wright, 25 September 1969, NA, CJ/5/2.
163. Londonderry Visit, 4 September 1969, NA, CJ/5/2.
164. Doherty, *Paddy Bogside*, pp. 187–91; E. McCann, *War and an Irish Town* (Harmondsworth: Penguin, 1974 edn.), pp. 72–3.
165. McCafferty, *Nell*, p. 180.
166. Meeting with DCDA, 19 September 1969, NA, CJ/5/2; INTSUM, 26 September to 3 October 1969.
167. O. Wright, Londonderry, 25 September 1969, NA, CJ/5/2; E. Gallagher to Holmes, 10 September 1969, NAI, DT/2000/6/660. What Gallagher heard in Derry shaped his next policy paper. E. Gallagher, Policy as a means to an end...,10 September 1969, NAI, DFA/2000/5/12.
168. E. Gallagher to Holmes, [25 October 1969], NAI, DT/2000/6/661.
169. O. Wright, Record of Conversation with Commander Anderson, 26 September 1969, NA, CJ/5/2.
170. O. Wright to J. Callaghan, 19 October 1969, NA, FCO/33/769. Around this time, Ken Whitaker, Governor of the General Central Bank of Ireland and a key adviser to Lynch, was proposing that the Taoiseach use 'words like' 'deep and legitimate desire for a united Ireland' rather than 'our claim to unity'. Keogh, *Jack Lynch*, p. 209.
171. *Londonderry Sentinel*, 20 August 1969. See also the interviews Proinsias Mac Aonghusa conducted with residents of the Fountain. Press cuttings, Imperial War Museum, Freeland Papers, Box 79/34/4.

9

From the Ashes of Bombay Street...

In September 1994, soon after the Provisional IRA had announced a 'complete cessation of military operations', the Belfast-born journalist David McKittrick wrote an article in the *Independent* that looked back to the riots of August 1969 in his home town. 'Bombay Street', he claimed, 'was in a real sense the birthplace of the Provisional IRA, which shortly afterwards broke away from the main IRA under the slogan "From the ashes of Bombay Street rose the Provisionals". They vowed that vulnerable Catholic areas would never again be left undefended'.[1] Contemporary unionist leaders, however, told a different story about what had happened. Prime Minister James Chichester-Clark insisted on 15 August 1969 that 'we confront here a deliberate conspiracy to subvert a democratically-elected government'.[2] This was a view shared by the likes of William Craig, Ian Paisley. John McKeague and other hardline unionists, too. In fact, a number of different factors combined to produce an explosive mixture. These included the growth in communal tension, which has been charted in the last Belfast chapter and was by no means the sole responsibility of the IRA; the clumsy interference of the Republic of Ireland; and the semi-detached policy of the British Government which, in the words of Home Secretary James Callaghan, was 'to influence while getting embroiled as little as possible', a contradictory and almost mutually exclusive approach.[3]

The IRA was certainly in no position to take on Stormont and its security forces. According to Billy McMillen, the Belfast Batallion in 1969 consisted of approximately 120 men who had only twenty-four weapons at their disposal, mostly short-range pistols. Raymond Quinn puts the figure at eighty full-time members and 200 auxiliaries and says that its 'arsenal' comprised two Thompson sub-machine guns, one Sten gun, a .303 Lee Enfield rifle and nine handguns.[4] The RUC's estimate ranged between 150 and 170 members and the City Commissioner would not commit himself with regard to its armament.[5] As early as 18 August 1969 the RUC admitted in a letter to the Ministry of Home Affairs that, although 'the I.R.A./Republican Movement have infiltrated and been manipulating the Civil Rights organisation with great energy, the speed of success of the latter in producing the present conditions in the streets has caught the I.R.A. largely unprepared in the military sense'.[6] What the IRA could do, though, was to light the spark which produced the explosion.

I

After Derry erupted into renewed violence on 12 and 13 August 1969, appeals for diversionary activities to draw the RUC away from the city emanated from the DCAC and the chair of NICRA, Frank Gogarty, called for such action on that night.[7] Gerry Adams tells us that the BHAC duly decided to hold a protest meeting at the Divis Flats on 13 August and on the same day McMillen ordered Republicans in Belfast to 'get people on the streets' to take the pressure off Derry. At 19:28 pm the Belfast police log recorded, 'White car Cortina...in vicinity of Unity Flats with loud speakers asking people to attend meeting at Divis Towers tonight to support riots in Derry'.[8]

Later in the evening a crowd – led, as we now know, by two IRA men, Joe McCann and Anthony Dornan – was moving from Divis Street up the Falls Road towards the RUC's Springfield Road barracks, where a deputation was received by the station sergeant to deliver a protest about events in Derry. The crowd then returned down the Falls to Divis Street and on towards the Hasting Street barracks which were bombarded by stones and petrol bombs. There then followed a police baton charge which drove the crowd back towards the Divis Flats.[9]

On hearing, just after 10:30 pm, that the crowd was heading over to Grosvenor Road, the Deputy Commissioner, Samuel Bradley, who feared that it might cross into a mixed area sent a platoon to stop it. This unit was met by gunfire and a hand grenade; the attackers were IRA volunteers.[10] Another IRA action on the Falls Road that night was the arson attack on Isaac Agnew's car showrooms. The police log reports at 23:32 pm that petrol bombs were thrown into them, looting was taking place and boys aged 14 or 15 years old were pulling vehicles out and setting fire to them. It was not young 'hooligans', however, who started the fire, but three IRA volunteers.[11]

It was a similar situation in Ardoyne, although guns were not fired there. Because of the trouble in the Lower Falls, the Crumlin Road had been relatively neglected by the RUC. District Inspector Montgomery told the Scarman Tribunal that only a sergeant and seven men were left at Hooker Street. Bottle throwing was reported at the Hooker Street-Disraeli Street interface as early as 7:16 pm on 13 August, but an urgent note only creeps into the police log four hours later when it was reported that rioting had begun. Protestants and Catholics had started throwing stones at one another and assistance was required. Father Marcellus Gillespie was out and about on the Catholic side of the Crumlin Road that night and he told the tribunal that he came upon a crowd 'who told me that they were told to try and draw the police off Bogside to reduce the pressure on Bogside, to create some sort of disturbance to keep the police occupied'. A degree of duress, as well as organization, is suggested by his subsequent remark that 'some of them actually asked me to persuade them to go home'.[12] The rioting continued in Ardoyne and on the Falls until well into the small hours of 14 August 1969. It was not until 4:20 am that the police log recorded 'all quiet now'.[13]

The effect that this rioting had upon local Protestant communities was considerable, especially when combined with the broadcast, at 9 pm on 13 August, of the Taoiseach, Jack Lynch, in which he declared that 'Irishmen in every part of this island' were concerned about what was taking place, that Stormont had 'lost control of the situation' and that his own government could 'no longer stand by and see innocent people injured and perhaps worse'.[14] The legitimacy or otherwise of not only the intervention from Dublin but also London's insistence that the situation was a domestic matter does not concern us here. What matters is that the interstate competition between the Republic of Ireland and the United Kingdom added to the sense of uncertainty in Belfast and the feeling that the relationship between the two communities there was in flux. This, in turn, encouraged some people to take up violence. Whereas the clashes on 13 August were confined to confrontations between the police and Catholic crowds, those on 14 and 15 August saw large-scale involvement of Protestant crowds and were much more violent. Indeed, all seven deaths occasioned by the rioting occurred during those two days.

The Republican interpretation of these events is summed up in a recent article by Roisin McManus in the *Andersonstown News*. 'This weekend', she wrote, 'marks the 40th anniversary of the pogroms of August 1969 when loyalists, B-Specials and the RUC invaded Catholic areas, shooting and burning as they went. In the hours that followed, three Catholics were shot dead as well as a Protestant rioter. As shots were fired into Catholic streets, nationalists had nothing but stones to defend themselves'.[15] Let us look at the use of the word 'pogrom' here. It is a Russian word meaning 'destruction' or 'devastation', and has been specifically applied to 'attacks carried out by the Christian population against the Jews in Russia between 1881 and 1921 while the civil and military authorities remained neutral and occasionally provided their secret or open support'. One of the worst pogroms occurred in Odessa in the first week in November 1905. It is estimated that over 300 were killed and thousands wounded. 'From the outset, these pogroms were inspired by government circles. The local authorities received instructions to give the pogromists a free hand and to protect them from the Jewish self-defence ... After a while, it became known that pamphlets calling for the pogroms had been printed on the press of the government secret police.'[16]

Although there was some superficial similarity between Belfast in 1969 and Odessa in 1905, it is hardly enough to justify the use of the word 'pogrom'. Both Catholics and Protestants suffered, albeit unequally, from damage to property[17] and there were deaths and injuries on both sides. The first death was, in fact, that of a Protestant. Herbert Roy was shot in the chest with a .38 calibre revolver bullet in Dover Street at about 12:30 am on 15 August. While he was undoubtedly part of a crowd which was trying to break out into Divis Street, the only eyewitness at his inquest stated that he was 'not taking part in anything' when he was shot.[18] McManus's lumping together of 'loyalists, B-Specials and the RUC' is clearly intended to lend support to the 'pogrom' thesis because the last two were agents of the state. However, despite serious lapses of discipline and impartiality on the part of both bodies, this does not mean that there was nothing to choose between them and the loyalist rioters, let alone that the Northern Ireland Government positively encouraged and even organized the rioting in the first place. Indeed, if one wishes to explore 'victimhood', while the RUC did not experience any fatalities, 76 of its members were injured, compared with 199 Protestant and 178 Catholic civilians. Given the relative size of each group, the police constituted the one which suffered the most. Finally, if 'nationalists had nothing but stones to defend themselves', it is odd that not only were both dead Protestants killed by gunfire, but another 61 were wounded by it.[19] Apparently first applied to attacks by Protestants upon Catholics in Belfast in 1920–22 by Father John Hassan, the word 'pogrom' was not a full and accurate description of the facts even then, let alone fifty years later.[20]

Another Republican myth – or, at least, one propagated by the Provisional IRA and its supporters – concerns the alleged failure of the pre-split IRA to defend the Catholic population from loyalist attacks. In fact, Brian Hanley and Scott Millar have provided ample evidence to show that, far from 'running away', the IRA stood and fought. As we have seen, the organization took the initiative on 13 August and on the following day, correctly anticipating a loyalist reaction, McMillen and his adjutant, Jim Sullivan, sent small groups of volunteers to the different Catholic areas and ordered them to engage in defensive actions.[21]

The most famous example of the latter took place at St Comgall's School in Divis Street on the night of 14/15 August 1969. Quinn tells the story in dramatic fashion. The area, he writes, was under attack from 'a 200-strong Protestant mob' which had come down Percy Street from the Shankill Road. 'The warm dark night', Quinn continues, 'was illuminated with the red flames from the burning terrace houses, the smell of burning crackling ashes mixed with the smoke filled air' and a small group of young IRA men in St Comgall's School made themselves a target by throwing petrol bombs at the mob. 'If the school burned... a direct line would be open into the Loney and St Peter's...'[22] When 'gunfire...began to hit down toward St Comgall's...the young defenders held on with fading hope'. However, 'that hope became one of confidence when seven armed men moved from the back of the school. One carried a Thompson [sub-machine gun] and he positioned himself above the front door on the roof. Others took up position on the ground floor of the school with a .303 rifle and pistols. The defence party included Billy McKee, Albert Price, Seamus Twomey and Liam Burke.' These men succeeded in driving the Protestants back.[23]

Is it mere coincidence that all those named in Quinn's account happened to be men who had left the IRA because they disagreed with the direction of the leadership and who subsequently became key figures in the Provisionals? We simply do not know how many men were involved in the defence of St Comgall's, let alone who they were. The *Scarman Report* refers to '3 or 4 men'. Joe Graham says he was one of them, but he does not mention the names of any of the others, referring only to 'a handful (literally) of other republicans'. Peter Taylor also mentions 'three or four'. Patrick Bishop and Eamonn Mallie, whose account pre-dates Quinn's and is basically the same as his, give no names either, while the editor of the posthumously published oral memoir of Brendan Hughes, who was also present as a guide around the school of which he had been a pupil, has excised the name of the man with the Thompson gun![24] While Quinn's account may be accurate, it is hard to avoid considering the possibility that its principal purpose is to confirm the Provisional IRA's narrative: namely, that Cathal Goulding's IRA was not up to a fight and had to be 'rescued' by men who had left it for that very reason.

Another iconic moment of the Belfast riots occurred in the Clonard district on 15 August and a vivid account of it is preserved in the chronicle of the monastery which overlooked the area. In the course of the previous evening, the monastery had received an anonymous telephone call threatening to burn the inhabitants out – but nothing happened. The following day, however, the chronicler records, 'Just after noon a sniper on the old linen mill behind the monastery was shooting at people on the street' and '[w]e learned from the people around that there was going to be real trouble'. At 3 pm the older men and the sick were evacuated from the monastery and sent to two of the brothers' houses nearby. Half an hour later rioting began in Cupar Street, the dividing line between the Falls and the Shankill. 'The protestants seem to have been well armed', the chronicler went on, and '[t]here was a lot of shooting from the Cupar Street side...'[25]

The monks tried to telephone the RUC for help, but could not get through because the power was off. The rector then went to the police station, 'but they more or less said they could do nothing' so the bells were rung to call more people to defend the monastery. At 4:30 pm, we read, fires were raging in Bombay Street, Kashmir Road and Cupar Street. 'No one can do anything about it. They are protecting by guns [those] who are throwing the petrol bombs. It seems certain now that the Monastery will be burnt. The Blessed Sacrament has been removed. We are all prepared to move when the worst happens'.[26]

The fact that British troops were already on the streets of Belfast gave the chronicler some hope, especially after about thirty soldiers arrived at the monastery at 7 pm and there was a lull in the fighting. An hour later, however, he reported that '[m]obs came on to Bombay Street again protected by guns and began one by one to set on fire all that remained of Bombay Street and Kashmir Road. They even got as far as setting o[n] fire five houses in Clonard Gardens. St Gall's School was ablaze'. What was more, '[t]he soldiers were useless. They called down Bombay Street, "Come out with your hands up: we won't shoot." They were answered with a hail of petrol bombs. One soldier was hit by a bullet. They retreated and fired a tear gas bomb and there was silence for a while, except for the crac[k]le of sixty or so houses burning. Eventually the shooting stopped and the fire in St Gall's was put out. Most of the houses were left to burn. They were beyond redemption'.[27]

The toll was indeed a heavy one. No less than twelve Catholics were wounded by gunfire between 4 pm and 5:45 pm in Bombay and Kashmir Streets.[28] In nearby Waterville Street a 15-year-old boy, Gerard McCauley, was shot dead. A member of the Fianna, the Republican youth movement, he was described as 'the first Republican activist to lose his life during the present phase of Ireland's freedom struggle'. While he was clearly helping in the defence of the Clonard area, there is nothing to suggest that he himself was armed. McCauley was shot from what the autopsy report described as more than close range by a medium or high velocity bullet.[29]

Thirty-eight houses in Bombay Street had to be demolished together with four in Kashmir Street and one each in Clonard Gardens and Cupar Street.[30] Despite the alleged ineffectiveness of the IRA, however, there was evidently enough firepower in the Clonard to turn the tide of battle. Indeed, between 6 pm and the small hours of 16 August, not a single Catholic was shot while 13 Protestants suffered gunshot wounds.[31] This was almost certainly due to the efforts of the IRA, for although the organization had received two severe blows on 15 August – its leadership (including McMillen) had been interned as a result of a government decision on the previous day and its ammunition had almost run out – there was a small number of volunteers present and, on this occasion, the evidence that they included McKee is a little stronger.[32]

II

If the IRA played an important part in the riots on the Catholic side, was there any equivalent organization on the Protestant side? If the UVF was involved, it has left no traces. The same cannot be said of McKeague's SDA. He told the tribunal that, even before the riots broke out, 'I took steps to find out what armament or if there was any in the particular area [the Crumlin Road], and anyone with any legal shotgun was asked to have this available to stop any infiltration into this area'. This proved unnecessary on 13 August 1969, but because there was only a small police presence there the following evening, six shotguns were brought out and barricades were erected in three streets on the Protestant side. The men with shotguns were posted behind each of them. When the Catholic crowd from Hooker Street attempted an incursion, he boasted, 'it was repulsed and the Protestant people went after them and gave them a lesson which I do not think they will ever forget'.[33]

McKeague also admitted to taking part in the rioting in Percy Street on the same night, even claiming that he and two of his men were responsible for devising a successful counter-attack against the Catholic crowd which enabled him to plant a Union Jack on the Falls Road.[34] Another man who was involved in the rioting in nearby Dover Street and who exercised his leadership skills by organizing the Protestant crowd was John McQuade, the ex-boxer and hardline Unionist MP for Woodvale at Stormont.[35]

As for Paisley he led some of his colleagues from the UCDC in a deputation to see Chichester-Clark in the early hours of 14 August to ask for the immediate mobilization of the B-Specials. Chichester-Clark warned that if this happened, Westminster would say that Stormont was unable to rule Northern Ireland and take over itself.[36] Paisley suggested the immediate formation of a people's militia instead. Chichester-Clark's response to that proposal is not known, but Paisley did advertise a meeting at his church on 15 August to collect names for the militia. Some 100 people reportedly turned up and Paisley later claimed that about 5,000 ultimately volunteered. However, as Mr Justice Scarman pointed out, this was 'the only occasion, of which we have evidence, of any action by the Ulster Constitution Defence Committee in the events under review'. He added, 'There is no evidence that the Ulster Protestant Volunteers played any part in the disturbances...'[37]

There was obviously some jealousy of McKeague's influence on the part of Paisley and other would-be loyalist leaders. On 26 August the Orange Order, the Unionist Party in west Belfast and the UCDC issued a joint statement in which they stressed that they had no connection with the SDA and that any public statement it had made in the past or would make in the future 'doesn't represent the views of opinions of the above associations or any loyalists or Protestants in this area'.[38]

What about the actions of the police? During an emergency debate at Stormont on 14 August, the pugnacious NILP MP for the Falls constituency and former IRA volunteer, Paddy Devlin, said that the RUC had done 'a remarkably good job' during the previous day's rioting in Belfast.[39] Devlin was contrasting the behaviour of the police in Belfast with that in Derry, but even so, one wonders whether he would have been so fulsome in his praise a day or so later. There is no doubt that the RUC resorted to excessive force, particularly on the nights of 14 and 15 August. The most obvious example was the use of Shorland armoured cars equipped with .30 calibre machine guns in Divis Street on the night of 14 August. As Scarman pointed out, these vehicles and their weapons were designed for patrolling border areas of Northern Ireland and not for use in an urban environment. Their firepower was awesome: 500–600 high velocity rounds a minute which could only be fired in bursts.[40] According to police records, well over 100 rounds of this lethal ammunition were discharged in the Divis Street/Falls Road area that night and one was responsible for the death of 9-year-old Patrick Rooney. The boy was sheltering with the rest of his family in a back bedroom of a flat in the Divis complex and was struck in the head by a high velocity bullet. A detailed ballistics report showed that the Rooney family's ground-floor flat had been hit by four such bullets which had passed through windows, doors and plasterboard walls before exiting the building altogether or lodging in a wall. Since there had been no intention to kill the child, his death was clearly an accident, but an accident caused by such recklessness on the part of the policemen responsible that it would surely have merited a charge of manslaughter had it been properly investigated.[41]

The other death at the Divis Flats that night was of Trooper Hugh McCabe, a 19-year-old British soldier who was on leave and back home with his wife in the complex. His body was not discovered until some time after his death, so it is not clear when he died as a result of being hit by a single, high velocity bullet which entered his body via his right cheek and exited from the back of his chest. The *Scarman Report* suggests that he was shot by a police marksman from the roof of the Hastings Street RUC barracks while 'assisting...others in assaulting with missiles the police in the street below'. His father testified at the inquest that his son 'had no connection whatsoever with any Republic[an] or illegal organization', but while there is no reason to dispute this statement, it does not mean that he was not participating in the violence. Another witness at the inquest, a first aid worker who inspected McCabe's body where it was lying, said that he had had difficulty 'in getting past a stack of crates containing petrol bombs' to reach it.[42]

In Ardoyne, seventy-five rounds of 9 mm Sterling sub-machine gun ammunition were fired on 14 and 15 August. Samuel McLarnon was killed with one round and Michael Lynch probably with another. McLarnon, a 47-year-old bus conductor, was inside his house in Herbert Street. His wife described at his inquest how she and her husband heard shooting outside, turned out the lights and drew the blinds in their living room, which faced on to the street. She went out of the room for a few moments and returned after hearing more gunfire to find her husband lying dead on the floor. The ballistics report stated that the bullet which killed him and which was recovered from his skull was a 9 mm round of the kind used in a number of weapons, including the Sterling sub-machine gun carried by the RUC. Two similar bullets were found embedded in the living room wall and others from houses on either side of the McLarnons'.[43] These details point towards a random burst of fire rather than a carefully aimed discharge.

The second fatality in Ardoyne that night was a 29-year-old labourer, Michael Lynch, who was one of a small group of local residents trying to dash across nearby Butler Street, where shooting was coming from the direction of the Crumlin Road. An eyewitness saw Lynch, who was just in front of him, fall to the ground. He saw blood on Lynch's shirt near the centre of his chest, but ran on in the belief that his companion would be able to get up and get away. Lynch did get up and staggered into a house in a neighbouring street, where it was found that he was badly wounded. Since an ambulance could not get through because of the rioting, Lynch was taken to hospital in a private car and was admitted at 2 am on 15 August. He died fourteen hours later. The bullet which killed him was not recovered, although the pathologist thought it was of 'medium or high velocity' and 'fired at short range', which led Scarman to conclude that 'in all probability' it came from an RUC Sterling.[44] Unlike McLarnon, Lynch was out in the street and he could have been taking part in the rioting, but there is no evidence that he was. The police came under fire on this occasion, which was their justification for using guns themselves, but it is significant that in addition to the two dead men, no fewer than twenty Catholics in Ardoyne were treated for bullet wounds that same night, while the only gunshot wound on the RUC side seems to have been a grazed ear. This suggests that the latter's response was grossly disproportionate. The death of McLarnon was probably accidental and that of Lynch possibly so, but as in the Rooney case, there was a need for further investigation which might have led to criminal charges. None, however, was forthcoming.[45]

There was one more fatal shooting in Ardoyne on the following afternoon, 15 August. Describing the mood of his parishioners to the tribunal, Father Marcellus said 'Everyone was in a state of panic. People were talking about how many were injured and who was dead. Some were boarding up their houses and others were moving out. Some were building barriers with paving stones'. The priest helped build one in Herbert Street and he witnessed a bus being hijacked on the Crumlin Road to make another. To make matters worse, the *Scarman Report* noted that, due to pressure elsewhere, there were no police officers or vehicles on duty in the Crumlin Road/Ardoyne area for a two-hour period in the late afternoon. This left the rival groups free to fight it out amongst themselves, which they duly did. Between 5:30 and 6:15 pm no fewer than seventeen people (ten Catholics and seven Protestants) were admitted to hospital with shotgun wounds. They included Martin Meehan of the IRA.[46] At 5:45 pm David Linton, a 48-year-old machinist from the Protestant Palmer Street, was brought into the Mater Hospital suffering from shotgun wounds in the head, neck, chest and right arm. Three of the pellets caused massive internal bleeding and Linton died some ten hours later. According to two eyewitnesses at his inquest, Linton was defending his street against an incursion from the other side of the Crumlin Road when he was shot and was not carrying a gun himself.[47]

Although the police returned to the area after 6 pm, rioting and shooting continued into the night. About twenty houses in Catholic Brookfield Street, abandoned earlier by their frightened residents, were looted and set on fire by Protestant rioters and another casualty of the night's violence was the Edenderry Inn, where the trouble in Ardoyne had begun three months earlier. Although British troops had arrived in Belfast on 15 August, they were not initially deployed in Ardoyne. Vivian Simpson, the Stormont MP for the area had appealed for them shortly after midnight on 15 August and, together with the Rector of the Holy Cross Church, went to the Cabinet Office on the afternoon of 16 August to repeat the request. The Cabinet's Joint Security Committee had already approached the GOC Northern Ireland, Lieutenant-General Sir Ian Freeland, on the same subject and troops arrived on the Crumlin Road at 6:30 pm that same day.[48] An uneasy calm gradually descended upon the city.

III

Amid the pages of statistics produced for the benefit of the Scarman Tribunal were lists of individuals arrested for participating and/or injured during the course of the rioting in Belfast. An examination of these enables the historian to construct a collective profile of those involved. In the case of those arrested, it is perhaps more useful to adopt a wider time-frame than the 13–16 August, when the police were more concerned with containing the violence than arresting the perpetrators. The figures cited, therefore, cover a three-month period starting from 16 May – i.e. the date of the first disturbance in Ardoyne. They show that rioters were overwhelmingly male: only six of those arrested out of a total of 150 were women. They were also young: 28 per cent were aged between 16 and 20, 37 per cent between 21 and 29 and 21 per cent between 30 and 39. Finally, they were overwhelmingly working class. Indeed, of the 143 for whom we have employment details, no less than fifty-seven (40 per cent) were classified as labourers. One man was described as a despatch clerk and another as a salesman, which was the sum total of the white-collar occupations. The second largest single category among those arrested was the unemployed, but no significance should be read into that. Not only were the riot areas ones of high social deprivation, but the proportion of unemployed in the sample – 7 per cent – was no different from that in Belfast as a whole.[49]

The profile of those injured in the rioting of 13–16 August is broadly similar, although it is obviously more difficult to tell whether those affected were merely victims as opposed to participants as well. Excluding members of the RUC, we have some data for 276 persons. There were more women, both numerically and proportionately, than in the case of those arrested, but since a third of them were in their 50s and 60s and were clearly suffering from the effects of acute anxiety rather than riot-inflicted injury, one should not exaggerate the significance of this. For the rest, there is again a preponderance of young males – with 24 per cent between the ages of 16 and 20, 31 per cent between 21 and 30 and 18 per cent between 30 and 39 – although it is not as great as in the case of those arrested. Since the available hospital records, unlike those for arrests, do not automatically include occupation, the historian has to try to ascertain this from other sources, in this case by matching patients' addresses with the entries in the annual Northern Ireland directory. As the latter only lists the head of household and sometimes not even that, the results can be disappointingly small, especially where so many younger people living with their families are involved. Nevertheless, the occupations of sixty-one patients can be found. Once again, labourers were well ahead of the field (twenty-three in total), while another thirty-five were in working class employment of one kind or another. The white collar and middle classes were represented by one businessman, one fire officer and one clerk.[50] This brief breakdown of social background is revealing in some ways, but it cannot provide the basis for an explanation of why certain people turned to violence. Beliefs mattered more than background.

This is further suggested by the geography of violence. Picking up on a comment in the *Scarman Report* concerning the 'remarkable fact... that the Belfast riots of August 1969 did not spread from the Falls and the Ardoyne into the rest of the City', Liam Kelly, in a brief article and longer essay, has sought to explain why areas which had previously enjoyed a reputation for violence, like Sandy Row and east Belfast, remained relatively quiet. He attributes this to a combination of factors, notably the efforts of local peace committees, some of which were drawn from both communities, and better relations between the police and the public than those which existed on the Falls and Crumlin Roads.[51] While Kelly's research provides many valuable insights and casts further doubt on the 'pogrom' thesis, it omits one remarkable factor. Whether a particular area erupted into major violence or not in August 1969 seems to have depended, to a significant extent, upon how far communal tensions could be exploited and even engineered by those with a particular political agenda. As we have seen, the IRA was active in the Falls and Ardoyne and the SDA on the Shankill. Both played an important role in the turn to violence. Such organizations had not as yet succeeded in putting down strong roots in other parts of Belfast. When they did, trouble followed.

IV

The deployment of British troops in Belfast, and elsewhere in Northern Ireland, too, gave Westminster the central role in future developments in the province. It was all very well for the two British Cabinet ministers principally involved to say 'Let's keep Chichester-Clark carrying the can' and 'I too want to avoid responsibility',[52] but the buck now stopped in London. Thus, all the available accounts of the Cabinet meeting of 19 August 1969 show that the British Government's sympathies lay overwhelmingly with the Catholic minority. Yet, as Defence Secretary Denis Healey also reminded them, the Protestants were the majority and 'if we put the majority of the population against us, we should be once again in the 1911–14 situation...'[53]

In spite of Prime Minister Harold Wilson's insistence that 'We must keep firmly in the middle of the road and be "firm, cool and fair"',[54] the presence of the army on the streets of Belfast soon antagonized the loyalists. It is often overlooked that the initial clashes between the army and the civilian population in Belfast were with Protestants. These took place on 7 September, 27 September, 4/5 October and 11/12 October – and the first shot fired at the army was by a loyalist on the third occasion. On the last date, during a massive riot on the Shankill Road, over a thousand shots were fired at the RUC and the army, killing a police constable, Victor Arbuckle, and wounding sixteen soldiers. The army returned fire, shooting and killing two Protestants, George Dickie and Herbert Hawe.[55] Some of the Protestant crowd were waving Union Jacks and shouting 'Englishmen go home' at the troops.[56]

The riot of 11/12 October was undoubtedly sparked off by the appearance of the Hunt Report on policing in Northern Ireland. A three-man committee, consisting of Lord Hunt, the conqueror of Mount Everest, and two senior British police officers, Robert Mark and Sir James Robertson, produced its report on 10 October after only six weeks' work. It reflected the widespread British suspicion of Northern Ireland's mechanism for preserving law and order and proposed the disbandment of the B-Specials and their replacement by a completely new and non-sectarian reserve force soon to be called the Ulster Defence Regiment (UDR), together with the disarmament of the RUC and its transformation into an English-style, 'normalized' police force.[57] It confirmed the belief among loyalists that the British Government and the army were 'soft' on the Catholics – which, in a way, they were.

General Freeland gave a revealing indication of his position in remarks he drew up for a staff conference in London. 'Many people, mainly Northern Ireland Protestants,' he stated, 'have said "Why didn't the Army restore Law and Order when they were brought in in August after the Police had lost control of the situation?"' What they meant by this, he continued, was '"Why didn't the Army counter the resistance of the Roman Catholics behind their barricades by force of arms and reduce this minority to their original state of second-class citizenship?"' This, Freeland argued, would have been impossible without a declaration of martial law, which was 'unthinkable in the UK, especially when imposed on part of the population who have a long-standing grievance against the Police and Government'. He saw his task, therefore, as keeping the peace and holding the ring while the new deal for the Catholic minority and police reorganization was carried out. 'If we had used force to reduce the Roman Catholic strongholds', he concluded, 'there would have been immediate escalation of the situation throughout the whole of Ireland and possibly elsewhere [i.e in Britain]'.[58]

Freeland's remarks here highlight how it is far too simplistic to assume that the British army saw Northern Ireland purely in colonial terms. Indeed, in June 1970 a high-ranking civil servant at the Ministry of Defence wrote to a colleague at the Home Office that the army may have previously thought 'in a colonial context' but that 'the Northern Ireland troubles' had shown that disturbances in 'what purport to be civilised countries' required the review of 'the whole of tactical doctrine for internal security operations'.[59] The General Staff bracketed together Northern Ireland with the ghetto uprisings in the United States, especially the Detroit riots of 1967, and campus unrest throughout the western world, specifically the protests at Kent State University in the spring of 1970 which had ended with the National Guard shooting dead four students.[60] When a Whitehall working party was set up in July 1970 to look into ways of improving 'the British Army's Internal Security (IS) techniques to meet situations similar to those in Northern Ireland', its members travelled to America, France, West Germany, Italy and Japan not to the Third World.[61]

V

Towards the end of 1969, the UVF began to emerge from the shadows. As early as 2 September, a statement purportedly emanating from 'Captain Stevenson, Chief of Staff, UVF' had appeared in the *Belfast Telegraph*. It claimed that 'battalions of the UVF are ready for action, and new battalions are being formed', but it was dismissed by both the RUC and Paisley's UCDC. On 19 October, however, following an explosion at an electricity sub-station in Donegal, UVF armbands were found on the severely burned body of a man, Thomas McDowell, discovered nearby. On 24 October the UVF claimed responsibility for the explosion, declaring that it was, in part, a reprisal for the stationing of Irish troops on the border following Lynch's speech and warning that, as long as the threat from Republic continued, its volunteers would strike at targets over the border.[62]

The following month, on 18 November, it was reported that the UVF had 'embarked on a recruiting campaign to augment its underground forces' and that '[c]anvassing has been going on among factory workers in certain parts of Belfast and some country areas to enlist men for the illegal organization. Compulsory contributions of 10 shillings a week are being levied for the purchase of firearms.' The campaign was linked, it was said, to the British Government's plan to replace the B-Specials with the UDR.[63] A subsequent article spoke of the UVF's twenty to thirty 'divisions', while at the same time suggesting that it was 'organisationally poor and numerically weak' – although well-armed![64]

The official picture was not much clearer. An RUC Special Branch report at the end of the year stated that 'it appears that the subversive elements in the ranks of extreme Protestants loosely referred to as the Ulster Volunteer Force, will never be identified as a body. They do not appear to have a constitution or terms of membership and their means of communication are confined to a very few letters carried by hand and the verbal passing of instructions...' The author of the report referred to 'an indication' that ten men awaiting trial on conspiracy charges arising from the sabotage of public utilities earlier in the year were the activists and that 'the remnants in Belfast are now in two separate groups clandestinely dealing in small quantities of arms, but at loggerheads with each other'. There was no intelligence on the identity of a leader or leaders. 'Indeed the contrary is true, that there does not appear to be a "leader" as such'.[65]

It would be easy dismiss this report as proof of the RUC's poor intelligence concerning extremist Protestant organizations about which the army habitually complained. However, the evidence to the Scarman Tribunal of Brigadier Peter Hudson, the CO of the Army's 39th Brigade which was responsible for Belfast, shows just how fissiparous loyalism was in the months that followed the deployment of British troops in the city. Asked whether there appeared to be any organization on the Protestant Shankill side, he replied, 'No effective organization. We found it very difficult indeed to get together a body of people who could talk with the same view. We tried for a long time to get, say, a dozen or 20 people representing, say, Shankill, Woodvale and [east Belfast], but failed. It was not easy. They were fragmented and all of different opinions'. Even the SDA 'never really seemed to us to be a body that had very much influence and it certainly didn't represent the whole of the Shankill, for instance;…other people with what one might almost call extremists views…disowned McKeague;…he was not acceptable to them, to the mass of the Shankill'.[66] None of this shows that the UVF did not exist or did not play a role in events; merely that it was not nearly as significant as it has been made out to be. Its heyday was to come later, after the Provisional IRA campaign had begun.[67]

VI

Things were very different on the Catholic side, where the various local defence committees which sprang up at the time of the rioting came together to form a Central Citizens Defence Committee (CCDC). The CCDC negotiated with the army on such crucial matters as the removal of the barricades and the re-entry of the RUC into Catholic areas. The CCDC was not a Republican body, although a prominent Republican, Sullivan, became its chair. As Adams later explained, Republicans 'came naturally into area leadership positions because they had standing in the community or because of their previous experience of agitational activity in unemployment and housing action and civil rights campaigning'.[68]

Recruitment to the IRA appears to have increased rapidly. '[Y]ou could have filled Falls Park with the amount of people who wanted to volunteer', one man reminisced to Hanley and Millar, while three senior RUC officers told the Hunt Committee in September 1969 that the number of IRA members in Belfast had probably doubled to between three and four hundred in the month since the riots.[69] Nevertheless, within a matter of months both the IRA and Sinn Féin had split. Belfast played a key role in this development. According to Adams, there were 'three broad tendencies within republican activism' in the city. The first was the leadership headed by McMillen and Sullivan and which continued, by and large, to follow the line laid down by Dublin. The second consisted of an older generation of Republicans, often referred to as 'the forties men', because they had joined the IRA in the 1940s. They had dropped out of the movement or resigned in protest against the 'politicizing' tendencies of the leadership, but turned out to offer their services during the August crisis. The dominant figures in this group were McKee, Twomey and Joe Cahill and their priority was armed struggle. Younger activists, like Adams himself, who had been involved in the new-style political and social agitation encouraged by Dublin, but who realized that developments in Northern Ireland required different priorities and different solutions, made up the third group.[70]

It was 'the forties men' who seized the initiative. According to one source, they met as early as 24 August and 'decided to remove Sullivan and McMillen as quickly as possible and work on replacing the Dublin leadership with "traditional" republicans'.[71] On 22 September they actually confronted McMillen and Sullivan – some say with guns in hand – to demand that the Belfast staff be enlarged by co-opting people who shared their views and that four members of the existing IRA leadership be removed, including Goulding.[72] Cahill claims that McMillen promised to discuss the dissidents' demands with Dublin, but when it was subsequently discovered that he 'had been instructed by Goulding and company to play along with the dissidents and keep General Headquarters Staff informed of what was happening' and particularly 'to find out if we had made any contacts for arms supplies', that was 'the final straw' and the dissidents set up their own separate and independent Northern Command.[73]

The split did not officially come, however, until Southern figures like Seán Mac Stíofáin, Ruairí Ó Brádaigh and Dáithí Ó Conaill unsuccessfully challenged the leadership at a special IRA convention in mid-December 1969 on the twin issues of forming a broad National Liberation Front with other left-wing groups and, more importantly, formally abandoning the hitherto sacrosanct principle of refusing to take up seats in the Dáil. The traditionalists reckoned that the meeting had been rigged because a number of delegates who could have been expected to vote with them failed to turn up. In addition, of course, Belfast was not represented, having decided to set up its own Northern Command. Immediately after the convention, Mac Stíofáin went to Belfast, where he spoke to a gathering of twenty sympathetic Republicans, who agreed with him that a new organization should be created. Another special Army convention was therefore summoned which was attended by representatives from Belfast, the minority who had voted against the Dublin leadership at the previous convention and those who had been excluded. It was this at meeting that the Provisional IRA was formally established, with Mac Stíofáin as its Chief of Staff and two Belfast men, Cahill and Leo Martin, on the Army Council. The split was completed in January 1970 when Provisional Sinn Féin was set up after a walk out from the Ard Fheis.[74]

The Provisional IRA was particularly strong in Belfast, probably because so many of its founders came from there. Cahill believed that there was another reason. When trying to recruit new members from the rest of Northern Ireland, he found that the rural units would not abandon their allegiance to the Dublin-based organization – soon to become known as the Official IRA – 'until they were certain they would get weapons...They were very reluctant to change horses in midstream, and would say, "When you can supply arms, get back to us". Despite everything, they were still hopeful that the Official IRA would supply arms'.[75] Hanley and Millar have detailed how the two factions engaged in an arms race, seeking funds and/or weapons from, among others, the Irish Government, the Irish Diaspora, Cuba, the Soviet Union, Hollywood film stars and even loyalists.[76] Principles, personalities and pistols were not the only things shaping the way that the split was developing. Like any civil war, the Republican one was about more than just the issues that were dividing the elite.

Within Belfast, the Official IRA continued to occupy a dominant position in the Lower Falls, thanks no doubt to the influence of McMillen and Sullivan, both of whom were from the area. Outside of that neighbourhood the only parts of the city where the Officials could be said to have rivalled the Provisionals in strength were the Markets and the western suburb of Turf Lodge, possibly because a large number of former Falls Road residents had been re-settled in the latter. Those who formed the Provisionals started organizing in Ardoyne as early as November. Meehan played a key role here. He had resigned from the IRA in disgust after the August riots because he felt that the area had not received sufficient assistance from the Belfast command, and his brand of muscular Republicanism found a natural home in the Provisionals. The Short Strand in east Belfast seems to have been a kind of no-man's-land between the two factions, while Ballymurphy remained in a state of limbo because Adams, whose position in this western suburb was crucial, had not yet made up his mind which side to back. He finally plumped for the Provisionals, who already held sway in the Unity Flats, the New Lodge area and the rest of Catholic west Belfast, apart from Turf Lodge.[77]

While the Republican movement was going through its reorganization, things seemed to be going well for the Catholic community in general. The British Government was overseeing and guaranteeing reforms which the community's representatives had long sought and British troops were protecting its areas from further depredations by Protestant crowds. The Hunt Report, the Clonard Chronicle recorded, 'marks a new era for Catholics in the North' and they were 'very impressed' by it.[78] An intelligence assessment approved by the Army's intelligence committee on 5 January 1970 stated that 'the majority of Catholics in the North have now little or no sympathy with the IRA type of attack. Now that the Civil Rights Association has paved the way for the reforms which are now working their way through Parliament, there is no point whatsoever in jeopardizing the gains already made by senseless acts of violence'. While Catholics in troubled areas would naturally accept IRA offers of protection and even offer to conceal weapons, the assessment concluded, 'there is no real affection for the IRA and the IRA themselves are aware of it'.[79]

Of course, this did not suit the Provisionals at all. Hughes, a new recruit to their ranks, remembered McKee, the Provisionals' commander in Belfast, 'saying that this is our opportunity now with the Brits on the streets, this is what we wanted, open confrontation with the Army. Get the Brits out through armed resistance, engage them in armed conflict and send them back across the water with their tanks and guns. That was the Republican objective.'[80] For people such as McKee, reform was a side issue if not a positive threat.

So, if the Provisionals' objectives were to be achieved, the Catholic community had to be turned against the British army. To some extent the army itself was helping the Provisionals achieve this very thing. As an 18-year-old in west Belfast, the journalist Malachi O'Doherty recalls an incident which occurred in September or October 1969. Walking home from a Sunday night dance, he and a group of his friends 'were drawn to the sound of shouting up ahead. It was a group of soldiers taunting some of the others who had come from the dance. I heard the soldiers calling them "stupid Micks".' While he could understand the rough behaviour of the troops when they were under attack later on, O'Doherty wrote, '[f]or them to have turned nasty before all that, just for the fun of it, seemed to say something fundamental about the untenability of using these men to bring peace...English soldiers calling Irishmen "stupid Micks" seemed to confirm the republican notion that there was old bad blood at work here...'[81]

Some of the dances and discos were put on by the British army as part of its programme for 'winning hearts and minds', but produced the opposite effect when the soldiers competed with the local boys for female attention. Adams subsequently criticized the troops 'attitude to womenfolk', and at the time he went so far as to organize a picket from the local Sinn Féin women's branch against a disco in Ballymurphy. This 'quickly deteriorated into shouting matches between British army squaddies, who were incensed by the protest, and the local women, who were incensed by the attitude of the British soldiers'. He claims that the protest put a stop to the discos, and adds significantly that 'it had given us our first opportunity to agitate publicly against British troops and we continued this low-intensity agitation through the spring of 1970'.[82]

VII

What the Provisionals really wanted, however, was some high-intensity action as opposed to 'low-intensity agitation'. This occurred at Easter 1970 and, since it was set off by an annual Junior Orange outing, was reminiscent of the disorders at the Unity Flats the previous year. On this occasion, though, the rioting occurred in Ballymurphy and Catholics took the lead. At approximately 9:15 pm on 31 March 1970, well after the local Junior Orange Band had passed, a gang of up to 200 youths began throwing bottles and stones at troops in the area of the Whiterock Road/Springfield Road crossroads. The disorder lasted until 1:30 am, four arrests were made and twenty-five soldiers were injured, one of whom had to be detained in hospital. The following night trouble began at about the same time and the RUC reported that 'a raiding party' of Catholics had crossed the Springfield Road into the Protestant New Barnsley estate. As the situation deteriorated, CS gas was used, for only the third time in Belfast[83], and barricades were thrown up at two road junctions leading from Ballymurphy out on to the Springfield Road. According to the British army's weekly intelligence summary, 'Military action was taken to clear demonstrators and petrol bomb throwers from the area...The troops used baton charges and 18 cartridges of CS gas between 0200-0300 hours. By 01.40 hours the area had been cleared and the barricades taken down...'[84]

A third night of rioting took place on 2/3 April 1970. Earlier in the day about seventy Catholic youths broke into homes on the Protestant side of the Springfield Road which had been vacated by residents on account of the previous disturbances. Families with children later moved in and the RUC made plans to evict them, but a local councillor managed to persuade them to leave peacefully. Two hostile crowds faced each other that night, with the RUC taking care of the Protestant one and the British army the Catholic. The former managed to persuade the Protestant crowd to disperse, but the Catholic one chose to attack the soldiers again. CS was used once more and by 2:30 am on 3 April the crowd had been cleared. Around fifty petrol bombs had been thrown at the troops and a cache of 150 more was discovered during a search of the area. Twenty-one arrests were made by the army, one of them a man carrying a .22 automatic rifle and fifty-three rounds of live ammunition.[85] These events there followed by a series of threats and counter-threats: General Freeland announced that petrol bombers could be shot dead if they persisted in their actions after due warning. The Provisional IRA then stated that if one Irish life was lost in this fashion, it would shoot members of the army where and when the opportunity arose, while the UVF threatened to shoot one Catholic for every soldier.[86]

In a memorandum, dated 3 April, the UK Representative, Ronald Burroughs, told his superiors that not only had an outbreak of violence in the area not been predicted, but it also could not have been because 'the root causes are still obscure'. Even the leaders of the Catholic community, he added, were at a loss to explain them. Their consequences, however, were clear: 'A Bogside type of situation developed in which hooligans turned their attention more towards the forces of law and order than towards their religious opponents'. And, in this case, the forces of law and order were the soldiers who 'had to face a series of hit and run assaults from highly mobile and elusive gangs of stone-throwing hooligans, the majority of whom were in their teens'.[87]

A few days later, a telegram from the Director of Intelligence in Northern Ireland to the Joint Intelligence Committee in London provided an attempt at an explanation. 'When hooligans took possession of houses evacuated by Protestants', he wrote, 'women and children were put in as squatters later. This was not [the] action of [a] teenage mob.' Provisional IRA volunteers and Republican sympathizers, he continued, were among those arrested and they were carrying offensive weapons and taking part in the violence. Finally, he noted, a meeting of 'Brady group Republicans' in the area had decided to 'cool down Bally-murphy temporarily', while promising to deal firmly with the Protestants in New Barnsley when the troops were occupied elsewhere. 'It is very much in [the] interests of IRA/extreme Republicans to get the army fighting with Catholics in order to destroy [the] army image as protectors of [the] Catholics. It is the IRA activists who want to assume this role.'[88]

It appears from another account that, if McKee had had his way, the Provisional IRA would have opened fire on the troops. According to Ed Moloney, 'When the Ballymurphy riots erupted, he ordered an armed unit from D Coy in the Lower Falls Road to go to Ballymurphy and take on the British army. When Adams found out, he was furious and detained McKee's men at gunpoint'. One of those held explained to Moloney, 'McKee wanted a gunfight, but Adams didn't. Adams wanted ordinary people involved in the rioting as a way of radicalizing them. That impressed me'.[89] It was not long before McKee was to get his gunfight, but it was not against the army and he was almost killed as a result of it.

NOTES

1. *Independent*, 19 September 1994.
2. The text of Chichester-Clark's statement may be found in Government of Northern Ireland, *Violence and Civil Disturbances in Northern Ireland in 1969 (Scarman Report), Volume II* (Belfast: HMSO, 1972), pp. 37–8.

3. B. Castle, *The Castle Diaries 1954–1970* (London: Weidenfeld and Nicolson, 1984), p. 640. The remark was made at a Cabinet meeting on 24 April 1969.

4. L. McMillen, 'The Role of the IRA in the North from 1962 to 1969', in *Liam McMillen: Separatist, Socialist, Republican, Respol Pamphlet, No. 21* (Dublin: Sinn Féin, n.d.), p. 10; R. Quinn, *A Rebel Voice: A History of Belfast Republicanism 1925–1972* (Belfast: Belfast Cultural and Local History Group, 1999), pp. 141–2.

5. Hunt Committee meetings with Commissioner Wolseley, District Inspector Millar and Inspector-General Peacocke, 12, 15 September 1969, London, National Archives (NA), CJ/3/57.

6. Unsigned letter, 18 August 1969, *Scarman Report, Volume II*, p. 53.

7. *Irish Times*, 13 August 1969.

8. G. Adams, *Before the Dawn: An Autobiography* (London: Heinemann, 1996), pp. 100–1; B. Hanley and S. Millar, *The Lost Revolution: The Story of the Official IRA and the Workers' Party* (Dublin: Penguin Ireland, 2009), p. 126; Police Logs, Belfast, McClay Library, Scarman Belfast exhibits.

9. Police Logs; Hanley and Millar, *Lost Revolution*, p. 126.

10. Police Logs; S. Bradley's evidence to the Scarman Tribunal, 20 October 1970, Belfast, McClay Library, Scarman minutes of evidence, p. 40; Hanley and Millar, *Lost Revolution*, p. 126.

11. Police Logs; J. Graham, *'Show Me the Man': The Authorised Biography of Martin Meehan* (Belfast: Rushlight Publications, 2008), p. 39.

12. S. Montgomery's evidence to the Scarman Tribunal, 26 May 1970, p. 17; M. Gillespie's evidence to the Scarman Tribunal, 27 April 1970, pp. 48–9.

13. Belfast Police Logs.

14. Lynch's speech is reproduced in *Scarman Report, Volume II*, pp. 43–4.

15. *Andersontown News*, 14 August 2009.

16. Y[ehuda] S[lutsky], 'Pogroms', in *Encyclopaedia Judaica, Volume 13* (Jerusalem: Keter Publishing, 1972), pp. 694–701.

17. Protestants occupied 16.5 per cent of the domestic properties damaged or destroyed, while Catholics occupied 83.5 per cent. In the case of commercial properties, most of the damage – with the important exception of licensed premises – was suffered by non-Catholics. *Scarman Report*, pp. 243–5.

18. Ibid., pp. 141–2; *Belfast Telegraph*, 26 November 1969.

19. Scarman Report, p. 242.

20. 'G.B. Kenna' (J. Hassan), *Facts and Figures: The Belfast Pogroms 1920–1922* (Dublin: O'Connell Publishing Company, 1922).

21. Hanley and Millar, *Lost Revolution*, p. 127; Adams, *Before the Dawn*, pp. 103–5. The reference to 'running away' refers to the slogan 'IRA = I Ran Away', which allegedly appeared on walls in Catholic areas of Belfast following the events of August 1969, but of which no contemporary record survives.

22. The Pound Loney was a Catholic district to the south of Divis Street. St Peter's was the Catholic cathedral.

23. Quinn, *Rebel Voice*, p. 144.

24. *Scarman Report*, pp. 156–7; Graham, *'Show Me the Man'*, p. 42; P. Taylor, *Provos: The IRA and Sinn Féin* (London: Bloomsbury, 1997), p. 53; P. Bishop and E. Mallie, *The Provisional IRA* (London: Corgi Books, 1988), p. 112; E. Moloney, *Voices from the Grave: Two Men's War in Ireland* (London: Faber, 2010), pp. 47–8. I myself have heard different names mentioned in connection with this episode.

25. Clonard Monastic Chronicle, 14 and 15 August 1969.

26. Ibid., 15 August 1969.

27. Ibid.

28. Belfast No. 55, Scarman Belfast Exhibits.

29. *Tírghrá: Ireland's Patriot Dead* (Dublin: no publisher given, 2002), p. 1; Press autopsy report, 16 August 1969, Belfast, BELF/6/1/1/23, PRONI. It emerges from the inquest report that the Clonard chronicler was wrong in claiming that McCauley had been shot in the back.

30. Belfast No. 14, Scarman Belfast Exhibits. It should be noted that the injured fireman was not rioting, but rather was on duty when his car was fire-bombed by a rioter.

31. Belfast No. 55.
32. Hanley and Millar, *Lost Revolution*, p. 128; Quinn, *Rebel Voice*, p. 147; Bishop and Mallie, *Provisional IRA*, pp. 116–17.
33. J. McKeague's evidence to Scarman Tribunal, 18 May 1971, pp. 58 and 60–63; J. McKeague's evidence to Scarman Tribunal, 7 June 1971, p. 87.
34. McKeague's evidence, 18 May 1971, p. 62.
35. *Scarman Report*, pp. 139–40.
36. The B-Specials were nevertheless mobilized on 14 August.
37. I. Paisley's evidence to the Scarman Tribunal, 17 June 1971, pp. 11–15; *Scarman Report*, p. 152.
38. S. Bruce, *The Red Hand: Protestant Paramilitaries in Northern Ireland* (Oxford: Oxford University Press, 1992), p. 38.
39. *Northern Ireland House of Commons Debates*, vol. 73, 14 August 1969, col. 2307.
40. *Scarman Report*, p. 172.
41. Schedule of Discharge of Firearms by Royal Ulster Constabulary in Belfast during the months of July and August 1969, Scarman Belfast Exhibits; Marshall autopsy report, 15 August 1969, PRONI, BELF/6/1/1/2.
42. *Scarman Report*, pp. 167–9; Marshall autopsy report; J. McCabe and F. Murney's depositions, 26 November 1969, PRONI, BELF/6/1/1/23.
43. M. McLarnon and S. Montgomery's depositions, 27 November 1969, PRONI, BELF/6/1/1/23; Price ballistics report, 15 January 1970, Scarman Belfast Exhibits.
44. Press autopsy report; L. Morris, A. McAfee and W. Rutherford's depositions, 27 November 1969, PRONI, BELF/6/1/1/23; *Scarman Report*, pp. 187–8.
45. Belfast No. 55; Belfast No. 35, Scarman Belfast Exhibits; *Scarman Report*, p. 215. More than twenty Catholics were wounded by gunfire during the period in question, but those injured by weapons not used by the police (e.g. shotguns or .22 rifles) have been excluded.
46. Gillespie's evidence, pp. 54–5; Belfast No. 55; *Scarman Report*, pp. 213.
47. Press autopsy report; Witness A and Witness B's depositions, 19 November 1969, PRONI, BELF/6/1/1/23.
48. *Scarman Report*, pp. 213–21.
49. Belfast Nos 20 and 24A, Scarman Belfast Exhibits.
50. Belfast No. 4, Scarman Belfast Exhibits.
51. L. Kelly, '"One Remarkable Fact": Why Most of Belfast Remained at Peace', *History Ireland*, July/August 2009, pp. 40–42; L. Kelly, 'Belfast, August 1969: The Limited and Localised Pattern(s) of Violence', in W. Sheehan and M. Cronin (eds), *Riotous Assemblies: Rebels, Riots and Revolts in Ireland* (Cork: Mercier Press, 2011), pp. 228–41.
52. Remarks by the Defence Secretary, Denis Healey, and the Home Secretary, James Callaghan, as cited by Tony Benn in his diary record of the Cabinet meeting of 19 August 1969. T. Benn, *Office without Power: Diaries 1968–72* (London: Hutchinson, 1988), p. 198.
53. Cabinet conclusions, 19 August 1969, Confidential Annex, NA, CAB/128/46; Castle, *Castle Diaries*, pp. 700–1; R. Crossman, *The Diaries of a Cabinet Minister, Volume III: Secretary of State for Social Services, 1968–1970* (London: Hamish Hamilton and Jonathan Cape, 1977), pp. 621–3; Benn, *Office without Power*, pp. 196–9.
54. Castle, *Castle Diaries*, p. 700.
55. I. Freeland, 'I[nternal] S[ecurity] Op[eration]s Northern Ireland', Chapter 3, paras 7, 11–12, London, Imperial War Museum, Freeland Papers, Box 79/34/3. See also undated Ballenden report on the Shankill Road Operations 11/12 October 1969, attached to Freeland letter, 18 October 1969, Imperial War Museum, Freeland Papers, Box 79/34/3.
56. *Irish News*, 13 October 1969.
57. Government of Northern Ireland, *Report of the Advisory Committee on Police in Northern Ireland (Hunt Report)*, (Belfast: HMSO, 1969).
58. 'Talk at CGS's Conference', attached to Freeland letter, 18 October 1969, Imperial War Museum, Freeland Papers, Box 79/34/3.
59. A. Hockaday to E. Wright, 25 June 1970, NA, HO/325/132.
60. E. Wright to R. Mark, 10 August 1970, NA, HO/325/132.

61. The Internal Security Tactical Doctrine Working Party – Terms of Reference, 21 July 1970, NA, HO/325/132.
62. *Irish News*, 22 October 1969; *Irish News*, 25 October 1969.
63. *Irish Press*, 18 November 1969.
64. *Irish Times*, 22 November 1969.
65. INTSUM, 1 January 1970, NA, WO/305/3783.
66. Brigadier Hudson's evidence to the Scarman Tribunal, 30 March 1971, pp. 25 and 76.
67. A former member of the UVF, who joined the organization in 1970, emphasized to me how 'elitist' it was in the early days, only recruiting after a lengthy selection process. In this respect, he suggested, it differed from the Ulster Defence Association which placed more weight upon numbers.
68. Adams, *Before the Dawn*, p. 113.
69. Hanley and Millar, *Lost Revolution*, p. 135; Hunt Committee meetings.
70. Adams, *Before the Dawn*, pp. 121–2.
71. Bishop and Mallie, *Provisional IRA*, p. 125.
72. B. Anderson, *Joe Cahill: A Life in the IRA* (Dublin: O'Brien Press, 2002), p. 180; Taylor, *Provos*, p. 61; Bishop and Mallie, *Provisional IRA*, p. 125.
73. Anderson, *Joe Cahill*, pp. 180–1.
74. Mac Stíofáin, *Memoirs*, pp. 133–43; Bishop and Mallie, *Provisional IRA*, pp. 135–37; R. White, *Ruairí Ó Brádaigh: The Life and Politics of an Irish Revolutionary* (Bloomington, IN: Indiana University Press, 2006), pp. 154–8. News of the split appeared in the *Sunday Press*, 28 December 1969.
75. Anderson, *Joe Cahill*, pp. 188–9.
76. Hanley and Millar, *Lost Revolution*, pp. 141–51. The machinations of Charles Haughey and Neil Blaney lie outside the scope of this book.
77. P. Beresford, 'The Official IRA and Republican Clubs in Northern Ireland 1968–1974 and their Relations with other Political and Paramilitary Groups', PhD thesis, University of Exeter, September 1979, pp. 263–6; Graham, '*Show Me the Man*', pp. 43–5; Taylor, *Provos*, pp. 62–3; Adams, *Before the Dawn*, p. 129. The RUC Special Branch estimated that in April 1970 the Official IRA had 28 members in Belfast and the Provisionals 312. INTSUM, 30 April 1970, NA, WO/305/3783.
78. Clonard Chronicle, 10 October 1969.
79. Northern Ireland Threat Assessment for Period 1 January 1970 to 30 June 1970, NA, DEFE/13/765.
80. K. Bean and M. Hayes (eds), *Republican Voices* (Monaghan: Seesyu Press, 2001), p. 50.
81. M. O'Doherty, *The Trouble with Guns: Republican Strategy and the Provisional IRA* (Belfast: Blackstaff Press, 1998), pp. 64–5.
82. G. Adams, *The Politics of Irish Freedom* (Dingle: Brandon, 1986), p. 54; Adams, *Before the Dawn*, p. 134.
83. It had been used against loyalists in September and October 1969.
84. INTSUM, 2 April 1970, NA, WO/305/3783.
85. INTSUM, 9 April 1970, NA, WO/305/3783. RUC Duty Officer's Report ending 9.00 am, 3 April 1970; Annex A to Director of Operations Brief 020800A to 030800 April 1970, PRONI, CAB/9B/317/7.
86. HONIP (70), No. 15, 10 April 1970, NA, CJ/4/269. HONIPs were weekly summaries of developments in Northern Ireland prepared for Cabinet members and other interested parties by the Home Office.
87. R. Burroughs memorandum, 3 April 1970, NA, CJ/3/18.
88. Herbert telegram, 7 April 1970, NA, PREM/13/3386. The term 'Brady group' was customarily used in British Army documents at this time to refer to the Provisional IRA, even though Ruairí Ó Brádaigh was not its Chief of Staff, but only a member of the Army Council. (He was, however, the Chairman of Provisional Sinn Féin.) The Official IRA was usually referred to as the 'Goulding group'.
89. E. Moloney, *A Secret History of the IRA* (London: Allen Lane, 2002), p. 88.

10

The Weekend of 27–28 June 1970

I

It was not until the last weekend of June 1970 that the Provisional IRA was able openly to demonstrate its growing strength. Because this coincided with a change of government in London – the Conservatives under Edward Heath replacing Labour under Harold Wilson following the General Election of 18 June 1970 – it is tempting to link the two events and argue that a tougher line was being taken against disorder in Northern Ireland. After all, for over a century, the Conservatives had been regarded as the natural ally of the province's Unionist establishment. Indeed, the party's official title remained the Conservative and Unionist Party and the Unionist MPs at Westminster took the Conservative whip, so forming part of the new government's majority.

The reality, however, was that the new Cabinet – as opposed to some of its backbenchers – had no more affection for Northern Ireland than its predecessor. Callaghan's successor as Home Secretary, Reginald Maudling, famously described it as 'a bloody awful country'; the Foreign Secretary and former Prime Minister, Sir Alec Douglas-Home, favoured pushing its population into a union with the Republic of Ireland; while Heath himself doubted whether Stormont would ever be able to devise a workable solution to the province's problems.[1] This does not suggest a deep-rooted commitment to the Unionist cause.

Indeed, the main preoccupation of both the Labour and Conservative Governments in June 1970 was the possible consequences of the marching season and in particular of the upcoming Orange Order parades in Belfast. On 15 June 1970, three days before the United Kingdom went to the polls, an important meeting had taken place at the Home Office between civil servants from that department and the

Ministry of Defence. General Freeland and Ronald Burroughs, the UK Representative in Northern Ireland, were also present.[2]

Freeland had been instructed by Callaghan to assess the possibility of banning the marches. He told the meeting, however, that 'Orangemen felt passionately about these parades and that if they were cancelled this would be regarded as a victory for the Republican cause'. He also made the valid point that this was all the more likely as an earlier ban on marches had been lifted the previous Easter in order to allow Catholics to parade. Any attempt by the government to ban the Orange marches at this stage, the General warned, 'would inevitably result in illegal marches and trouble on the streets which could not be controlled' and he expressed concern that if this happened, 'the credibility of the security forces would be destroyed and…all progress made over the last nine months would be thrown away'. Burroughs supported Freeland. '[O]nly the extremists on both sides would welcome a ban and subsequent disorder', he said. The left would see in it 'prospects for the end of partition and the right something akin to UDI' (the Rhodesian parallel was also in the mind of British officials).[3]

The permanent head of the Home Office, Sir Philip Allen, who was chairing the meeting, said that Callaghan intended to go to Northern Ireland after the election when, among other things, he would urge the Orange Order to call off the parades. Both Freeland and Burroughs opposed any such visit before the main parades on 12 July and the meeting concluded that the Home Secretary should be advised not to ban them.[4] It is of course impossible to know whether Callaghan would have rejected the unanimous advice of his senior political and military advisers on the ground in Northern Ireland if the Labour Party had won the election and he had remained Home Secretary, but it is worth pointing out that in his first speech from the Opposition front bench on 3 July 1970, Callaghan did not call for a ban, although he did appeal to the Orange Order 'to say seriously whether they believe it to be in the best interests of good government and in the interests of the security of the ordinary people that they should march on 13th July'.[5]

Whatever Callaghan might or might not have done, a meeting of senior Conservative ministers and their advisers on 22 June 1970 agreed to send the reinforcements Freeland had requested and which the Chiefs of Staff had approved. The meeting also briefly considered the question of marches and parades in general and there was a consensus that 'the present situation, in which one faction was allowed to carry out provocative marches and demonstrations in the territory of the other, was an invitation to disorder and should not be allowed to continue indefinitely'. If they could not be banned altogether, attempts should be made to re-route them in order 'to prevent the Protestants from trailing their coats in Roman Catholic areas and vice versa'. This was a further indication that the Conservative leadership was no more partial to the Protestant community on this issue than it was to the Catholic one, and while Westminster was urged to seek 'every opportunity' to bolster the authority of Stormont, it was suggested that it should do everything in its power 'to maintain the momentum of reform'. It is clear from these decisions that there was no change in British policy. Like its Labour predecessor, the Heath Government wanted to keep going with reform by proxy and to keep away from direct rule. It was also agreed that Maudling should go to Northern Ireland as soon as possible, but even before his visit the situation there had begun to deteriorate.[6]

II

An Orange parade was scheduled for Belfast on the afternoon and evening of 26 June 1970. Led by Loyal Orange Lodge No.1216, the parade's route took it up the Crumlin Road and past the dangerous interface between the Shankill and Ardoyne districts, the scene of so much violence the previous year. The Ardoyne Citizens Defence Committee had warned the authorities that there would be trouble if an Orange march came up the Crumlin Road, but as nothing had happened in response to other marches in the area, the latest warning was dismissed by the principal military unit involved, 45 Royal Marine Commando, as 'probably a bit of Irish blarney'. Precautions were nevertheless taken and troops and police were deployed in the area. This proved to be a wise move because violence erupted around 8:30 pm and lasted through much of the night. Although the marines agreed that the behaviour of the marchers and their supporters was extremely provocative, they were also clear that people in the Catholic crowd had been the first to resort to violence by hurling stones, bottles and even chunks of metal at their opponents.[7]

On 27 June 1970, there were not only Orange marches, but a Republican funeral. Hugh McAteer, an IRA Chief of Staff during the

Second World War and brother of the Nationalist leader, had died suddenly and was being buried in the Milltown Cemetery. Both the Official and the Provisional IRA were represented. Indeed, the leadership of the Provisional IRA, in the persons of Seán Mac Stíofáin, Ruairí Ó Brádaigh and Dáithí Ó Conaill, were all present and as well as attending the funeral they had discussions with the Belfast Provisionals.[8] One wonders to what extent the disturbances of that day were in any way influenced by their presence.

On the afternoon of 27 June 1970, the so-called Whiterock Parade, which followed a circuitous route to and from an Orange hall on the Springfield Road, duly took place. This march was also scheduled to pass Catholic districts at a number of points, including Cupar Street, another place where violence had occurred during August 1969. The army had received intelligence that the Official IRA was planning to disrupt the parade in Cupar Street[9] and the authorities had succeeded in persuading the organizers to make a slight diversion so that the marchers did not come straight out of this street on to the lower Springfield Road, but instead emerged a few hundred yards further up. This minor adjustment did not, however, prevent an outbreak of violence. A RUC witness, Constable Wilson, who was on duty in the Springfield Road, described what happened from his perspective. 'At approximately 3:30 pm', he said, 'the start of the Parade rounded the corner of Mayo Street and headed up the Springfield Road. They were met immediately by a shower of missiles thrown by a large party of opposition some 15 to 20 yards below Mayo Street'. The Protestant crowd then picked up missiles and retaliated, which prompted a baton charge by troops, who were also on duty. Shortly afterwards 'a number of shots' were fired from within the Catholic crowd, a number of Protestants surged forward once more and the army fired several canisters of CS gas.[10]

A British army report supported Wilson's version of events. 'At the junction [with the Springfield Road]', it stated, 'a crowd of Republican opposition engaged the leading elements [of the parade] with "The Soldier's Song", a bottle and stones in that order; the marchers replied with stones following receipt of the bottle. Then, at least 4 rounds of 9 mm ammunition were fired.' The report speculated whether this was the attack originally planned by the Official IRA for Cupar Street, adding that '[m]ilitary observers in plain clothes who were in the Catholic crowd saw small groups of civilians conferring before the incident and heard a civilian say, "Don't worry the right boys are up in front".[11]

On the other hand, the *Guardian*'s correspondent, Simon Winchester, who was also present during the riot, lays the blame for what happened on the marchers. 'The Orangemen', he writes, 'were prepared for trouble: one could say with some fairness that they initiated it'. He recalls 'watching the huge accumulation of personal weaponry passing before my eyes', including bricks stuffed into bandsmen's pockets and empty milk bottles grasped in free hands. He even drew the attention of a policeman to 'one man, five foot of wrinkled hatred...with no fewer than six housebricks held in his two hands'. The policeman allegedly turned to Winchester and said, with a grin and a wink, 'You know...I never saw a thing. Not a single thing.' At the same time, however, Winchester does not record that people in the Protestant crowd threw their missiles first. Indeed, his earliest mention of stone-throwing as opposed to carrying refers to the Catholic crowd's attack upon the marchers. He also observes that during the riot, which lasted about two hours, '[a] petrol bomb, launched by a Catholic from the Clonard, set a bakery ablaze'.[12]

One man lost his life as a result of the riot on the Springfield Road that afternoon. He was William Thomas Reid, aged 46, a foreman iron-turner, who was married with three children. At his inquest, his wife testified that she and her husband had set out from home at about 2:15 pm to walk alongside the parade. As the couple approached the junction of Mayo Street with the Springfield Road, she became aware that there was trouble ahead and turned back. Just as she did so, 'there was a ferocious attack by hundreds of people who were standing on the other side of the Springfield Road with stones and a variety of other missiles' and she was hit on the hand as she raised it to her head to protect herself. She became separated from her husband in the melee and returned home. It was not until 5:45 pm that she heard from her son that her husband had been struck on the head by a missile and had been taken to the nearby Royal Victoria Hospital, where he died six days later.[13]

Whether Reid was involved in the rioting when he was struck is unclear,[14] but prevailing notions of manliness required women to be kept away from violence and not to be brought out for an afternoon of street fighting. There were two other women who accompanied the Reids on their outing and they also turned back as soon as the missiles began to fly.[15] This suggests that there were people on the Protestant side of the Springfield Road who did not anticipate the violence which occurred.

No sooner had trouble died down on the Springfield Road than it flared up again on the Crumlin Road – and, if the Official IRA had been involved earlier in the day, it was the Provisionals who picked up the baton later on. Just before 5 pm, 45 Royal Marine Commando reported that Protestant and Catholic crowds on either side of the Crumlin Road were hurling stones at one another. Ten minutes later, the message came that the crowds had increased in size, that shots had been heard in Hooker and Herbert Streets and that a woman in Protestant Bray Street had been hit. The unit's ambulance was said to be on its way. After it arrived one of the medical orderlies on board was shot through the cheek. Further entries in the 39th Brigade Log reveal the rapidly deteriorating situation. At 5:24 pm there was a report of shooting from a rooftop in Herbert Street into Bray Street; at 5:36 pm of 'men with guns' coming out of Herbert Street; and at 5:49 pm of shots from another Catholic street and of a man in a white Cortina handing out petrol bombs on the Crumlin Road. Within an hour of the riot starting, 45 Commando's No. 2 Company had itself come under fire and one marine had been injured.[16]

A total of three Protestants were killed on the Crumlin Road that evening. It is impossible to be sure about the precise sequence of events, but all three seem to have been killed during the shooting described above. At the inquest of one of the three, a 34-year-old plater Daniel Loughins, an eyewitness testified that he had seen 'two masked men come out of Herbert Street firing pistols in our direction. Loughins fell to the ground with what appeared to be a head wound'. The gunmen then turned their attention to Bray Street, one street up from Palmer Street and began to fire down it.[17]

The other two shootings took place at the mouth of Disraeli Street, one street down from Palmer Street. The two victims were Alexander Gould, an unemployed 19-year-old barman, and William Kincaid, a 28-year-old process operator. Witnesses stated that both men had been shot by gunmen from Hooker Street. A police officer who arrived on the scene shortly after Gould's death called for an ambulance at 5:15 pm. Both he and the ambulance driver referred to the confusion of the crowd in Disraeli Street when they arrived. Gould and Kincaid had each been killed by .38 revolver rounds. The former had been hit in the middle of the forehead and the latter in the chest, midway between the nipples, which suggests a combination of good marksmanship, cool-headedness and close proximity on the part of the gunman or gunmen involved.[18] No one disputes that the latter were members of the Provisional IRA.

Although there were no more fatalities in the area, there was a lot more violence. News of the shootings worked to mobilize many more people. The chief sub-editor of the *Belfast Telegraph*, Desmond McMullen, found 'huge mobs, crazed by a vicious combination of drink and hatred' in the Shankill Road 'searching for anyone or anything to attack with whatever missiles came to hand'. But, as McMullen himself acknowledged, most of the attacks were directed against a political target: 'their' army for failing to defend them. The marines were called 'English bastards' and 'Fenian lovers'. Asked what it felt like to be abused by both sides, a young marine laughed and replied, 'I didn't think much about religion before I came here. But now I'm a confirmed atheist'.[19] Even the UVF made a fleeting reappearance. In a telephone message relayed from the RUC to Northern Ireland army headquarters at 7:15 pm. the mysterious figure of 'Captain Johnston' referred to events earlier in the evening as 'obviously a takeover by the IRA' and warned that 'the UVF is equipped with [the] latest equipment, [and] 8,500 men are ready to take over in half an hour'.[20]

Prevented by the security forces from crossing the Crumlin Road into Ardoyne, the Protestant crowd turned to other targets. 'Realizing that they were contained in the area of the Crumlin Road/Disraeli Street,' the history of 45 Royal Marine Commando recorded, the crowd 'moved east [and] back on to the Crumlin Road where they commenced burning cars, looting and setting fire to property including a petrol station a launderette and a tyre store'. They then proceeded to Tennent Street police station, the location of the Commandos' headquarters, and laid siege to it. Shooting broke out and the senior RUC officer at the station was hit in the neck and face by a shotgun blast at a range of five yards. A marine was also hit, but he was lucky. The bullet pierced his riot shield, travelled on into the pouch on his belt and ended up in his rifle cleaning box. Fire was returned and the crowd withdrew. When dawn broke, 'the Crumlin Road looked like a battleground. Bottles, stones, marbles, ballbearings and bullets were found littered all over the area and the air was thick with smoke from burnt out cars, petrol stations and other buildings…Yet again Belfast Corporation dustmen came along to sweep up the wreckage and people started going to church'.[21]

Commenting on this episode to his biographer, Martin Meehan, the commander of the Ardoyne Provisionals, declared that

> the IRA had proved beyond a shadow of a doubt that what they said they were going to do, they had done. There would never be another day like the 15th of August 1969, when Ardoyne was left open to RUC and Loyalist attack and unable to defend itself. The date – 27th of June 1970 – is more significant for that than anything else. As a result the whole broad spectrum of the nationalist people actually supported what the IRA was doing. Everybody, man, woman and child came out and supported us in any way possible. I never saw support like it in my life. It was unbelievable.[22]

This assumes, of course, that the loyalists originally intended to attack Ardoyne in June 1970, as they had done in August 1969. But, while Republicans like Meehan may have thought this was so, there is no evidence that he was right. Indeed, as we shall see, the British were firmly convinced that while individuals and groups on the Protestant side had been mainly responsible for the trouble in 1969, Catholics were to blame for what happened ten months later.[23] Even if one gives the Ardoyne Provisionals the benefit of the doubt and does not accuse them of pursuing a strategy of provocation, there was in fact no need for them to take the action they did, as the RUC and the Commandos had the situation under control and the intervention of the Republicans only made matters worse. Meehan was also a little premature in suggesting that the night of 27/28 June 1970 consolidated Catholic support for the Provisional IRA in Ardoyne, for it is significant that it was Catholic women from Ardoyne and not Protestant women from Woodvale who brought tea to the exhausted men of 45 Royal Marine Commando on the morning after the rioting.[24] The Provisional IRA's claim to represent the local community was still just that: a claim.

III

Rioting was not confined to north Belfast on the night of 27/28 June 1970. Just across the River Lagan in east Belfast was the Catholic enclave of the Short Strand, bounded by the Albertbridge Road, Bryson Street, the Lower Newtownards Road and Short Strand itself, and which was dominated by the steeple of St Matthew's Catholic church at the corner of Bryson Street and the Newtownards Road. Orange bands from all over Belfast took part in the Whiterock Parade on the afternoon of 27 June 1970 and in the early evening one of them, the Gertrude Street Flute Band, marched up the Newtownards Road. 'Passing the "notorious" Catholic Seaforde Street close to the [St Matthew's] chapel,' writes Raymond Quinn, 'it launched into its usual zest [sic] of "Kick the Pope" tunes. Stones began to fly in each direction as the Irish flag was waved from Seaforde Street. As in Ardoyne earlier, shots rang out and fire was returned without injury. The situation died down quite suddenly...'[25]

According to District Inspector John Hammond and County Inspector George Moore, however, the Irish Tricolour did not appear until five hours *after* the passing of the Gertrude Street Band which, according to Hammond, took place at about 6:15 pm. A Protestant eyewitness subsequently recalled, moreover, that 'Residents from Short Strand watched the parade and shouted "Orange bastards" as the parade passed by. Republicans...threw stones and other missiles at the parade and the crowds around me'. 'Naturally', he added, 'we returned the missiles thrown'. According to this witness, the police, who were present, gradually gained control of the situation and the crowds dispersed at about 7 pm.[26] A Catholic eyewitness, on the other hand, claimed that '[a] hail of pennies and particles of glass were thrown into Seaforde Street' by the Protestant crowd as the Gertrude Street band passed and that a similar barrage occurred some ten minutes later. This witness complained that the police – whose strength he put at five – made no attempt to stop this Protestant attack, but concentrated upon persuading the residents of Seaforde Street to return to their homes.[27] If there were indeed only five RUC officers on duty, this was perhaps not surprising.

Whoever began the stone-throwing, there was clearly an ugly confrontation between members of the two communities when the Gertrude Street Band passed along the Newtownards Road. It is extremely doubtful, however, whether firearms were discharged by either side on this occasion. If they had been, the RUC would have reported it to the army and the details would have been recorded in the army logs. However, there is no reference to any gunfire in the area during the early evening of 27 June in either the Northern Ireland Headquarters log or that of the 39th Infantry Brigade, while civilian sources, including the St Matthew's parish chronicle, also suggest that there was no shooting until much later in the evening.[28]

The tension in the area eased somewhat after the Gertrude Street Flute Band incident. Further trouble was clearly expected, however. According to a Catholic account, at around 8 pm 'a member of the St. Matthew's C.D.C. was summoned to a meeting in Mountpottinger R.U.C. Barracks and advised to expect trouble that night'.[29] This is borne out by an entry in the 39th Brigade Log which recorded that at 8:24 pm the local District Inspector, who was based at Mountpottinger, was 'extremely worried' about the situation and concerned lest 'all the work done in the last year will be destroyed in one night'. He felt that 'something may well develop (very quickly) in Ballymacarrett to relieve the situation in West and Central Belfast'. Soon after 10 pm, two Catholics who were trusted by the RUC warned the District Inspector to expect trouble on the Newtownards Road in half an hour or so.[30]

They were right. As the pubs emptied on to the Newtownards Road, crowds began to gather. A Catholic witness said that he saw about 200 people moving towards Seaforde Street, 'shouting the usual anti-Catholic slogans'. '[S]ome were shouting "we'll burn the fenians out!"' The small number of policemen present, he claimed, did little to disperse this crowd, but instead stationed themselves across the mouth of Seaforde Street.[31] One of those officers, District Inspector Hammond, in his statement to the inquest on one of the victims of the subsequent shooting, maintained that just before 11 pm people had gathered at Gertrude Street and at the corner of Wolff Street and the Newtownards Road. There was also a crowd in Seaforde Street. Its existence was reported to the army and the 39th Brigade log states that the police were trying to disperse it.[32]

At about 11.20 pm another senior policeman, County Inspector Moore, arrived on the scene, where he saw District Inspector Nichol trying to control the crowd on the north side of the Newtownards Road while Hammond was doing the same on the south side at Seaforde Street. According to Moore, the people in Seaforde Street were hostile and were accusing Protestants of damaging and looting Catholic premises on the Newtownards Road. He tried to reassure them that their fears were groundless, but they did not believe him and began throwing missiles at him, whereupon he hastily retreated up Seaforde Street and on to the Newtownards Road. It was at this point, according to both Hammond and Moore, that the Irish Tricolour was hoisted on the roof of a vacant shop at the corner of Seaforde Street and the Newtownards Road.[33]

As the angry Protestants, provoked by the appearance of the Irish Tricolour, surged forward, Moore claims that he managed to intercept a man who was about to throw a stone at the Catholics. But, just as Moore was about to take him into custody, another man ran out of Seaforde Street and fired into the Protestant crowd.[34] On the other side of the Newtownards Road, May Campbell, who was walking home with her husband after a drink at the 'Talk of the Town' bar on Bridge End, also noticed the man come out of Seaforde Street. She saw him get down on one knee and was about to ask her husband what he was doing when a bullet struck her in the left leg, putting her in hospital for four weeks. Hammond, who also witnessed the shooting, saw two men, as well as Mrs Campbell, fall to the ground. At 11:35 pm the 39th Brigade log recorded a message from the RUC: 'shooting in Seaforde Street. Several people reported injured'. The support company of the 2nd battalion of the Queen's Regiment was put on immediate alert.[35]

Some of the Catholics in the Short Strand had certainly taken precautions to counter any trouble which might occur. In particular, the Provisional IRA was ready for action. A member of the local battalion staff told Quinn that he had already been warned on the Friday to be prepared for the following evening 'as there was a good chance that things might "kick off"'. At 6:30 pm on 27 June 1970, after he had returned from work and eaten, he was called upon at home by the battalion commander and told to 'get ready'. He went to Seaforde Street, where most of the battalion staff had assembled. 'Our local Company who totalled around 30 volunteers', he went on, 'were split up into two sections, one being deployed around Seaforde Street, the other to the Short Strand end of the district. Other volunteers were simply told to remain in their homes on stand-by'. In addition there were six to eight members of the Cumann na mBan, the IRA's women's auxiliaries which had gone with the Provisionals in the split, and two sections of the Fianna Éireann, its youth movement. Their job was to act as runners with either messages or ammunition.[36]

In the appropriately named Chemical Street, teenage girls filled buckets with a solution of water and vinegar – an antidote to the effects of CS gas – and, as we shall see, first-aid facilities and a family refuge were set up in the school at the rear of the St Matthew's church complex. Billy McKee was also warned of impending trouble in the Short Strand and arrived in the area shortly after 10 pm to assess the situation in person. Tom O'Donnell, another member of the Belfast Staff and a resident of the Short Strand himself, requested further weapons and McKee promptly ordered the car in which he had travelled to return to west Belfast and find some. It returned with six M1 carbines and five full magazines for each one.[37]

Following the outbreak of shooting in Seaforde Street, Moore testified that the Protestant crowd scattered, ambulances were sent for and the wounded were evacuated to houses in nearby streets. 'While waiting for the ambulances', he continued, 'heavy firing was directed out of Seaforde Street, in automatic and single shots'. After the ambulances had left, a group of Protestants gathered at the end of Kenilworth Street, whereupon firing broke out from the grounds of St Matthew's church and another man was hit. 'Heavy firing continued from the Chapel grounds', Moore noted, and as the police (unarmed following the Hunt reforms) were unable to do anything about the situation, they withdrew. He timed the decision at 12:30 am and it is recorded in the log at Northern Ireland army headquarters at 12:54 pm.[38]

Moore added that the Protestants had already begun to return fire by the time the RUC withdrew, but maintained that it was not 'heavy'.[39] Shortly before the police pulled back one of their number allegedly told a Protestant taxi driver, as they both took shelter from the gunfire on the Newtownards Road, '[F]or God['s] sake if you have anything go and get it'. The message was clear. '[I]t was now a free for all', the taxi driver recalled. He knew a friend who had an old Lee Enfield rifle from the Second World War. Another friend knew someone else who had an even older weapon, a rifle that had been smuggled in for the original UVF in 1912. When they returned to the scene, the taxi driver and his friend returned the fire coming from St Matthew's, moving from position to position both to confuse the enemy and to ensure greater self-protection. He estimated that about fifty rounds were fired from the Lee Enfield during the next couple of hours and noticed that other Protestants were also returning fire, notably from the doctors' surgery at the corner of Bryson Street and the Newtownards Road.[40]

By this time, the shooting had already claimed its first fatality. At about 11:45 pm, five men had left the Buffs Club on the Albertbridge Road after a night's drinking. They made their way towards the home of one of their number for some non-alcoholic refreshment. Their route took them along Bryson Street. Just as they turned into it at about midnight, however, there was, in the words of one of them, 'a burst of automatic gunfire from the direction of Kilmood Street' and James McCurrie, a married 44-year-old labourer with four children and another on the way, was cut down. By a terrible coincidence, it was McCurrie's own home towards which the men were walking. As McCurrie's friends dived for cover behind the wall and railings of the school which stood at the corner of Beechfield and Bryson Streets, it seems that they were not fully aware of what had happened to their companion. They called his name, but got no reply, and shortly afterwards two of them ventured to put their heads around the corner of Bryson Street once more, only to be met with another burst of automatic fire. They then retreated to the Newtownards Road, where they informed a policeman of what had happened. The same man told the inquest on McCurrie that 'if we had known there was trouble in the area we would have went home [by] a different route'. He added, 'I never heard shots on Saturday night until the burst of gunfire which was aimed at us in Bryson Street'. A third member of the party said, 'None of the five of us had any guns and we definitely done no shooting'. He too claimed that he had heard no gunfire beforehand and was unaware of any trouble in the area.[41]

The sequence of these events is confirmed by the army logs. At one minute past midnight the 39th Brigade log noted: 'Shots reported from Bryson Street. Long burst of automatic fire'. Six minutes later there was a report of a '[b]ody lying in Bryson Street suffering from gunshot wounds'.[42] This was undoubtedly McCurrie. The person who discovered him was Mrs Annie Blackmore, who told the inquest on his death that she was out looking for her own husband when she entered Bryson Street. As she passed Kilmood Street, about half-a-dozen armed men came out of it and one of them told her to keep down because of the shooting. When she said that she was looking for her husband, the man pointed to a body lying in the gateway of Beechfield School. Having ascertained that it was not her husband, she and another man moved the body into Beechfield Street. A police officer appeared and rang for an ambulance, after which McCurrie was then moved again into a nearby house.[43]

The men whom Mrs Blackmore encountered at the junction of Bryson and Kilmood Streets were almost certainly among the IRA volunteers defending the area, while the man who spoke to her was probably the one who had shot and killed McCurrie. Mrs Blackmore said that he was carrying 'a short gun about two feet long', whereas his companions were carrying longer weapons, 'like rifles'. Evidence produced at his inquest suggested that McCurrie had been killed by a 9 mm bullet. Twenty-four spent cases of this type of ammunition were found near the junction of Kilmood Street with Bryson Street the following morning, which is consistent with both the two bursts of 'automatic gunfire' described by McCurrie's friends and Mrs Blackmore's reference to 'a short gun'.[44]

There is no contemporary evidence that McCurrie and his friends were carrying weapons or that they had any aggressive intentions.[45] It is of course possible that the IRA volunteers saw a group of five men entering Bryson Street from the Protestant side as suspicious and potentially dangerous. Even so, to open fire on them with a sub-machine gun without warning was at best a display of panic and at worst a deliberate attempt to kill regardless.

As the RUC were withdrawing from the area, the British army, in the shape of the company of the 2nd Queen's Regiment which had been placed on alert just over an hour before, arrived.[46] The Provisional IRA was well aware of the army's movements, thanks to the activities of Paddy Kennedy, the Republican Labour MP for Belfast Central. Quinn relates how McKee, who was worried about possible intervention by the army and the consequent loss of volunteers and weapons, asked Kennedy to go to the Mountpottinger RUC station in his capacity as a Stormont MP 'and using a veil of concern at the situation to try and find out if troops would be deployed into the district'. Kennedy was accompanied by another man who later testified that they saw an army major and a number of police officers. The major replied that troops would be sent into the area, whereupon McKee instructed O'Donnell 'to have weapons off the streets and back in their "dumps" as soon as possible'.[47]

He need not have worried: the troops were initially more concerned with preventing the hijacking of buses on the other side of the Short Strand for use as barricades. A platoon was despatched to the bus depot for this purpose at 1:45 am.[48] There certainly appears to have been plenty of shooting in that area too. Quinn's Battalion Staff informant told him that he was initially stationed there. A few yards away, at the top of the Albertbridge Road, the Armagh House, a Catholic-owned pub, 'was well on fire and the [loyalist] mob was attacking firemen as they attempted to tackle the blaze'. He and a member of the local vigilantes opened fire on the loyalists with .38 pistols. A little later the two men moved to a position 'which gave us a better field of fire...' Two other Provisional IRA volunteers were there, including Joe Surgenor. 'We were coming under fire', Quinn's informant recalled, 'and one Loyalist who was using a Sterling 9 mm sub-machine gun appeared "to know what he was doing", so I asked Joe to position himself at an upstairs window with his .303 Lee Enfield rifle to see if we "could get a fix on him".' At about 2:30 am, however, when 'the situation was under control', Quinn's informant left for Seaforde Street and the St Matthew's church complex.[49]

Those in charge of the troops, moreover, were understandably anxious not to expose their men to the hazards of a full-scale firefight, especially at night, without further reconnaissance and reinforcement. The *Belfast Telegraph*'s McMullen, who on hearing that rioting had broken out in the Short Strand had left the Crumlin Road to cross the Lagan with three journalists from London, found the soldiers positioned in the vicinity of their makeshift headquarters on a patch of waste ground off Bridge End. 'If what we had seen earlier was a living nightmare', McMullen wrote, 'then this was hell itself'. Soldiers, crouching behind a gable wall, told the reporters that there was a gun battle going on and they themselves heard at least 100 shots within the next five minutes. Apparently, the troops were waiting for the arrival of some armoured cars before going into the area.[50]

Undaunted, the journalists edged along the south side of the Newtownards Road in 'utter darkness' (taking out the street lighting was now a common tactic), dodging from doorway to doorway. At the junction of Seaforde Street, they were fired upon and McMullen called upon his colleagues to join him in running back towards the protection of the army. As they did so, a further shot rang out and one of two men he had noticed running down the Newtownards Road towards them fell, screaming with pain. A soldier dashed out from behind the gable to rescue the wounded man, only to find himself attacked by the man's companion, who shouted: 'Where have you bastards been?' as he rained blows upon the unfortunate Good Samaritan. Eventually, the wounded man, who had been hit in the leg, was given first aid by the army and despatched to hospital.[51]

At 1:32 am, 39th Brigade Headquarters radioed Mountpottinger to say that a report had been received stating that the Sexton's house in the grounds of St Matthew's church had been 'blown up'. It had in fact been set on fire by members of the Protestant crowd. Exactly when this occurred is not clear. Quinn's account implies that it was earlier in the evening as does the parish chronicle; but Moore testified that it was not on fire when he left the area at 12:30 am, although it was when he returned two hours later, and one of those who was providing first aid inside the St Matthew's complex confirmed that it was 'well alight' by then.[52]

Three quarters of an hour earlier, a second man had been fatally wounded. This was Robert Neill, a 38-year-old sheet metal worker of Central Street. A witness at his inquest stated that he had seen Neill at about 1:45 am on the corner of Central Street and the Newtownards Road. '[T]he next thing I saw,' the witness continued, 'was him being helped round the corner by two fellows whom I don't know. Somebody shouted "Bobby Neill has been shot", and I ran up to give them a hand'. Neill was taken into a nearby house – whether it was his own is not stated – and an ambulance was sent for to take him to hospital. It took some time to come and, in fact, the driver told the inquest that he did not receive the call until 2:32 am. The autopsy report showed that Neill had been killed by a 9 mm bullet, which had entered the left-hand side of his back and passed through both lungs and the spine before lodging in the muscles of his right armpit. It was the opinion of the pathologist that the shot was probably a ricochet. His death may have been due to the fact that, as another witness put it, 'he had a wee drop of drink on him' and had simply failed to take sufficient cover. As in the case of McCurrie, there is no evidence to suggest that he was carrying a weapon or participating in the rioting.[53]

Some fifteen minutes after Neill was mortally wounded – i.e. at around 2 am – a third man suffered the same fate. This time he was a Catholic. Quinn makes the episode sound like a scene in a Western when a wagon train is making its last stand against a raiding party. According to his account, a defiant McKee, assisted by Henry McIlhone, a 33-year-old scaffold rigger from nearby Sheriff Street, shouted at the

Protestant mob 'to come on in' to the St Matthew's grounds in the hope that this show of bravado, plus the memory of the heavy gunfire they had encountered earlier, would in fact deter them from doing so. When McKee saw not a mob but two armed men advancing from the direction of the Newtownards Road, he ordered McIlhone to open fire and in the exchange of shots which followed, both men were hit.[54]

Earlier in the evening, a classroom in the St Matthew's Boys' Primary School in Seaforde Street had been turned into a first-aid post. It was staffed mainly by the Knights of Malta. There was also a GP, Dr John Mellotte, who had been called in to attend to some children who had taken refuge in the school. When the news came through that two men had been shot in the grounds of St Matthew's, Mellotte and James Allison, a lieutenant in the Knights, hurried to the site with a stretcher to see what they could do to help. They encountered a group of seven or eight men, presumably IRA volunteers, one of whom deliberately prevented Dr Mellotte from going any further on the grounds that he was 'more valuable' in the first-aid post. Allison, however, was allowed through and it was he and one of the other men who brought McIlhone and then McKee to the primary school, where they were given first-aid before being transferred to the Mater Hospital on the Crumlin Road. McIlhone died of a gunshot wound in which the bullet entered the right side of his neck and exited from the top of his left shoulder, which had passed through his spine, damaging the spinal cord on the way. He had also been shot through both feet.[55] The badly wounded McKee, however, lived to fight another day and became a living legend in the process.

In the Provisional IRA's 1973 account of the origins of the Troubles, McIlhone was described as an 'I.R.A. auxiliary'. Almost immediately, however, the Provisionals issued a statement to the effect that this was a mistake and that 'Mr McIlhone was not at any time a member of this organization and was in fact an innocent bystander when he was shot dead'.[56] Notwithstanding the allegation by District Inspector Hammond at his inquest that McIlhone was the man who had opened fire on the Protestant crowd at the junction of Seaforde Street and the Newtownards Road earlier in the evening, the 1973 denial is undoubtedly correct. A judge ruled in June 1975 that not only was Hammond's identification of McIlhone as the gunman unreliable, but that he was not even carrying a gun. As a result, his widow qualified for £10,000 compensation from the state for his death. More recently, the Police Service of Northern Ireland's Historical Enquiries Team has concluded that not only was McIlhone unarmed, but that he was shot by Republicans while attempting to put out a fire in the church grounds.[57]

Despite this the Republican movement reverted to its original position. McIlhone's name appears on the Provisional IRA's role of honour, where it is stated there that although he was not a member of the organization, he was included 'as a mark of respect to a great Irish man by Republican comrades who fought alongside him in the defence of the Short Strand on that historic day'. McKee, moreover, has insisted that his original account is correct and that McIlhone was shot by 'loyalist gunmen'.[58] Belfast was not the American West. But, here too, there is a tendency when the legend becomes fact to print the legend.[59]

Apart from the shooting in the vicinity of St Matthew's chapel, 'a large crowd of looters' was reported at the Newtownards Road end of Bryson Street at 2:05 am and half an hour later it was stated that the Catholic-owned Lynch's Bar on the Newtownards Road had been set alight. The RUC, who were now back in the area, appealed for more troops 'or all the shops will be burnt down'. The Protestant crowd was clearly incensed by what they regarded as the army's lack of action against the gunmen in the St Matthew's complex. Indeed, when the army managed to fire the first rounds of CS gas into the church grounds at 2:37 am, it was recorded that the '[c]rowd [was] now happy'.[60]

The fighting went on until daybreak when, in the words of Quinn's battalion staff informant, 'the girls of Cumann na mBan were handed our weapons to take out of the district about 8 am over to the Markets district to avoid capture in any raids into the area by the British Army'.[61] Troops also reported spasmodic shooting throughout the night until about 5:30 or 6 am.[62] For all the residents of Ballymacarrett – Protestant and Catholic alike – the night of 27/28 June 1970 was a night to remember.

IV

Unfortunately for the historian, however, it has been collectively remembered in different and indeed contradictory ways. Peter Taylor discovered just how different individual memories were while researching his BBC documentary trilogy on the Troubles at the end of the 1990s.

In the first series (which dealt with the Provisional IRA and Sinn Féin), he had presented '[t]he widely accepted view of this violent encounter…that loyalist mobs attacked the [St Matthew's] church with petrol bombs until the Provisional IRA came to the rescue'. When he came to make the second series on loyalism, however, Taylor was 'taken to task by angry local [Protestant] residents. He was told that he had 'fallen for IRA propaganda' and that it was the 'loyalists in the area [who] had come under attack from nationalists and [who] were only defending themselves'. The depth of feeling with which this view was expressed, wrote Taylor, 'suggested that there might be some truth in what they said' and he duly reported it in the relevant programme.[63]

Now that much more documentation has become available, it is time to take a further look at who produced the violence. Whatever their disagreements, both sides share the view that it was the hoisting of the Irish Tricolour on the corner of Seaforde Street which led to the outbreak of shooting. According to the loyalist version of events, '[t]he spark that lit the fire, the waving of the Tricolour[,] was all part and parcel of a pre-meditated republican plan. A Tricolour was waved at Protestants to goad them into a fight.'[64] If this sounds far-fetched, consider the Republican justification for hoisting the flag. It was, we are told, 'a ploy to establish as to whether or not [there] were armed men among the crowd. The answer was quick in coming as a bullet was fired through the flag'.[65] The Provisionals did not need to resort to such a risky initiative in order to discover whether members of the Protestant crowd were armed. They would have found out soon enough. The raising of the Tricolour makes much more sense as a deliberate provocation designed to produce a hostile reaction from what was by all accounts a drunken Protestant crowd. As one Catholic account put it, '*Naturally enough* [my italics], there was a frenzied reaction from the Orange mob…'[66]

The Provisional IRA certainly seems to have been better prepared and better organized than the loyalists. McKee told Taylor that his men had fired 800 rounds on the night of 27/28 June 1970. He knew this, he said, because the Provisional IRA's quartermaster had told him so.[67] Then there were the casualties. The three people who were killed all died at the hands of the Provisional IRA. Neither of the two dead Protestants was carrying a weapon and they were not attacking the Catholic area when they were shot. As for the wounded, Quinn tells us that forty Protestants from Ballymacarrett had gunshot wounds, while the only Catholic to be injured by gunfire was McKee.[68] All this suggests that the Protestants were both unprepared and heavily outgunned.

Finally, McKee's attitude towards the army was revealing. When seeking to discover if and when troops would arrive on the scene, he seemed more concerned about dispersing his men and concealing their weapons than with the fate of the local Catholic community. This suggests that there was rather more to the Battle of St Matthew's than the heroic defence of a threatened minority. This was certainly the view of the army. 'The fact that the Ballymacarrett shooting broke out at such an inopportune time, in a location where troops were not stationed, and where no trouble had occurred for many months', stated its weekly intelligence summary, gave 'an indication of pre-planning'. McKee's reported presence added 'weight to the evidence that the events of the night 27/28 June were stage-managed by the IRA as part of a deliberate plan to overstretch, and thereby discredit, the Security Forces'.[69] This would account for the statement, said to have been made by the commander of 39th Brigade in reply to repeated requests from the CCDC to intervene in the fighting in east Belfast, that 'the military had no desire to be caught in cross-fire and also they suspected that the situation might be a trap'.[70]

More important than the discrediting of the security forces, however, was its obverse: the strengthening of the credibility of the Provisional IRA. As Quinn puts it, 'Bombay Street, Cupar Street and Conway Street had been avenged in the Short Strand. In Ardoyne there was also a sense of relief, as the I.R.A. found itself being embraced by its people as never before'. Moreover, as Quinn goes on to emphasize, it was the Provisionals and not the Officials who were being embraced. 'The Provisionals,' he writes, 'much to the dismay of the Official I.R.A. command was establishing itself as the "army of the people".'[71]

Relations between the two IRAs had in fact deteriorated in Belfast during the spring of 1970. An army intelligence report of 30 April 1970 mentioned a string of incidents involving 'violent rivalry' between the two factions, culminating in the attempted assassination of Billy McMillen four days before. A week later it was reported that there had been intimidation of Provisionals by Officials in the Lower Falls and that there had been a meeting in which women from the affected families had sought help from Sullivan in his capacity as chair of the CCDC. Since he was also McMillen's second-in-command in the Official IRA, they did not receive much joy, and several families fled the area. A meeting was arranged on 1 May 1970 with the help of local clergy and a truce was concluded.[72] Like revolutionary groups waging armed struggles elsewhere in the post-war world, the Provisionals and the Officials were using violence to compete with each other.[73] The events of 27/28 June 1970 did not improve matters and the Official IRA condemned the Provisionals for their action. 'The hatred and bitterness engendered by the killing of six Protestant civilians', it stated, 'can only increase the likelihood of further pogroms in the future' and, in a reference to the Falls Road curfew imposed by the Army on 3/4 July 1970 following the discovery of an Official IRA arms cache, it added that '[t]he Falls, the best organized, most peaceful and least bigoted area in Belfast has paid the price for the bigoted sectarian actions of the previous week for which they were in no way responsible'.[74]

Unionists were even more angry about the events of 27/28 June 1970, as Maudling quickly discovered on his first official visit to the province on 30 June 1970. At a meeting with the Northern Ireland Cabinet on the opening day of his visit, minister after minister criticized the way in which the disturbances had been handled and how this had weakened the government's position. Prime Minister James Chichester-Clark felt that it was 'essential that the Army should deal toughly, and be seen to deal toughly, with thugs and gunmen'. Brian Faulkner, the Minister of Development, said that he had personally visited the disturbed areas and had encountered demands by Catholics and Protestants alike that 'the police and army should deal toughly with hooligans'. Roy Bradford, the Minister of Commerce, said that '[t]he old system of police baton charges and "B" specials may have been crude, but they did protect the Protestant population', while the Chief Whip emphasized that in the last three days the credibility of the government had been strained to breaking point and that immediate action was needed to demonstrate that law and order would be maintained. All that Maudling could say in response to this barrage of criticism was that 'he recognized there was a very real problem and that it appeared that neither the police on their present instructions nor the army as at present equipped were in a position to deal with it'. He promised to discuss the matter with both Freeland and Sir Arthur Young, the British policeman who had taken over from Peacocke as head of the RUC

following the Hunt Report, 'to see whether there was scope for clari-
fying the roles of police and army'.[75]

An equally bruising reception awaited the Home Secretary when he
met Unionist Party backbenchers on 1 July 1970. As the anonymous
author of the minutes of the meeting recorded, '[t]he points made were
almost exclusively concerned with the action of the army and police in
the past weekend. Criticism of the G.O.C. was vehement and, in some
cases, personal. Several demanded his replacement; the more moderate
called for new instructions.' Young also came under fire, with one MP
describing him as 'a big laugh'. Joshua Cardwell, whose Mountpottinger constituency included the Short Strand, criticized the army's
inaction in east Belfast. They might as well have been 'the boys'
brigade', he contemptuously observed.[76] It was the same story when
Maudling saw Joseph Cairns, the Unionist Mayor of Belfast. Cairns
expressed his disappointment at the army's security policy. 'They were
not acting quickly enough', he complained, 'and nor were they firm
enough in the action they should take'. Things had been better, he
suggested, when order had been maintained by the RUC and the
B-Specials.[77]

At the grass-roots level there was more than talk. Almost exactly fifty
years earlier, in July 1920, Catholic workers had been ejected from Belfast
shipyards and for a short time it looked as though serious trouble
was about to occur there again. On the morning of 29 June 1970, a
meeting of Protestant workers, variously estimated at between 100 and
300, convened at the Harland and Wolff yard. Angry at the deaths and
injuries incurred by their community over the previous weekend,
particularly the death of Loughins, who had worked at the yard, they
ordered Catholic workers off the premises. One Catholic, who had
worked at Harland and Wolff for twenty years, was told by a group of
men, 'You're a Fenian bastard. If you don't get out you'll get what our
boys got at the weekend'. When others approached the management
for advice, they were advised to leave for their own safety. However, as
a result of intervention by the government and the trade unions,
together with a threat by the chairman of Harland and Wolff that those
involved in intimidation faced instant dismissal, most of the Catholics
were back at work by the end of the week.[78]

More sinister repercussions followed. We have seen that the Protestants were outgunned by the IRA in east Belfast on the night of 27/28

June 1970 and if it was true that 'Captain Johnston's' UVF was really capable of mobilizing 8,500 well-armed men 'to take over in half an hour', where were they? Protestants subsequently denied that the UVF even existed in east Belfast in June 1970 and in his rebuttal of their account Quinn significantly does not deny this, but merely points out that the Protestants had more guns at their disposal than they admitted.[79] One of the Protestants involved in the fighting, however, stated that after the weekend of violence 'myself along with others got together and approached people who then put us in touch with the UVF [and] I along with others formed and started recruiting for the Ulster Volunteer Force in east Belfast'.[80]

There appears to have been a similar development in the north of the city. Following the events of 27/28 June 1970, we read, 'a small group of young loyalists from the Shankill and Oldpark met in a house off Manor Street to band together and organize for the future'. They met secretly with John McKeague and 'quickly acquired some handguns and small arms from various sources'. McKeague introduced them to other loyalists from east Belfast – where, of course, he lived – and north Down and it was eventually decided to call the new grouping the Red Hand Commando.[81] Polarization was more a product of violence than the cause of it. Although the first British soldier was not killed until 6 February 1971, it was not for want of trying by either branch of the IRA. McKee's dream of confronting 'the Brits' on the streets of Belfast was coming true; for others, the Troubles in Belfast was a waking nightmare in which over 1,500 people would die.[82]

NOTES

1. *Sunday Times* Insight Team, *Ulster*, (London: André Deutsch, 1972), p. 213; L Baston, *Reggie: The Life of Reginald Maudling* (Stroud: Sutton Publishing, 2004), pp. 364–65; E. Heath, *The Course of My Life: My Autobiography* (London: Hodder and Stoughton, 1998), p. 436; Minutes of Ministerial Committee on Northern Ireland, 13 July 1970, London, National Archives (NA), CAB/124/3011.
2. Unsigned note of meeting at Home Office, 15 June 1970, NA, DEFE/13/731.
3. Ibid.
4. Ibid.
5. *House of Commons Debates*, vol. 803, 3 July 1970, cols 220–21.
6. Minutes of Ministerial Meeting on Northern Ireland, 22 June 1970, NA, CAB/164/877.
7. 45 Commando Royal Marines News Letter, January 1968–December 1970, pp. 13–14, NA, ADM/301/26. See also *Belfast Telegraph*, 27 June 1970 and *Irish Times*, 27 June 1970.
8. S. Mac Stíofáin, *Memoirs of a Revolutionary* (Edinburgh: Gordon Cremonesi, 1975), p. 152.

9. INTSUM, 2 July 1970, NA, WO/305/3783.
10. Wilson statement, Reid Inquest, Belfast, Public Record Office of Northern Ireland (PRONI), BELF/6/1/1/24.
11. HQ Northern Ireland, Duty Officer's Log, 27 June 1970, NA, WO/305/3771; INTSUM, 2 July 1970, NA, WO/305/3783.
12. S. Winchester, *In Holy Terror* (London: Faber, 1974), pp. 56–8. He also mentions the shooting, but does not indicate who was responsible.
13. E. Reid's statement, Reid Inquest, PRONI, BELF/6/1/1/24. See also A. Reid's statement, Reid Inquest, PRONI, BELF/6/1/1/24.
14. Constable Wilson, who saw him fall, did not say that he was. Wilson's statement, Reid Inquest, PRONI, BELF/6/1/1/24.
15. M. Oliver's statement and M. Beattie's statement, Reid Inquest, PRONI, BELF/6/1/1/24.
16. 39th Brigade, Duty Officer's Log, 27 June 1970, NA, WO/305/4237.
17. W. Carlisle's statement, Loughins Inquest, PRONI, BELF/6/1/1/23. Another witness, George Mawhinney, said that Loughins was on the Protestant side of the Crumlin Road, which seems more likely. G. Mawhinney's statement, Loughins Inquest, PRONI, BELF/6/1/1/23.
18. C. Hamilton's statement, D. Elliott's statement J. Wood's statement, Marshall autopsy report, Gould Inquest, PRONI, BELF/6/1/1/23; N. Hamilton's statement, Marshall autopsy report, Kincaid Inquest, PRONI, BELF/6/1/1/23.
19. *Belfast Telegraph*, 29 June 1970.
20. HQ Northern Ireland Log, 27 June 1970, NA, WO/305/3771.
21. 45 Commando Newsletter, p, 15.
22. J. Graham, *'Show Me the Man': The Authorised Biography of Martin Meehan* (Belfast: Rushlight Publications, 2008), p. 47.
23. 45 Commando Newsletter, p. 27.
24. Ibid., p. 15.
25. R. Quinn, *A Rebel Voice: A History of Belfast Republicanism 1925–72* (Belfast: Belfast Cultural and Local History Group, 1999), p. 161.
26. Hammond's statement, McIlhone Inquest, PRONI, BELF/6/1/1.24; Moore's statement, McIlhone Inquest, PRONI, BELF/6/1/1.24; Anon., *Murder in Ballymacarrett – The Untold Story* (Belfast: East Belfast Historical and Cultural Society, 2003 edn.), p. 18.
27. Anon., *The Battle of St. Matthew's, 27th–28th June 1970*, (Belfast: n.p., [1971]), Chapter 7, pp. 2–3. The author appears to have been someone on or close to the local defence committee.
28. St Matthew's Parish Chronicon, 28 June 1970; P. McAtamney's statement, E. Heaney's statement and J. Allison's statement, McIlhone Inquest, PRONI, BELF/6/1/1/24.
29. Anon., *Battle of St Matthew's*, Chapter 7, p. 3.
30. 39th Brigade Log, 27 June 1970.
31. Anon., *Battle of St. Matthew's*, Chapter 7, p. 4.
32. Hammond's statement.
33. Ibid.; Moore's statement. Hammond's timing is a little different from Moore's, but not significantly so.
34. Hammond stated that the man fired five shots from a .45 revolver.
35. Hammond's statement; Moore's statement; Anon., *Murder in Ballymacarrett*, p. 15; 39th Brigade Log, 27 June 1970. Mrs Campbell states in Anon., *Murder in Ballymacarrett* that she was shot at 10 pm, but this appears to be a false memory on her part.
36. R. Quinn, *The Rising of the Phoenix: The Creation of the Provisional I.R.A.; The Historic Battle of St. Matthew's; The Falls Road Curfew*, (Belfast: Bryson Publications, 2007 edn.), p. 66.
37. Quinn *Rebel Voice*, pp. 161–2. The M1's magazine contained either 15 or 30 rounds.
38. Moore's statement; HQ Northern Ireland Log, 28 June 1970, NA, WO/305/3771. The 39th Brigade log adds at 12:31 am that the RUC was pinned down in Pitt Street by heavy fire from both the Chapel grounds and the Hayes Potato Factory at the bottom of Austin Street. 39th Brigade Log, 28 June 1970.
39. Moore's statement.
40. Anon., *Murder in Ballymacarrett*, pp. 23–4.

41. Algie's statement, Farr's statement, Guiller's statement and Wilson's statement, McCurrie Inquest, PRONI, BELF/6/1/1/24. See also the interview with McCurrie's widow on the *Murder in Ballymacarrett* DVD. In this she confirms that the route followed by the five men was the one her husband normally took when returning home from the Buffs Club.
42. 39th Brigade Log.
43. Blackmore's statement, McCurrie Inquest, PRONI, BELF/6/1/1/24.
44. Grier's statement, McCurrie Inquest, PRONI, BELF/6/1/1/24. Quinn's battalion staff informant told him that, apart from the weapons introduced by McKee, the Provisionals in the Short Strand had access to the following weapons in their own arms dumps: 2 M1 carbines, 2 Stens, 2 Winchesters (rifles), 2 Thompson sub-machine guns, 'some Lee Enfields [rifles]' and 'several handguns [pistols and revolvers]'. Anon., *Battle of St Matthew's*, p. 68.
45. A letter sent by the head of the Historical Enquiries team to McCurrie's widow in 2010 stated that 'there is no intelligence or evidence to show that James [McCurrie] had ever been involved in any illegal activity, or had association with any paramilitary organisation'. *Belfast Telegraph*, 23 June 2010.
46. HQ Northern Ireland Log, 28 June 1970, NA, WO/305/3771.
47. Quinn, *A Rebel Voice*, p. 163; Anon., *Battle of St. Matthew's*, Chapter 7, p. 5. Kennedy's presence at Mountpottinger RUC station is confirmed in the 39th Brigade Log at 1:50 am, where he is recorded as promising to 'try to calm things down' and requesting the 'retention of [a] military presence in [the] Roman Catholic end of the Newtownards Road'. 39th Brigade Log, 28 June 1970.
48. 39th Brigade Log, 28 June 1970.
49. Quinn, *Rising of the Phoenix*, p. 67.
50. *Belfast Telegraph*, 29 June 1970.
51. Ibid.
52. Quinn, *Rebel Voice*, p. 162; St Matthew's Parish Chronicon, 28 June 1970; Moore statement's and Allison's statement, McIlhone Inquest, PRONI, BELF/6/1/1/24; 39th Brigade Log, 28 June 1970.
53. Dougherty's statement, Matthews's statement, Rutherford's statement, Carson autopsy report, Neill Inquest, PRONI, BELF/6/1/1/24.
54. Quinn, *Rebel Voice*, pp. 163–4. See also P. Taylor, *Provos: The IRA and Sinn Féin* (London: Bloomsbury, 1997), pp. 76–7.
55. Quinn, *Rebel Voice*, p. 164; Heaney's statement; Allison's statement; Carson autopsy report; McAllister's statement and Mellotte's statement, McIlhone Inquest, PRONI, BELF/6/1/1/24. I have found no evidence to support Quinn's claim that loyalists tried to obstruct the ambulance taking McIlhone and McKee to the hospital, although there is an entry in one of the army logs, timed 2:20 am, which stated that the RUC were holding an ambulance at Mountpottinger.
56. 'P. Ó Néill', *Freedom Struggle by the Provisional IRA* (Dublin: Irish Republican Publicity Bureau, 1973), p. 25; *Irish News*, 8 September 1973.
57. Hammond's statement; *Sunday Times*, 24 May 2009.
58. *Belfast Graves*, pp. 68–9; *Andersonstown News*, 21 January 2010.
59. The situation was further complicated by the suggestion that the man who killed McIlhone was Denis Donaldson, an IRA volunteer whom the RUC subsequently 'turned' into becoming a key informer. McKee denied that Donaldson was involved and, on this point, there is no good reason to disbelieve him. *Sunday Times*, 24 May 2009; *Andersonstown News*, 21 January 2010.
60. HQ Northern Ireland Log, 28 June 1970; 39th Brigade Log, 28 June 1970.
61. Quinn, *Rising of the Phoenix*, p. 68.
62. HQ Northern Ireland Log, 28 June 1970.
63. P. Taylor, *Loyalists*, (London: Bloomsbury, 1999), pp. 79–80. For his earlier account, see Taylor, *Provos*, pp. 75–77.
64. Anon., *Murder in Ballymacarrett*, p. 14.
65. [R. Quinn], *Lagan Enclave: A History of Conflict in the Short Strand 1886–1997* (Belfast: Ballymacarrett Research Group, 1997), p. 58. This explanation was not included in Quinn's subsequent publications.

66. Anon., *Battle of St. Matthew's*, Chapter 7, p. 4.
67. Taylor, *Provos*, p. 76. The army put the figure even higher at 1,150. 39th Brigade Log, 28 June 1970.
68. Quinn, *Rebel Voice*, p. 66.
69. INTSUM, 2 July 1970, NA, WO 305/3783. Burroughs had already informed Whitehall that 'if the Protestants were the main aggressors [in August 1969], on this occasion there is convincing evidence that the Catholic side was initially to blame...' Both sides had used guns, 'but the first shots were fired from the Catholic side'. R. Burroughs telegram, 29 June 1970, NA, FCO/33/1076.
70. Anon., *Battle of St. Matthew's*, Chapter 7, pp. 5–6.
71. Quinn, *Rebel Voice*, p. 165. In *Rising of the Phoenix* (p. 63), Quinn admits that there were two Officials from the Falls in the Short Strand on the night of 27/28 June 1970. He says nothing about local Officials.
72. INTSUM, 30 April 1970, and INTSUM, 7 May 1970, NA, WO/305/3783.
73. A. Lawrence, 'Triggering Nationalist Violence Competition and Conflict in Uprisings against Colonial Rule', *International Security*, 35, 2 (Fall 2010), pp. 88–122.
74. *Irish Times*, 7 July 1970; G. Warner, 'The Falls Road Curfew Revisited'. *Irish Studies Review*, 14, 3, (August 2006), pp. 325–42.
75. Unsigned minute of conversation, 9 July 1970, NA, CJ/4/21.
76. Unsigned minute of conversation, 9 July 1970, NA, CJ/4/21 (this is a separate document from the one cited in the previous note).
77. Hopkins minute, 3 July 1970, NA, CJ/4/21.
78. Unsigned memorandum, [n.d.], NA, CJ/4/27; *Irish Times*, 30 June 1970. According to the memorandum, there were 500 Catholics at Harland and Wolff out of a total workforce of 10,500.
79. Anon., *Murder in Ballymacarrett*, pp. 19 and 25; Quinn, *Rising of the Phoenix*, pp. 70–1.
80. Anon., *Murder in Ballymacarrett*, p. 25.
81. 'The History of the Red Hand Commando', www.freewebs.com/red-hand/history. htm (last accessed 1 March 2008).
82. http://www.wesleyjohnston.com/users/ireland/past/troubles/troubles_stats.html#locaton (last accessed 18 May 2011). Deaths in Belfast were just under 44 per cent of the total.

Endings

'All human histories are provisional; none will have the last word'

– Joyce Appleby, Lynn Hunt and Margaret Jacob

'[M]any people in Ireland retain a strong sense of their received version of history as a personal possession', observes Patrick Maume, 'and react angrily to what they experience as attempted dispossession.'[1] But, neither Irish land nor Irish history is ultimately owned by people in Ireland (facts that may be unpalatable to many): property is tied up in the international markets and the past is tied up with transnational developments. Consequently, Ian McBride, for example, has chosen to 'write the history of Ireland from the outside in – to begin, that is, with the central features of eighteenth-century Europe and to trace the ways in which they were mapped onto the Irish situation'.[2] Similarly, we have chosen to address a question that has global relevance (how is the violence of the start of a civil war produced?) by studying two local cases (the start of the Troubles in Belfast and Derry). This has necessarily meant breaking with constitutional nationalist, republican, socialist and unionist narratives – from the beginning of our book through to its endings. We have not chosen to end with, say, the killing of three off-duty British soldiers in Belfast, internment, the killing of eleven civilians by the British army in Ballymurphy, Bloody Sunday or direct rule. Instead, we have taken the political scientist Stathis Kalyvas's general definition of civil war, applied it to Belfast and Derry and, accordingly, constructed our separate endings. Kalyvas's definition is 'agnostic about causes', yet some readers may still be offended that we have chosen to end when we have and that we have ended at different times because it does not fit with their version of how the Troubles is to be explained.[3] After all, endings as well as beginnings lock in narrative meaning. All that we can do here is stress once again that we are not exploring the origins of the Troubles, that we are not presenting the full story of these years and that we are not drawing attention away from people's suffering.

This book has engaged with scholarly debates that are both more general and more particular than the ones which are related to the causes of the Northern Irish conflict. We have chosen to cross over disciplinary divides and join our neighbours across the academy – political scientists, sociologists, anthropologists, psychologists and economists – in trying to better understand political violence. In the preceding chapters, we have had something to say about whether violence should be conceived as a degree of conflict or a form of conflict; about how non-violent action works; about the range of constitutional, non-violent and violent strategies and about how they can be used in combination; about whether an increase in protest comes from a build up of frustration or from fresh power to fight for change; about the links between riots and elections; about the puzzling impact of repression; about what leads certain crowd events to become violent; about the reasoning behind the selection of violent strategies; about political action outside movements and institutions; about the relationship between polarization and violence; about the part played by narrative in the turn to violence; about the connection between international politics and internal conflict; and about the effectiveness of violence.

But, for all that, we nonetheless remain historians first and foremost. Confronted with what Peter Mandler describes as 'the profound strangeness and diversity of the past', we are therefore reluctant to push our arguments too far. In this book, we have simply presented the most convincing interpretation of what happened in Belfast and Derry at the start of the Troubles that we could construct from available sources. We will not pretend that we have produced a general history (a history of its capital and second cities is not a history of Northern Ireland) let alone general theories which can be applied across time and across cultures (our goal has been to suggest questions to scholars working on related subjects, not to set down models for them to follow). This should not be mistaken for a lack of ambition. Given that the humanities and social sciences are being made to draw inspiration from the markets, historians should perhaps aspire to be the regulators; when academics from other disciplines occasionally show, in Mandler's words, 'universalizing hubris', claiming to have 'unlocked the secrets of human behaviour', historians can tender a check.[4] To paraphrase the longest-serving Chairman of the United States Federal Reserve, our job should be to take away the punch bowl just as the party gets going.[5] Sadly, there are many, many people in Ireland today who can easily recognize just how important it is for such a job to be done properly.

We offer no apologies for making the story of the start of the Troubles harder to simplify, harder to contain and harder to use. It is not our book's function to aid the search for a useable past, to nourish a narrative of peace and reconciliation or struggle and liberation. The relevance of the past, we would argue, actually lies in its alien character. Reflecting on what was once perceived to be both possible and impossible expands our imagination and offers us new ways of looking critically not just at our own time but at ourselves, too. Although we have to accept that we can only hope to understand the past through what traces it has left behind of itself in the present and within the constraints imposed by our own culture (broadly defined), such scepticism can have its comforts. The world will keep changing, and so will the ways in which historians study the past. There will always be something new to be said about the start of the Troubles.

NOTES

1. P. Maume, 'Irish Political History: Guidelines and Reflections', in M. McAuliffe, K. O'Donnell and L. Lane (eds), *Palgrave Advances in Irish History* (Basingstoke: Palgrave Macmillan, 2009), pp. 1–48, p. 2.
2. I. McBride, *Eighteenth-Century Ireland* (Dublin: Gill & Macmillan, 2009), p. 20.
3. S. Kalyvas, *The Logic of Violence in Civil War* (Cambridge: Cambridge University Press, 2006), p. 17.
4. P. Mandler, 'The Problem with Cultural History', *Cultural and Social History*, 1, 1 (January 2004), pp. 94–117, p. 116.
5. *New York Times*, 23 December 2007.

Index